EMPLOYEE ASSISTANCE PROGRAMS

ABOUT THE EDITORS

WILLIAM G. EMENER is a Distinguished Research Professor in, and a former Chair of, the Department of Rehabilitation and Mental Health Counseling, *and* a former Associate Dean at the University of South Florida, Tampa, Florida. He has worked as a rehabilitation counselor and supervisor as well as a rehabilitation counselor educator and program director at three other universities (Murray State University, Florida State University, and the University of Kentucky). Dr. Emener's publications and writings include seven research monographs, 14 books, book chapters in 15 different texts, over 60 nonpublished professional papers, over 100 authored/co-authored articles in 17 different professional refereed journals, and over 95 professional papers presented at professional association meetings. He has been an editor/co-editor of over 20 special publications, and was Co-Editor of the *Journal of Applied Rehabilitation Counseling* from 1978-1982. Dr. Emener's recognitions include being a recipient of the *1980 American Rehabilitation Counseling Association Research Award*, and a recipient of the National Rehabilitation Administration Association's *The Advancement of Research in Rehabilitation Administration Award*. He was the 1983-1984 President of the National Rehabilitation Administration Association and the 1989-1990 President of the National Council on Rehabilitation Education. Dr. Emener has had a private practice as a licensed psychologist for the past 30 years (in Florida and Kentucky) and currently practices as a licensed psychologist in St. Petersburg, Florida with specializations in employee assistance programs, couples counseling, and addictions/substance abuse counseling.

WILIAM S. HUTCHISON, JR., M.S.W., Ph.D. is a Professor of Social Work of the School of Social Work at the University of South Florida. He earned his Ph.D. in Adult Education with a cognate in Staff Development and Training in 1992 from the University of South Florida. In addition, he received his M.S.W. degree from the University of Georgia and his B.A. in psychology from David Lipscomb College. He has worked as a clinical social worker in health, mental health, alcohol and drugs, and child welfare treatment settings. His clinical practice in these settings has included individual, couple, family, group, and psychodrama treatment methods. He has taught social work practice in four universities and two colleges including Duke University Department of Psychiatry and the University of North Carolina–Chapel Hill. Dr. Hutchison has authored and co-authored 10 treatment training manuals, co-authored *Counseling the Troubled Person in Industry*, and has presented numerous invited papers on social work practice at professional meetings. He is a member of the National Association of Social Workers and the Academy of Certified Social Workers. In addition, he is a Board Certified Diplomat in Clinical Social Work and a licensed clinical social worker (LCSW). He is Director of Clinical Service Associates, PA, a corporation providing mental health, employee assistance, and wellness programs in Tampa, Florida.

MICHAEL A. RICHARD is an Assistant Professor in the Department of Rehabilitation and Mental Health Counseling at the University of South Florida– Sarasota/Manatee, where he has also served on several university committees and provides ongoing advising to the University Counseling Center. He worked as a vocational evaluator, rehabilitation counselor, and behavioral program supervisor in the private sector for over 12 years prior to obtaining his Doctorate. He also taught graduate and undergraduate courses in rehabilitation counseling as well as providing undergraduate student advising at Emporia State University for three years. He received his B.S. degree from Athens College, his M.Ed. from Auburn University and his Ph.D. from The Florida State University. He is a Certified Rehabilitation Counselor and has worked extensively in the field as Rehabilitation and Mental Health Professional. His research interests include consumer satisfaction assessment of counseling services and diversity training for counselors.

Third Edition

EMPLOYEE ASSISTANCE PROGRAMS

Wellness/Enhancement Programming

Edited by

WILLIAM G. EMENER

WILLIAM S. HUTCHISON, JR.

MICHAEL A. RICHARD

CHARLES C THOMAS • PUBLISHER, LTD.
Springfield • Illinois • U.S.A.

Published and Distributed Throughout the World by

CHARLES C THOMAS • PUBLISHER, LTD.
2600 South First Street
Springfield, Illinois 62794-9265

©2003 by CHARLES C THOMAS • PUBLISHER, LTD.

ISBN 0-398-07397-X (hard)
ISBN 0-398-07398-8 (paper)

Library of Congress Catalog Card Number:

Printed in the United States of America
MM-R-3

Library of Congress Cataloging in Publication Data

Employee assistance programs : wellness/enhancement programming -- 3rd ed. / edited by
William G. Emener, William S. Hutchison, Jr., Michael A. Richard
    p. cm.
Includes bibliographical references and index.
ISBN 0-398-07397-X (hard) − ISBN 0-398-07398-8 (pbk)
1. Employee assistance programs--United States. I. Emener, William G. (William
George) II. Hutchison, William S. III. Richard, Michael A.

HF5549.5.E42E47 2003
658.3'82--dc21

           2003040178

With humility and the utmost respect, this book is dedicated to the millions of employees and families throughout the United States whose work and lives have dramatically changed since 9-11, yet continue to dignify our country every day by working, serving, producing, and living the American way.

Thank you,
Bill, Bill, and Mike

CONTRIBUTORS

WILLIAM BLOUNT, Ph.D.
University of South Florida
Department of Criminology
Tampa, Florida

MAX L. BROMLEY, Ed.D.
University of South Florida
Department of Criminology
Tampa, Florida

ALISSE C. CAMAZINE
Love, Lacks & Paule
St. Louis, Missouri

B. ROBERT CHALLENGER
Tampa, Florida

HELEN DAHLHAUSER
Clearwater, Florida

JOHN L. DALY
Department of Government and
International Affairs
University of South Florida
Tampa, Florida

FRED DICKMAN, Ed.D.
(Deceased)
University of South Florida
Department of Rehabilitation and
Mental Health Counseling
Tampa, Florida

CHARLOTTE G. DIXON
Department of Rehabilitation and
Mental Health Counseling
Tampa, Florida

WILLIAM G. EMENER, Ph.D.,
CRC
University of South Florida
Department of Rehabilitation and
Mental Health Counseling
Tampa, Florida

MARK EVANS
EVA-Tone, Inc.
Clearwater, Florida

J. ERIC GENTRY, M.A.
University of South Florida
School of Social Work
Tampa, Florida

RICHARD E. GENTRY, ESQ.
South St. Augustine, Florida

BEN HAYES, B.A.
St. Petersburg, Florida

WILLIAM S. HUTCHISON,
JR., M.S.W., Ph.D.
University of South Florida
School of Social Work
Tampa, Florida

JAN LIGON, M.S.W.
The University of Georgia
School of Social Work
Athens, Georgia

JOSEPH MOLEA, M.D.
Medical Director
Health Care Connections
Tampa, Florida

CARNOT E. NELSON, Ph.D.
University of South Florida
Department of Psychology
Tampa, Florida

RANDY K. OTTO
Mental Health Law and Policy
Florida Mental Health Institute
Tampa, Florida

JOHN PETRILA
Mental Health Law and Policy
Florida Mental Health Institute
Tampa, Florida

MICHAEL G. RANK, Ph.D.
University of South Florida
School of Social Work
Tampa, Florida

MICHAEL A. RICHARD, Ph.D.
University of South Florida
Department of Rehabilitation and
Mental Health Counseling
Sarasota, Florida

JUDITH K. SCHEMM, M.S., LPCT
Employee Assistance Programs
Newman Regional Health
Emporia, Kansas

MONA SCHONBRUNN
Longboat Key, Florida

THOMAS P. SCHROEDER, C.C.P.
Diocese of St. Petersburg
Department of Human Resources
St. Petersburg, Florida

KEELY L. SPRUILL, MA/CAS
Lee County Schools
Sanford, North Carolina

MICHAEL R. TELVEN, President
Workplace Dimensions, Inc.
Tampa, Florida

HARRISON M. TRICE, Ph.D.
Cornell University
Ithaca, New York

SUSAN VICKERSTAFF
Susan Craft Vickerstaff, Ph.D., L.C.S.W.
The University of Tennessee at Martin
Department of Sociology, Anthropology,
Social Work and Criminal Justice
Martin, Tennessee

TENNYSON J. WRIGHT, Ph.D.
University of South Florida
Department of Rehabilitation and
Mental Health Counseling
Tampa, Florida

BONNIE L. YEGIDIS, Ph.D.
The University of Georgia
School of Social Work
Athens, Georgia

FOREWORD

The field of Employee Assistance (EA) is faced with many challenges and opportunities. To place this Third Edition of *Employee Assistance Programs* into perspective, one must only look at the First and Second Editions. The First Edition addressed issues such as growth in the EA field and explored certification and credentialing. Occupational alcoholism programs were prominently discussed. Those were the hot topics of the day.

The Second Edition explored how the fields of EA and Human Resources could partner to better address employee concerns. Helping a work organization improve the bottom line was seen as a competitive advantage for that organization.

It is evident in this Third Edition that EA professionals can be a valuable resource in ways not imagined in the past. September 11th changed the world. That single event catapulted EA and the support we can give work organizations. The number of requests from the media and the workplace overwhelmed International Employee Assistance Professionals Association. Employers now include EA practitioners in their crisis management planning and consult with us on a variety of other issues ranging from organizational change, sexual harassment, workplace trauma and violence, substance abuse, and mental health issues.

Our role is very vital in assisting employers to manage and support their greatest asset which is its human capital. In the future, when the Fourth Edition is written, I expect topics of importance will be different, yet comparably challenging.

This Third Edition of *Employee Assistance Programs* will add to the existing body of knowledge. The current issues and trends discussed demonstrate the field of employee assistance is dynamic and changing—as are our work organizations.

Linda Sturdivant, M.Ed., CEAP, President
International Employee Assistance Professionals Association 2000-2002

FOREWORD TO THE SECOND EDITION

The nature of business is changing from a manufacturing-based economy to a service- and information-based economy and as these changes take place, the work force is undergoing a dramatic shift. It is becoming older and more female. It is becoming better educated. Its values are changing and its emphasis is shifting more toward family life and the home.

Business must accommodate these changes if it is to survive and remain viable. No longer are family issues, for example, something that corporate executives can ignore and expect employees to deal with on their own or on their own time. Restructuring the business to deal with these and other employee concerns and personal problems is not an exercise in altruism; it is a way of improving the bottom line, a means to increased competitiveness. Competition of the future will not focus solely on attracting and keeping customers for a company's products; it will include attracting and keeping the best of a dwindling pool of potential employees who create those products. Employee assistance programs (EAPS), from an employer's viewpoint are becoming essential to the success of today's businesses.

For these reasons the employee assistance professional is becoming more and more an integral part of the corporate policy-making team. The chief executive officers and union leaders are looking to these professionals for guidance and in maintaining thE most important resource of all: the people who make a company work.

This second edition has been carefully updated and constructed to help employee assistance and human resource professionals do their jobs better. It is a distillation of many years of experience and aims to give the building blocks for a successful EAP. Its approach to this complex subject is practical, not academic, and while no two EAPs are exactly alike, the fundamentals in this book will apply to all work sites.

The profession of employee assistance has developed extensively over 25 years, and today's employers can build on the experiences of major Employee Assistance Programs firms that have developed effective EAPs by trial and error. This book has been written with the help of many people, including human resources, research, EAPs, labor, law enforcement, and clinical and managed care professionals. In the end, this book is about how to help people live happier, more productive lives by providing them with the resources to deal with personal problems–to the advantage of all concerned.

George T. Watkins, M.A., CEAP
Publisher
EAP Digest Magazine

FOREWORD TO THE FIRST EDITION

Over the past several years there has been tremendous growth in all phases of the Employee Assistance Programming field. The rapid growth in programs initiated, designed, and implemented by, with, and for both labor and management, has placed a great demand upon the qualified resources now available. If we are to meet this growing demand, indeed, the quality, quantity, and opportunity to attract qualified professionals working in the field needs to be enhanced and increased.

We are on the threshold of professional certification and credentialing, EAP curricula for colleges and universities, and a growing host of workshops, seminars, and conferences–all on EAPs. All of this necessitates a significantly larger library of available resources and knowledge bases, relative to all phases of the Employee Assistance Program enterprise.

This book represents the effort of numerous experienced and noted EAP practitioners in the fields of Occupational Alcoholism and Employee Assistance Programming. It is through these types of undertakings and the willingness of professionals to share knowledge, skills, and expertise that will enhance the growth of the EAP field and enable it to flourish and reach its professional potential. Thus, the authors are to be commended for their initiatives and leadership to "pass it along" and maximize our abilities to assist a special group of our citizenry–our troubled employees.

John J. Hennessey
President of ALMACA 1984-86

PREFACE

The current spiraling and escalating rate of *change* within the business and working world, fueled by the events as well as those emanating from September 11, 2001, indeed were the impetus and driving force behind the initiative and development of this Third Edition. Energized by the genuine encouragement of Mr. Michael Thomas (from Charles C Thomas, Publisher) to consider a Third Edition, Bill Emener and Bill Hutchison reviewed the successes of the First Edition (in 1988) and the Second Edition (in 1997) and fittingly contemplated the numerous challenges of producing an equally successful Third Edition. Their first stroke of genius was in soliciting the assistance of a good friend and colleague, Mike Richard. As the reader will notice, the three of us authored and/or co-authored half (18/36) of the chapters in this Third Edition. Bill and Bill are indebted to Mike's active involvement, excellent work, and overall contributions as can be witnessed herein.

While savoring the still pertinent and meaningful 18 chapters originally written for the First Edition and the five chapters written specifically for the Second Edition, the other 13 (36%) chapters are "new" and were written specifically for this Third Edition. It is important to note, moreover, that six (1/3rd) of the new chapters are in the seven-chapter, "Part VI, Special Issues." Furthermore, the seventh chapter (from the First, 1988 Edition) in Part VI has a "new" Comment/Update. We share these specific realities of this Third Edition because they indeed reflect the aforementioned spiraling and escalating rate of change over the past six years.

It is with utmost respect and appreciation that we acknowledge the 26 first-class professionals who collectively joined in producing this 36-chapter Third Edition. Importantly, of our 26 colleagues who authored and co-authored chapters with and for us, 14 of them authored and co-authored this Third Edition's 13 "new" chapters and 4 "new" Comments/Updates. Thus, we respectfully and humbly suggest that this Third Edition is "cutting edge" for today and tomorrow.

The challenge of producing this Third Edition indeed was arduous and challenging. We believe, nonetheless, that for today's and tomorrow's EAP professionals, the challenge of improving and enhancing the lives of workers and their families through efficient and effective employee assistance programs is even more challenging. We are confident they will be successful.

Moreover, we trust that this Third Edition will meaningfully help them with their critically important endeavors.

William G. Emener
William S. Hutchison, Jr.
Michael A. Richard

PREFACE TO THE SECOND EDITION

The dawn of the second edition of this book was born during a conversation between its two editors, Bill Emener and Bill Hutchison, specifically when their dialogue turned to their departed friend and colleague, Dr. J. Fred Dickman. Grieving can be painful at times, yet the energy it can engender can likewise be productive. Such was the case during this aforementioned conversation. "What better way to honor Fred than to carry on his dream of providing important cutting edge information to students, colleagues, and fellow professionals."

The editing processes that ensued were guided by three definitive goals for this second edition: (1) to honorously savor the historical and developmental considerations of the past; (2) to surface and discuss the avant-garde issues and developmental accomplishments of the present; and (3) to update and hone our predictions, concerns, and recommendations regarding the future. Needless to say, these three expectations indeed were challenging.

This second edition has the same titled eight Parts as did the first edition. A careful study of the 40 chapters in the first edition, however, rendered a decision to reprint 26 of the chapters from the first edition, unedited and unabridged. (Four of these 26 chapters actually had been reprinted from the first edition of our first edited book in 1985, *Counseling the Troubled Person in Industry.*) Two chapters from the first edition were edited and updated by their author(s) specifically for this second edition. Thus, 12 chapters from the first edition were eliminated from this second edition. Four of the 26 unedited and unabridged chapters from the first edition are accompanied in this edition by a "Comment/Update" authored by carefully chosen professionals from the field having specialized expertise and experience in the respective areas of the chapters. Six of the 33 chapters in this second edition were authored by experts especially for this edition. In sum, it is the belief of the editors that the three goals for this second edition are accomplished in the blending and special tailoring of attention to the past, the present, and the future.

As addressed throughout this volume, and specifically in the "future directions" writings in the last chapter, employee assistance programs have made and are continuing to make meaningful, helpful impacts on the lives of employees and on the efficiency and effectiveness of American business and industry. We are confident, moreover, that you, the reader, the student, the professional of today, will successfully confront the unique challenges facing the future of employee assistance programs. And when it is necessary and appropriate for a third edition of this book to be prepared, we trust that we will again rise to the occasion and successfully confront that challenge. Together, we can move closer to seeing Fred's dream come true.

William S. Hutchison
William G. Emener

PREFACE TO THE FIRST EDITION

The genesis for this text commensurate with the intentions of most human service professionals, emanated from our compassionate and genuine commitment to ameliorate self-destruction, pain, and sorrow. Collectively, we have provided 110 years of human services to individuals and families in need of special professional assistance. Our actual work on this volume, however, was initiated by perceived and real needs for it within the Employee Assistance Program movement. The personal and intrinsic satisfaction we derive from helping others provided the impetus and energy for this endeavor; our individual and collective research, scholarship, and clinical experience provided the wisdom and guidance.

In 1978, faculty in the College of Social and Behavioral Sciences at the University of South Florida began offering masters level courses on alcoholism and alcoholism counseling. These courses have been in such demand that the first editor of this book, Fred Dickman, was released half time for teaching them and continuing curriculum developments. Concomitantly, the third editor, Bill Hutchison, was developing and teaching specialized courses in substance abuse and family intervention. In the past two years, their respective departments, Rehabilitation Counseling and Social Work, have focused concentration tracks in these areas with special considerations in the industrial work world. Fred, who also coordinates industrial EAP programs, and Bill, who also consults with EAP programs, realized a student demand for coursework specific to EAPs. Thus, during the summer of 1983 they offered a special EAP course. While being overwhelmed by large enrollments, they also observed a scattered dearth of professional literature specific to EAPs. During a professional conference with their colleague, Bill Emener, a counseling psychologist who also worked with industry and EAP clientele, the idea for the first book, *Counseling the Troubled Person in Industry*, eventually emerged into a reality.

Since publication of *Counseling the Troubled Person in Industry*, Bob Challenger emerged on the scene. As First Vice President of the Institute for Human Resources, Bob has become an invaluable asset to the EAP community in Florida in general and the Tampa Bay Area in particular. He became a co-teacher in the EAP course cosponsored by the Departments of Social Work and Rehabilitation Counseling at the University of South Florida. Bob brings 40 years of experience in the EAP field which is evident in his efforts as an author and co-editor of this new book. Among the numerous purposes of this book, one has loomed in the forefront: to provide a meaningful updated collection of readings basic to the understanding, development, implementation, evaluation, and future continuation of Employee Assistance Programs in the United States. In short, this book is designed to serve as a basic text covering the important aspects and critical issues concerning EAP professionals.

In many ways, this is an original text. An analysis of the specific contents of this book (i.e., its 40 chapters), indeed delineates its existence as an original work on our behalf as its authors. Ten chapters are carefully selected reprints of previously published works by experts in the field. The four of us contributed to three of the 14 authored and co-authored chapters which were written specifically for this book by leading, nationally recognized experts. Moreover, the four of us authored and co-authored (exclusively) three chapters which were previously published works, and authored and/or co-authored 19 chapters which were originally written for this book (three of them with professionals other than ourselves). Overall, the four of us individually and collectively authored and/or co-authored 25 of the 40 chapters in this volume. We are very appreciative of our professional colleagues and associates throughout the United States who assisted us with this endeavor. We enjoy full responsibility for our final selection of all previously published chapters and our choices of the authors of all original chapters in this book. Nonetheless, it must be noted that the specific content of each chapter remains the sole responsibility of the author(s) of each chapter.

Part I provides a background, historical appreciation, and philosophical orientation for EAPs in the United States. Part II articulates and refines the basic ingredients, components, administrative aspects, and critical attributes of a successful EAP. Part III surveys the predominant characteristics of EAP clientele and the clinical approaches designed to ameliorate the problems and difficulties that EAP clients tend to be experiencing when they come for assistance. Part IV discusses basic aspects of program evaluation relevant to an EAP. Part V discusses the EAP professional and professional education, training, and development with emphasis upon the growing demand for professionalism in the EAP movement. Part VI looks at special issues currently in debate including legal aspects of EAPs and drug testing in industry as an EAP dilemma. Part VII highlights a few selected examples of EAP populations requiring special attention and procedures while the last part looks at future directions of the EAP movement.

Admittedly, our intentions were ambitious and could very well have been beyond what reality would allow in one single volume. Fittingly, we ask you, the reader, to study the contents of this book and join us in our initiatives and endeavors to continue to develop the best EAP programs we can, conduct them in the most efficient and effective manner possible, appropriately evaluate them, and thus ensure their continuing developments into the future. Millions of America's workers and their families, as well as American industry itself, have, are, and will continue to benefit from EAPs. With reasons such as these, our labors of love shall prove to be eminently worthy of our efforts.

B. Robert Challenger
Fred Dickman
William G. Emener
William S. Hutchison

ACKNOWLEDGMENTS

The opportunity to write and edit the Third Edition of this book has been exciting and challenging. So, too, is the identification of all the individuals who contributed to the successful completion of this project. We have attempted to be inclusive and if we fail to acknowledge one of the book's contributors, we apologize for the blunder.

First and foremost we wish to thank our deceased colleagues, Fred Dickman and Robert Challenger (posthumously) for contributions to the original text and their roles as pioneers in the EAP profession. We miss you both!

We particularly want to recognize the contributions of Deborah Hart who scanned the carried-over chapters from the Second Edition on to a CD, never complaining when we increased the pages originally agreed upon while doing formatting we did not request. Deborah truly performed beyond the call of duty. Francene Brannon, thank you as well for scanning and typing three of the book's chapters for the new edition.

Bill Emener is truly indebted to his three children, their significant others, and his two grandchildren for their unconditional presence in his life, unerring support, and an occasional spit-up on a new shirt which facilitates respectful humility and grounding.

Bill Hutchison thanks his wife Glenda, his father, Bill Sr., daughters Angie and Keely, and his grandson Aidan for the joy of unconditional love.

Michael Richard particularly recognizes Judith K. Schemm, his wife, friend, and co-author for her love and patience, and he especially wants to thank his mother for a life full of inspiration.

The 13 new chapters in this Third Edition were carefully written to reflect the exponential growth in the employee assistance field. The scholarly contributions by each of the following writers are greatly appreciated: John Daly, Charlotte Dixon, J. Eric Gentry, Henrietta Mencoein, Joseph Molea, Randy Otto, John Petrilla, Michael G. Rank, Keely Spruill, Susan Vickerstaff, and Tennyson Wright.

The new Comments/Updates expanding on selected Second Edition chapters involve carefully selected professionals in the EAP field. For their timely and on target contributions we express sincere appreciation to Judith K. Schemm, Thomas Schroeder, and Mike Telvan.

We are especially honored to have the Foreword to this Third Edition written by the 2000-2002 President of the *International Employee Assistance Professionals Association*, Ms. Linda Sturdivant. In it she eloquently expresses her vision and wisdom. A hearty "Thank-you" to Linda!

To our Chairs, Dr. Charlotte Dixon and Dr. Bill Rowe, to Dean's Renu Khator and Peter French, to our other colleagues, and especially to our students, we thank you for your support, understanding, patience, and encouragement. We also recognize the integrity and leadership of many others in the University of South Florida's administration who assisted with words and action.

This work would not exist without the courage of our clients and the contributions of fellow EAP professionals who repeatedly make clear a central truth—"people heal people." Indeed, we are grateful to learn so much every day from our colleagues as well as those we attempt to help and assist.

CONTENTS

Part I: History and Philosophy

Part II: Structure and Organization

Part III: Client Characteristics and Services

Part IV: Program Planning and Evaluation

Part V: Professional Training and Development

Part VIII: Future Directions

EMPLOYEE ASSISTANCE PROGRAMS

Part I

HISTORY AND PHILOSOPHY

Chapter 1

A HISTORY OF JOB-BASED ALCOHOLISM PROGRAMS 1900–1955

HARRISON M. TRICE and MONA SCHONBRUNN

The early history of job-based alcoholism programs can be traced to efforts to eliminate alcohol from the workplace that were prevalent into the early years of the twentieth century, and to subsequent socioeconomic factors which mandated a change in long-accepted behaviors and employer policies. Numerous forces, including World War II and its impact on the labor market, led to the need for rehabilitating alcoholics in the work force, a need recognized by a number of sensitive and innovative industrial physicians. Evidence supports the conclusion, however, that without the existence of Alcoholics Anonymous, and the dedication and almost superhuman efforts of some of its members in developing and supporting the early programs, few of these programs would have survived.

In an attempt to describe partially the events, forces, and individuals involved in the formative period of occupational alcoholism programs during the 1940s and 1950s, the authors have collected material from a variety of sources, including many firsthand accounts from persons directly concerned in early program development. It is hoped that this material will promote increasing interest in the history of job-based alcoholism programs and generate further input from sources that can contribute to knowledge about this movement which has had such a strong impact on the progress of alcoholism intervention practices.

INTRODUCTION

Although there has been a trend in recent years to eulogize the "new" and to discredit the early focus of job-based programs on alcoholism, there is a growing interest in the history of this movement. Many practitioners express a curiosity about the earlier efforts, often believing them to be rich in anecdote and interesting personalities, and perhaps searching for the increased sense . . . derived from knowledge about one's predecessors.

In an effort to partially describe some of the forces, events, and persons who were involved in the early formative period of the 1940s and 1950s, we have been collecting data from a variety of sources. First and foremost, we attempted to locate and secure the recollections of those persons involved in early programs who are still alive. Where we found such people, we tried to secure a taped, face-to-face interview, or alternatively, asked them to tape for us, following uniform guidelines. In other cases the persons wrote their recollections in letterform.

Our next source was the literature of the period and, to a degree, of the first decades of this century prior to World War II. In addition, we visited the General Service Office of Alcoholics Anony-

Note: Reprinted with permission from the authors and the *Journal of Drug Issues, Inc.*, Spring 1981, pp. 171-198. This chapter is reprinted from *Employee Assistance Programs: A Basic Text* (1988) with permission of the author, the book's editors (Dickman, Emener, & Hutchison, Jr.), and the publisher (Charles C Thomas, Publisher, Ltd.).

mous and were provided with copies of relevant correspondence (anonymous). The Christopher D. Smithers Foundation allowed us to make use of their historical materials. Yvelin Gardner, long-time Associate Director of the National Council on Alcoholism (NCA), used his files and those of NCA to help us. We also gained access to the collection of papers of Mrs. Marty Mann, founder and for years Executive Director of NCA, in the archives of Syracuse University Library. We were fortunate in securing the cooperation of Lewis F. Presnall, former Director of Industrial Services at NCA; Presnall provided us with five background tapes. Also, J. George S., one-time Director of the Milwaukee Information and Referral Center, shared historical recollections with us.

Despite all this help, we felt rather uneasy about

many of our descriptions and ask readers to realize that this article is our first effort to pull together the materials we have collected over the past five years. For those who believe we are in error, and we are sure we have made errors relative to specific points and conclusions, we make a special request. Since this article represents a first "take," so-to-speak, we extend to you an invitation: Please share with us whatever historical materials you have; we will treat them in a professional manner and use them to correct or supplement what we have begun here. We should all profit from a more abundant knowledge of early program formation and the dedicated pioneers who led the way in this important and innovative movement toward the rehabilitation of alcoholic employees.

EARLY ROOTS OF JOB-BASED PROGRAMS

Ironically, the common use of alcohol as a mainstay of the workplace was the ground in which the first roots of job-based programs took hold. Throughout much of the first half of the nineteenth century, workers in practically all occupations drank on the job, frequently at the employer's expense, and often during specific times set aside for imbibing (Krout, 1925; Furnas, 1965). In the southern United States, for example, men often took off from work for "elevenders," a whiskey and brandy version of the coffee break (Janson, 1935). In England, dock workers during this period, and on into the twentieth century, typically had at least four or five drinking breaks with "practically no restrictions on the worker's access to liquor during the hours of labor" (Sullivan, 1906:508). These practices were even more evident in eighteenth century England. In London during this century, it was commonplace for workers in many trades to be directly dependent upon tavern keepers, since taverns were the employment agencies of that period. In one extreme instance, men who worked on coal-carrying ships were almost required to drink specific amounts each day; the cost of the assigned amount was taken from wages—whether it was drunk or not (George, 1925). Other employers sold drinks in

the workplace and frequently charged these costs against wages.

Apparently, such drinking was deeply embedded in both the leisure and job behavior of working class people . . . permeated much, if not all, of frontier life, where there was "liberal and frequently excessive consumption of alcohol" (Winkler, 1968:415). The repeated waves of immigrants had somewhat different, but generally supportive drinking norms. These served to reinforce the widespread use of alcohol in some form, both on and off the job (Sinclair, 1962). Despite numerous efforts to remove this practice from worker behavior (Gutman, 1977), it persisted well into the latter part of that century and on into the twentieth (Stivers, 1976).

Probably the first expression of concern for on-the-job drinking, and dealing with the problem in a nonpunitive sense, came from the Washingtonians (Fehlandt, 1904). This society—in some ways a forerunner of Alcoholics Anonymous (AA) in that it advocated total abstinence, group meetings, and the "carrying of the message"—flourished for a brief time in the mid-1800s, until political and religious entanglements led to its demise. It did, however, very early on, set something of a precedent for the heavy involvement of AA in job-based programs during the 1940s and 50s. It was a policy among Washingtonians that "each one bring one," and working men were a primary target. Members frequently would seek out excessive drinkers from their work settings, often asking employers and co-workers for suggestions about whom to approach with their message. For example, during the Civil War, and immediately thereafter, Washingtonians became active among the employees of a prominent Chicago publishing and printing house.

Because there is a strong concentration in the literature on "problem drinking," and a neglect of functional or "payoff drinking" (Bacon, 1976; Trice and Beyer, 1977), little is known about the positive functions of alcohol use in working class life. Apparently, however, there were perceived to be many. As a result, the first intensive effort to excise alcohol from the workplace, which came from farmers and employers from the 1880s to the 1920s who were attempting to discipline and organize a dependable, predictable workforce (Gutman, 1977), was a lengthy and difficult task, fraught with intense value judgments. It is within this context that the first roots of job-based programs can be found. Despite strong and deep-seated opposition, the early decades of this century saw the disappearance of condoned drinking on the job.

All segments of American society had become caught up in the Temperance Movement. Employers, in particular, were committed to the removal of alcohol in order to eliminate one of the main problems in socializing a reliable workforce. Among the most prominent examples were the employers in the steel industry (Hendrick, 1916), where all sorts of persuasions–including discharge–were used to stop drinking in the workplace. By the turn of the century numerous American railroads required total abstinence, both on and off the job (Timberlake, 1963). Directly reinforcing the Temperance Movement efforts was the "gospel of efficiency" (Haber, 1964, IX) that came to be the predominant ideology of the second and third decades of the twentieth century. One form of this "gospel" was commercial efficiency. Apart from the moralistically desirable personal characteristics of discipline, self-reliance,

and hard work, there was the ideal of the profit-making, efficient, commercial enterprise that utilized the efficient worker and operated within an efficient community. That ideal then spread to housewives, clergymen, and teachers. Taylorism was the epitome of this ideology within the workplace. This set of carefully calculated studies of how jobs could be most efficiently done, with the least amount of time spent, created an atmosphere in which there was precious little acceptance for time off for a beer! There was even less tolerance for unproductive workers, regardless of why they were that way. Alcohol became anathema to efficiency.

Equally potent was the emergence of workmen's compensation in the various states. Under these laws, employers were held financially responsible for many of the injuries incurred by employees on the job–regardless of who was actually at fault. Thus, there was a heightened concern and fear that drinking workers would injure either themselves, fellow workers, or both. In sum, the Temperance Movement, Taylorism, and Workmen's Compensation combined to drive alcohol from the workplace.

These efforts rapidly became fraught with punitive measures which soon carried over in many quarters to judgmental attitudes of anger and disgust for individuals who drank to intoxication, even though off the job. It may not be an exaggeration to conclude that much of the stigma that came to be attached to alcoholism arose from these repressive efforts to drive alcohol from the job environment.

Whatever the motives, a genuine concern for the effects of alcohol intoxication, of problem drinking, and of alcoholism on performance marked this period and was in sharp contrast to the long-standing encouragement or acceptance by employers of drinking on the job. A concerted drive to bring awareness of these problems to industry was evident during the first two decades of the century. Sullivan (1906) stated that "industrial alcoholism" was a particularly debilitating form, derived from workers' use of alcohol as an aid to heavy labor. Citing the high rates of alcohol-related pathologies among English dock workers, where industrial drinking was high, and the low rates of similar disorders among coal miners, where such drinking was low, he urged that on-the-job use of alcohol be eliminated rather than encouraged. According to him, such a program would strike at the main source of alcoholism. The American Museum of Safety published, and sold to employers on a large scale, a compilation of European methods for discouraging drinking while working. It stressed, providing some evidence, that the major reason for such company actions should be the loss of efficiency and increased chances for accidents if drinking occurred in a mechanized workplace (Tolman, 1911).

Following this, in 1915, *The Outlook* published a succinct account of how 63 large firms in the Midwest had discovered that alcohol in almost any quantities damaged efficiency, and how they used all manner of ways, including discharge, to discourage its use. This effort was attributed to the "new campaign for scientific efficiency in industry." A review of the evidence that had accumulated during this period was one of the first publications of the Yale Center of Alcohol Studies in the early forties (*Quarterly Journal of Studies on Alcohol,* 1942). In many ways it was an enlargement and refinement of an earlier approach, attributed to an unidentified vice president of a large iron works during the early teens. He explained the positive effects of the evangelist Bill Sunday on work productivity by saying that religion had little to do with it. "The thing that made those men efficient was cutting out the drink" (Theiss, 1914:856). Thus, impaired job performance became a major focus on the concern about drinking on the job during these decades prior to World War II, although a great deal of awareness had already emerged just prior to World War I. Those who came to emphasize the point were first and foremost work world people; moreover, they were not staff people such as medical or personnel; nor were they persons from the outside who sought to influence employers. Rather, they were largely line managers, whose chief concern was "getting the job done." More basic, however, is the fact that these very early efforts were exclusively directed toward alcohol and alcohol problems only. Even though other personal problems were to attract

much attention later in Employee Assistance Programs the origin of job-based programs was undeniably in alcohol problems within the workplace.

The Early and Mid-Forties: Actual Programs Emerge

Three potent forces combined during this period to capitalize on the already present and widespread concern about the effects of alcohol on job efficiency. First was the birth and sudden growth of Alcoholics Anonymous (AA). Second, influential and dedicated medical directors came to support and actively initiate programs during this period, providing a high status leadership to the emerging programs. Third, this development converged with the unique labor market conditions during World War II.

In 1938, there were three AA groups and approximately 100 members. By 1944, the movement had 10,000 members in just over 300 groups in America and Canada. Widespread favorable publicity about the "Big Book," *Alcoholics Anonymous,* created a wave of interest about AA during 1939 and 1940. An article in the *Saturday Evening Post* in 1941 accelerated the sale of the book and a flood of interest in AA activity (Trice, 1958). In 1945, a film, "Problem Drinkers," in the *March of Time* documentary series, focused on AA, the newly formed National Committee for Education on Alcoholism (NCEA), and the Yale Center of Alcohol Studies.

Probably of equal significance was the fact that AA had come to the attention of a few influential medical directors and industrial physicians who became very prominent in developing many of the early programs. From the recollections of our various sources come numerous names of company medical directors during this period. One source believes that Dr. Daniel Lynch, Medical Director of the New England Telephone Company in the thirties, "could be the very first in point of time who conducted a program for alcoholics in industry; he was conducting his one-man Medical Director program as early as the mid-thirties." Other sources mention Dr. George Gehrmann of DuPont, Dr. John L. Norris of Eastman Kodak, Dr.

John Witmer and Dr. S. Charles Franco of Consolidated Edison, Dr. W. Harvey Cruickshank of Bell Canada, Dr. James Roberts of New England Electric, Dr. Clyde Greene of Pacific Telephone and Telegraph, Dr. Robert Page of Standard Oil of New Jersey, Dr. Harold Meyer of Illinois Bell Telephone, and Dr. James Lloyd of North American Aviation. We will discuss some of these individuals and programs in more detail in a later section.

To a very large degree, underlying motivation for rehabilitative action came from the unusual labor market conditions during World War II. The enormous production requirements of the war resulted in a careful measurement of productivity at a time when many companies were "scraping the bottom of the barrel" for employees. Under the pressure for the "fullest possible production" (Stevenson, 1942:661), significant losses of efficiency by only a few workers created a noticeable problem. Fox (1944:257) described the personnel demands as a "drastic change from a period of recession to one of maximum production (which) brought many new problems to industry, including those arising from the employment of workers who would hardly be hired under normal conditions." As a result, many cases of problem drinking and alcoholism, which would otherwise have remained largely outside, the typical workplace, came to the attention of managers and medical directors. For example, Dr. James Roberts of the New England Electric Company said that during the war years the company was desperately in need of employees, especially at the wage earning level, and began recruiting from employment agencies in the Bowery area of New York. Many of these employees were near skid row types, and efforts to devise rehabilitation for them was unsatisfactory. Dr. Roberts underscored that the company program evolved from necessity rather than benevolence. Aside from the need to hire "marginal" workers, other factors also contributed to management's awareness of alcohol-related problems in the workplace during the war years. As the association between alcohol abuse and absenteeism became more and more obvious (Industrial Medicine, 1943), this became the most significant part of the awareness (Jukes, 1943). Shift work also

produced on-the-job drinking with its safety and disciplinary problems. Rapid, sudden expansion of productivity necessitated long working hours, making for a use of alcohol and for management's toleration of it that was reminiscent of a century earlier.

There were also indications that conditions just after the war exacerbated employee drinking problems. One factor was the problem of readjustment for millions of returning soldiers. Another was the large scale readjustment of industry and business itself to peacetime conditions. Henry A. Mielcarek, Director of Personnel Services at Allis Chalmers during the postwar period, observed that these problems continued on into the fifties (Mielcarek, 1951).

Although labor conditions had a great deal of influence on the development of the early "near programs," union involvement was practically nonexistent. It should be noted that true management involvement was also minimal during this time. The truly early programs were often so "informal" and "unwritten," that only those directly involved knew what was going on. For example, great pains were taken at DuPont for three or four years after program inception to "keep quiet what was being done." [Quotation marks, without a designation, indicate a direct quote from one of our sources.] If management was kept uninformed, labor unions were consulted even less. Although union organization and strength were well advanced during this period, it was not until the late forties and early fifties that unions became involved. Even then it was largely on their own initiative. There is evidence that for quite some time programs were seen as management-based. When Eastman Kodak and DuPont made their programs public, no union was involved, and as other companies explored programs following the war, this same attitude prevailed. Although this was slowly to change, it set a pattern for future programming, and one that was to be a source of much confusion and conflict.

Pioneer Companies:
The Unheralded and the Famous

There is substantial evidence in our accumulated materials that there were numerous employers who were taking some form of action approaching a program during the war years. Some branches of the military also appeared to be taking steps to combat alcoholism. Rather early on the Merchant Marine found that combat pressures were so strong for some men that they resorted to heavy alcohol use. As a result, this service developed its own rehabilitation centers and encouraged an open recognition of the problem (JIF, 1947). There is also some evidence in our materials that the U.S. Navy had a similar concern.

Among companies who may have been developing some form of program—often dubbed "informal" or "quasi-private"—during or just after World War II, some appear at least twice in our materials, but are difficult to corroborate. Among these are the Hudson Department Store of Detroit and Thompson Aircraft Products of Cleveland. Similarly, Schlitz Brewery received some mention, but the lead is difficult to substantiate.

Most tangible evidence exists concerning a cluster of companies who appear to have had some of the basic ingredients of alcoholism programs in the early forties. The Pacific Telephone and Telegraph Company in 1940 made one of its many modifications and additions to its employee benefit plan; it decided that disability directly or indirectly due to intoxication or use of alcohol would be covered by the plan; prior to this such coverage had been discretionary. The New England Electric Company, responding to many of the pressures of World War II, began an organized effort to control and rehabilitate problem drinkers in the mid-forties. There are also indications that the Illinois Bell Telephone Company began working with alcoholics toward the end of the war. The work "was done quietly with no formal management support." In other words, the approach was a rehabilitative one, but it was "unwritten." Just why there was so much emphasis on "keeping it quiet" during this period is a question never answered by our sources; however, one may guess that the stigma attached to alcoholism played an important part.

In the Western Electric Company a series of memos in the early forties set forth a rehabilitative approach, although the company made no formal public statement. One source indicated that such guidelines existed in the late 1930s when he began working for Western Electric. According to this source, unions were cooperative from the beginning—an exception to the general rule of not involving unions.

Although there is some evidence that an "unwritten policy" had existed earlier, the Caterpillar Tractor Company's "formal" efforts to deal with alcoholism began in 1945. In that year, the company's medical department and personnel from the Medical College of Cornell University developed a comprehensive, company-wide mental health program that included alcoholism (Vonachen et al., 1946). In many ways, this was an early Employee Assistance Program (EAP) rather than a plan which focused solely on the alcoholic employee. It seems to be the only example of an explicitly EAP approach in this entire period, though one survey observed that "there is also a marked trend to integrate industrial alcoholism activities with broader health and personal programs" (Henderson and Straus, 1952). This reference may have been to the kind of personnel counseling programs that also were active in Western Electric's Hawthorne plant, and in the Chino Mines Division of Kennecott Copper Company. Our evidence, however, suggests a sharp separation between these programs and job-based alcoholism ones. Alcoholism programs focused on alcoholism and alcoholism only—other drugs were rarely, if ever, mentioned in the literature or other source material.

Other early approaches also seemed to be moving toward the status of a program, yet are largely unheralded as such today. The first semiformalized effort on the West Coast was started by North American Aviation in 1944. Webb Hale, Manager of Personnel Administration, instituted the program with Earl S. (where private or AA sources were used, an effort has been made to respect AA members' anonymity in the spirit of AA's traditions by using the first name and the first initial of the last name. We especially tried to follow this policy with living AA members who helped us), a recovering alcoholic, was employed as a counselor and soon began to work with various other company locations. Although there is a question in our materials about how much top management recognized this "program," there still was some formalization.

Just after the war, Dr. W. Harvey Cruickshank of Bell Telephone of Canada became interested in the problem of alcoholism in the workplace. However, a program was not formalized for some years to come, due in large part to management resistance.

Against this background of unheralded employers who were taking bits and pieces of programmatic action in the war years, and immediately thereafter, it is revealing to look at the widely publicized "pioneers." Probably the most celebrated are those at E.I. DuPont de Nemours and Company and at the Eastman Kodak Corporation. They are linked together for a good reason. Apparently, Dr. John L. Norris of Eastman Kodak and Dr. George H. Gehrmann of DuPont played very similar roles at about the same time in the very early forties, although they never met until a conference in 1949. Both were much impressed with the effectiveness of AA in arresting problem drinking among employees and encouraged the use of AA by utilizing the services of recovering alcoholics who worked in the plant. However, while both of these often publicized "pioneers" started from much the same point, they nevertheless diverged considerably in their approaches in program development with one moving toward a more formalized internal program with a policy statement and coordinator, while the other initiated an informal network of information and action directed toward outside community agencies.

Dr. Gehrmann developed the DuPont program with the help of a member of AA, David M., who was hired specifically for that purpose. Dr. Gehrmann's interest was in part due to several severe drinking problems among highly valuable DuPont employees. Also, important was the interest of high status managers in the company. Apparently the activity at DuPont became more formalized as the war ended.

In contrast, the situation at Kodak remained informal during this period, with the medical department and a network of AA members inside the company operating with the "quiet acceptance" of management. Nor is there evidence that

an awareness of alcoholism among higher status employees operated at Kodak, although it might have done so. In any case, Dr. Norris developed the tie with AA in a way that emphasized it as a community resource, and followed through with this approach by helping to form one of the first Councils of Alcoholism, in Rochester, New York, under whose aegis an outpatient clinic was established.

Given this examination of the history of both the publicized and unpublicized early programs, it is difficult to speak of a "first." Clearly, North American Aviation on the West Coast developed the basic elements of a program at about the same time as did DuPont and Kodak on the East Coast, and in somewhat the same way. Other companies were also active, with many having dedicated, energetic AA persons working with them, but many always remained "informal." DuPont and Eastman Kodak operated a very low-key program indeed during the late war years and immediately thereafter, but both had medical directors who used their status and expertise to initiate, innovate, and break precedent. Perhaps this sponsorship by relatively influential staff officers constituted the major differences, insuring some continuity and recognition. This may be particularly true of Dr. Gehrmann, who decided to concentrate internally. He thereby slowly built a program inside DuPont, rather than relating primarily to community resources and agencies.

This notion of an "in-house" program received support from the next pioneer company to emerge, the Consolidated Edison Company of New York. In many ways it represents a transition from the informal, unwritten practices that characterized the start of the earlier programs. Early in 1947, Consolidated Edison officially recognized alcoholism as a medical disorder and set up a three-fold procedure for dealing with it. Behind this decision were factors quite different from those operating at Kodak and DuPont. Dr. John J. Witmer, Vice President of Industrial Relations in 1947, seemed to be a moving force, although there is some evidence that the Chairman of the Board, Ralph Tapscott, initiated the idea following complaints about the discharge of a long-term problem drinking employee from a local clergyman. Dr.

Witmer had consulted on several occasions with Dr. Gehrmann of DuPont, as well as with Professor Selden Bacon of Yale. Unlike the case with DuPont and Kodak, there is a conspicuous absence of reference to counselors, AA groups, or AA members within the company. Instead, an influential medical director and department, encouraged by top management, apparently devised the plan largely on their own, a play relying heavily on the authority of the company to legitimately intervene. In many ways, what is now called "occupational programming" had come into being. For example, there is good reason to believe that the union was quite active, and that the company incorporated it into the planning. The company also took the position that they would openly describe their policy, despite some unfavorable publicity. In terms of modern day programs, it may well be that Consolidated Edison was really "number one."

AA Pioneers

There are two persons who can truly be called pioneers in job-based programs. The earliest, and truly the first, was the previously mentioned David M., who started a one-man, persistent campaign within the Remington Arms Company of Bridgeport, Connecticut, a subsidiary of the DuPont Company. He was to continue this work inside that same company until his retirement in 1967. Although he came to have some influence outside DuPont (he was invited to participate in the industrial seminar at Yale, the first University of Wisconsin Summer School, and later on at Rutgers University industrial workshops) he nevertheless was largely a pioneer within the company. He can be called an "inside" change agent. The second pioneer, Ralph "Lefty" Henderson, was a sharp contrast. From his position as industrial consultant with the Yale Center of Alcohol Studies, he began in 1948 to range far and wide, contacting and encouraging organizations by the dozens, traveling practically all over the country to start programs. If David M. was "Mr. Inside," Lefty Henderson was "Mr. Outside."

Both came from the same background of severe, chronic alcoholism and recovery through

Alcoholics Anonymous. Both were products of the very early period of AA's growth–both joining AA in 1940–and both manifested an almost superhuman tenacity and persistence, restrained by a worldly-wise finesse. Both had high status and influential collaborators who should share in their pioneer standing. Certainly this is true of David M.'s association with Dr. George H. Gehrmann, long-time Medical Director at DuPont. Henderson's affiliation was with Professor Seldon D. Bacon, Director of the Yale Center of Alcohol Studies. Although Bacon's direct involvement was much shorter than that of Gehrmann, it was for a time intense. Perhaps the Fates also deserve recognition for bringing the individuals of these two pairs together. There is little doubt that, despite many differences in background and status, there was a compatibility, a "chemistry," in each pair that sparked action.

David M.: A Dedicated Inside Change Agent

Dave M. was the first industrial counselor hired to work with alcoholic employees. His early experience in the industrial environment and determined efforts at the Remington Arms Company are best described in his own words:

> One of the officers of the tennis club (where I worked) was Vice President of the Remington Arms Company and I told him about this very vivid and wonderful experience of AA. I told him that I wanted to get out of tennis and that I felt industry could use something of this kind. He seemed quite understanding and he said certainly the members of the Club had noticed quite a difference. I advertised in the paper that an AA group was starting in the Bridgeport-Fairfield area. Then came along a case of a shift supervisor in Remington Arms. This man responded very well, so I went to the Vice President and asked him if I could approach the people at Remington Arms to see if they would rehire this supervisor. I saw the head of personnel and the welfare man. They were both very understanding, but then they took it up with the Medical Director; Dr. was adamant that the man would not be allowed to return to work at Remington Arms. Dr. had fired him and he was going to stay fired.
>
> That summer I finished my work at tennis hop-

ing to get started in industry with Remington Arms, but I found out that I only had my first citizenship papers. I had to wait until March. I went from September (I'd given up my job at Aiken) to March without any work of any kind because there was nothing to do without my second citizenship papers. Finally I did start with Remington Arms in March 1942. I particularly wanted to get into the shop to get a better idea of industry in general. I was put on a job as an inspector, inspecting bullet jackets as they were made. I started at 75 ¢ an hour after I'd been making $5.00 to $6.00 an hour at tennis. [for five months] my job was working from 11:00 at night until 7:00 in the morning. It was quite a rich experience. I picked up a couple of alcoholics and got them interested in coming to our AA meeting in Bridgeport.

Then with quite an effort, I got transferred to the personnel department as a terminator/exit interviewer. I met with people who were leaving the company after being fired, or going into the service, or becoming pregnant. In this particular job the alcoholic had to come through me and this was where we were able to get them interested in coming into AA. Before I left Remington Arms, I was able to keep 22 employees working steady and sober with AA.

When I was in personnel, I contacted about 3 or 4 of the manufacturing supervisors—top men—and told them about my experience and asked if they had any employees with a drinking problem and said I'd be only too pleased to help. In my particular office I was soon able to get supervisors to give these people who were being let go another chance and the success rate was extremely high. They were very pleased, but when I approached top management in Remington Arms about what more could be done officially, I was told that there was not enough of a problem to justify a program. I asked permission to approach the DuPont Company, in Wilmington, Delaware. I had to go through Dr. _____ to be allowed to approach DuPont, the parent company. Again, I got a very emphatic no from Dr. _____. In September 1942, I got a letter of introduction to two of the bigshots in Wilmington: Mr. Maurice DuPont Lee and Emile DuPont. I got the letter of introduction from a Vice President of the Guarantee Trust Co. who at this time was active in AA himself. I made arrangements and went down to see Mr. Lee and Mr. DuPont. I explained the work that had been done at Remington. They were very gracious, and thanked me for the time and effort, but they didn't feel that drinking was a major problem. They said

they had picked up a few cases over the years that could have been helped, but they could see no need for anything in the way of a program.

On the way down to make the visit, I had stopped at the AA clubhouse in Philadelphia. I got friendly with one of the members there and I told him about the work I'd done at Remington Arms and my intention of going to DuPont. He said the Medical Director of DuPont, Dr. Gehrmann, had been to two or three meetings and that he was red hot as far as AA was concerned. The AA said I should be sure to see Dr. Gehrmann while I was in Wilmington.

After I had been to see Mr. Lee and Mr. DuPont, I went over to Medical, but Dr. Gehrmann happened to be out of town, so I didn't see him. Two weeks later, I got a letter from Mr. Lee thanking me again but saying that they could see nothing in the way of a program in the future. Naturally, I was quite disappointed. About 3 weeks after that I got a layoff notice. Remington Arms was cutting back from 15,000 to 7,000 practically overnight. So by December 1, 1943, I had a month's notice to leave. With that, I got on the phone to call Dr. Gehrmann and explain that I was in AA, that I had been in AA 3 years, and what I'd done at Remington Arms. Gehrmann's answer was 'By God, you're just the guy I'm looking for. . . .' He said he'd been to some AA meetings in Philadelphia, was deeply impressed, and would like to get a group started in the company or in Wilmington. He said, 'I'll arrange for you to come down and talk it over and see what we can do about a transfer.' So, that's what happened. I went down and saw Dr. Gehrmann and we seemed quite pleased with each other. In the meantime, I talked it over with Bill Wilson and I said 'If I take a job like this would I be a professional AA?' He said 'No, not unless you actually took money for direct therapy. If a company wants to hire someone to give information and to teach them about the problem and give some direction there is no one more qualified than the recovered alcoholic.' So, in that case I felt free, and he said he thought it would be a wonderful thing if I could work something out.

Dr. Gehrmann wanted to set me up in Medical, but I suggested I stay anonymous and find a job that would keep me busy. In the meantime, I'd start a group in Wilmington that could absorb any DuPont employee. I transferred there in January 1944.

Once "on board," Dave M. quietly, but with determination and Dr. Gehrmann's backing, began to approach employees. Apparently supervisors would confront employees with poor performance, decide whether the problem was alcohol-related or not, and refer at once to the medical department. Henrietta Gehrmann, the widow of the medical director, stated that "Dr. G. gave him (Dave M.) names of men he was to approach." He would tell these employees about the AA group he and a few others had started in Wilmington, Delaware. At the same time he made it clear that it was the employee's choice to decide whether to join or not. In the meantime the employee would have the general help of the medical department, but unless he took steps to overcome his problem he would be discharged. These points, and others such as probation for three months, came to be formalized by Gehrmann over the next four years into company policy and procedure (Gehrmann, 1955). This tough "constructive coercion" position is one that has been substantially muted into what is today called "constructive confrontation" (Beyer and Trice, 1980).

Dave M. was a naturalized citizen of the U.S. He was born in the north of Ireland and lived in England until he was 21 where he was educated and developed his love for tennis. He came to this country in 1923 during the Prohibition era. By 1928–29 he had become an active alcoholic, growing worse and worse over a twelve-year period. During this time, he made his living as a coach and professional tennis player. He learned about AA when he read an article about the group in *Liberty Magazine.* He sent away for the AA book and in early 1940 and, greatly impressed by it, contacted the organization.

Dave M. was in his early forties when, after joining AA, he worked for Remington Arms, and then transferred to DuPont. For a quarter of a century, he pursued the growth and development of the alcoholism program within DuPont and its many locations and subsidiaries, making this his major life's work until he retired in 1967. Bill W., the co-founder of AA, in a letter to Dave M. in 1968 refers to "the marvelous job that you turned in as the first pioneer of alcoholic rehabilitation in industry." There seems little doubt that he was a true innovator, joined by another innovator—a dedicated, powerful medical director—to launch a new and practical approach to alcoholism.

We know much less about what Dr. Gehrmann's experiences and attitudes were during the late 1930s and early 1940s, but there are some clues. At the time Dave M. called him in 1943, he had, like Dr. Norris, experienced numerous failures with alcoholic employees. He later declared that "for twenty-eight years I struggled without AA and my results were zero; with AA over the past five years, I got 65 percent (recovery)" (National Industrial Conference Board, 1958:36). Also like Dr. Norris, he was much impressed by AA and the results it had achieved. He had referred professional employees to it and had himself attended some meetings. He was at the time a well-established professional and an administrative officer in the company, and had been with DuPont since 1915, about 25 years, allowing for service during World War I. He had been medical director since 1926 and was not to retire until 1955. Of the numerous industrial physicians who played a role in the emergence of job-based programs, he was probably one of the best positioned to initiate the innovation and keep it alive.

There is also good reason to believe that some of the top management at DuPont was sympathetic, although not necessarily convinced. Dr. Thomas Hogshead, a psychiatrist in private practice in Wilmington, and who knew the principals involved, has identified Maurice DuPont Lee as a person "who was also quite instrumental in the inauguration and development of this program." Maurice DuPont Lee's interest may have come about because of a chance meeting, while on vacation with Bill W. Other sources mention Henry DuPont and Emile DuPont as also having been sympathetic. In any case, there apparently was no opposition to what Dr. Gehrmann and Dave M. were doing; although there may not have been active encouragement. The best conclusion is that, as far as the company policy was concerned, Dr. Gehrmann "carried the ball" alone.

Ralph "Lefty" Henderson: A Peripatetic and Influential "Outside Change Agent"

Many of the early forces operating to produce

job-based programs culminated in the person and work of Ralph McComb Henderson. For the last ten years of his life (1948–1958) he was the industrial consultant for the Yale Center for Alcohol Studies, traveling constantly in an effort to influence both small and large companies, and unions as well, to take positive rehabilitative action toward their problem-drinking employees. Probably no other single person invested as much time, effort, and energy to this general task. R. Brinkley Smithers stated that Henderson aided greatly in installing programs in numerous small companies in New Haven and vicinity where the Yale Center was located. Professor Milton Maxwell, who succeeded Henderson at Yale, observed in 1958 that Henderson "had a small or large hand in just about every occupational program in existence." Mark Keller, long-time editor of the *Journal of Studies on Alcohol*, describes him as "our man for industry and he was often on the road promoting the Yale Plan for Business and Industry." He goes on to say that he believes Henderson to be the main initiator, with Professor Selden Bacon of Yale, of the Allis Chalmers program in Milwaukee. Bacon himself spent much time in the early fifties on the road with Henderson, explaining the Yale Plan and soliciting funds for an industrial unit at the Yale Center. Bacon describes him as an "itchy-foot AA who was eager to get to the big boys and tell them the facts of life about boozers," and as "a frequent traveler who, when on the road, talked and talked and talked and was enormously welcome as a talker."

Henderson could be termed the first occupational program consultant (OPC) with a territory that covered the Northeast, the Midwest, and probably even beyond. Lewis Presnall, in fact, tells of him visiting the Chino Mines Division of Kennecott Copper in Hurley, New Mexico, in the early fifties. Henderson's second wife, Esther, relates how he was often invited to the Minneapolis-St. Paul area where he consulted with numerous industrial representatives. She says that he "traveled all over creation—I wouldn't be surprised if he used American Legion contacts, law contacts, contacts made when he was in industry, but above all AA contacts, and of course the NCA staff; he was getting in touch with various people

in industry all over America."

George S. describes several visits that Henderson made to the Milwaukee area. Accompanying him on these visits were such prominent persons as Marty Mann, Leo Greenberg, and Selden Bacon. According to George S., Henderson played an "integral part in setting up the Milwaukee effort." Under the auspices of the Milwaukee Information and Referral Center, the first meetings in the area to discuss job-based programs were set up to include 14 employers, among whom were International Harvester, Huebsch Manufacturing, Trackson Co., Wisconsin Electric, A.O. Smith, American Laundry, Schlitz Brewery, Cudahy Packing Co., Allis Chalmers, and Marathon Paper. Apparently strongly influenced by Henderson, George S. stimulated a cooperative network of companies who agreed to participate in a demonstration program of the Yale Plan. This may well have been the first consortium. Henderson first came to Milwaukee in 1950, and upon his third trip there (two years later) was badly injured in a car accident. Because of this, and George S.'s departure from Milwaukee in 1953, the program for all practical purposes lapsed at this point.

Henderson's work in the Northeast is described by Charles Rietdyke, who as Coordinator of Supervisory Training at the Scovill Manufacturing Company in Waterbury, Connecticut, worked with Henderson to develop Scovill's alcoholism policy. Rietdyke describes Henderson's influence in starting programs at Scovill, Armco Steel, and Waterbury Brass Works in the early fifties. Elizabeth Whitney (now Elizabeth Whitney Post), detailed Henderson's dedication and enthusiasm in making numerous trips to Boston to talk with industrial groups and fraternal organizations. Like George S. in Milwaukee, she was greatly influenced and aided by Henderson in her work among New England companies. Henderson also had a substantial effect on the developing policy at Standard Oil of New Jersey. The AA General Services Office used his name, with that of Dave M. as a reference person, in answering mail inquiries about job-based programs in the early fifties. Seldon Bacon estimates he corresponded with over 50 companies and unions during that time.

Even before taking the Yale position, however, Henderson's travels had been extensive to say the least. The year before joining the Yale Center (1947), he had worked as a field representative of the then National Committee for Education on Alcoholism. During that year, according to his annual report, he visited 43 different cities in 14 different states and one in Canada, often two and three times. In the early 1940s, when Henderson worked for the Wedge Pipe Company in New Orleans, "he made speeches to business and industrial groups all over the South," as well as literally hundreds of AA talks. Beyond doubt Ralph "Lefty" Henderson sowed the seeds of job-based programs wider and further than anyone before him, and probably anyone since.

Henderson's personality apparently fitted his mobility in that he was outgoing, gregarious, and extroverted. Those who saw him in action usually had similar impressions and their descriptions were always very affectionate in tone. To one observer, he was "a bear-like man, a friendly, husky St. Bernard with a twinkle in his eye." Yet another vividly described him as a very persuasive "unmade bed." To another, he was a "gruff, eager beaver AA who told it like it was." One informant described how Henderson, on one occasion, had to be corrected on "scientific matters" while lecturing at the summer school, and that he boasted in an AA talk in 1954 that he was "proud that I'm no scholar." He was, however, a well-educated, colorful, and dynamic speaker who could command both humor and respect. One of the students in his industrial seminar in 1954 likened him to Will Rogers or Wallace Beery, describing how he used commanding gestures with "ham-like hands." Bacon said Henderson "was the most magnificent platform artist I ever saw." Apparently his earlier skills as a trial lawyer had found new and different expressions.

He was born in Armour, South Dakota in 1895; in 1919, he graduated from Law School at the State University. After private practice in his own law firm as a trial lawyer, he became active in the American Legion–he had served in World War I. In 1933–34, he was made State Commander of the Legion and soon thereafter was Assistant Attorney General of South Dakota for a brief time. In 1939, he was a State Chairman for the Republican National Convention and participated in the nomination of Alf Landon.

He developed a severe drinking problem during this period of his life. In one of his taped AA talks in 1954, he estimated that there were "seven or eight years when I was just lost from my associates, lost from my family, and actually lost to myself." He and his first wife were separated and ultimately divorced. In the late thirties he experienced skid row in many states. His turning point came in 1939 when a municipal judge in Chicago precipitated a crisis by threatening to "put him away" if he didn't join AA. Also his wife-to-be, Esther, provided moral support and encouraged him to learn about and locate AA. At that time AA was, in his words, "rather hard to find." When he did finally make contact, according to his AA story, he discovered the judge was already a member himself!

Upon affiliating with AA in 1940, he took a job with the Wedge Pipe Company of Chicago. He worked out of the firm's New Orleans office and was, according to his obituary (*Quarterly Journal of Studies on Alcohol* 1958:374) an "industrial personnel specialist." Having spent the war years in this capacity he probably saw firsthand some of the ways in which a specific workplace dealt with problem-drinking employees. In 1946, the company transferred him back to Chicago where a new phase of his life began. He married for the second time, and in 1947 both he and his wife attended the Yale Summer School Alcohol Studies. While there, Esther Henderson accepted a position as Secretary/Treasurer with Professor Selden Bacon at the Center of Alcohol Studies. Ralph Henderson took a position as Assistant to the Executive Director of NCEA, Mrs. Marty Mann. During 1947 he traveled extensively for NCEA throughout the Southeast, Northeast, and Midwest, establishing a mobile pattern, which soon accelerated and became his trademark. The following year, 1948, he accepted an offer from the Yale Center to serve as their industrial consultant.

From 1948 until 1958, Henderson developed the work world approach to problem drinking at the Yale Center. He lectured at the summer school, conducting an industrial seminar there, and engaged in what could be termed "outreach" to a wide variety of employers and unions. During his first years at Yale, he sketched out, with Selden Bacon, the "Yale Plan for Business and Industry" (Henderson and Bacon, 1953). In this article he developed a concept that was to become widely used, the "half man" description of alcoholic employees. The Plan contained a series of specific suggested policy guidelines a company could follow to openly deal with the problem-drinking employee, containing sections on the pivotal role of line supervisors, location of coordinators in the company, and counseling-referral. It put frequent emphasis upon alcoholism as a health problem and upon the alcoholic as a sick person. As mentioned previously, the Plan was a focal point for a series of conferences in Milwaukee, Wisconsin under the auspices of the Milwaukee Information and Referral Center. Henderson acted as a "spark plug" in the entire effort although it later collapsed. Apparently only one company carried through and that was Allis Chalmers, which was to produce a classic example that would be cited and studied worldwide. The death of Henderson in 1958 meant the loss of an energetic pioneer who had both a keen personal knowledge of alcoholism and a working knowledge of, and experiences with, the dynamics of the workplace—a combination of attributes that was often to be in short supply as job-based programs grew in numbers and size in the coming years.

There are certainly other AA "pioneers" of job-based alcoholism programs about whom we unfortunately have less background information. One such person is Warren T., the first counselor with the Great Northern Railroad (presently Burlington Northern Railroad) in the early fifties. We have some tantalizing glimpses of his earlier pioneering efforts through Dave M., and the AA General Services Headquarters in New York, but few solid facts. In the AA files, we find a letter written in March 1943, signed Warren T., which reads, "I am now in the loan department, under a personnel manager who is a most tolerant person, and I am to take care of the alcoholic problems. This I believe is the first firm to take on an AA for

that sole purpose. I have been here on the new job four days and have conferred with 17 cases (which I write up) of men who admit their alcohol problem and are looking for help." He then refers to the "shipyard" where he works. Dave M. says that Warren T. worked for the Kaiser Shipyards near Oakland, California in a job not unlike the one Dave M. had with Remington Arms in 1941. That is, he was in the personnel department where he could readily encounter employees with drinking problems. Although his letter fails to mention these assumed details, they nevertheless seem plausible. In spite of the optimistic tone of the letter to AA Headquarters, Dave M. has said that Warren T. had trouble getting management support—the same problem which he himself had with Remington Arms. Whether or not Warren T. was able to continue in this type of work after the shipyards closed down in 1946 is unclear.

On the other hand, in a speech at the Twentieth Anniversary Convention of Alcoholics Anonymous in St. Louis in 1955, he remarked that "I've worked on this problem in industry for more than 12 years. . . ." But in a July 1951 letter to AA headquarters, telling them of his appointment at Great Northern he observes that "I am most grateful for the opportunity to again get back into active work of this type that I like so well."

One thing seems clear. Warren T. was an experienced man with employed alcoholics when he came to work for Great Northern, and that he gained this experience on the West Coast during the forties. Much like Dave M. he was motivated by his AA affiliation. He worked in a somewhat more receptive company, but started approximately two years later, and probably had to cease his efforts because the war ended and management was unwilling to go formal. In contrast, Dave M.'s job accelerated following the war. In any event, it seems likely that Dave M. (1941) was followed by Warren T. (1943), with Henderson capping off the AA pioneers of this period (1949).

Two other AA members, Elizabeth W. in Boston and George S. in Milwaukee, also played an important role in the field of alcoholism programming in the mid-1940s, but with a somewhat different focus. Both approached the question of job-based programs from the standpoint of broad-based community action organization. Their approach contrasted with both Dave M.'s and Warren T.'s and to some degree with Henderson, who were all more oriented to single, specific work organizations. George S. left Milwaukee in 1953 and continued his community-based approach in Canada. Elizabeth W., however, continued to generate considerable activity over a long period of time among local work organizations in the Boston area. For a quarter of a century, she served as the Executive Director of the Greater Boston Council on Alcoholism, an organization she founded in 1945. The Council, the first volunteer community health organization in the U.S. to deal with alcoholism, became the first affiliate of NCA. She recognized early on the importance of working together with industry in order to effectively rehabilitate alcoholics. Through the Greater Boston Council on Alcoholism she established the Consultation and Guidance Service on Alcoholism for Business and Industry, a service designed to educate companies in the greater Boston area on the problem of alcoholism and provide them with information about community treatment facilities. For five years the Greater Boston Council co-sponsored a two-credit course for personnel workers entitled "Problem Drinkers in Business and Industry" together with Boston University and the Personnel Managers Club of the Chamber of Commerce. One-day institutes were presented at the Harvard Business School,

Tufts, and MIT during a seven-year period.

Among the many companies in the Boston area with which she worked are Dow Chemical, Bell Telephone, General Electric, Hood Milk, Raytheon, Woolworth, Allis Chalmers, First National Bank of Boston, Eastern Gas and Fuel, New England Electric, Foxboro Company, New England Telephone, and Liberty Mutual. The widespread support that Boston industry committed to the efforts of the Boston Council is a reflection of the capabilities of Elizabeth W.

Elizabeth W. is the most prominent woman in the early period of job-based programs, although by no means the only one. Although Marty Mann's concentration was not specifically directed to such programs, she constantly supported and "did everything possible to promote them," throughout her long career as founder of NCA. Other women worked in more specialized ways. Warren T.'s wife, Alice, worked directly with her husband, while Esther Henderson worked as an administrator and sympathetic supporter of Ralph Henderson. Also, during the surge of interest in the Milwaukee area, two industrial nurses were particularly active: Phoebe Brown of the Schlitz Brewery and Kathleen Russell of International Harvester. At approximately the same time, Metropolitan Life Insurance Company in New York appointed Dr. Lydia Giberson as a member of the President's staff to counsel on medical-behavioral problems.

THE UPSURGE OF PROGRAMS–LATE FORTIES AND EARLY FIFTIES

In a broader view, a more discernible coherence in efforts to develop job-based alcoholism programs emerged as the 1950s approached, with a resultant burgeoning of activity. There was a sharp increase in the number of formal, written policies and a diminution of the "quietly started" ones. A number of factors were involved.

Major Contributing Factors

AA continued to provide a widespread impetus; its General Services Office continued to respond to inquiries about job-based programs

from both members and nonmembers. Between 1949 and 1954, there was an increase of almost 50 percent in the number of inquiries about work-world programs, although inquiries leveled off. AA itself continued to grow during these years. By 1950, there were approximately 90,000 members in 3,000 groups spread throughout the world (Trice, 1958).

The efforts of the Yale Center were sharply increasing. Not only did the major part of Ralph Henderson's work take place during this time, but he was often joined by Selden Bacon. The latter recalls the entire effort as a "tremendous campaign," saying, "I personally visited 40 or 50 directors (or presidents or executive vice presidents) of the 65 largest corporations in America and discussed this alleged problem with all of them at considerable length; this traipsing around may have had some impact; we may never know." The Yale group devised a card file about large employers, used by both Bacon and Henderson, but there were many turndowns and "deaf ears." Efforts during 1948–50 produced a tentative plan for one giant corporation. The entire thing collapsed because "the top man was a teetotaler." Yet inquiries grew. Among those who became interested were the Department of Labor and the Federal Security Agency.

In the early fifties, the Christopher D. Smithers Foundation was established; in October 1952 it was formally incorporated. It soon became—and remains today—the only private foundation actively promoting education and action program on alcoholism. Although its focus was much broader than industrial alcoholism, it soon came to regard industry as a major arena for programs and prevention efforts. Moreover, its early emphasis was on the need for labor and management participation in joint planning and action. It actively encouraged labor-management committees in the National Council on Alcoholism and developed foundation bulletins directed toward job-based programs (Smithers Foundation, 1977). The Foundation collected information on individual company programs, which resulted in the first publication that surveyed the developments of the forties and fifties (Smithers Foundation, 1958). Since this early beginning, the Foundation, and its President, R. Brinkley Smithers, have actively supported and helped to develop job-based programs.

Publicity also began to play a part in the upsurge of activities. At least two companies, Allis Chalmers and Consolidated Edison, openly publicized their programs. Henderson received good press coverage on the subject indicating that his subject matter was newsworthy. Charles P. Frazier, a New York City journalist and later Director of Education for the Christopher D. Smithers Foundation, wrote a series of articles that attracted much attention and came to be dubbed "The Billion Dollar Hangover." Copyrighted by the United Features Syndicate, the three-piece series appeared in over 250 newspapers and magazines. In his introduction, Frazier wrote: "Alcoholism has grown to be a billion-dollar-a-year headache in industry and a few enterprising companies have taken steps to combat it therapeutically" (Frazier, 1957).

In addition, there was radio coverage starting in 1950. Elizabeth W., Executive Director of the Greater Boston Council on Alcoholism, produced and moderated a weekly radio program entitled "Alcoholism is Everybody's Business." She interviewed various community leaders, many of whom were leaders in business and industry, on the program. She also invited speakers from various industrial companies from all over the country to be interviewed. Among her guests were industrial physicians, psychologists, and nurses who discussed the problem of and programs for the alcoholic employee. This long-running radio program had a listening audience of 150,000.

During this period, the American Association of Industrial Physicians and Surgeons (currently known as the American Occupational Medical Association) formed a Committee on Alcoholism. In 1950, its name was changed to the Committee on Problem Drinking and Dr. R. Gordon Bell of Toronto became its chairman. The committee's efforts were directed toward changing the disinterested and negative attitude held by numerous members of the industrial medical community toward the alcoholic employee. Membership on the committee included such well-known physicians as Dr. James Roberts of New England Electric, Dr. Harvey Cruickshank of Bell Telephone of Canada and Dr. Edward Byneski of General Electric in Cincinnati. During the Association's 1949 annual meeting, a symposium addressing the topic "Alcoholism as a Medical Problem in Industry," was presented by Drs. Gehrmann and Norris.

More concrete action came from Consolidated Edison Company in New York City during the same period of time. Dr. Franco was instrumental in establishing the Consultation Clinic for Alcoholism at University Hospital, New York University Bellevue Medical Center. Many other industrial physicians in the New York City metropolitan area soon joined with Dr. Franco in referring problem=drinking employees to the Clinic.

Consistent with these developments was the inclusion of materials on alcoholism in textbooks on occupational medicine. Dr. Gehrmann authored a chapter for a widely circulated book that described the DuPont Company program (Gehrmann, 1954). Ten years earlier, the watchword had been "keep it quiet," even for Gehrmann. Now programs for alcoholic employees were part of a textbook. Other forms of institutionalization of programs also occurred among industrial physicians during this period. Dr. John Witmer passed on the developing program at Consolidated Edison to Dr. S. Charles Franco in 1951 who in the early seventies passed it on to a younger associate of his, Dr. Thomas Doyle. At DuPont, when Dr. George Gehrmann retired, Dr. Gerald Gordon followed him and continued to work with Dave M. At Illinois Bell, Dr. Harold Meyer turned the program over to Dr. Robert Hilker who directed it during the seventies. At Eastman Kodak, upon the retirement of Dr. John Norris, Dr. William Hoskin carried the program forward.

These developments were accompanied by an outcropping of special conferences that focused on the topic of alcoholism in the workplace. In addition, more broadly-oriented Summer Schools of Alcohol Studies followed the lead of the Yale School by including in their programs, lectures, and seminars on the subject. The University of Wisconsin's Adult Extension Division, for example, began to sponsor a week-long conference on alcoholism in 1949; Henderson held a session there on industrial alcoholism throughout the early fifties. The University of Utah presented a similar conference. In the same year the Chicago Committee on Alcoholism sponsored the first national conference on the subject of problem drinking and the workplace. Entitled "The Problem of Alcoholism in Industry" it featured both Drs. Gehrmann and Norris.

Between 1949 and 1951, the Milwaukee Information and Referral Center sponsored a series of conferences that involved at least 18 companies in the Milwaukee area. In 1951, an Institute on Alcoholism was established at Marquette University's Labor College. That year Henry Mielcarek presented a session at the Institute, which described the origins and procedures of the Allis Chalmers program. By 1952, the previously mentioned course for personnel managers established by Elizabeth W. at Boston University entitled "The Problem Drinker in Business and Industry" was instituted.

A natural concomitant of these conferences was the emergence of relevant research. In 1946, Dr. Elvin M. Jellinek made his now famous *What Shall We Do About Alcoholism* speech to the Economics Club of Detroit. Published in 1947 (Jellinek, 1947), it contained a series of carefully calculated estimates of the impact of problem drinking on employee absenteeism, job-related accidents, and its costs to business and government. (It is interesting to note that the same issue of the journal carrying Dr. Jellinek's speech also carried a speech about how Alcoholics Anonymous came into being and was organized.) An enlargement of these facts and estimates soon followed. Bacon published articles directed toward both industrial physicians and business people that expanded on the factual points in Jellinek's speech and pointed out the dollar and cents costs of alcoholism to employers (Bacon, 1948; 1951).

In 1950, the Yale Center set up an Industrial Research Council on Alcoholism with representatives from prominent companies. From this group came a pioneering piece of research in 1951 that was to break with the global, overall estimates that characterized the earlier reports and effectively dispelled the skid row stereotype of the alcoholic. The research, carried out by Robert Straus and Selden Bacon of the Yale Center of Alcohol Studies on 2,000 male patients from nine outpatient clinics, produced evidence that there was a "hitherto unrecognized segment of alcoholics who display a relatively high degree of social and occupational integration" (Straus and Bacon, 1951:238). This was a landmark piece of research, often cited even today, setting the stage for the legitimacy of job-based programs. It played a pivotal role, together with earlier research, in the formation of the Yale Plan for Business and Industry, and was the backdrop against which Henderson developed his widely used "half-man" description of problem drinking employees.

Less profound, but nevertheless useful research also appeared as part of the general upswing of activities. Allis Chalmers (1950) published a follow-up report of the first eight months of its program. Seventy-one cases were studied; of these, 51 employees were still working and had so curtailed their drinking that it did not interfere with their jobs. The remaining employees were in various undetermined categories. Only five employees had to be discharged. This was perhaps the first evaluation of a company program. It set the pattern of unusual success that was to be frequently reported in future years. The Allis Chalmers program also provided data for an empirical study of absenteeism: the 174 disciplinary cases involving use of alcohol at the time the program began were absent an average of 26 days annually (O'Brien, 1949). A few years earlier, Benson Y. Landis (1945:212), commenting on data about the absenteeism of factory workers relative to drinking, reported they had lost, "on the average 3 days per month, or 36 (days) per year." Other published research attempted to make estimates of the actual number of alcoholic employees in a given workplace (Page, et al., 1952).

Surveys were not neglected in the upswing of research activity. The Greater Boston Council on Alcoholism conducted a survey of 400 Boston area companies in 1952 in an effort to determine industrial interest in job-based programming. Eighty five of the companies surveyed indicated their interest in job-based programming. Eighty-five of the companies surveyed indicated their interest in an alcoholism program that could be incorporated into their company health policy. The Opinion Research Corporation, Princeton, N.J. (1952) conducted a survey for the Licensed Beverage Industry. The results of this study, which sampled medical and personnel directors from 433 manufacturing companies, reported that in their opinion "chronic alcoholism" was not considered an important problem. And a 1954 Kansas survey of 364 companies reported a policy of immediate dismissal for detected alcoholics (Community Studies, 1954).

Although job-based programs tended to be seen initially as purely management-oriented,

union involvement and interest became manifest during the late forties and early fifties. This trend emerged despite the fact that the Yale Plan made no mention of unions. Typical of the early management-based orientation was the statement of Dr. Robert Page, Medical Director of Standard Oil of New Jersey, that a program "must be oriented, sold all down the line, and carried out by management." As R. Brinkley Smithers observed, this had often been an obstacle in implementing programs during the early period. Since that time, not only has union interest increased, but more programs have direct union involvement.

Leo Perlis, longtime Director of the Department of Community Services, AFL-CIO, recounts how alcoholism became a part of the CIO Community Services "agenda" beginning in late 1948 along with heart disease, cancer, and "all sorts of problems." Unions were actively involved in a number of seminars during the late 1940s and early 1950s. During 1948 and 1949 the CIO Community Services Committee sponsored a series of seminars and workshops where they had large locals. The Steel Workers of America held two conferences in Youngstown, Ohio in 1950. In 1953, the Utility Workers of America, CIO, and the International Brotherhood of Electrical Workers, AFL, jointly sponsored several meetings on the topic "Problem Drinking and Industry" at the New York Academy of Medicine. Perlis met and conferred a number of times with Mrs. Marty Mann, Executive Director of NCA. An outcome of these meetings was the publication of a pamphlet entitled "What Every Worker Should Know about Alcoholism." This was the first labor printed publication on the subject of alcoholism.

Also important was the effort to place labor representatives on the Board of Directors of NCA. Berkeley Watterson, staff member from CIO Community Services, was an NCA Board member in the early fifties, and Walter Reuther, President of the United Automobile Workers, was an early member also. Interestingly enough, there was some resistance from the Brewery Workers Union—who feared that the entire operation might be prohibitionist. Apparently this fear faded when members learned of the disease concept of alcoholism. Perlis summarized the early period as follows: "Our own records show that we first initiated a nationwide program on alcoholism in 1950. That was under the auspices of the National CIO Community Services Committee. While there was no great enthusiasm among union leaders, there was even less enthusiasm among corporate executives. This was so even though we proposed joint union-management sponsorship and a policy to keep alcoholism outside the controversial area of collective bargaining."

The CIO sent a number of its community services representatives to the Yale Summer School of Alcohol Studies in the early fifties. Henderson, using the CIO pamphlet, encouraged union representatives to be active in his industrial seminars and generally recognized the value of the union in job-based programs. In a 1953 letter he expressed this point succinctly. "The mere fact that the union recognizes the problem and has gone on record will be a great help in the development of programs in plants where the CIO is involved." Bacon recalls a lengthy discussion he had with officers of the Steel Workers Union; members were initially undecided on the issue of problem-drinking behavior; finally they agreed it was indeed a union problem. Meanwhile, local counselors of Community Services in New York City and Chicago had begun openly to work with alcoholism cases. In Buffalo, N.Y., the Steelworkers Local availed themselves of the knowledge and advice of Dr. Marvin Block, a widely recognized authority on the medical aspects of alcoholism, who was instrumental in initiating many alcoholism programs.

But these union achievements came at the expense of some internal conflict. Because unions were first and foremost political organizations there were real risks involved for union officers who might appear to be embracing a policy that was often seen as management inspired or controlled. For example, unions at Allis Chalmers were not involved in the initial planning of the program in the late forties. They heard about it only when the publicity occurred, and angrily threatened a strike. Matters became so bad in 1949 and 1950 that Walter Reuther, President of the United Automobile Worker, was asked to mediate. He convinced management that they

should go over the entire plan with the union. When an agreement to consult with union officials was reached, and union representatives were included in training sessions, the conflict over the program ceased and there was general union support. Surprisingly, the two unions involved said that if management did not set up a program, they would.

The Programs

The late 1940s and early 1950s saw the emergence of a large number of company programs and policies on alcoholism. Selden Bacon, referring to the emergence of open, more explicit efforts, says: "I think this sort of thing was going on all over in the fifties." Programs that developed during this period were often more formalized than earlier efforts. The alcoholism programs that were started at Allis Chalmers in Wisconsin, at Bell Telephone in Canada, at the Great Northern Railroad in Minnesota are among the best known programs of the time period.

Of these three companies, the most publicized program was at the Allis Chalmers Manufacturing Company. As with many of the earlier efforts, an AA member, George S., was a key figure in starting the program. In 1948, he organized the Milwaukee Information and Referral Center and directed his attention toward business and industry. Presumably he got a favorable reception from top management in Allis Chalmers, or perhaps he stimulated it. In any event, Walter Geist, company president during the late forties seemed to be quite motivated. An informational flyer on the Allis Chalmers program states that "Since October 1947 our company has had a plan for the rehabilitation of alcoholic employees. . . ." Henry Mielcarek, then Personnel Services Manager, described how "in March 1948 a committee was appointed to study alcoholism at Allis Chalmers" (Mielcarek, 1951:152–153). However, as often happens, there came a lull in activity for almost two years. George S., however, continued to urge Geist to launch a program. Early in 1949 Geist directed Mielcarek to get a plan together and the latter reports that "In May, 1950, an experienced counselor, a former secretary of the local AA group, was employed to handle the situation" (Mielcarek, 1951: 152–153). The program was set up in the Personnel Services Division, which also administered a wide variety of employee benefits: home benefits, physical illness benefits, retirement, recreation, and "general counseling." Initially the Medical Department was not involved, although "two or three years later" they did begin to participate, but how and to what degree is unclear.

The public relations department, on the other hand, took an active interest from the start. One observer noted that "the P.R. aspect of the program was a big factor in moving it from the drawing board to actual operation." According to several of our sources the program was publicly announced before it was actually in operation. One informant recounts how the public relations and advertising people—particularly one person— "saw all kinds of potential in it. . . . He spared no effort and no dollars and it became known worldwide; and almost overnight they had visitors from all over coming to learn how they dealt with alcoholics."

Henry Mielcarek himself traveled to Wilmington to visit with Dr. Gehrmann and also attended the Yale Summer School. He seemed to have accepted the strategy, to a degree, of DuPont and Consolidated Edison: "In our alcoholic approach, we have used the philosophy that it is our job to straighten the man out and not to punish him" (Mielcarek, 1951:159). One anecdote that seems to be fairly accurate is about his effect on a sales convention of heavy machine manufacturers in Kansas City (or St. Louis) in 1949. He included in his talk a description of the Allis Chalmers plan and this immediately generated some new accounts, especially from the deep South where some dealers thought Allis Chalmers already had an active program. One version of that incident has Mielcarek "making a great sales pitch and dominating the total sales convention." It is clear that public relations had come to play a prominent part in job-based alcoholism programs. More and more it would become a regular part, making for a sharp reversal of the "keep it quiet" atmosphere that had characterized practically all of the efforts of the early forties. As a matter of fact, it had

become so much a part that when the first AA counselor hired for the Allis Chalmers program had a bad "slip" it created "some real live problems." Another important feature was the role of the labor unions in the Allis Chalmers program. As mentioned previously, the initial lack of union involvement almost precipitated a strike. For this reason, unions were involved in early program development at Allis Chalmers, probably for the first time.

In contrast to the Allis Chalmers program, the program that emerged at Bell Telephone in Toronto, Canada, was almost purely a medical department matter, without any AA or personnel department involvement. It grew largely from the experiences and knowledge of one man: Dr. W. Harvey Cruickshank. Dr. Cruickshank's correspondence has provided us with much insight into the behavior and attitude of Canadian industry during the forties. Just prior to the war, when he was taking his degree in psychiatry, "attempts at rehabilitation were seldom considered and most never successful," and the AA movement was not yet active. During the war, Dr. Cruickshank worked with both the Ontario Department of Health and the Canadian Army Medical Corps in Canada and overseas. In neither case did anyone "give alcoholism or alcohol a second thought." But later, during the postwar changes in Canada, with the impetus toward industrial medicine engendered by the war and the improvement in economic conditions, with rising pensions and sickness benefits, he observed a growing awareness of the "great cost of employee marginal ill health and absences." As a result, top management became more and more oriented to the "human resources of the business."

Against this background, Dr. Cruickshank took a position as Medical Director of Bell Canada immediately following the war. However, it was not alcoholism that at first concerned him. Rather he was originally interested in the "main causes of illness and absences and their effects upon the business." His studies quickly identified the absent-prone and sickness-prone employee who accounted for a large percentage of the disruptive problems. Dr. Cruickshank recalls that as he and his staff "began to study in detail the absent-prone employee we ran head-on into the problem of alcoholism and, after seeing the extent of it began to spend more and more time on it." Such a position implied that rehabilitation should receive greater attention than it had previously. Slowly, from 1947 to 1950, he and his staff began to train and inform managers, but "it was slow going." There was resistance at all levels, though the medical department found that a "fair number (of problem drinkers) could be rehabilitated."

Because there were over 8,000 managers, there arose in the late forties a real need for an official company policy to guide managers in detecting and referring problem-drinking employees. Gradually, Dr. Cruickshank and his staff thrashed out a policy statement that alcoholism was a health problem, that it was treatable, that the condition be considered eligible for sickness benefits, and that disciplinary actions be delayed until health factors had been adequately reviewed. "By 1950, we had quite a large number of success stories among some very highly skilled and talented people and the skeptics became less vocal," he wrote. But it was not until there had been a "lot of selling on the part of a great number of people at all levels" that a formal policy became possible. This was in 1951. Although AA had become very active during this time and "spread far and wide," its services were apparently not used. Dr. Cruickshank also writes that he knew "of no significant initiatives by personnel staff people," and that, although there was union support, even the "trade union movement had not really taken any initiative in this area." It is obvious that the program began and remained based in the medical department in this company.

Another prominent example of the emergence of stable programs during this period was that developed at the Great Northern Railroad. John M. Budd, the company president, had become aware of a definite problem among his employees as early as 1951 and hired Warren T. as the company's first alcoholism counselor. Budd had come up through the ranks and had seen firsthand, and

at all levels, the problems that alcohol could create in running a railroad. Thus, he was intensely interested and Warren T. reported directly to him. Not only did the Great Northern program enjoy this unusually strong management support, but it appears to have had a broader scope than others in some ways. As mentioned earlier, Warren T.'s wife, Alice, played a part in this, working in "debt adjustment" at Great Northern, where she helped with the debt-ridden nature of problem drinkers as well as with their creditors. In 1956, Les V. succeeded Warren T. His wife, Kay, also worked with him, but added a new development: she was a charter member of Al-Anon and so introduced the family dimension to their approach. They covered an enormous system of 25,000 miles on a regular basis, slowly winning support from the railroad unions.

The period saw the appearance of numerous, relatively formal, open policy approaches which are less well-known than those at Allis Chalmers, Bell Canada and Great Northern. The number of these companies further demonstrated the rapid upswing of activity in the latter part of the forties and early fifties.[2]

There was even some activity in the military at this time, though it can hardly be termed either open or explicit. In 1949 and 1950, T/Sgt. William Swegan attended the Yale Center of Alcohol Studies. A chaplain on the Mitchell Air Force Base, N.Y. (Major Thomas Adams) helped him secure a leave of absence for six weeks and $150.00 for expenses. For the refresher in 1950 he received a five-day leave, but not monetary support. After much delay, Sgt. Swegan managed to secure a transfer to Lackland Air Force Base in San Antonio, Texas in 1953, where he was fortunate in working with an interested psychiatrist, Dr. Louis West. A "small experimental program was initiated in 1953 at the 700th USAF Hospital with the approval of the Hospital and Base Commanders and the Office of the Surgeon General (West and Swegan, 1956: 1004).

SOME CONCLUSIONS

The roots of job-based alcoholism programs can be traced back to the late nineteenth/early twentieth century efforts by employers to eliminate the long-accepted use of alcohol in the workplace. Even though these efforts were largely successful, the process took roughly 50 years, and the repressive measures used created stereotypes that may well have contributed substantially to the stigma surrounding the disorder of alcoholism. Actual programs came into being in an effort to reduce this stigma and treat the problem-drinking employee in a constructive, rehabilitative fashion rather than a punitive one. Programs sprang from the workplace itself and from employers' concern about job efficiency, workmen's compensation, and mechanization. Moreover, they grew solely from a concern for alcohol use, and rarely, if ever, dealt with other kinds of drugs or personal problems.

Three forces combined in the late thirties and during the war years to escalate these concerns into embryonic programs. These were the rapid rise of Alcoholics Anonymous, the sudden and enlarged need for workers during the war, and the concern of industrial physicians. Persons who were active and highly committed innovators capitalized upon these ingredients during the war, molding them into specific, but "quiet" programs. These formative forces spun off additional ones immediately after the war. Some top managements became interested; various unions and their community services programs became openly active. The "keep it quiet" theme of the early forties rapidly gave way to more open publicity in the latter part of the decade. The Yale Center of Alcohol Studies became very active, efforts of AA members grew rapidly, and industrial physicians organized their interests more formally than before. Serious research efforts appeared and found their way into program planning. By the mid-fifties there were full-blown efforts underway in at least 50 or 60 companies and unions. Ten years earlier there had been only the quasi-secret activities of a handful of dedicated AAs and influential industrial physicians.

The dim shape of an intervention strategy for combating alcoholism in the workplace had surfaced during this short, but active period. The Yale Plan had made no mention of poor work performance and relied largely upon supervisors as liaisons with counselors and referral agents, but it did urge the developments of AA groups, even within the plant itself. There was, however, no connection seen between the AA notion of "hitting bottom" and using the authority of the workplace to precipitate this in the Plan.

Others, however, were making the connection. Dr. Witmer at Consolidated Edison tended to reject the prevailing notion that pressure from the workplace hindered rather than helped. Rather, he advocated that company pressure on the problem-drinking employee to do something about his drinking and his poor performance be used to promote acceptance of help and treatment. At DuPont, Dave M. was telling alcoholic employees that the company's concern involved job performance deterioration and a desire to protect its investment in the employee. Dr. Gehrmann went further and openly advocated that supervisors directly confront problem drinking employees, telling them the company could no longer tolerate poor performance because of drinking, that discharge could ensue, but that AA and medical help would be available while the employee made up his or her mind. The outlines of what was later to be called constructive confrontation had been sketched out and an intervention strategy was born (Beyer and Trice, 1980).

Finally, it is obvious that many of these early efforts disappeared; we know little about them or why they died. Two speculations are, however, supported by historical evidence. First, where there was a combination of top management encouragement, a motivated high status staff person, and a dedicated AA counselor, there seems to have been more continuity. Secondly, and more basic, when a program had these ingredients, and also planned for its own continuance by institutionalizing and formalizing its efforts, it tended to survive. In contrast, when it relied heavily upon the zeal and dedication of one person, regardless of who he/she was, it was likely to disappear.

NOTES

1. The following individuals and organizations contributed to this study. There were many others, however, too numerous to list here, whose contributions were invaluable. Tapes were provided by those with an asterisk.

   AA General Services Office, Selden Bacon*, Charles J. Barron, R. Gordon Bell*, Marvin Block, John M. Budd, John Carney, The Christopher D. Smithers Foundation, William Cowan, W. Harvey Cruickshank, Ralph Daniels*, S. Charles Franco*, Charles Frazier*, Yevlin Gardner*, Henrietta Gehrmann, Claude Green, Esther Henderson, R. J. Robert Hilker, Thomas Hogshead, John Kaczmarowski, Mark Keller, William Knaut, Earl H. Loomis, Marty Mann Collection of Private Papers, University of Syracuse Library, Syracuse, NY, Milton Maxwell*, David Meharg*, Harold Meyer, Virgil J. Meyers*, John L. Norris*, Leo Perlis*, R. H. Porter*, Lewis Presnall*, Charles Rietdyke*, James Roberts, R. Brinkley Smithers*, George Strachan*, William Swegan, C. L. (Les) Vaughan, Elizabeth (Post) Whitney*.

2. Armco Steel Corporation of Ohio, Bell Telephone of Detroit, Bethlehem Steel Co., Chino Mines Division of Kennecott Copper, Chicago Rawhide Company, Cone Mills Corporation, Greensboro, NC, Corning Glass Works, Corning, NY, Detroit Edison, Dow Chemical, Midland, Michigan, Equitable Life, New York City, General Electric, Lynn, Massachusetts, Inland Steel Company, International Harvester, Peoria, Illinois, Kemper Insurance Company, Liberty Mutual of Boston, Lockheed Aircraft, Burbank, California, Metropolitan Life, New York City, New England Electric Company, Westboro, Massachusetts, New England Telephone, Boston, New York Telephone, New York City, New York City Transit Authority, Norton Company, Worchester, Massachusetts, Peoples Gas Light and Coke Company, Chicago, Raytheon Corp., Boston, Scovill Manufacturing Company, Waterbury, Connecticut, Southern New England Telephone Company, New Haven, Connecticut, Standard Oil Company of New Jersey, Waterbury Brass Company in Connecticut.

REFERENCES

Allis-Chalmers Manufacturing Company (1950). Results to Date–March 15, 1950. Milwaukee, Wis.: Privately Printed. (March 15).

Bacon, S. (1948). Alcoholism in Industry. *Industrial Medicine, 17:* 161–167.

Bacon, S. (1951). Alcoholism and Industry. *The Civitan Magazine,* March, 3–57.

Bacon, S. (1976). Concepts. Pp. 57–134 in Filstead, W. J., J. J. Rossi, & M. Keller (eds.) *Alcohol and alcohol problems.* Cambridge, MA: Ballinger Publishing Co.

Beyer, J., & Trice, H. (1980). The design and implementation of job-based alcoholism programs: Constructive confrontation strategies and how they work. Papers Presented for N.I.A.A.A. Research Workshop on Alcoholism in the Workplace, Reston, Virginia, May 24, 1980, Government Printing Office, Forthcoming.

Community Studies, Inc. (1954). Alcoholism Survey: State of Kansas. Kansas City, pp. 76–80.

Fehlandt, A. (1904). *A century of drink reform in the United States.* Cincinnati: Jennings and Graham Publishers.

Fox, J. (1944). Some implications of expansion in war industries. *Quarterly Journal of Studies on Alcohol, 3,* 646–649.

Frazier, C. P. (1957). Firms fight alcohol waste. *New York World Telegram and Sun,* April 8, 9, 10.

Furnas, C. (1965). *The life and times of the late Demon Rum.* New York: Capricorn Books.

Gehrmann, G., & Norris, J. (1949). Alcoholism in Industry–Symposium: Thirty-Fourth Annual Meeting, American Association of Industrial Physicians and Surgeons, Detroit, Michigan, April 16.

Gehrmann, G. (1954). The rehabilitation of the alcoholic in industry. In A. Fleming & C. A. D' Alonzo, *Modern occupational medicine.* Philadelphia: Lea & Febiger.

Gehrmann, G. (1955). How DuPont combats alcoholism. *Petroleum Refiner,* July, pp. 23–28.

George, M. D. (1925). *London life in the 18th century.* New York: Knopf.

Gutman, H. (1977). *Work, culture, and society in industrializing america.* New York: Vintage Books.

Haber, S. (1964). *Efficiency and uplift.* Chicago: University of Chicago Press.

Henderson, R., & Straus, R. (1952). Alcoholism: 1941–1951. A survey of activities in research, education and therapy. *Quarterly Journal of Studies on*

Alcohol, 13, 472–495.

Henderson, R., & Bacon, S. (1953). Problem drinking: The Yale plan for business and industry. *Quarterly Journal of Studies on Alcohol, 14.* 247–262.

Hendrick, B. (1916). How business fights alcohol. *Harper's Monthly Magazine,* August: 425–431.

Industrial Medicine (1943). Absenteeism–Unauthorized time away from the job. 12:338–341.

Janson, C. (1935). *The stranger in America, 1798–1806.* New York: Press of the Pioneers.

Jellinek, E. J. (1947). What shall we do about alcoholism? *Vital Speeches, 13,* 252–254.

J.I.F. (1947). Alcoholism: An occupational disease of seamen. *Quarterly Journal of Studies on Alcohol, 8,* 498–505.

Jukes, R. (1943). Industrial absenteeism; Its medical phase. *Industrial Medicine, 12,* 553–556.

Krout, J. (1925). *The origins of prohibition.* New York: Alfred A. Knopf.

Landis, B. (1945). Some Economic Aspects of Inebriety. In *Alcohol science and society.* New Haven: Yale University Press, pp. 212–268.

Mielcarek, H. (1951). Alcoholism in Industry. In *Proceedings of the Institute on Alcoholism,* October 10–December 12, Marquette University Labor College, pp. 150–161. Milwaukee, Wisconsin.

National Industrial Conference Board (1958). *The Alcoholic Worker.* Studies in Personnel Policy, number 166. New York: National Industrial Conference Board.

Norris, J. L. (1968). *Alcoholism in Industry: Lecture in Honor of Dr. George Gehrmann.* Annual Meeting of the American Academy of Occupational Medicine. Boston, February 8th.

O'Brien, C. (1949). Alcoholism among disciplinary cases. *Quarterly Journal of Studies on Alcohol, 10,* 268–278.

Opinion Research Corporation (1952). *Chronic alcoholism in industry as viewed by medical and personnel directors.* Princeton, NJ, privately printed.

The Outlook (1915). Alcohol and efficiency. Vol. III, Oct. 13, p. 350.

Page, R., Thorpe, J. J., & Caldwell, D. W. (1952). The problem drinker in industry. *Quarterly Journal of Studies on Alcohol, 13,* 370–396.

Quarterly Journal of Studies on Alcohol (1942). Alcohol and industrial efficiency. Lay Supplement #3, New Haven, Conn.

Sinclair, A. (1963). *Prohibition: The era of excess.* Boston: Little, Brown and Co.

Smithers Foundation, The Christopher D. (1958). *A basic outline for a company program.* New York.

Smithers Foundation, The Christopher D. (1977). *25th Anniversary Report: Pioneering in the disease of alcoholism.* Mill Neck, New York.

Smithers Foundation, The Christopher D. (1979). *Pioneers we have known in the field of alcoholism.* Mill Neck, NY.

Stevenson, R. (1942). Absenteeism in an industrial plant due to alcoholism. *Quarterly Journal of Studies on Alcohol, 2,* 661–668.

Stivers, R. (1976). *A hair of the dog.* University Park, PA: Penn State University Press.

Straus, R., & Bacon, S. (1951). Alcoholism and social stability. *Quarterly Journal of Studies on Alcohol, 12,* 231–260.

Sullivan, W. C. (1906). Industry and alcoholism. *Journal of Mental Science, 52:*505–514.

Theiss, L. (1914). Industry vs. alcohol. *The Outlook, 107,* 856–861.

Timberlake, J. (1963). *Prohibition and the Progressive Movement, 1900–1920.* Cambridge: Harvard University Press.

Tolman, W. (1911). *Alcoholism in industry.* New York: American Museum of Safety.

Trice, H. (1958). Alcoholics Anonymous. *Annals of American Academy of Political and Social Science, 315,* 108–116.

Trice, H. (1959). The problem drinker on the job. Bulletin #40. New York State School of Industrial and Labor Relations, Cornell University, Ithaca, NY.

Trice, H., & Beyer, J. (1977). A sociological property of drugs. *Journal of Studies on Alcohol, 38:*58–74.

Vonachen, H., Mittelmann, B., & Kronenberg, M. (1946). A comprehensive mental hygiene program at Caterpillar Tractor Co. *Industrial Medicine, 15,* 179–184.

West, L., & Swegan, W. (1956). An approach to alcoholism in the military service. *American Journal of Psychiatry, 112,* 1004–1009.

Winkler, A. (1968). Drinking on the American Frontier. *Quarterly Journal of Studies on Alcohol, 129,* 413–445.

Chapter 2

EMPLOYEE ASSISTANCE PROGRAMS: A HISTORICAL SKETCH

FRED DICKMAN and B. ROBERT CHALLENGER

It is well documented that the employee assistance program (EAP) movement has gained astounding momentum in recent years with EAPs in over half of the largest industries found in Fortune's "500" (Busch, 1981; Dickman & Emener, 1982; Land, 1981; Roman, 1981; Sonnenstuhl & O'Donnell, 1980). Increasing numbers of smaller (250 employees) companies are interested in EAPs (Phillips, 1983), and community observation reveals that mental health centers, alcoholism treatment centers, social service agencies, etc. are literally rushing to get "into the act" and secure EAP contracts with industry. A strong and viable association, Association of Labor and Management Administrators and Consultants on Alcoholism (ALMACA), exists for EAP professional personnel. Undoubtedly, the movement will grow and as it does, at least some broad knowledge of its history and early philosophy is important.

History and Philosophy

EAP history is intertwined closely with that of Alcoholics Anonymous (AA). AA, it is well known, began in Akron, Ohio on June 10, 1935 when Bill Wilson talked for hours with Dr. Bob Smith in an attempt to help himself stay sober. Bill, a stockbroker from New York, had five months "release" from the "compulsion."

Following a business failure on a trip to Akron, he was craving a drink (Kissin & Begleiter, 1970). This meeting was essentially the founding of AA, as each man learned he could stay sober by talking about his alcoholism to another. When it is recalled that in 1935 alcoholic people were given up by medical and psychological practitioners as "incurable" and, as a rule, were institutionalized under life commitment, this chance encounter seems nothing short of miraculous (Leach & Norris, 1977).

By 1939, the AA movement had spread throughout the midwestern and northeastern United States, and more people were getting into "recovery." Many of these recovering people were members of the work force, and it is reasonable to assume their transformation was not lost on factory supervisors and higher level management.

One alcoholic worker was eager to communicate his experience, strength and hope to his fellow suffering worker (Trice & Schonbrunn, 1981). Hence, the EAP movement began—amateurishly if you will—with one recovering alcoholic worker sharing his recovery with another.

These occupational alcoholism programs (OAPs) were so successful in terms of saving money, of increased production, and of ultimately "rehabilitated" skilled workers, that it was reasonable to assume that such an approach to alcoholism problems would be effective for other

Note: The original version of this chapter was prepared specially for *Counseling the Troubled Employee in Industry* (1985) as Chapter 1, pp. 7–12. For purposes of being accurately avant-garde, it was updated by its authors and reproduced in this book with their permission as well as the permission of the publisher (Charles C Thomas, Publisher, Ltd.). This chapter is reprinted from *Employee Assistance Programs: A Basic Text* (1988) with permission of the author, the book's editors (Dickman, Emener, & Hutchison, Jr.) and the publisher (Charles C Thomas, Publisher, Ltd.).

human problems as well.

In 1962, the Kemper Group launched its program of rehabilitation of its alcoholic personnel and expanded the program's thrust to reach families of alcoholic workers and to persons with "other living problems." This enlarged scope of OAPs led to the modern employee assistance program (EAP) known as the "broad brush" approach to human problems in industry. This approach basically increases the services of the assistance program to include marriage and family problems, emotional problems, financial and legal problems, and other problems with drugs in addition to alcohol. This became the typical industrial counseling approach by the end of the 1970s, and during the 1970s, the broad brush approach exploded.

The tremendous growth in the 1970s of EAPs was accompanied by (and perhaps contributed to) the following:

1. The Hughes Act

In 1969, Senator Harold Hughes of Idaho deplored the lack of federal and state involvement in the treatment of alcoholism. The next year Congress passed the Federal Comprehensive Alcohol Abuse and Alcoholism Prevention Treatment and Rehabilitation Act and created the National Institute of Alcoholism and Alcohol Abuse (NIAAA) to administer monies and provide leadership in the alcoholism field. The next year (1971) most states followed federal lead and enacted legislation to decriminalize public intoxication and treat alcoholism as a medical disease rather than a legal issue.

2. NIAAA

In 1971, the National Institute of Alcoholism and Alcohol Abuse (NIAAA), commissioned to treat and research alcoholism, saw the workplace as a potentially effective early intervener. Consequently, establishment of EAPs in each of the various states had a high priority. Grants were made to the various state alcoholism authorities to train and hire EAP specialists. Through these grants, many mental health districts and community alcoholism services hired specialists and instituted efforts to reach smaller, local industries as individuals randomly reached national industry in the 1940s, 1950s, and 1960s. (Trice & Schonbrunn, 1981)

3. National Council on Alcoholism

In the 1970s, the NCA established the Occupational Alcoholism Bureau and under the leadership of Ross Yon Wiegand began to publish helpful materials, sponsor seminars, and conferences and spread the EAP concept.

4. ALMACA

Another major thrust of the 1970s was the organization of the Association of Labor and Management Administrators and Consultants on Alcoholism (ALMACA) in 1971. ALMACA provided a forum for dissemination and enhancement of knowledge among professionals, published a directory of specialists, and generally increased community and industrial awareness of the EAP concept today.

5. Treatment Centers

The proliferation of alcoholism treatment centers since the Hughes Act of 1970 is nothing short of phenomenal. In 1969, there were three treatment centers in Florida, one publicly funded by the state, and two privately funded. Today, the author knows of twenty-plus private centers in four counties—just in the Tampa Bay area. Each of these centers has an EAP specialist whose major endeavor is to reach industry. These private centers are in addition to several public agencies in this same location. Perusing national magazines and professional journals, it is not difficult to see this same phenomenon throughout the nation. There is no way to accurately estimate just how many EAP endeavors exist at the present time.

6. Change Human Services Funding

Another force fueling the EAP fire at the present time may be the most significant EAP event of the 1980s. This involves public centers and private practitioners. The economic situation of the early 1980s and, to a real extent, governmental philosophy have forced significant cutbacks in every phase of human services. Public mental health agencies, alcohol/drug treatment centers, and private counseling firms tend to see future survival in a partnership with industry and are eager to enter the EAP field. This event is labeled potentially most significant, as it may well change the major philosophy and thrust of the EAP movement.

As noted, the early movement provided an innovative and effective approach to alcoholism identification and treatment by means of early intervention and confrontation. Its philosophy was that alcoholism was treatable, and since the average alcoholic industrial employee was a ten-year skilled worker, the bottom line was that to remediate this employee ultimately saved the company money (Brisolara, 1979; Land, 1981). This philosophy developed (World War II and two decades beyond) when a premium was placed on high productivity and during a period in which there was a shortage of trained persons. This, coupled with the fact that OAP/EAP personnel had a high commitment to alcoholism rehabilitation, made for strong motivation to identify and treat the alcoholic workers.

The situation may now be changing. Skilled workers are waiting in line for jobs, and EAP personnel often do not have the training or the commitment of their predecessors to identify and rehabilitate alcoholic people. In addition, many managers in local industry do not want to believe they have alcohol/drug problems among their work force. A change, or at least confusion, may be witnessed in the philosophy and thrust of the EAP of the 1980s. What will take its place?

7. Reduction of Stigma

Significant in the 1970s and 1980s is a reduction of the stigma pertaining to alcoholism. In 1976 at the National Council on Alcoholism annual meeting, 50 prominent Americans publicly proclaimed their recovery from addiction to alcoholism. Since that time countless other nationally known persons have done the same. This has led to a gradual reduction in the stigma attached to alcoholism and directly influenced the growth of the EAP concept.

A new concept is gaining momentum and may threaten or even supplant the EAP movement. This is increasingly known as the employee enhancement program (EEP). It claims preventive capabilities by concentrating on stress management, holistic health concepts, and other "addiction" problems such as smoking, overeating, overworking, etc. It purports that if stress is controlled and employees are taught healthy lifestyles, such problems dealt with by OAPs and EAPs may be

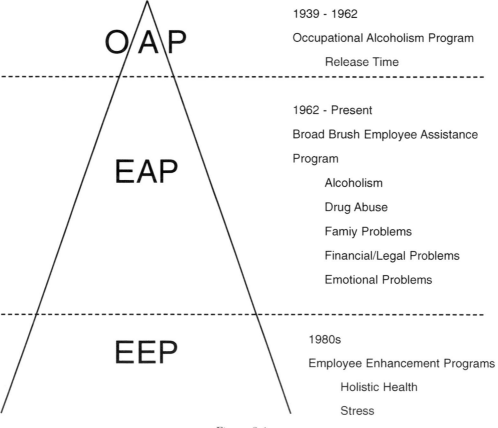

1939 - 1962

Occupational Alcoholism Program

Release Time

1962 - Present

Broad Brush Employee Assistance

Program

 Alcoholism

 Drug Abuse

 Famiy Problems

 Financial/Legal Problems

 Emotional Problems

1980s

Employee Enhancement Programs

 Holistic Health

 Stress

Figure 2-1.

prevented. However controversial this new thrust may be, no one doubts that it may be the "industrial counseling" concept of the 1980s (see Fig. 2-1). Hopefully, this new "preventive" approach will add to the old and that remedial work with alcoholics and–other troubled employees will continue to be refined and enhanced.

REFERENCES

Brisolara, A. (1979). *The alcoholic employee: A handbook of useful guidelines.* New York: Human Sciences Press.

Busch, E. J. (1981). Developing an employee assistance program. *Personnel Journal, 60* (9), 708–711.

Dickman, F., & Emener, W. G. (1982). Employee assistance programs–basic concepts, attributes and an evaluation. *Personnel Administrator, 27* (8), 55, 56, 58–61.

Kissin, B., & Begleiter, H. (Eds.) (1977). *Treatment and rehabilitation of the chronic alcoholic.* New York: Plenum Press.

Land, T. (1981). Global strategy: Confronting alcoholism at the workplace. *Alcoholism, 1* (6), 41–42.

Leach, B., & Norris, J. L. (1977). Factors in the development of Alcoholics Anonymous (AA). In B. Kissin & H. Begleiter (Eds.): *Treatment and rehabilitation of the chronic alcoholic.* New York: Plenum Press.

Phillips, E. A. (1983). Employee assistance programs: A survey of selected firms in Pinellas County, unpublished survey.

Roman, P. M. (1981). From employee alcoholism to employee assistance. *Journal of Studies on Alcohol, 42* (3), 244–272.

Sonnenstuhl, W. J., & O'Donnell, J. E. (1980). EAP's: The why's and how's of planning them. *Personnel Administrator, 25* (11), 35–36.

Trice, H. M., & Schonbrunn, M. (1981). A history of job-based alcoholism programs: 1900–1955. *Journal of Drug Issues.*

Chapter 3

THE NEED AND RATIONALE FOR EMPLOYEE ASSISTANCE PROGRAMS

WILLIAM S. HUTCHISON, JR. and SUSAN VICKERSTAFF

The origins of present-day Employee Assistance Programs (EAPs) can be traced back to the world of American industry in the late 1800s. By the end of the nineteenth century, industrial technology allowed businesses to become so large that there was a widening gap between management and labor. Decreased personal contact between workers and managers along with increasing numbers of women and immigrants in the labor force made it obvious that past autocratic ways of dealing with work-related issues were no longer going to be effective. Previously reliable employees began demonstrating dissatisfaction with working conditions by changing jobs, refusing to cooperate, and threatening to unionize.

Obviously, this atmosphere posed a serious threat to industry's ability to thrive. In response, management created a system of programs and hired individuals to provide services to address what management saw as problems in the lives of their workers. This system became known as a welfare movement and obviously dealt with work-related concerns and also with more personal issues (Popple, 1981).

Recognizing that large numbers of immigrants, women, and young workers had little or no experience, one of the first services offered was training. Schools built and operated by business provided education in basic reading and writing as well as training in skills needed to succeed in specific work sites. Immigrants were helped to learn the language and culture. On-site medical clinics provided treatment for work-related injuries as well as for health problems that would interfere with a worker's performance. Low cost meals, housing and material goods were made available to workers in financial need. "Wholesome" recreational opportunities were created in an attempt to keep workers, especially women, out of trouble (Brandes, 1970).

The provision of welfare services to employees by industry increased rapidly. According to the United States Bureau of Labor Statistics (1928), by 1926 approximately 80 percent of the 1,500 largest businesses in America were providing at least one program for workers and 50 percent were providing comprehensive services. Businesses hired individuals called welfare secretaries who were responsible for providing these services.

America's economic conditions in the 1920s and 1930s created even more need for these welfare services. Unfortunately, even as the number of programs increased, labor was becoming dissatisfied with the manner in which services were provided. The welfare secretary began to be distrusted and viewed as a management tool for controlling the workers. This negative view combined with the economic downturn during the Great Depression led to a decrease in the number of programs and services offered (Wyers & Kaulukukui, 1984).

One type of service did continue to grow during the 1920s and 1930s through World War II: industrial alcoholism programs. By the 1950s, it had become obvious that many work-related problems were related to alcohol abuse or dependence. Many large corporations in America no longer hired on-site equivalents of the welfare secretary but instead focused on the identification of workers whose drinking was causing problems. These workers were then referred to treatment resources such as Alcoholics Anonymous.

This model of identification and referral in the industrial alcoholism programs is the most influential forerunner of today's EAP. The focus is first on identifying those employees whose problems, whether related to alcohol or other personal issues, are causing deterioration in their work performance and productivity and second on linking them with appropriate treatment and support services (Hartwell, Steele, et al., 1996).

The need for preventive and treatment services for employees continued to expand through the remainder of the twentieth century (Emener, l997). The Hughes Act recognized that alcoholism and (by extrapolation) drug addictions were diseases needing treatment rather than incarceration and condemnation (Dickman, l997).

Simultaneously, an explosion in the cost of health care along with increased competition from overseas forced U.S. corporations to seek cost containment of health insurance benefits to maintain economic profitability and price competitiveness. This led to the development of managed health care whose prototype was the Medicare program of Diagnostic Related Groupings (DRG,S) which set dollar amount limits on reimbursement of treatment for all medical and mental health conditions (Segal & Brzuzy, 1998).

Automatization and computer technology appeared on the economic scene and resulted in an explosion of change in work organization and productivity which lasted until 2001, when a number of factors slowed the economy and created a recession (Emener, 2002). However, the need and demand for employee assistance and wellness programs expanded so that by the 90s some 90 percent of Fortune 500 companies had EAPs. This demand recognized the value of EAPs including recognition as to how these programs could assist workers in coping with rapid workplace change. Some of the problems created by these changes included increased need for day and child care, eldercare, as well as programs to reduce other health care costs such as smoking cessation, weight reduction, physical fitness, and stress management (Hutchison, 1997).

Newer challenges emerged at the workplace including murder (post office and Columbine High School shootings), terrorism (bombing of the Murrah Office building in Oklahoma City and the Twin Towers in New York City as well as the bioterrorism of Anthrax). All of the survivors (those who were physically present), their families and friends who were not, and those of us who witnessed the visual media were affected significantly depending on proximity, loss, emotional, and mental vulnerability. Critical Incident Stress Debriefings increased as did the demand for individual services and challenged EAP providers (DeGrando, 2002).

Economic recession, the abuse of religious position and corporate fraud magnified the traumas of terrorism. Layoffs, cutback in retiree health benefits, globalization of the economy with increased need for cultural competent communication and business practices all provided expanding need for EAP/wellness programs (Darling, 2002). EAPs are playing major roles in developing new services to respond to these arising needs. Some examples include interpreter services, cultural competence training, Sexual Harassment Prevention Training, Violence Awareness and Prevention Training, Pre-Retirement and Retirement Training and Outplacement Services Assistance.

EAPs are also viewed as a primary solution to health care cost containment by "providing early intervention" by helping employees and their families find earlier solutions (e.g., weight reduction before type II diabetes develops). Likewise, consulting with the worksite can produce such results (Darling, 2002). For instance, it is known that shift work can produce circadian rhythm disturbances that may lead to serious sleep disorders. Programs can be developed that teach employees sleep adaptation techniques as well as working with employers to consider alternative forms of scheduling to better attain production goals.

Thus, the continued need for EAP services is reflected through expanded service types and this consultative partnership.

REFERENCES

Brandes, S. D. (1970). *American welfare capitalism: 1880–1940.* Chicago: University of Chicago Press.

Darling, H. (2002). Rising health care costs. *Exchange, 32* (2), March/April.

DeGrande, L. (2002). Creating a template for the future. *Exchange, 32* (4), July/August, 22–23.

Dickman, J. F. (1997). EAP's: A historical sketch. In Hutchison, Jr. & W.G. Emener (Eds.), *Employee assistance programs: A basic text* (2nd Edition). Springfield, IL: Charles C Thomas, Publisher, Ltd.

Emener, W. G., & Hutchison, Jr., W. S. (1997). Future perspectives–1997. In Hutchison, Jr. & W. G. Emener (Eds.), *Employee assistance programs: A basic text* (2nd Edition). Springfield, IL: Charles C Thomas, Publisher, Ltd.

Goin, M. K. (2002). Learning from adversity: Raising the profile of workplace mental health. *Exchange, 32* (4), July/August, 19.

Googins, B., & Godfrey, J. (1987). *Occupational social work.* Englewood Cliffs, NJ: Prentice-Hall.

Hartwell, T. D., & Steele, P. et al. (1986). Aiding troubled employees: The prevalence, cost, and characteristics of employee assistance programs in the United States. *American Journal of Public Health,* June.

Hutchison, W. (1997). Working with families through employee assistance programs and wellness programs. In Hutchison, Jr. & W. G. Emener (Eds.), *Employee assistance programs: A basic text* (2nd Edition). Springfield, IL: Charles C Thomas, Publisher, Ltd.

Popple, P. R. (1981). Social work practice in business and industry, 1875–1930. *Social Service Review* (June), 257–269.

United States Bureau of Labor Statistics. (1928). Health and recreation activities in industrial establishments, 1926. *Bulletin Number 458.* Washington, DC: U.S. Government Printing Office, 86.

Wyers, N. L., & Kaulukukui, M. (1984). Social services in the workplace: Rhetoric vs. reality. *Social Work, 29* (March–April), 167–172.

Part II

STRUCTURE AND ORGANIZATION

Chapter 4

WORK ORGANIZATIONS: STRUCTURE AND ORGANIZATIONAL DYNAMICS CRITICAL TO EMPLOYEE ASSISTANCE PROGRAMS

CARNOT E. NELSON and WILLIAM G. EMENER

Central to the initiatives, missions, goals, and objectives of employee assistance programs is a uniquely defined and targeted constituency group-troubled employees in work organizations. Fittingly, employee assistance program professionals, in order to be effective and efficient in their efforts of assisting troubled employees, must understand work organizations. Importantly, an understanding of a work organization demands a thorough comprehension and appreciation of both its structure and organizational dynamics. Nonetheless, work organizations do not exist in isolation; rather, they are influenced by many "outside" organizations and individuals. For example, a primary outside organization that highly influences a work organization and its respective employee assistance program is a labor union (Beyer, Trice & Hunt, 1980; Dickman & Emener, 1982; Emener & Dickman, 1983; McWilliams, 1985). The overall, guiding purposes of this chapter are twofold: (a) to examine the structure of business and industry and labor unions; and, (b) to describe and discuss key organizational dynamics of industrial organizations. It should be noted that throughout this chapter the terms work organization, business, and industry are used interchangeably.

Structure

A typical definition of an organization includes the planned coordination of the activities of two or more people in order to achieve some common and explicit goal through a division of labor and a hierarchy of authority (Robbins, 1983). Thus, even though they may differ in many ways (e.g., size, goals, activities, and ownership), General Motors, a university, and a local doctor's office can be viewed as organizations. Importantly, each of these three work organizations has a common characteristic—they have structure.

The concept of structure denotes the way in which an organization combines its human resources for its goal-directed activities. Structure can be viewed as consisting of three primary dimensions: (1) complexity, (2) formalization, and (3) centralization. **Complexity** refers to the differentiation within an organization—the greater the differentiation, the greater the complexity. There are three types of differentiation: (a) horizontal, (b) vertical, and, (c) spatial. Horizontal differentiation is concerned with the differences between work units in terms of tasks performed and the requisite education and training of the individuals working within them. Vertical differentiation refers to the number of steps in the chain of command within an organization (more complex organizations tend to have more steps). When an organization has plants and offices in a number of different geographical locations, this is considered spatial differentiation. **Formalization** refers to the degree to which jobs in an organization are standardized or the degree to which individuals working in the

Note: This chapter is reprinted from *Employee Assistance Programs: A Basic Text*, Second Edition (1997) with permission of the author, the book's editors (W.S. Hutchison, Jr. & W.G. Emener) and the publisher (Charles C Thomas, Publisher, Ltd.).

organization have individual discretion over what they should do, and how and when they should do it. **Centralization** is concerned with the degree to which formal decision-making powers are concentrated in a single position within an organization. Thus, it is eminently important for employee assistance professionals to be very cognizant of an organization's complexity (e.g., how is it differentiated?), its formalization (e.g., what levels of autonomous functioning do various groups of employees have?), and its degree of centralization (e.g., where and within whom is decision-making power vested?) in the processes of initiating, developing, implementing, and evaluating an employee assistance program.

There are four basic determinants of organizational structure: (a) its size, (b) technology, (c) environment, and (d) power-control. Large organizations (e.g., Westinghouse), by their very size, tend to be complex in that there is a vast amount of all three types of differentiation. Moreover, large organizations tend to be decentralized and formalized. The former primarily due to the fact that no one individual could keep track of all decisions that have to be made (not to mention the vast amount of information that would have to be maintained in order to make so many decisions). "Control" in large organizations tends to be developed through formalization with the utilization of specialized implementation techniques such as detailed job descriptions, formal rules and regulations, and standardized operating procedures.

The technology of an organization refers to what it does–how it transforms "inputs" into "outputs"–how it produces products from raw materials. Within an organization, there can be many levels of technology, which can be understood in terms of their amounts of routinization. For example, some job tasks such as those found on assembly lines can be viewed as highly routinized; the job tasks of research chemist, on the other hand, tend to be very nonroutinized. Fittingly, highly routinized jobs tend to be very formal while nonroutinized jobs typically are not. Thus, while not implying an overgeneralization, it hereby can be appreciated that an employee assistance program for predominately assembly line industry understandably would have different perspectives on its EAP clients than an employee assistance program for a chemical research company.

The environment of an organization also influences its structure. In order for an organization to survive, it must adapt to (or at least accommodate to) its environment. In placid environments with little change, for example, a centralized, complex, and formal organization would tend to function most efficiently. In rapidly changing environments, on the other hand, highly decentralized structures would tend to be preferred in order to provide the needed flexibility to confront and accommodate the rapidly changing environmental conditions and constituencies. It recently has been critical for employee assistance programs in the airline and banking industries, for example, to be cognizant of the turbulent environments in which these two large industries strive for survival and viability.

Although the phenomenon of "power" will be discussed in detail later in this chapter, at this point it is important to note that the power-control explanation of organizational design focuses on the politics within the organization. Quite frequently within an organization, there are individuals and/or units seeking to enhance and further their own interests. Central to this observation is that those in power in an organization tend to prefer an organizational structure that maximizes their control within (or over) the organization. Thus, a manager may make a decision that minimally satisfies or enhances the organization while maximizing his or her interests (e.g., level and span of control). From an overall perspective, it is important to remember that **business is structured top-down**.

Operationally, authority is vested in the ownership of a company and then delegated to boards of directors, chief executive officers, managers, supervisors, etc. While remaining open-minded in their perceptions of leaders in business and industry, it is also important for employee assistance program professionals to be cognizant of not only who people are, but where they are in the company as well.

Culture

According to Schein (1990), organizational culture is a pattern of basic assumptions that are invented, discovered, or developed by a group as it learns to cope with its problems of external adaptation and internal integration. This pattern of assumptions, if it works well, is adopted and taught to new members as they enter the organization. An organization's culture can be thought of as "the way we do things around here." Each organization has its own unique culture. Organizational culture is a socially-constructed concept that provides organization members with a way of understanding events. The use of symbols, sagas, and stories is a major component of organizational culture.

Symbols are essential elements of managing people in organizations. Symbols are important for control and motivation in any social system. For example, in some organizations, wearing a special pin is a symbol of achievement. Even in child-focused groups such as the Girl Scouts or Boy Scouts, symbols are important. Symbols provide a way to control and guide behavior in the direction that the organization chooses.

Sagas and stories usually involve a retelling of how the organization was started or of some great accomplishments by someone in the organization. In many cases, the stories involve relating how someone's hard work and sacrifice resulted in a major benefit for the company or society. The stories and sagas are passed along and as with most stories are distorted and exaggerated. The stories and sagas serve much the same purpose as the symbols—they can be used to control and motivate people.

Schein (1990) recommended that organizations and managers learn to use organizational culture to control and motivate employees. However, he cautioned that organizational culture, once established, is only changed with great effort.

Labor Unions

As mentioned at the beginning of this chapter, labor unions play vital and pivotal roles in the employee assistance programs where they exist.

Dickman and Emener (1982), for example, boldly stated: "An EAP cannot be meaningful if it is not backed by the employees' labor unit" (p. 56). With regard to structural considerations of work organizations, however, it is important to remember that whereas in industry authority flows "top-down," in unions power flows "bottom-up." In a union, the workers it represents are its members—thus, the goals and accomplishments of the union must reflect the members' interests. In unions, the leadership is elected by the members and contracts typically are ratified by the members.

The labor movement in the United States exists at three levels: (a) local unions, (b) national unions, and, (c) labor federations. Prior to discussing these three components of labor, however, an important distinction that cross-cuts all of labor must be noted. In general, there are two types of unions: (1) craft unions, and (2) industry unions. An example of the former would be the carpenters' union; an example of the latter would be the auto workers' union.

The local union is the formal organization through which the member deals with his or her employer on a day-to-day basis. Typically, "locals" represent workers in a single industry or job classification in a single locality, and frequently bargain with a single employer. Smaller locals that deal with a single employer typically elect part-time officers to run the union. Locals that deal with multiple employers, as is frequently found with construction unions, employ a business agent who is charged with the responsibility to see that the members' contractual rights are not being violated and for referring members to available employment. In industrial organizations, the key union officer is the "steward." He or she is responsible for ensuring that management (especially first-line supervisors) complies with the union contract. Also, the steward represents the employee when grievances are aired, and in most instances it is the union representative with whom employee assistance program professionals work with the closest.

The national or international union is the body that holds the basic authority within the labor movement. Interestingly, most local unions are chartered by a parent national union, and many local activities are constrained, governed and/or must be approved by the respective national (parent) union. For example, local unions usually are required to obtain permission from their national unions before striking or ratifying a contract. The employees of national (parent) unions tend to be full-time employees and work hard to assist their local unions in a wide variety of activities. Thus, while it is critical for employee assistance program professionals to develop close working relationships with local union officials (e.g., the stewards and elected officers), it is also very important for them to develop good relationships with representatives of respective national (parent) unions.

The structure of national unions, depending upon the nature of the industry involved, varies widely. For example, the United Auto Workers has national departments, each representing one of the major auto manufacturers. Because the auto industry is centralized, so is the national union representing auto workers. The Carpenter's Union, on the other hand, tends to bargain at the local or regional level because the industry is decentralized.

The American Federation of Labor and the Congress of Industrial Organizations (AFL-CIO) is a federation of 99 national unions. Although it has many missions, goals, and objectives, it basically is designed to facilitate some overall direction to the labor movement and provide technical assistance to its national unions. There are also state and local labor organizations that are affiliated with local unions; however, these organizations tend to be primarily involved in political and lobbying activities.

McWilliams (1985), in articulating the benefits of a joint union-management employee assistance program, poignantly stated, "Programs [EAPs] achieve maximum effectiveness only when unions and managements are joint partners–when the program is neither a 'union' program nor a 'management' program but a joint 'people' program" (p. 56).

Employee assistance program professionals not only recognize the meaningfulness of this cooperative relationship between management and labor, but also are committed to enhancing it. The more knowledgeable, understanding and appre-

ciative employee assistance professionals are the structure of work organizations and labor unions, and **how they interface and work together and with each other**, the more effective and efficient they will be in providing meaningful employee assistance programs for troubled employees.

Organizational Dynamics

Power

A key element in understanding how an organization functions is power. In terms of organizational functioning, the concept of power (as used by the authors of this chapter) refers to an interpersonal or intergroup relationship in which one individual or group has the ability to cause another individual or group to take an action that would not be taken otherwise (Steers, 1984). Obviously, power is closely related to the concepts of authority and leadership. Authority includes the right or legitimacy of seeking compliance to one's requests that is absent in the concept of power. Leadership, on the other hand, refers to the ability to influence another person above that required by the situation. It, indeed, is critical for employee assistance program professionals to know who is in authority or who is in the position of leadership. Nonetheless, it is also important to know whom or which group has what power.

According to French and Raven (1968), there are five bases of social power; these will provide the grounding for the following discussions of power in organizations. **Reward power** exists when person A perceives that person B controls his or her rewards. In **coercive power**, person B perceives that person A will punish him or her if B does not comply with A's request.

A most important source of power within organizations is **legitimate power**. Here, person B perceives that person A has the right to exert power and B has an obligation to comply. This, of course, is what is meant by authority. When person B complies with person A's request because B admires or likes A, this is referred to as **referent power**. The fifth source of power is called **expert power** and exists when person B perceives that person A has knowledge or expertise relevant to him or her. The ability to recognize and understand the variety of types and sources of power is very important to the employee assistance program professional. For example, if one employee or a group of employees are having difficulties relating to another employee(s) in their work area and the situation becomes troublesome, it would seem appropriate to suggest that the employee(s) discuss the matter with the individual central to the situation. Should the response to such a suggestion be akin to, "I/we can't because that person has too much power," it would be very beneficial to explore the type and magnitude of the power that the individual is perceived to have. Given the basic differences among French and Raven's (1968) five sources of power in organizations, differential intervention/remediation strategies would be needed in each individual situation. What works in one power situation may be totally ineffective in another power situation.

Politics

Closely associated with the concept of power is politics. In terms of the relevance of power and politics in the work organizations germane to employee assistance programs, the concept of "politics" basically will refer to the resolution of differing preferences in conflicts over the allocation of scarce and valued resources (Steers, 1984, p. 314). Many organizations, businesses, and industries circa 1987 are highly political entities for two understandable reasons (among others). First, resources are scarce. Today, a common business slogan is "lean and mean." Companies like AT&T, for example, are "downsizing" (i.e., reducing staff). Second, rapid changes in the environment call for increasing numbers of nonprogrammed decisions–decisions that are novel or unstructured (vis-à-vis decisions that are more routine and structured). Moreover, politics become more prevalent when: (a) the goals of a department, unit or organization are ambiguous; (b) the external environment is more complex; and, (c) during periods of organizational change. It is important for employee assistance program professionals to be acutely aware of the politics in the

work organizations that their employee assistance programs serve. Among the many reasons why such awareness is important are: (a) the professionals would be better postured for accurately predicting changes in the organizations that may affect the employee groups they serve; (b) they would be more insightful in assisting their clients (employees) in understanding resulting changes and impacts; and, (c) they would be in a more advantageous position of assisting organizations in understanding ways and means by which the organizations could be more caring about the employees being affected by resulting changes in the organizations.

Decision Making

A key element in any organization is decision making. In the context of the phenomena being addressed in this chapter, "decision making" is being referred to as a process of selecting among alternatives. For example, it is very appropriate for an employee assistance professional to be curious about "Who makes what decisions within the organization?," and "How and by what processes are such decisions made?" Interestingly, Heller (1973) pointed out that: (a) if a decision is important for the organization, a nonparticipative style of decision making is likely to be used; (b) if a decision is important to the subordinates in the organization in terms of their work, a more participative decision-making approach would likely be used and (c) if the organization's decision makers believe that the subordinates in the organization have something to contribute to the decision making and/or its implementation, then participative decision making is even more likely to be used. Another way of viewing this is to consider topics of importance to the organization as "managerial decisions" and decisions concerning the employees' (subordinates') work as "technical decisions."

Two basic models of decision making are the "economic man model" and the "bounded rationality model." The economic man model assumes that people are economically rational (i.e., they desire to maximize gains and minimize losses), and that they do this in an orderly and systematic manner. Fundamentally, this model posits that people discern the symptoms of a problem, define the problem to be solved, develop criteria to evaluate alternatives, systematically explore all alternatives, evaluate each alternative, select the "best" alternative, and finally implement the decision. Although on the surface, this model appears reasonable and appealing, it is woefully inadequate in describing actual and/or typical decision-making behavior. First, it assumes that individuals or groups can gather all the relevant information necessary to make a given decision. Second, it assumes that all relevant information can be stored and processed. Obviously, these assumptions are false and actually can be misleading to employee assistance program professionals in their attempts to comprehend decision making in business, industries, and work organizations.

Simon (1957) presented a much more relevant and appropriate model for the employee assistance program professional, the "bounded rationality model," which assumes that people consider alternative solutions sequentially. Operationally, this model postulates that if a solution meets a minimum set of criteria, then it is accepted; if not, then another solution is examined. (It is important to note here that it is not the "best" solution that is sought; rather, it is a "satisfactory" solution that is sought.) Decision makers are assumed to use "heuristics"–rules that guide the search for alternatives into areas with high probabilities of yielding satisfactory solutions. For example, a company will tend to promote employees who have attained certain scores on selected performance measures because in the past employees with such scores have succeeded.

Employee assistance program professionals have found that their knowledgeable awareness of decision-making phenomena is very useful in their understanding of the organizations that their programs serve. Moreover, such expertise can facilitate helpful self-insights into how employee assistance program professionals, themselves, make their own day-to-day decisions.

Communications

Communication can be considered the "life blood of an organization." In fact, five decades ago

Barnard (1938) postulated that communication is the basis of organizations and that without–communication organizations cannot function. The following section of this chapter will examine the relationship between organizational structure and communication, the direction(s) of communication within organizations, and selected problems in organizational communication.

Communication networks portray the impact of organizational structure on communications. Additionally, communications networks reveal the paths of communication between and/or among individuals in a group. Consider, for example, the difference between the "chain" versus the "wheel" types of communication networks. In the chain, each member of the group can only communicate to two other members (except at the ends). The typical "chain of command" communication in work organizations is a good illustration of this communication mode. In this type of network, however, the centralization of power is high and the satisfaction of group members tends to be low. The wheel type of communication network can be conceptualized as a wheel–with a hub and spokes. In this mode, members of the group all communicate with the same (one) person. A common work organization illustration of this type can be found in formal work groups where all members communicate (individually) with their leader, e.g., their foreman or unit supervisor. As mentioned earlier, in this mode there is a highly centralized form of authority and satisfaction among its members tends to be low. "Common," or complete communication, on the other hand, allow everyone on the group to communicate freely with everyone else. This communication network type can be observed, for example, in a human development/ training seminar for first-line supervisors. There is no centralization of authority and power, and satisfaction of the members tends to be high. Employee assistance program professionals conducting seminars such as these, need to be cognizant of the fact that the communication network mode that the supervisors may experience in the seminar (i.e., the common type) is most likely quite different from the type of communication network they experience when they have their monthly meetings with their division manager (i.e., the wheel type). These structures also differ in terms of their relationship to the accuracy of communication. In the chain, for example, written communication tends to be high on accuracy and verbal communication tends to be low on accuracy.

Communication in organizations can flow three ways: horizontally, upward, and downward. **Horizontal communication** involves communication between or among individuals at the same level within the organization. There are two types of horizontal communication: (a) within subunit; and, (b) between subunit. Within subunit communication typically is informal and focuses on the coordination of work activities. For example, rehabilitation counselors and social workers within a district office may work together very closely on a special project calling for high levels of within subunit cooperation and coordination. Between subunit communication, both face-to-face and written (e.g., between district offices), although not sanctioned in bureaucratic organizations, tends to be common. Between subunit communication such as this has been referred to as "Fayol's Bridge"– without it the communication system would become completely clogged. For example, in a bureaucratic hierarchy such as a governmental agency, direct communication between or among different subunits (e.g., district offices) typically is difficult to develop because in a bureaucratic hierarchy communications predominately are directed upward in the chain of command until the point where the hierarchies of the two subunits come together (e.g., the regional office). The between subunit type of communication thus saves time, enhances good cooperation, and allows for the development of reasonable solutions to complex problems and situations. However, it should be noted that this type of communication can lead to conflict; for example, different subunits may view the world differently and have different vocabularies.

Upward communication flow is not very common in most traditional work organizations; it tends to be circumscribed. For example, subordinates are very careful of what they say to their superiors. Employees tend to tell their superiors what their superiors want to hear. Moreover, they tend to emphasize the positive and eliminate or downplay the negative in upward communication. Essentially, the element of trust plays a major role in the accuracy and honesty of upward communication; usually, the higher the level of trust, the higher level of accurate and honest upward communication.

Downward communication involves five important elements (Katz & Kahn, 1978). First is "job instruction" which basically refers to the employee being taught and/or told what he or she is expected to do. Second is the "rationale for the task" and an understanding of where it fits into the total organization. Third is "information" regarding rules and regulations, policies, procedures, and practices within the organization. The fourth element is the giving of feedback to the individual employee regarding his or her performance. The fifth element involves an attempt on behalf of the organization to indoctrinate subordinates into the organization's goals and values.

As most experienced employee assistance program professionals know, there are numerous problems and difficulties in organizational communications. The following four, however, appear to be especially relevant to their work. **Omission** occurs when aspects of a message are either not (a) sent by the sender, (b) understood by the receiver, (c) accurately transmitted by a middle or interim person, or (d) understood completely by the recipient. **Distortion** is the alteration of the meaning of messages as they pass through the organization. **Overload** occurs when an individual receives too many messages to adequately understand and respond appropriately (it must be remembered that a person's capacity to comprehend and remember information is finite). The substance, style, and tone of communications can have interfering emotional influences on a receiver to the extent that such an experience renders the communication cycle as ineffective. In such cases, the receiver typically has **unrealistic expectations** regarding the communication, disappointment as well as a whole cadre of other kinds of emotional reactions emerge, and the receiver understandably focuses his or her attention on the essence of the communication rather than its substance. For example, an employee assistance program counselor may meet with an upset employee who says, "My manager has been a good friend of mine for years, yet he sends me these stuffy, pushy, cold-sounding and demanding memos!" Here is where a helpful EAP counselor can facilitate an understanding of the communication style appropriate and necessary for this employee's manager (in view of his position in, and the nature of, the organization—vis-à-vis his friendship with his subordinate).

Labor Relations and Collective Bargaining

How an organization treats its employees is an important aspect of organization dynamics. Fittingly, this is also an important consideration for employee assistance programs! In organizations where unions are involved, relationships between management and unions are referred to as **labor unions**. The key element to such relationships is the development and implementation of collective bargaining agreements. **Collective bargaining** is a human institution in which the representatives of management and employees establish the terms and conditions of employment (Mills & McCormick, 1985). The process of collective bargaining is the primary means through which labor and management come to terms and settle disputes. Whenever possible, representatives from an organization's employee assistance program should have a consultative role in the development of the organization's collective bargaining agreement(s) in order to assure a synergistic relationship among three missions and goals of the three arms of the enterprise: management, labor and the employee assistance program (Dickman & Emener, 1982; Emener & Dickman, 1983).

The collective bargaining agreement typically covers a wide variety of topics. First and foremost are wage and benefit issues. Included here are not just pay per hour but a variety of fringe benefits as well (e.g., health and dental insurance, vacations, holidays, pensions, etc.). Interestingly, because of burgeoning medical and other health care costs, documented advancements, benefits, and appreciations of employee assistance and wellness programs, and assorted cultural phenomena such as a

rise in the leisure ethic, employers are becoming much more concerned with benefits than previously. Fittingly, nonwage issues increasingly are becoming integral parts of collective bargaining agreements. Issues such as these include hours of work, length of contracts, management and union rights, procedures for disciplining and discharging employees, grievance and arbitration procedures, seniority and job security, and working conditions and safety. Obviously, the development of a collective bargaining agreement is a complex process in which both sides are adversaries who must cooperate if the company is to prosper and an acceptable contract is to be reached. Assuring that the contract is in keeping with the missions and objectives of the organization's employee assistance program (e.g., especially in terms of how it relates to troubled employees), constitutes a very important consultative role on behalf of the employee assistance program professional.

Resource Allocation

Much valuable information can be learned about an organization from an understanding of how it allocates its resources. The ultimate goals and priorities of an organization become clear and concrete in the process(es) of resource allocation. In almost every case, an organization's resources are finite, and how and in what ways an organization allocates its resources constitute key managerial functions.

Among the variety of resources of an organization, the following five are not only precious to most organizations but also highly relevant to the initiatives and activities of employee assistance program professionals. The first is time—how should an employee spend his or her time on the job? Most jobs involve a variety of job tasks—what are the priorities by which an employee's tasks should be initiated and/or completed? An organization has a finite amount of **financial resources**—how should they be allocated? For example, should a company increase employees' salaries, dividends to stockholders, purchase new equipment, take over another company, "save it for a rainy day," etc.? **Personnel** is another resource that must be allocated. For example, should a terminated employee be replaced or should that line be transferred to another unit within the company?

When "times are bad" and there has to be a reduction in the work force, who gets fired? **Materials** also are considered a valuable resource to an organization. For example, should a new computer system be purchased for the front office, or should new typewriters be purchased for the front office, or should new typewriters be purchased for all the unit offices? What will be the differential effects and impacts of these two alternative purchases? Finally, there are **physical resources**. What types of new buildings need to be constructed or what existing building should be renovated? Again, what would be the rationale for such alternatives–e.g., the predicted effects on work output, the status needs of management, the job satisfaction level of on-line employee, etc.? Importantly, it can be extremely beneficial to everyone concerned when an organization's employee assistance program's professionals are formally or informally consulted when resource allocation decisions need to be made. There is no substitute for accurate predictions of the outcome effects of such decisions, and the adage "an ounce of prevention is worth a pound of cure" assuredly verifies this assertion.

CONCLUDING COMMENT

This chapter has examined key structural components of business and industry, and described and discussed dominant considerations of the organizational dynamics of industrial organizations–all of which are relevant, critical, and pivotal to the work of employee assistance program professionals. Obviously, the space available in one chapter can only scratch the surface in terms of all of the phenomena known, understood, and appreciated by the successful employee assistance program professional. Fittingly, employee assistance program professionals are urged to develop a professional lifestyle in which they will always be a "student" of organizational structure and organizational dynamics. The world is ever changing–rapidly changing–and remaining on top of "what's going on" in the work organizations that their employee assistance programs serve, is tantamount to being an efficient and effective employee assistance program professional.

REFERENCES

Barnard, C. (1938). *The functions of the executive.* Cambridge, MA: Harvard University Press.

Beyer, L. M., Trice, H. M., & Hunt, R. (1980). Impact of federal sector unions on supervisor's use of personnel policies. *Industrial and Labor Relations Review, 33,* 212–231.

Corneil, W. (1982). Initiating a joint labor management EAP. *EAP Digest, 2* (5), 22–27.

Dickman, F., & Emener, W. G. (1982). Employee assistance programs: Basic concepts, attributes and an evaluation. *Personnel Administrator, 27* (8), 55–62.

Emener, W. G., & Dickman, F. (1983). Corporate caring: EAPs solve personnel problems for business

benefits. *Management World, 12* (1), 36–38.

French, I. R. P., & Raven, B. (1968). The basis of social power. In D. Cartwright & A. Zanden (Eds.), *Group dynamics.* New York: Harper and Row.

Heller, F. A. (1973). Leadership decision making and contingency theory, Industrial *Relations, 12,* 183–199.

Katz, D., & Kahn, R. L. (1978). *The social psychology of organizations,* rev. ed. New York: John Wiley and Sons.

McWilliams, E. D. (1985). The values of a joint union-management program. In J. F. Dickman, W. G. Emener, & W. S. Hutchison, Jr. (Eds.), *Counseling the troubled person in industry.* Springfield, IL: Charles C

Acknowledgement: Sincerest appreciation is extended to Margaret A. Darrow, a Masters Candidate in the Department of Rehabilitation Counseling at the University of South Florida, for her technical assistance and critical reading of earlier drafts of this chapter.

Thomas, Publisher, Ltd.

Mills, D. A., & McCormick, J. (1985). *Industrial relations in transition: Cases and context.* New York: John Wiley and Sons.

Robbins, S. P. (1983). *Organizational behavior: Concepts, controversies and applications* (2nd ed.). Englewood Cliffs, NJ: Prentice-Hall.

Schein, E. N. (1990). Organizational Culture. *American Psychologist, 45,* 109–119.

Simon, H. A. (1957). *Administrative behavior* (2nd ed.). New York: The Free Press.

Steers, R. M. (1984). *Introduction to organizational behavior.* Glenview, IL: Scott, Foresman and Company.

Chapter 5

INGREDIENTS OF AN EFFECTIVE EMPLOYEE ASSISTANCE PROGRAM

FRED DICKMAN

Employee Assistance Programs (EAP) are extesive and widespread (U.S. National Institute on Alcohol Abuse and Alcoholism). In addition, their goals, structures, and types of personnel vary extensively in order to meet the specific program needs for which they were developed (Beyer & Trice, 1978). Yet, to reach a high degree of effectiveness, every EAP requires identifiable minimum ingredients (Dickman & Emener, 1981; Dunkin, 1982). These necessary ingredients and their specific uniqueness comprise the primary thrust of this chapter.

I. MANAGEMENT ENDORSEMENTS. It is absolutely necessary that management, at its highest level, endorse and actively support their Employee Assistance Program (EAP). To begin with, backing simply from middle management and/or the Industrial Relations Department is not enough. Management endorsement and active involvement from the very top of the corporate structure is required if an EAP is even to get off the ground. This is true whether the industry is a large corporation such as General Motors or whether it is to serve a small distributorship such as one with 50 employees.

Top management backing can insure that the following will happen:

- Doors will open to EAP personnel at all other levels of management.
- Adequate financial support to begin the EAP will be made available for mail-outs, lower supervisory training, and initial diagnostic sessions.
- Enthusiastic support of middle and lower management more likely will model and reflect top management initiative.
- A beginning to enlist the support of local top management will be maximized.

In this author's experience, no elaboration is strong enough to stress the above principle. He coordinates, on a local level, four EAPs, all of which abide by this first principle by beginning the EAP with support at the highest corporate level. This has meant he has had access and friendly receptivity to top level local management. From the beginning and throughout the past five years this enthusiastic support is largely responsible for each of the local branches achieving a penetration rate of 8 percent and very high employee, management and labor satisfaction with the program (Dickman & Emener, 1982).

II. LABOR ENDORSEMENTS. Organized labor on a national level has wholeheartedly endorsed the EAP concept, and other experts in the field have expounded the value of labor-management cooperation in implementing an effective program (Beyer, Trice, & Hunt, 1980; McWilliams, 1978). Such cooperation, in this author's experience, is crucial when the industry involved is union organized and will increase EAP participation by a meaningful degree. The following anecdotes illustrate this point.

Two of the several EAPs with which the author is under contract to coordinate in the Tampa Bay

Note: This chapter is reprinted from *Counseling the Troubled Person in Industry* (1985) with permission of the author, the book's editors (Dickman, Emener, and Hutchison, Jr.), and the publisher (Charles C Thomas, Publisher, Ltd.).

area are union shops. Both unionized companies had national union EAP endorsement but local business managers were cautious and hesitant. Such reticence could have hindered the progress of this "new idea" at the area. Fortunately, opportunities to demonstrate EAP value came early.

Two illustrative incidents in one shop involved alcoholism and both occurred late in 1979. In the first incident, the author was "beeped" by his answering service in the middle of a Saturday morning. It appeared that a worker (with seven years of seniority) had had an emotional breakdown during the midnight shift. During a disagreement with a foreman, he had "lost it" and thrown a bottle at the foreman (which fortunately missed but crashed through a plate glass window of the foreman's office). The caller (to the EAP office) was a labor steward who quickly asked, "Could the worker be seen?" He was seen an hour later, initially diagnosed as "withdrawal–acute," and was referred that day to a treatment center. It was clear he was blacked-out during most of his shift. He was treated, suspended for several months (the EAP is often an alternative to discipline but not a substitute), continued in a recovery program, returned to work, and today is a fully functioning sober, effective employee. No doubt his job, seniority and expertise would have been lost had not the labor steward acted quickly and had the EAP not been there.

The other incident concerned an older, skilled employee who was brought to the EAP office by another labor steward. The employee was intoxicated and was attempting to start his car to drive home at the end of his shift. The steward persuaded the worker to let him drive and went directly to the EAP office. He was persuaded to go that day to a treatment center and today is a recovering employee of 20 years seniority who is rated to be even more competent than he had been. In both cases, families and co-workers were aware of these two person's problems, but did not know what to do, or how to do it, before the company (and union) provided the EAP.

As of this writing, four years later, these cases have been replicated with the EAP identifying and securing proper treatment for alcoholism, drug abuse, and many other productivity-reducing problems. And incidentally, local union management, at all levels, is solidly behind the program, and provides 20–25 percent of the referrals. Where labor is involved it is imperative to secure its support.

III. POLICY STATEMENT. Every industry instituting an EAP must have a clear policy statement as to the philosophy and intent of the program. The policy statement makes it clear that human problems are inevitable, that these problems often interfere with work performance, and that, rather than terminate the impaired, troubled employee, the company would prefer to restore the employee to full capacity by providing the appropriate assistance in a confidential and professional manner. An effective policy statement makes clear the following:

- To have problems is human, and the workplace is not immune.
- The company prefers the interfering problem to be dealt with professionally as early as possible.
- Problems brought to the EAP will be treated confidentially and will not become a part of an employee's personnel file.
- Alcoholism and other drug abuse is a disease to be treated, and not a behavior to be punished.
- The EAP exists to assist employees and their families, not as a substitute for usual disciplinary principles and policies.
- In no case will the employee be coerced to use the EAP.

These basic principles are necessary as minimum components of the company's statement that its employees are its most valuable asset. In addition, these principles, properly stated, serve to protect employees who choose to use the EAP.

IV. CONFIDENTIALITY. Confidentiality is the cornerstone of an effective EAP. All employees have the right to seek help for their problems and know that their problems will be kept in the strictest confidence. In addition, when a worker is referred to the EAP by a supervisor (rather than self-referred), he or she needs to know that under no circumstances will this information be noted in any official files. Further, any employee needs to know that nothing of the nature of his or her problem will get back to supervisors or anyone else. Unless absolute confidentiality is kept at all levels, the EAP will not be successful. It is that simple. Only the employee himself or herself may (and often does) reveal his or her treatment (often the best EAP referral source) but no one else may, including the referring supervisor or labor steward, a manager, or, of course, the EAP personnel who are bound by professional ethics. Holding to this important ethic and principle overtly is not enough. There are many ways to break confidentiality in an Employee Assistance Program inadvertently.

Following, in a tongue-in-cheek fashion, are some of the ways this can be done:

1. How to Break Client Confidentiality Without Even Trying: Schedule clients from the same industry too close together. Usually the EAP counseling office is offsite. This in itself protects confidentiality. Yet if two or more clients from the same company are scheduled too close together the probability is increased they will see each other. Even if neither employee cares who knows who uses the EAP, once word of this "chance encounter" gets back to the plant, credibility as to advertised confidentiality is lessened, if not destroyed. In any event, the EAP appointment secretary must take every precaution to make sure back-to-back appointments are avoided for employees from the same industry.

This problem becomes especially acute when the EAP contractor or coordinator gives service to several companies and is part of a large counseling team. Such an arrangement is helpful in that the contracting counselor or EAP coordinator has a pool of specialists nearby to whom he or she can refer employees and thereby match the client with a counselor having specifically needed expertise. When this occurs, over a period of time several clients from the same company may be in at least medium-term treatment. This means several clients may be coming to the EAP center to see several different counselors at the same time period, increasing the odds of clients from the same company being in the same waiting room at the same time. Someone has to be assigned to make sure this does not occur. This discussion could go

on and on but the point remains clear: Don't let scheduling break the client's confidentiality. He or she may go back and tell the whole work force—and some do!

2. Keep Rigid Intake/Counseling Hours: Another good way to break client confidentiality and credibility is to have a narrow nine-to-five intake schedule. This means the client has to ask for time off which usually requires telling someone to get excused from work. Since most (80–85%) EAP clients are self-referred, they require an appointment time when they are off work. This becomes complicated when work time is in shifts, which run around the clock. Consequently, it is important for the EAP office to be open and appointments available at night. This is also true for ongoing counseling. The counselor with whom the client is eventually to work must have flexible hours.

3. Randomly Assign Clients to Groups: For many years the author has led after-care and ongoing recovery groups for alcoholic persons and their spouses. He has found this modality in conjunction with AA involvement an excellent one for ongoing treatment and generally stipulates this program for his substance abuse clients.

A good way to break confidentiality of a client, whether already in the groups (which are open-ended) or newly-entering, is to just "let it happen." Instead, when clients of the same industry are involved, each must be told he or she may see someone from his or her worksite without, of course, revealing who the someone is. Usually in the alcoholism field, clients realize they are "in it together" and grant permission for the new person to come in and vice-versa. However, if there is any objection either way, other treatment opportunities must be identified.

4. Handle Insurance Locally: Most plants or sites have a person assigned to process insurance. This is helpful in that the fellow employee can expedite claims and usually takes a personal interest. However, when the client is seen by a therapist to whom a referral was made from the EAP office, or when the client is seen by someone in the EAP office, this procedure can jeopardize confidentiality. This problem can be resolved easily by arranging for a special (specific) person in the insurance office to process all EAP client claims. This author has found this to be a satisfactory way to solve this problem, and that the company and the insurance company readily comply with this method. Most importantly, clients report satisfaction and relief with this procedure.

5. Let Hospital Admittance Clerks Verify Employment: Hospitals and treatment centers are happy to get referrals but they often insist upon verifying current employment by calling the local plant. Since most EAP referrals are to mental health centers or alcoholism/other drug treatment centers, a call to the switchboard, industrial relations, or the plant manager can be embarrassing to the employee. It is a simple matter for the EAP contractor to have a good enough relationship with the institution to pave the way for the client and eliminate this problem.

6. Plant (Site) Visitation: A good way to increase EAP visibility is for the coordinator/contractor to regularly visit the plant. However, if he or she seeks out only current or former clients, this activity can start rumors and people may shy away from being associated with the "shrink" or the plant "alcohol man." If care has been taken to do extensive supervisor and labor steward training, this problem can be meaningfully minimized as there is someone to see. And once some alcoholic persons are helped into recovery, this group (as a rule) is the best EAP advertiser. Alcoholic people, in this author's experience, once recovering, not only are not afraid to share their treatment and AA experience, but on the contrary—they tend to talk to everyone who will listen. This is a good nucleus to whom to say "Hi" while visiting. Actually this author's experience is that most employees are receptive to seeing the EAP person. Yet, care must be maintained to protect the anonymity of clients.

7. Contacting Clients at Work: Sometimes appointments have to be changed and the client must be contacted. The general rule is to call at home if possible. If time does not allow this and the client must be contacted at work, caution is in order. It's best to have a first name, usually the secretary's, and a number rather than say "please have him call the EAP office as soon as possible."

8. Tell Referring Supervisors More Than Necessary: The usual procedure, spelled out in the policy statement, is for supervisors to be told three things when a supervisor referral is made:
  a. The employee kept the appointment;
  b. He or she does or does not need treatment (If he or she is to be hospitalized or referred to a treatment center, the supervisor is told approximately the time the employee will be away from work); and
  c. He or she has accepted or rejected recommended treatment.

No other information is required and, as a matter of fact, any information about the nature of the problem is unethical and may be illegal.

Admittedly this section on confidentiality is detailed and perhaps tedious. Yet the message, hopefully, is clear. Every effort must be made to protect worker confidentiality or the program will falter. Keeping trust with the client is crucial.

V. SUPERVISOR AND LABOR STEWARD TRAINING. It is recommended that supervisor training be conducted at least once a year and certainly extensively as the program is initially instituted. Further, it is a helpful practice to have labor stewards and supervisors in training groups together (recommended size 15). This stresses the fact that the EAP is a joint management-labor venture. Likewise when top local management is oriented to the program, local labor executives should be included for the same reason.

Content of the sessions should include the following:

1. Alcoholism Awareness: Company policy typically states that alcoholism is a disease and that it is treatable. Other important concepts should include a thorough discussion of enabling behavior, effect on productivity, accidents, the family, etc.

The supervisor needs to be warned **not to**

diagnose but to look for signs of trouble, which include absenteeism, erratic behavior, tardiness, irritability, and a **drop in productivity**. The supervisor needs to know that what an employee does off time is his or her personal business. Yet, the supervisor needs to know that poor and erratic productivity often can be a sign of problems. He or she needs to be taught to more keenly observe work performance **only** and base referral on that alone. Large numbers of EAP studies evidence that this method of referral has rehabilitated more alcoholic persons than any other vehicle (Phillips, Purvis & Older, 1980).

2. Family and Other Problems: Problems hinder productivity and are human. No employee is immune. This is typically an EAP company policy. Again the supervisor/labor steward does not have to diagnose. Work performance alone is enough to refer an employee to the EAP.

3. Drug Abuse: Like alcoholism, drug abuse is a disease–company policy. Again, the supervisor should be taught to act only on work performance with one exception. While alcohol is legal, drugs are not. Observing illegal drug consumption, therefore, is a different problem than observing an employee with a bottle. The supervisor should be advised to report this behavior. Nonetheless, an EAP referral is still in order.

4. Any Problem a Referral Situation: Often employees confide in supervisors or labor stewards. This can complicate their lives by trying to be "nice guys" and trying to do counseling "in house." They are not trained; neither do they have the time. They should be encouraged to use the EAP. That's what it is there for.

5. No Problem Too Small: This author has found that many employees believe they have to be "in crisis" to contact the EAP. Yet many of these "small" problems are, in reality, not so small. Supervisors and stewards need to hear (as do eventually the other employees) that a "little" problem can grow and that what bothers a person is important to him or her and therefore is important to EAP personnel.

6. Policy Statement and Philosophy: In essence, training should cover the content of the policy statement. If that statement is adequately complete, its elucidation will cover the content of the training.

7. Practical Issues to be Covered:

a. How to make a referral;
b. Off-hours practice;
c. Emergency calls–24-hour coverage;
d. Confidentiality of the program;
e. Cost to employers;
f. Insurance coverage of the company policy;
g. EAP consultation available; and
h. What feedback they can expect.

8. Killing with Kindness: A final word is required about "enabling." Many supervisors and stewards are from the ranks. They are friends of their employees. Hence, they may overlook behavior, cajole, counsel, and out-and-out cover up. They, like all of us, need to learn that you don't help a friend with these behaviors. As a matter of fact, we "friends" will kill each other with "kindness." When this principle is understood, the EAP program is off the ground.

VI. FINANCIAL ASPECTS AND INSURANCE COVERAGE. In each of the several local companies for which the author coordinates an EAP, the company pays for the first three visits. He has not escalated the cost of these visits for five years in an effort toward cost containment and to work with each company to make it easier for employees to make that first effort. Like most people, employees are fearful of counseling, psychotherapeutic, and psychiatric costs. When employees know that going to the EAP may cost them something but that it won't break them, they will be more apt to accept a referral or (as most do) refer themselves or members of their families.

In addition, insurance must be helpful in paying for any inpatient or ongoing outpatient visits they or their family may need. In each of the companies the author serves, the insurance has been arranged to cover at a rate of 80/20 percent which means the employee pays no more than 20 percent (or minimally) for treatment. Each of these programs has an 8–10 percent penetration rate for five years and this insurance arrangement certainly has proven to help. Preliminary evaluations tend to show that money is saved over a long period of time, especially in the treatment of alcoholism. Recovered alcoholic people use their insurance less, have fewer accidents; are sick less (fewer alcohol-related illnesses) (Asma, 1975; Pell & D'Alonzo, 1970). These same observations probably hold true for other strictly functional illnesses but have not been as well-tested.

Another important factor is that there should be an "okay to pay" list provided by the EAP coordinator and accepted by the insurance company. Typically and currently, insurance payments are made for services provided by a psychiatrist or psychologist. Yet some problems are better treated by other specialists, i.e., marriage and family counselors, alcoholism counselors, drug abuse specialists, sex therapists, rehabilitationists, social workers, nutrition specialists, and others. The EAP coordinator should have a list of such competent specialists to whom to refer, and the company (which pays the premiums) should urge the insurance company to accept a special "okay to pay" list of professionals.

Last, but most important, is the issue of third-party payments for the treatment of alcoholism. Since 1956, the American Medical Association has declared alcoholism a **primary**, **chronic**, **progressive disease**. Yet, many insurance companies ignore this and **exclude** alcoholism and other drug abuse from treatment, especially outpatient treatment. Yet, 40 percent of a good EAP caseload is for this disease and seven out of 10 of these can be effectively treated with little or no time lost from work.

VII. PROFESSIONAL PERSONNEL. The EAP Coordinator needs to possess expertise in the following general rehabilitation areas:

1. Alcoholism and Alcohol Treatment: It is important to note that the entire EAP movement began with efforts to rehabilitate alcoholic employees (Roman, 1981). This was so successful the movement was broadened to include other employee problems. However, occupational alcoholism (modern-day EAP) is still the best intervener in the treatment of alcoholism. To lose this thrust would be not only a blow to the national alcoholism treatment movement, but such loss would weaken the EAP (Dickman & Phillips, in press).

2. Marriage and Family Counseling: Relationship problems comprise the second largest expected EAP caseload (McClellan, 1982). It is important that the EAP personnel be knowledgeable in this area and have referral sources to remediate these problems.

3. General Emotional Problems: The EAP Coordinator needs to have a grasp of the more typical emotional syndromes such as depression, anxiety, and stress reactions and have ready access to specialists relevant to rehabilitative treatment modalities in these areas.

4. Other Typical Problems: Financial, legal, trouble with other employees, etc. are but a few of the problems brought to the EAP. Again, ready referral sources need to be available.

5. Basic Interview/Counseling Techniques and Case Management: The EAP Coordinator is the hub around which the services will be delivered. This specialist requires interviewing, diagnostic, counseling, and referral skills. Obviously he or she also needs to know the community and which are the good treatment facilities and who are the more appropriate or better specialists.

VIII. BROAD SERVICE COMPONENTS. The EAP must be designed to helpfully respond to a wide variety of employees' problems (e.g., alcohol, drug abuse, personal, family, financial, grief, mental health, medical, legal, etc.). Such a concept is known" as the "broad brush" approach to industrial counseling as distinct from the historically earlier occupational alcoholism programs (see chapter on history in Part I of this book). The advantage of the broad brush approach is obvious. More employees get help with problems, which definitely have an effect on productivity and the employees' well-being (Dickman & Emener, 1982).

An obvious disadvantage is that practically such an approach attracts private practitioners who have little background in EAP and often no training in alcoholism and other drug abuse rehabilitation. There is supportive evidence that without these skills such a practitioner will not enhance alcoholism awareness nor will he or she properly diagnose alcoholism and other drug problems when confronted with them in an intake situation (Dahlhauser et al., 1983).

IX. ACCESSIBILITY. Employees need to be able to get to their EAP site in a timely, convenient, and efficient manner. In the opinion of this author the off-site model is more effective in that such a model better protects the confidentiality of the client. (This issue is more deeply presented in Part II of this book). Along with accessibility, 24-hour service is critical.

X. EAP AWARENESS. The EAP requires constant marketing to be effective. Some of the ways this is done are the following:
1. Supervisor training;

2. Talks before shifts;
3. Home mailouts;
4. Plant (site) visitations; and
5. Presentations (such as union meetings, departmental meetings, and motivational meetings).

These opportunities to market the EAP are invaluable. In the author's experience every time one of the above occurs (mailout, visitation, supervisor seminar, etc.), calls for service increase.

XI. PROGRAM EVALUATION. The entirety of Part IV of this book involves evaluation. Too much cannot be said about this endeavor; it is crucial to any effective program. The company and the EAP office need to know if the program is working and if it's doing what it purports to do. Some evaluation questions involve the following:
1. Penetration rates;
2. Cost effectiveness;
3. Nature of client populations;
4. Client satisfaction;
5. Management and union satisfactoriness;
6. Medical cost saving; and
7. Productivity gain.

CONCLUDING COMMENT

These are critical attributes. If they are all in place the EAP will be effective and everybody wins–the employee, employee families, management, labor, and the human service personnel.

COMMENT/UPDATE

JUDITH K. SCHEMM

Employee Assistance Programs (EAPs) and professionals have welcomed the new millennium. They continue to perform in their historical role of working with employees and addictions, but they have also invited the challenges of solution-based therapy, Critical Incident Stress Debriefing, online analysis and long-term counseling. EAP professionals today are much more than substance abuse counselors of the past. The role has evolved to offer services to employees and employers, which address an array of personal and corporate needs. Employers are increasingly recognizing the benefits of EAP intervention and they continue to ask EAPs to do more. This expansion of service means that EAPs of today are in a period of growth and transition.

EAPs have traditionally been closely associated with Alcoholics Anonymous (AA). EAP professionals continue in this familiar relationship, but are no longer limited to AA. New and diverse 12-step support groups have been developed to address the changing face of addiction, such as sex addictions, food addictions, gambling, and Internet addiction. The EAP professional has become more knowledgeable about these new compulsions and the impact each can and does have on the workplace. The impact of alcohol abuse on the workplace remains a key issue for the EAP professional, as billions of dollars are lost each year due to absenteeism and accidents contributed to alcohol or drug use. Treatment continues to be seen as an important component of service provision, but prevention capabilities have proliferated in the workplace. Organizations are offering incentives to employees to live healthier lives. Stress management, antismoking campaigns, free health screenings, and drug abuse awareness programs are prevention-based efforts seen in the workplace. The EAP counselor has become a proponent for prevention, offering a plethora of referral options and workshops targeting employees experiencing such stressors. The emphasis on prevention becomes more evident when one considers that the office of the National Drug Control Policy oversees more than $19 billion targeted for antidrug programming.

In recent years smaller businesses have sought the help of Employee Assistance Programs. EAPs are no longer limited to the Fortune 500 companies. The competition between EAPs often results in lower pricing and consequently smaller companies find it is affordable to provide EAP services for troubled employees. Of special interest is the role of EAP services used as a back-up to drug testing done at the work site. Businesses have realized that the expense of replacing employees who test positive is a less viable and more expensive option. Therefore, instead of termination for a positive drug test, referral to an EAP provider for a second chance has become the more normal response.

Since September 11, 2001 violence in the workplace has become a significant area of focus for EAP professionals. In response to this need EAP professionals are seeking more training in Critical Incident Stress Debriefing and Posttraumatic Stress Disorder. EAP professionals find themselves on the front-line after violent acts or disasters. Violence has threatened feelings of security in the workplace, offices have been mailed poisons, employees have been attacked by significant others, disgruntled workers have killed innocent employees. The workplace has been visited by terror and trauma. Today's EAP professionals are prepared to deal with the impact of these events. EAP counselors are now schooled on appropriate responses to trauma and are able to educate employers as to the necessary course of action. This includes providing the needed interventions to facilitate the process of adjustment and acceptance for workers impacted by violence and trauma. The need for an EAP's presence has never been more apparent. The primary goal is to assure employees regain adequate well-being and mental health. The concerns of the employer include employee issues of stress, anxiety, and risky alcohol use.

Another new challenge for EAP provider is the emergent multigenerational workforce. The growing age difference among workers presents a new challenge to EAP professionals. The census bureau reports 19 percent of men and 10percent of women over the age of 65 are still working (Watkins, 2002).[1] The problems encountered by older workers include conflicts with younger supervisors, and limited experience with high tech work requirements. These conflicts are often a challenge for the EAP provider.

A related issue involves the challenges faced by workers whom assume the role of multigenerational caregiving. Caregiving takes a heavy toll on individuals and even more so if they have a job. For many workers, mostly women, this situation is a growing concern due to the impact on family and work. Employers are also increasingly concerned as caregiving can lead to lost time and impacts the bottom line. Among those who have provided hands-on care, 67 percent reported it has significantly affected their family life, and 41 percent said it interfered with their work. According to an August 2001 AARP survey, 44 percent of the nation's 76 million baby boomers have responsibility for both aging parents and children" (O'Toole & Pannen, 2002).[2]

The make-up of the workplace is also changing as more women and minorities enter the work force. It has estimated that the population of the United States will be 50 percent non-white by the year 2050. When persons who are not male or white EAP professionals enter the work force, they have had to acquire multicultural expertise. The need for such skills will only grow given the anticipated shift in population demographics.

Tollfree numbers have emerged as a new way for workers to seek counseling without leaving their desks. Although its effectiveness has been questioned, more therapy and EAP services are and will continue to be provided via teleconference and the Internet. This is most evident, as there has been an increase in web-based client education with electronic linking to service providers. In a recent study conducted at the University of Maryland at Baltimore, employees reported being more motivated to use online, integrated work-life EAPs as they were able to obtain immediate access to needed information about personal and professional issues. Findings also revealed that 92 percent found online recourses helpful or extremely helpful and of these, 93 percent reported they were likely to visit the site again. The specific reasons for using such services were to gain information and assessment of problems (Watkins, 2002). EAP professionals are upgrading computer skills as the profession encounters the information age. Obviously, in the future, the ethical and programmatic issues related to these services will continue to require the careful attention and consideration of employee assistance professionals and professional organizations.

The conventional wisdom in the EAP marketplace believes that on site EAPs will have lower utilization rates than off-site programs, primarily due to concerns about confidentiality. This conventional wisdom appears to be flawed. A 1999 study, which compared utilization rates for on- and off-site, EAPs reported that on-site programs had higher utilization. The average rates for onsite utilization ranged from 7 percent to 7.7 percent, while off-site programs averaged utilization rates from 4 percent to 5 percent (Sharar & White, 2001).[3] The roles and delivery opportunities of EAPs are changing, but the expectations of employers for solutions and results continue. The basic spirit in this era of transition for EAPs remains the same. It has created its niche. EAPs have a comfortable place as the liaison between employee and employer. In that context EAP professionals will continue to provide the means for bridging the gap between work and life. In fact, the role and appreciation of EAP professionals can be expected to expand.

ENDNOTES

1. Watkins, G. (2002). The multi-generational workforce. *EAP Digest 23* (4) 7.
2. O'Toole, B., & Pannen, M. L. (2002). Eldercare: The new frontier. *EAP Digest 22* (2).
3. Sharar, D. A., & White, W. (2001) EAP Ethics and Quality. *EAP Digest, 21* (4) 16–19.

REFERENCES

Asma, E. F. (1975). Long-term experience with rehabilitation of alcoholic employees. In R. Williams & G. Moffat (Eds.) *Occupational Alcoholism Programs.* Springfield, IL: Charles C Thomas, Publisher, Ltd. (175–193).

Beyer, J., & Trice, H. (1978). *Implementing change: Alcoholism policies in work organizations.* New York: Free Press.

Beyer, J. M., Trice, H. M., & Hunt, R. (1980). Impact of federal sector unions on supervisor's use of personnel policies. *Industrial and Labor Relations Review, 33,* 212–231.

Dahlhauser, H. F., Dickman, F., Emener, W. G., & Yegidis-Lewis, B. (1982). Alcohol and drug abuse awareness: Implications for intake interviewing, submitted for publication.

Dickman, F., & Emener, W. G. (1982). Employee assistance programs: Basic concepts, critical attributes, and an evaluation. *Personnel Administrator, 27* (5), 55, 56, 58–62.

Dunkin, W. S. (1982). *The EAP Manual.* The National Council on Alcoholism, Inc.

McClellan, K. (1982). An overview of occupational alcoholism issues for the 80s. *Journal of Drug Education, 12* (1).

Pell, S., & D'Alonzo, C. A. (1980). Sickness absenteeism of alcoholics. *Journal of Occupational Medicine, 12,* 198–210.

Phillips, D. A., Purvis, A. J., & Older, H. J. (1980). *Turning supervisors on (To employee counseling programs),* Hazelton Foundation, Inc.

U.S. National Institute on Alcohol Abuse and Alcoholism. Alcohol and health: technical support document. Third special report to Congress. (DHEW Pub. No. ADM–79–832).

Chapter 6

UNION INVOLVEMENT: A KEY INGREDIENT TO SUCCESSFUL EMPLOYEE ASSISTANCE PROGRAMS

FRED DICKMAN and WILLIAM G. EMENER

Indeed, no basic text on employee assistance programs would be complete without stressing the need for cooperative program involvement on behalf of both management and labor. Such cooperative involvement should occur all throughout an employee assistance program–its inception, planning, implementation, evaluation, program refinement, and continuation. By far, most employee assistance programs are management conceived, financed, and managed. Nonetheless, some employee assistance programs such as the Postal Workers Alcoholism Programs and Eastern Airlines Machinists Program are union managed. Whichever is the case, however, experience repeatedly had demonstrated that an employee assistance program's success ultimately is contingent upon **mutual cooperation** between the two–union and management. This concept and its importance was expounded as early as the beginning of the 1960s when farsighted union leaders like Leo Perlis, Director of Community Services for the AFL-CIO, pointed out that **more workers could be reached by union and management working together** than by either entity working alone (McWilliams, 1978). Other experts in the field also have stressed union and management cooperation: "Organized labor on a national level has wholeheartedly endorsed the EAP concept, and other experts in the field have expounded the value of labor-management cooperation in implementing an effective program (Beyer, Trice & Hunt, 1980; McWilliams, 1978)." (Dickman, 1985,

p. 40) It is interesting to note, moreover, that some experts even have argued that an employee assistance program has no place in a company or business without labor-management cooperation:

However, we do not wish to imply that "cooperation" just means that management creates a program and the union endorses it. While it is true that management will have to do more work than the union, no results are likely to emerge unless the program is a *joint* one. Company management and company unions must be involved right from the start and must back each other up all the way through. Otherwise, the program may not be sold, and adversary situations–which are out of place where an individual's health or sickness is concerned–will be inevitable (Sadler & Horst, 1972, p. 5).

In addition to mutual involvement on behalf of both labor and management, a demonstrated and genuine genre of **trust** must exist between them in order for an employee assistance program to be successful. In his discussion regarding the initiation of a joint labor-management EAP, Corneil (1982) stated:

Mutual trust and relative power are central issues to this step [starting an EAP]. If the trust level is low, perhaps due to a history of labor-management proposals that never quite worked out as planned, this step, and indeed the entire process to date, will have been characterized by suspicion and testing out of each other's motives. (p. 24)

Note: This chapter is reprinted from *Counseling the Troubled Person in Industry* (1985) with permission of the author, the book's editors (Dickman, Emener, & Hutchison, Jr.), and the publisher (Charles C Thomas, Publisher, Ltd.).

Thus, an important a priori contention on behalf of the authors of this chapter is that these two elements on behalf of both union and management, **mutual involvement and trust**, can almost ensure an employee assistance program's success and create exceptional benefits for all concerned. Relevant to this contention, the remainder of this chapter will identify and discuss specific: (a) benefits to the union; (b) benefits to management; (c) benefits to the employee assistance program; and (d) benefits to employees. The chapter will then conclude with a recommended conceptualization of the interfacing linkages among these three critical employee assistance programming entities, the union, management and the EAP, and the employees.

Benefits to the Union

1. Consistency with the Union's Mission. Typically, a union's primary stated purpose is to help its workers (members). This is also the primary purpose of an employee assistance program. Thus, when a union supports the efforts of an EAP, it essentially is doing what it is primarily designed to do—help employees (its members). Sadler and Horst (1972) articulated this notion when they stated: "The unions, too [in addition to management] have a vital reason for cooperating. The program [the EAP] is designed to help workers, and helping workers is the stated reason for the union's existence" (p. 5).

2. Building of Cohesiveness. In most instances, a union's strength and power, which comes from its members, is contingent upon the members' perceptions of the extent to which the union is "caring"—the extent to which it cares about the well-being and wellness of its members. An excellent way for a union to demonstrate its "caring" for its members (and also thereby communicating its "caring" message) is through meaningful involvement in a successful employee assistance program which is helpful to employees (the union's members). And, as most unions appreciate, this is an important message to communicate.

3. "Real Help" Versus "Sympathy." To help initiate, plan, support, implement, evaluate, and improve an effective employee assistance program, is an excellent way for a union to say (figuratively): "We want to support each member's access to expert assistance." In his discussion of an EAP's responsiveness to substance abuse problems, McWilliams (1985) addressed the importance of not just being sympathetic: "Unions, because of their relationship with their members, can give understanding and a sympathetic offer of assistance, counseling, and treatment. Yet, there is overwhelming evidence that alcoholics rarely respond to sympathy" (p. 54). Almost all experts in the field of alcoholism rehabilitation purport that employee assistance programs are very effective interveners in stopping active alcoholic behavior and maintainers of long-term recovery. Simplistically stated, when a special tool is needed to repair a special piece of equipment, you engage the use of a specialist, e.g., a machinist; when a person or a family breaks down, you engage the use of a specialist, e.g., a licensed counselor.

4. "Help" Versus "Arbitration": Another Option. Arbitration is expensive–not only to management but to the union as well. For example, the business manager, the employee, and the steward typically are all involved (usually on their own time). Too often, the situation emerges as a "win-lose" situation, and frequently "to win" or "to lose" is not the solution for the employee. This is almost always true for the alcohol/drug abusing worker who needs "help" rather than "fairness;" this many times is also true in instances when employees have other kinds of problems as well. Recently, in discussing union vs. management handling of employees problems, McWilliams (1985) stated: "No matter who wins, the employee is the loser. A union victory, in effect, kills the member with kindness. A management victory, in the absence of an enlightened joint program [an EAP], might result in punitive action rather than in urgently needed treatment" (p. 54).

Reasons such as these above four offer compelling reasons for unions to play an active role in the initiation, planning, implementation, evaluation, and refinement of employee assistance programs. Moreover, a healthy work force can enhance more overall productivity. Evidence is abundant that EAPs save the company money and thereby increase profits. The bottom line consideration for a union is that higher wages are more easily negotiated from a profitable than a non-profitable company.

Benefits to Management

When mutual involvement and trust pervade the cooperative activities of both labor and management, there are specific benefits that can be realized by management. The following five are among such management benefits and tend to represent those found to be highly appreciated by management.

1. Increased Cooperation. Employee assistance programs involve key personnel in what is frequently called "supervisory training." This training typically focuses on intervention techniques, referral procedures, signs to look for in the troubled employee, and reviews and discussions of company policies and procedures, among others. Importantly, supervisors and management representatives and stewards and other labor representatives are typically trained together, and training experiences such as these facilitate closer cooperation and increased "togetherness" among leaders within the environment that is good for the company.

2. Enhanced Morale. "Low Morale" frequently is discussed on American business pages as being meaningfully related to reductions in productivity. Other related concerns include high absenteeism, high turnover, and apathy. Nonetheless, it has been experienced that when union and management cooperatively work together to help troubled employees and their families through the auspices of an effective employee assistance program, worker morale tends to increase and be more positive (Dickman & Emener, 1982). On behalf of the management of a company, this spin-off outcome would appear to be very appealing.

3. More Troubled Workers Are Helped. For numerous reasons (e.g., philosophical, utilitarian), companies want to help their troubled employees. Identifying them, convincing them that they need assistance, and then helping them,' is easier said than done. Nonetheless, when union and management cooperatively work together with an employee assistance program, the likelihood of a higher penetration rate exists, and hence a greater likelihood of reaching more troubled workers who need help.

4. Enhanced Productivity. In the final analysis, helping workers toward being more fully functioning individuals will have a positive impact on productivity (Corneil, 1982; Dickman & Emener, 1982). The troubled on-the-line worker and others in the work force assuredly do not represent all of the variables related to less than potential productivity levels. On the other hand, however, a company's "happy and trouble free" workers do represent chief reasons for a fuller productive enterprise.

5. Increased Alternatives and Options to Problem Resolution. Surveys conducted by the authors of this chapter (e.g., Dickman & Emener, 1982), among others, clearly indicate that both high level managers and union officials alike do not enjoy disciplinary processes and procedures. Fittingly, one of their consistently reported areas of "satisfactoriness with" and "liking of" employee assistance programs is that the programs provide an option other than disciplinary action regarding a troubled employee. They are aware that the employee who requires disciplinary action and/or arbitration, often is troubled in some way, and that in many instances it is better, more effective, and cheaper to explore a "helping alternative" via the EAP than to go immediately to a disciplinary and/or arbitration alternative. Basically, it has been experienced that while it is not the only alternative, when appropriate, the "helping alternative via the EAP" is the preferred mode of action.

Reasons such as these above five, while not all inclusive, provide compelling rationale for management to work cooperatively and closely with labor in initiating, planning, implementing, evaluating, and refining employee assistance programming for workers. In effect, management has much to gain and very little (if anything) to lose.

Benefits to the Employee Assistance Program

As the leaders and developers of an employee assistance program plan implement, evaluate, and refine their program, it is critical for them not only to involve union and management but also to facilitate cooperative and trusting relationships among all those involved. Identifiable, mutual, and cooperative tasks and activities are not only beneficial to the union and management but to the EAP itself. The following five are noteworthy and deserving of special attention.

1. Increased Probability of Success. As discussed earlier in this chapter, the active, mutual, and cooperative involvement of both union and management with an employee assistance program, increases the program's probability for success. This, without a doubt, is important to the program. Corneil (1982), for example, discussed six developmental stages of a joint labor-management EAP [viz: (a) commitment; (b) policy; (c) procedure; (d) communication; (e) training; and (f) evaluation)], and stated: "If the site manager and supervisors and the membership of the local union do not support the EAP and are not willing to be actively involved in leadership, chances of success are limited" (p. 25).

2. Increased Referrals. A well-run and effective employee assistance program will have an 8 to 10 percent penetration rate (Dickman & Emener, 1982). More pointedly, this means that an effective EAP should serve approximately 8 to 10 percent of the total number of individuals who have access to it (e.g., employees and their immediate family members). Achieving a penetration rate such as this without full labor and management cooperation and involvement is very unlikely. An employee assistance program must be postured to respond to the needs of its constituency group (i.e., the employees); moreover, it must facilitate the employees' **demands** for it (i.e., their use of it).

3. Freedom of Movement in the Plant and the Union Hall. The authors of this chapter have had, and currently have, a variety of experiences in working with employee assistance programs in companies with union shops. In those situations in which the employee assistance program enjoys active, mutual, wholehearted, and supportive involvement from both the union and management, one important benefit is that the EAP contractor or manager has free movement throughout the plant and access to union meetings. This privilege of free and full visitation greatly enhances many important aspects of the program such as marketing of the EAP, follow-up, employee's perceptions of the program, and penetration rates.

4. Joint Training Sessions. The training sessions typically conducted by employee assistance program staff are attended by representatives from both labor and management. Not only does this provide serendipitous opportunities for cooperative interaction on behalf of the union and management representatives, but on behalf of the EAP staff as well. For example, the EAP professional enjoys the opportunity: to work with both the supervisors from management and the union stewards in a noncrisis, nonproblem-oriented situation; to train mixed intervention teams focusing on employee concerns; to educate and market the program; and above all, to **assist critical plant leadership on knowing "how not to enable the troubled worker."** This is absolutely invaluable if seriously troubled employees are to be identified and helped. Frankel (1985), in his discussion of alcoholism treatment in the partial hospital or day program, addressed this issue very well:

A labor-management employee assistance program helps eliminate many of the pitfalls characteristic of other types of intervention. Alcoholism is dealt with by labor and management under the same rules followed with other illness. It says that we are willing to help you deal with this illness by setting up the machinery to make it easy for you to get competent help and treatment. It confronts the employee with realistic and observable dimensions such as job performance and absenteeism. It eliminates cover-up and links one of a person's key worlds within which he or she operates (work world) with the treatment of his or her illness. (p. 133)

5. Early Intervention. Dickman and Emener (1982) conducted an evaluation research survey on one employee assistance program population with a focus on consumer satisfaction. In addition to finding a high degree of reported satisfaction with the employee assistance program, most participants also reported that they would not have tended to their problem as early as they did had it not been for the existence of, and the assistance they received from, the EAP. This particular EAP was strongly supported by both labor and management from its beginning and throughout, and it was concluded that this cooperation and involvement was a significant influence on the employees' reported early intervention experiences.

There are many more benefits of mutual involvement and trust on behalf of labor and management for an employee assistance program. These above five only scratch the surface. The important thing is for the professionals in an employee assistance program to not only remember that there are many, many benefits that result from fostering mutual cooperation and trust on behalf of labor and management, but also that there are no valid reasons for not fostering it.

Benefits to the Employee

In the ultimate sense, the vast majority of the previously discussed benefits of mutual cooperation and trust on behalf of labor and management (i.e., to the union, to management, and to the EAP), will directly and indirectly result in benefits to the employee. Nonetheless, there are numerous identifiable benefits to the employee, and the following five appear to be worthy of special attention.

1. A Well-Run EAP. First of all, it is important to remember that the mere existence of a good employee assistance program, in and of itself, is a meaningful employee benefit. Moreover, those

that are joint labor-management supported tend to be more efficient, more effective, and helpful to a larger proportion of the employees and their families who have access to them (Corneil, 1982; Dickman & Emener, 1982; Emener & Dickman, 1983). Joint labor-management-supported EAPs also tend to facilitate the existence of other positive qualities within the workplace (e.g., high morale), and with the existence of joint labor-management support conditions the longevity and continuance of the EAP assuredly is on more solid ground. It can be quite comforting and assuring to all those concerned to see healthy labor-management relations supporting a company's EAP; on the contrary, fear and concern that labor and management may get into a hassle and kill the company's EAP can be very debilitating.

2. Real Help in Response to One's "Cry for Help." In most instances, it takes caring, trained, and cooperating individuals to recognize and helpfully respond to a hurting employee's crying out for help. For example, many authorities in the field of alcoholism (consult Johnson, 1980) believe that the person troubled with alcohol or other drugs suffers from a "catch 22" situation: part of the person wants to hide and not be found out, and another part of the person wants to be identified and helped. When union and management cooperatively and in trusting ways work together with an effective employee assistance program, the latter alternative is more likely to be the affected outcome. Trice, Hunt, and Beyer (1977) articulated the key mechanisms operating in situations such as this:

> While the real objective of an industrialized alcoholism program is to assist the problem drinker, dealing with him/her in a unionized work setting requires overcoming the traditional advisory relationship between union and management. Problem drinkers usually seek to deny or rationalize their drinking problem, often becoming effective manipulators. Should the drinker detect an opportunity to playoff the union against management, he/she can "divide and conquer," thus seriously damaging the effectiveness of the confrontation. (p. 104)

Thus, as this illustrates, the importance of the union, the management and the EAP professionals cooperatively working together cannot be underscored enough.

3. Stigma Reduction. When both labor and management jointly communicate and demonstrate that "to be troubled is to be human," a much more trusting environment exists and employees tend to feel more comfortable asking for and accepting help and assistance. It is not easy for an employee and/or a family to admit that they need help. The cultural stigma that suggests that people should be able to solve their own problems without help from others can be a very powerful influence on a troubled employee and render him or her as being reluctant to seek assistance. However, when a person's **supervisor and labor steward** jointly recommend that he or she seek assistance from the employee assistance program, an altogether different atmosphere exists–one which is ultimately much more helpful to the troubled employee.

4. Feeling Cared For as a Person. No one advocates coddling, especially in the workplace. At the same time, however, a worker does not like to feel as if he or she is "a dispensable tool," "a number," or "a temporarily needed piece of machinery." When employees have feelings like these, morale tends to go down, job satisfaction dwindles, and quite often productivity suffers. Nonetheless, in environments where labor, man-

agement and the employee assistance program cooperatively, trustingly, and mutually work together, employees are more apt to feel that others (e.g., their union stewards, their supervisors) care about them as people. This environmental attitude, in turn, tends to enhance morale, job satisfaction, and productivity.

5. Affordable Access to Help. One of the primary reasons why employees seek help and assistance early from an employee assistance program (e.g., before their problems get out of hand) is that they can afford to (Dickman & Emener, 1982). Effective EAPs are well financed, at least to the extent that feared economic hardship is not an upfront deterrent to seeking help and assistance. "Affordability," in terms of the perceptions of troubled employees, also means that they can seek assistance and help without immediate fears that it could cost them their jobs (or benefits, opportunities for promotion, etc.). In an ideal employee assistance program environment, troubled employees do not consider whether or not they can afford to seek help and assistance, they consider why they cannot afford not to seek help and assistance. Hopefully, their considerations produce the conclusion, "I have a lot to gain and nothing to lose."

As suggested earlier, joint union-management-supported employee assistance programs produce numerous direct and indirect benefits for employees. These above five represent but a few of them.

CONCLUSION

In its purest form, an employee assistance program is the third arm of industry. As portrayed in Figure 9-1 (p. 99) labor, management, and the employee assistance program meaningfully interface with each other. The most important aspect of this conceptualization of the three arms of industry, however, is that **the employee is central to all three**. This assertion stems from the notion that the human being, the employee, is industry's most precious, valuable, and essential resource. Fittingly, labor (the union), management (the company), and

the employee assistance program should feel compelled to cooperatively, mutually, and trustingly work together to have the best employee assistance program they can have–what better way is there to protect their most precious resource? Should this be the case, everyone wins! Emener and Dickman (1983) captured this valuable workplace genre with a quote from a company official:

A business manager of one unionized plant has personally made appointments and brought several workers to the EAP. He stated: "The EAP is not a company or a union outfit. It is for the well being of each of us. Let's support it for ourselves and our families." This is management backing of a high sort and exemplifies the role a well-run EAP can play in the morale of everyone. (p. 38)

As suggested throughout this chapter, when labor and management cooperatively support an employee assistance program, everyone wins.

REFERENCES

Beyer, J. M., Trice, H. M., & Hunt, R. (1980). Impact of federal sector unions on supervisor's use of personnel policies. *Industrial and Labor Relations Review, 33,* 212–231.

Corneil, W. (1982). Initiating a joint labor management EAP. *EAP Digest, 2* (5), 22–17.

Dickman, F. (1985). Ingredients of an effective EAP. In J. F. Dickman, W. G. Emener, & W. S. Hutchison, Jr. (Eds.), *Counseling the troubled person in industry.* Springfield, IL: Charles C Thomas, Publisher, Ltd.

Dickman, F., & Emener, W. G. (1982). Employee assistance programs: Basic concepts, attributes, and an evaluation. *Personnel Administrator, 27* (8), 55–62.

Emener, W. G., & Dickman, F. (1983). Corporate caring: EAPs solve personal problems for business benefits. *Management World, 12* (1), 36–38.

Frankel, G. (1985). Alcoholism treatment in the partial hospital or day program. In J. F. Dickman, W. G. Emener, & W. S. Hutchison, Jr. (Eds.), *Counseling the troubled person in industry.* Springfield, IL: Charles C Thomas, Publisher, Ltd.

Johnson, V. (1980). *I'll quit tomorrow.* San Francisco, CA: Harper & Row Publishers.

McWilliams, E. D. (1978). The values of a joint union-management program. *Labor-Management Alcoholism Journal, 8* (3).

McWilliams, E. D. (1985). The values of a joint union-management program. In J. F. Dickman, W. G. Emener, & W. S. Hutchison, Jr. (Eds.), *Counseling the troubled person in industry.* Springfield, IL: Charles C Thomas, Publisher, Ltd.

Sadler, M., & Horst, J. F. (1972). Company/union programs for alcoholics. *Harvard Business Review, 50* (5), 1–8.

Sutermeister, M. (1963). *People and productivity.* New York: McGraw-Hill.

Trice, H. M., Hunt, R. E., & Beyer, J. M. (1977). Alcoholism programs in unionized work settings: Problems and prospects in union-management cooperation. *Journal of Drug Issues, 7* (2), 103–115.

Chapter 7

A NATIONAL EMPLOYEE ASSISTANCE PROGRAM: THE CERIDIAN EXPERIENCE

CERIDIAN

What is the most essential factor affecting an organization's competitiveness and productivity in today's global economy? Is it geography? Affordable capital? Access to the latest technology? Without a doubt, all of these are important. But the most important factor in a company's productivity is the *human element*–its management and employees, its partners and suppliers. Salaries and benefits are usually the largest line items in the budgets of most businesses.

Since the mid-1990s, the U.S. economy registered trend productivity growth of about 2.5 percent, well above the 1.4 percent average of the previous two decades.[1] Organizations' competitiveness depends on this trend of ongoing productivity growth. "Even though the private sector has shed more than a million jobs, companies have still managed to turn out goods and services that consumers want at prices that they can afford because of rising productivity. Rising productivity has enabled companies to meet the demands for products while reducing their work forces."[2] However, this productivity surge is a double-edged sword and has profound implications for employees and employers.

U.S. workers enjoyed steady growth in wages and benefits through the 90s and their productivity continued to rise. But they also put in progressively longer days and spent less time with their families. Continuous reorganizations and downsizing made them feel more uncertain and fearful about job security. As long as wages continued to rise, people tolerated the pressure. In 2002, however, wage increases went flat in three-quarters of U.S. firms and actually declined at some.[3] Leaders are correct to be concerned about sagging morale and productivity if they must freeze or cut people's financial compensation. If they must restructure their organizations, leaders are right to care about the willingness of people to put up with ongoing change and their ability to deal with it positively and creatively.

These productivity gains mean that employees need to work longer, harder, and smarter–which has significant consequences for people. This has spurred the growing popularity of employee assistance programs (EAPs) and work-life programs (WLPs) as important elements in the so-called "productivity miracle." Motivated, satisfied, and healthy employees are more productive, and EAPs and WLPs have been instrumental in helping reduce human resources-related barriers to productivity. EAPs and WLPs have been and will continue to be an important means for motivating competitive levels of performance, productivity, and profit in the modern corporation.

In order to remain vital, EAPs must demonstrate their value to the organizations that they serve. The new economy demands nonstop change. Work-life balance and employees' physical and emotional health are all critical parts of the equation. As this description of the Ceridian experience will show, a company's human resources offer the greatest opportunities for performance and productivity improvement. Implementing integrated employee assistance programs, with work-life and health and wellness programs is possibly the best means of realizing those opportunities.

Impediments to Productivity

Tired and overworked employees have trouble balancing the demands of work and family. Troubled, distracted, and stressed employees tend to have more unscheduled absences and higher medical expenses; more workers' compensation claims; make more mistakes and create more waste. In Ceridian's work with a wide spectrum of employers, we see many impediments to productivity. For example:

- **Reorganizations and Downsizing:** Since 1985 well over 85 percent of *Fortune* 500 companies have experienced major reorganizations and downsizing.[4] As more workers are laid off as a result of mergers and reorganizations, surviving workers worry about their own security. A survey sponsored by UNUM Life Insurance Company and conducted by researchers at Johns Hopkins University also shows a clear correlation between mergers and layoffs and high mental and neurological insurance claims–in fact, there was a 33 percent higher claim incidence among employees whose firms have restructured.[5] Such worrying also takes time away from the job. There is also the fact that after downsizing, fewer workers are left to do the same amount of work.

- **Child Care:** Forty percent of women in the workplace have children under age 18, and the number of children living in single-parent and dual income households is growing. Child care is a serious problem for many working parents, mainly due to the expense. A study by the Economic Policy Institute (EPI) reported that placing a child in a daycare center full-time can cost $4,000 to $10,000 a year–an amount well beyond the means of many low-wage families, even those with two working parents. The study report observed: "In 49 states, child care costs are greater than the tuition of public colleges."[6] Even when they are able to find affordable child care, parents worry about its quality. Experts estimate that most U.S. children are in child care situations that can be rated only poor or mediocre.

A study by the American Business Collaboration (ABC) for Quality Dependent Care suggests employers that help their employees find good child care may reap productivity gains. The survey of employees working at ABC-member companies found that 63 percent of the workers believe that their productivity is up because of the child care programs their employers provide.[7]

- **Elder Care:** Changing demographics are causing the emergence of new groups of dependent care providers. The leading edge of 78 million baby boomers–those born between 1946 and 1964–is now entering an age when their parents will have limitations and needs for care.[8]

The so-called "sandwich generation" is a growing group of adult children who are caring for aging parents while raising their own families. There are more than 9 million Americans in this situation today, with 40 percent of them between the ages of 35 to 49.[9] Over half the adult population either is now or expects to be family caregivers.[10] Yet, as the number of elderly needing care increases, the pool of family caregivers is dwindling from 11 potential caregivers for each person needing care to just four per elder in 2050. This will make elder care a more pervasive and intense issue for more employers.[11]

According to a Met Life study, caring for an elderly relative typically takes at least eight hours a week and spans eight years, and the problem is expected to mushroom as the number of middle-aged workers grows and their parents live longer.[12] Caring for sick, aging, and disabled family members cause absenteeism, financial hardship, depression, and turnover among employed caregivers. Caregiving costs U.S. businesses between $11.4 billion and $29 billion annually in productivity, according to a study of more than 1,500 employees.[13] Caregiving can force employees to take time off from their jobs, pass up promotions or "plum" assignments, retire early, or even quit. About one in five employed caregivers (18% of those under age 65) quit their jobs to provide care. Another 42 percent reduced the number of hours they work.[14] No wonder, then, that six in ten (61%) of "intense" family caregivers (those providing 21 or more hours of care per week) showed clinical symptoms of depression.[15]

- **Absenteeism:** Unscheduled absences are very costly to business firms and governmental bodies. A survey by CCH, Inc., a business research firm, and Harris Interactive found that absenteeism costs in 2001 to be about $775 per employee per year, which typically may cost $10,000 annually for small organizations and more than $3 million for large companies.[16]

Of chronic concern to employers is how to address the nonhealth-related reasons that keep workers off the job. In fact, while personal illness remains the single most common reason for last-minute worker no-shows (32 percent), reasons other than illness accounted for over two-thirds (68 percent) of unscheduled absences. These included family issues (21 percent), stress (19 percent), personal needs (11 percent) and entitlement mentality (9 percent). Another 8 percent of employees had unplanned absences from work for other reasons, such as bad weather or transportation problems.[17]

- **Aging Work Force:** Demographic trends are converging to create a projected labor shortage over the next few years. In the decade ending in 2006, the number of workers between the ages of 45 and 54 will grow by more than 50 percent, while the number between the ages of 25 and 34 will drop by 9 percent.[18] Americans are living longer and can expect a longer period of healthy, active life after the traditional retirement age of 55–65. These trends combine to predict a shift toward an older work force. The number of mid-career workers will shrink over the next several years, while the number of workers over 55 will grow.[19] Of great advantage to employers are the facts that older employees show less absenteeism, lower turnover, fewer accidents, higher job satisfaction and more positive work values than younger workers do. In all but a few areas they usually are more experienced.

This aging trend will be felt in the workplace in four principal ways. First, the number of employees with elder care responsibilities will rise significantly. Second, retirement policies and practices will need to change as employers seek to retain their experienced talent and as the baby-boom generation seeks to redefine the nature of retirement. Third, older workers will weigh their options and seek work that is both financially and personally rewarding. And fourth, there are significant challenges in leading and motivating an intergenerational work force with its competing values, attitudes toward work, work styles, etc. EAPs can help employers and employees with a wide range of issues affecting the aging work force—from caregiving and resources for older adults, to mid-life transitions and life planning for "the new retirement."

- **Substance Abuse and Depression:** Alcohol is the single most used and abused drug in America. According to the National Institute on Alcohol Abuse and Alcoholism (NIAAA), nearly 14 million Americans (1 in every 13 adults) abuse alcohol or are alcoholics.[20] Numerous studies and reports have been issued on the workplace costs of alcoholism and alcohol abuse, and report costs that range from $33 billion to $68 billion per year.[21] Alcohol is a major factor in injuries at home, at work, and on the road. Nearly half of all traffic fatalities involve alcohol. It is recognized as the direct cause of 15 percent of accidents at work.[22] In the workplace, the costs of alcoholism and alcohol abuse manifest themselves in absenteeism, which is estimated to be 4 to 8 times greater among alcoholics and alcohol abusers. Other family members of alcoholics also have greater rates of absenteeism.[23] Alcoholism accounts for more than 500 million lost workdays each year, according to the Bureau of National Affairs.

Likewise, an estimated 12.8 million Americans (about 6 percent of the household population 12 and older) currently use illegal drugs. More than a third of all Americans over the age of twelve have tried an illicit drug. Seventy-one percent of all illicit drug users aged eighteen and older (7.4 million adults) are employed, including 5.4 million full-time workers and 1.9 million part-time workers. No doubt, drug users decrease workplace productivity. The National Institutes of Health (NIH) estimates that the economic cost of alcohol and drug abuse was $246 billion in 1992, the most recent year for which sufficient data were available.

Depression is just as costly as substance abuse. According to the Bureau of National Affairs, a loss of 200 million workdays each year is due to depression.[24] There are more than 20 million people in the U.S. who suffer from depression. A study at the Massachusetts Institute of Technology put the annual cost of depression in the U.S. at $44 billion–as much as coronary heart disease. This amounts to roughly $6,000 for each depressed worker–and it is employers that end up paying 70 percent of the costs. Medical treatment accounts for $12.4 billion (28%) for therapists, doctors, and drugs. Suicide costs an additional $7.5 billion (17%) through lost manpower. And $24.1 billion (55%) of the cost of depression is due to lower productivity.[25]

- **Rising Health Care Costs:** The U.S. has a voluntary, employer-sponsored health care system, which is under tremendous pressure today. The increasing cost of health care, in addition to the aging work force–have helped make health insurance the most expensive single employee benefit. It is estimated that health care costs $5,000 per employee, and $7,000 per family per year. In 2002, there was a 13 percent "spike" in average health care costs, and many experts are predicting 20 percent increases in the future. Public policy will likely support more employer-employee cost-sharing in the future, with more options for tax deferred dollars for medical expenses. Yet employers must take other measures as well to contain health care costs.

Research shows that health costs are 70 percent higher for employees who are depressed and 46 percent higher for those who are stressed. Add to that the fact that one out of 20 employees is fighting depression at any given time, and one employee in four often feels stressed at work. It is easy to appreciate how pervasive–and costly–mental health issues can be. Today, a great number of employers offer EAP services, according to the U.S. Department of Labor. Typical before-and-after studies indicate that companies with EAPs report cost savings associated with health care, substance abuse, workers' compensation, and disability claims. They also report reduced turnover and absenteeism.

- **Workplace Violence:** Workplace violence is any act against an employee that creates a hostile work environment and negatively affects the employee, either physically or psychologically. Such acts include all types of physical or verbal assaults, threats, coercion, intimidation and harassment. Workplace violence is the number one security concern facing American business, according to the ninth annual study of *Fortune* 1000 corporate security professionals conducted by Pinkerton Consulting AND Investigations.[26] The National Institute for Occupational Safety and Health (NIOSH) reports that homicide, due to workplace violence, is the leading cause of death for women in the workplace and the second leading cause of death for men.

The Northwestern Life Insurance Company found that one out of four full-time workers had been harassed, threatened or attacked on the job, leaving the victim angry, fearful, stressed or depressed. Co-workers accounted for most of the harassment; customers were responsible for additional attacks. A 1994 study by the U.S. Department of Justice, Bureau of Justice Statistics, states that those victimized due to assaults occurring in the workplace costs about a half million employees 1,751,100 days of work each year, an average of 3.5 days per crime. This missed work resulted in over $55,000,000 in lost wages annually, not including days covered by sick and annual leave.[27]

In another study conducted in 1995, the Workplace Research Institute found that the annual cost to American businesses exceeds $36 billion. The calculations included the monetary cost of lot productivity, loss of life, injuries, counseling, legal fees, court awards, management time spent dealing with the crises, and other factors resulting in actual cash losses to a business suffering from any type of workplace violence. Legal actions following an incident of workplace violence often involve negligent hiring, retention, and management, as well as inadequate security. With average out-of-court settlements costing employers $500,000 and average jury awards at $3 million, it makes sound business sense to reduce the potential for workplace violence and thus avoid exposure to litigation.[28]

As all of this data suggests, people are hurting and the result are increased workers' compensation claims, more accidents, higher absenteeism and turnover, and lower quality and productivity. These problems cost employers hundreds of billions of dollars each year. More important, however, are the missed opportunities and potential growth which are lost when financial and human resources are diverted from productive activity.

It makes solid economic sense that helping people to maintain a healthy work-life balance and cope with the stresses of change will be major avenues for corporate and economic growth. Ceridian's integrated EAP, work-life, and health and wellness services help employers to provide services and support so employees can successfully deal with problems, enjoy a healthy work/life balance, and be more productive and satisfied at work.

However, like any other industry, businesses thrive if they are aligned with trends in their markets. EAPs need to look at the current and upcoming workplace trends and develop strategic plans accordingly. The pace of the industry has quickened over the past few years, with growing competition and consistent requests that EAPs deliver new products to meet employer needs.

These workplace trends represent significant opportunities for the EAPs to provide innovative services to respond to the changing workplace trends. For example; EAPs can help organizations recognize and prepare for managing multigenerational and aging work forces, offer retirement planning information, assist employees in evaluating nursing homes, and provide more proactive risk management services including ethics hotlines.

History of Ceridian's EAP Business

Ceridian's Corporate History

Ceridian helps client companies optimize the productivity of their human resources investment through managed business solutions for human resources and employee effectiveness. Ceridian Corporation serves businesses and employees in the United States, Canada, and Europe.

Ceridian offers employers a single source for solutions that benefit both employers and employees. Ceridian's focus is to offer services and tools for building an enabled and capable work force and organization by providing employee effectiveness services to remove any remaining barriers to productivity.

Ceridian Corporation grew out of Control Data Corporation and the assets that company acquired from IBM, two of the pioneering companies of the early Information Age. Control Data acquired IBM's wholly-owned independent subsidiary, the Service Bureau Corporation, in 1973 and thereby entered the human resources services arena. A year later, the company established an in-house employee assistance program to serve the 50,000 employees who then worked at Control Data. At that time, substance abuse, relationship issues and work situations interfered with the ability of many employees to effectively perform their jobs. The impact on Control Data's bottom line was significant, so the company designed the first EAP in the U.S. with access to masters-level consultants 24 hours a day, seven days a week. The new program was called Employee Advisory Resources (EAR). At first the program relied on face-to-face meetings between the employees and EAP counselors at the worksite. However, the on-site presence was found to discourage use of the service by employees. So telephone access was added, making EAR a multimode delivery service, and usage immediately increased.

The decade of the 80s was a building time for Control Data's human resources services business. The company began marketing EAR externally in 1981.

In late 1991, Ceridian acquired the Hazelden counseling service, a major move that enabled EAR to become a national EAP provider. The acquisition included the Hazelden customer base and its counselors, which increased the EAR staff by 50 percent. Other important benefits of the acquisition were: (1) counselors with experience in chemical abuse; (2) an excellent in-person model for service delivery; and (3) a nationwide network of affiliates.

In 1992, Control Data Corporation split into two independent companies: Control Data Systems, Inc. and Ceridian Corporation. Control Data Systems kept Control Data's hardware business. Ceridian built its business around a core of human resources services offerings, including EAR. Ceridian then began an aggressive effort, which continues to this day: being the single-source provider of the most comprehensive solutions covering the full range of human resources administration and management.

In the second half of the 90s, Ceridian made important acquisitions to strengthen its employee effectiveness offerings including EAR. Ceridian acquired The Partnership Group, a work-life provider, and EAA, an EAP and training firm, in 1996 and the work-life division of Work/Family Directions in 1998. Work/Family Directions and The Partnership Group were both founders and leaders of the work-life industry. In 1999, Ceridian acquired the Jernberg Corporation, an EAP firm. These acquisitions rounded out a suite of employee solutions that address a full range of issues, from employee recruitment and retention to productivity and commitment. Ceridian thus became the first company to offer organizations a single source for all their EAP, work-life, and health and wellness needs.

Ceridian's strategy remains simple: to track market and demographic trends, to heed independent research and performance theory across all lines of industry, and most importantly, to listen to customers who, as employers, are always looking for innovative ways to solve workplace challenges. Today, Ceridian's LifeWorks* business supports more than 20,000 clients and over 9 million employee lives. These clients include about half of *Working Mother* magazine's "100 Best Companies for Working Mothers" (including all of the top 10), more than 40 percent of all Fortune 100 companies, and more than 20 percent of all *Fortune* 500 firms.

Development of the EAP Industry

It may be that employee assistance programs (EAPs) are one of the most important workplace innovations of the twentieth century, according to Nan Van den Bergh in *Emerging Trends for EAPs in the 21st Century*.[29] In the early years, EAPs—more commonly known as occupational alcoholism programs—were primarily focused on alcohol abuse intervention and recovery and directed toward maintaining a sober work force by intervening with alcoholics early on in their disease. In 1972, there were just 300 national occupational alcoholism programs.[30] Most were internal programs, as was Control Data's, and relied on face-to-face counselors meeting with employees at the workplace during normal business hours.

In the mid to late 90s there was a movement away from internal programs. External programs allowed for greater economies of scale and were often instituted as organizations reorganized and streamlined their organizations. It is estimated that by 1996 there were approximately 20,000 EAPs, with 81 percent being external programs. According to a 1996 survey by the Employee Assistance Program Association (EAPA), approximately 80 percent of *Fortune* 500 companies have an EAP; 76 percent of U.S. companies with more than 1,000 employees have an EAP, and 33 percent of all workplaces with more than 50 employees offer employee assistance services. Using these figures to calculate access, more than 55 percent of the U.S. work force has employee assistance services available to them.[31]

As the number of EAPs has grown, the breadth of services and methods of delivery have changed. Beginning in the 80s and accelerating in the 90s, the focus of EAPs broadened to include workers' family and household members and any situation that effects an employee's ability to concentrate and be productive at work. Today's EAP enhances work site culture with the goals to increase productivity, improve morale, and decrease absenteeism, accidents, and turnover. No longer restricted to issues of alcoholism and substance abuse, EAPs have expanded their offerings to include child, elder, and dependent care services; preventive health and intervention services; mid-life and retirement support, convenience services; critical incident interventions and violence prevention services; management consultation; health and wellness promotion; etc.[32]

With this broadening of services, there has been a de-stigmatization of workers' using EAP services. Whereas early EAPs were focused on the employee mental health and substance abuse concerns, today's EAPs are focused on a broad array of challenges that employees face, which can impact their productivity and satisfaction on the job. Combined with a wide array of flexible, plug-and-play features, EAPs are increasingly viewed as positive elements in compensation and incentive programs to enhance employee attraction, motivation, and retention.

As EAPs evolve, there is an opportunity for EAP providers to work with employers to not only identify the future trends that will be impacting the work force, but also to produce services that will address these issues. At the same time EAPs will be asked to demonstrate their value by providing more outcome data that supports positive results. This information sharing can be helpful to current as well as long term planning as employers look at the characteristics and needs of the future work force.

Evolution of Productivity Practice

There has been a dramatic change in management and work—from bureaucratic or command-and-control management that simply demanded compliance from workers, to more empowering forms of management that ask workers to be innovative and do "smart" work. From the early 1900s to today, individual responsibility and discretion have been increasingly vested in the individual worker. The individual employee is now the basic unit of measurement for productivity improvement.

It is generally accepted today that releasing individual employees' full potential and instilling a responsibility-oriented culture are the best ways to compete in a "do more with less" business climate. This concept is known as "Employee Empowerment." Empowerment emphasizes information sharing, self-managed work teams, and the creation of worker autonomy. With such paramount emphasis on the individual in a productivity-oriented system, the use of EAP's that are integrated with work-life, and health and wellness programs help eliminate the impediments to productivity in individuals' lives, and free them up to focus on the job.

As employees take more responsibility for their productivity and well-being, education and training for both employees and managers will be crucial. For employees, training on such topics as how to understand different generations in the workplace and communicate effectively and career navigation will be important. On the manager side, the training may even be more extensive, including managing cross functional teams and projects, and managing "empowered" employees, which has been referred to as the "new individualism," The traditional manager role has changed and requires that managers adopt a new mindset. EAPs can provide the resources to help managers work within the boundaries of the new management model, which supports the new individualism.

Technological Developments in EAP

The power of technology is doubling every 18 months. Today's $900 laptop computer is many times more powerful than a $10 million mainframe computer was in the mid-seventies. As a result, computers are being installed into our homes and workplaces faster than any previous technology. More and more people now have access to computers and the Internet than ever before. In today's fast-paced world, and with the evolution of the Internet Highway, people have become accustomed to immediate service and response any time and anywhere.

The Internet has emerged as the first new mass medium in a generation and arguably the fastest-growing new technology in history. Harris Poll data, gathered in April 2001, indicates that almost 100 million adults go online to look for health care information (approximately 50% of all adult internet users).[33] Of these searches for "Health Topics," 41% are looking for behavioral health topics (over 40 million users).[34] The limits of HMO's and the limitlessness of the Internet have lately made self-help even more appealing. Last year Americans surfed more than 12,000 Web sites devoted to mental health. As stated above an estimated 40% of all health-related Internet inquiries are on mental health topics and depression is the number-one most researched illness on the Web."[35]

The Internet provides EAPs a chance to de-stigmatize behavioral health. While a person may not hesitate to ask a friend or neighbor to recommend a pediatrician, he would be very reluctant to ask about a psychotherapist. Moreover in today's fast-paced environment, the Internet gives users immediate gratification, by providing information around-the-clock, accessible from the office, home, or on the road.

Now Ceridian is bringing to bear the power, convenience, and privacy of the Internet through LifeWorks® Online. Self-assessment tools on LifeWorks® Online give employees an easy and confidential way to get an initial self-assessment with problems such as, stress, depression, anxiety, alcohol abuse, debt, caregiver stress and more. These Web-enabled, interactive tools which have been adapted for LifeWorks® Online, give immediate feedback on the likelihood of a problem, along with helpful resources and practical information targeted to the needs identified in the assessment. The combination of clinical reliability, ease of use (the tools take between two and four minutes to complete), and immediate response with customized information makes these tools uniquely effective in helping employees address significant mental health and daily living problems.

Ceridian's LifeWorks® Offerings

Ceridian provides a comprehensive, fully integrated employee assistance work-life, and health and wellness program. These services include

assessment, referral, and short-term problem resolution; legal and financial advice; elder and child care resource and referral; online resources with self-assessment tools, bulletin boards, moderated chats and seminars; expatriate and international EAP services; health and wellness consultation and education; concierge and convenience services; and consulting and training.

Today, some companies still obtain EAP, work-life, and health and wellness services from separate vendors. This usually ends up being costly, time consuming and counterproductive for program administrators. By providing a truly integrated portfolio of services, Ceridian provides a single access point with one account executive to coordinate all implementation, promotion, and ongoing program administration; an all-inclusive quality program that ensures consistent quality across all services and locations; integrated reporting that presents unified activity and ROI reports that build a complete picture for productivity planning.

Some of the main reasons people use Ceridian LifeWorks® services are:

- Career and vocational concerns
- Emotional concerns (depression, anxiety, stress)
- Relationship issues (couples and family relationships)
- Legal matters (divorce and separation, child custody, consumer protection)
- Parenting and child care (resource and referral, in-home nanny)
- Financial matters (budgeting, debt management, home buying/renting)
- Work and management consultations (co-worker relationships, mandated referrals)
- Convenience services (community resources and activities, consumer purchases)
- Older adults referrals and resources (home health and in-home care, assisted living)
- Substance abuse (alcohol, drugs, and concerns about others)

Ceridian provides toll-free telephone support for these and other concerns 24 hours per day, 365 days per year. A qualified consultant manages every case. Professional consultants listen to concerns, provide assessments, and work with employees to develop action plans within the context of their employers' benefit plans and—when necessary—human resource policies. Consultants receive ongoing in-service training, carry credentials (such as a state or national license or a board or other professional certification) to bring the appropriate level of help to every caller. Services are offered in English, Spanish, and French—plus language translation is available in 140 languages and dialects. If a caller is hearing impaired, Ceridian provides TTY/TDD phone access. Ceridian's goal is to offer easy access. With an integrated approach, Ceridian's consultants address the whole person—rather than assume that each problem, question, or issue is isolated and simple to solve. With its wide range of in-house resources, Ceridian meets the varied work and life demands of the whole individual.

Ceridian LifeWorks® offers both telephone-based service and face-to-face services. Clients and their employees can choose which mode of access they would prefer. In-person EAP sessions are provided through Ceridian's network of credentialed EAP providers in the United States, Canada, Puerto Rico, and abroad. Hundreds of booklets, tip sheets, and audio recordings are available for distribution to employees by various means. Lunch-and-learn seminars and skills-building workshops are also available for managers and employees. Plus, LifeWorks® Online provides immediate access to information and support for those who prefer the convenience and confidentiality of the Internet. Live chats and Web-based seminars are available. Its state-of-the art technology platform allows LifeWorks® Online to seamlessly integrate with Ceridian's high-touch services. Telephonically, in-person, online, via recordings, in print are just some of the ways Ceridian users can get the help they need.

The flexibility to support employees wherever, whenever and in whatever format best suits them is even more critical when it comes to delivering global services. Ceridian has the capabilities to effectively address employers' needs and provide benefits to employees both domestically and internationally. A specialty expatriate team was founded in 1998 and provides comprehensive support to U.S. employees and their families wherever they are posted. Ceridian's international EAP and expatriate EAP services provide a worldwide access through its service center in London, and through a global network of highly qualified clinicians in over 100 countries.

Ceridian LifeWorks Services helps employers manage their work forces better, and more cost-effectively. Also, account management, reporting, and promotional resources minimize employers' administrative burdens and maximize quality and the ability to assess results. This means less paperwork, and more effective program response and coordination.

How Ceridian's EAP Services Work

A cornerstone of Ceridian's service philosophy is the easy availability of help—so counselors are always available by telephone, Internet, and in-person—whatever means the employee prefers.

Because of today's busy schedules and fast-paced lifestyles, many people prefer to use the phone for the easiest and most natural way to get help. Experienced and trained consultants answer all calls 24 hours a day, every day. Consultants fluent in Spanish and fully experienced in dealing with cross-cultural issues staff a dedicated service center for Spanish-speaking employees. Ceridian's service center in Canada provides services in French and English.

An EAP counselor conducts an initial screening collecting basic demographic information, ascertains the reason for the call, assesses the employee's situation and evaluates for immediate risk and responds accordingly and determines the proper specialist to whom the caller should be connected.

Yet before the employee discloses any information, the counselor explains the limits of confidentiality and the guidelines, which apply. The counselor explains that no information linking the caller to the reason for the call—or acknowledging that a particular person called—can be released without written permission of the caller. The employee is told that only consultants with direct involvement in a case or in a supervisory role will ever be able to access the caller's case information.

Confidentiality is maintained within the legal limits of the applicable state and federal laws as well as throughout the entire client reporting process. For example, homicidal and suicidal ideation and intent, or suspected child, elder or disabled person's abuse must be reported to the proper authorities.

Regardless of where an individual is directed for help, experienced counselors manage the case every step of the way—from the initial assessment through follow-up, including comprehensive assessment, referral, and short-term problem resolution. For example, if callers need elder care or child care, they are routed to an appropriate specialist. If callers need legal or financial advice, they are routed to a legal team, which includes attorneys, or a team of certified financial planners and advisors. Ceridian's counselors include masters-level specialists in the areas of substance abuse, mental health, management consultation and critical incident stress management services, etc.

Ceridian LifeWorks Stories

Note: Due to the confidentiality of Ceridian's LifeWorks Services, the following examples are composites based on numerous typical cases.

Elder care assessment: At any given time, 26 percent of a typical company's work force may be providing care for chronically ill, disabled, or aged friends or family members.
- **One manager's story:** Steve, a 62-year-old shipping manager with a major industrial corporation, has been very concerned about his mother's health since his father died six years ago. As an only child—himself divorced and living alone—the responsibility for his mother's care falls on Steven's shoulders alone. Overwhelmed by his caregiving responsibilities, the strain began to show in Steve's job performance. There were many times when he had to leave work unexpectedly to deal with emergency issues including medication foul-ups, a serious fall, and several false alarms.

"I wondered how much longer I could manage this situation with my Mom," Steve recalled to a Ceridian consultant. "I lived only a couple miles away from my mother, but had to be over there all the time. Also, there was so much that could go wrong during the day while I was at work. The worst thing was her inability to cook for herself and to keep herself clean. Would she remember to take her pills? Would she burn the house down? I would think about these things all day long, even at work.

"I had just about come to the end of my rope when my company made the Ceridian LifeWorks elder care benefit available. What a relief it's been to have the help! I feel better at work now knowing that my mother has the care she needs."
- **Elder care need:** Steve's mother Edith is 85 years old and lives alone in her home of 49 years. Like so many people her age, her social circle has grown very small through the death, frailty, and mental diminishment of peers. Aside from her son Steve, Edith would see few, if any people in the course of a month. "When my dad was alive, her lack of friends didn't seem to matter," Steve said. "But after he died, Mom was alone in her house almost all the time.

Steve said that his mother's condition deteriorated rapidly. Though a meticulous housekeeper in the past, Edith now allowed her home to become littered and dirty and she had difficulty managing most activities of daily living (ADLs). Increasingly, she relied on Steve for her every need. But he was becoming exhausted and wanted to investigate other living arrangements for his mother.
- **Solution:** An elder assessment and elder care program plan were provided by Ceridian LifeWorks. The assessment gathered information on Edith's interests, activities, and lifestyle; her legal and financial situation including insurance coverage, retirement benefits, and estate plan; her health condition including medications and health care history; her ability to perform household and self-care tasks. After investigating the situation from both the son's and the mother's perspectives, the assessment concluded that Edith's health insurance, finances, and legal planning were adequate to meet her needs. However, a review of functional issues

indicated that his mothers greatest need was for help in managing her ADLs in order to remain safe and independent. The assessment also concluded she was at high risk for physical falls and memory and reasoning problems.

The solution for all these issues was to hire a daily companion and homemaker until Edith could eventually be relocated to an assisted living facility. In the meantime, though, she can remain at home where she is most comfortable and content—and her son can focus more time and attention on his own needs of life and career.

Integrated EAP and Health and Wellness

Why are integrated EAP and Health and Wellness programs becoming so prevalent in today's workplace?

- **One executive's story:** Jerry is a 54-year-old senior executive with a large financial services company. Jerry is married with two children in college. His professional life is heavily booked, fast-paced, intellectually demanding—and he revels in it. His work is so much fun, he said, it's been a struggle over the years to balance career and family life. However, more than ever work is interfering with Jerry's family life and he spends long days and nights in meetings and his wife is beginning to resent the time he spends at work. On top of all of this he was having health problems for the first time in his life.
- **EAP and health and wellness need:** Jerry first began thinking about doing something about his health as a result of a short detour he took one day on the way back from the company cafeteria. His company had arranged for Ceridian LifeWorks to provide free on-site health screenings for employees in addition to a free health risk assessment. "I saw one of their signs in the hallway, my next meeting wasn't for another hour, and I decided what the heck? I stopped in—on a whim, really—to see what it was all about." A few days later he was dismayed to learn not only was he 60 pounds overweight, but he had high blood pressure and high cholesterol, too. What the screening had

not disclosed—but what Jerry had known for months—was that he had developed a hernia.

"The LifeWorks screening was a wake-up call for me," Jerry said. "Driving home a few nights later, I realized that by letting my health slide I was risking everything that was important to me—my marriage, my family, and my career." He decided he would call Ceridian LifeWorks to get help with his health and marriage issues.

- **Solution:** Jerry called his Ceridian LifeWorks employee assistance program. He was reassured when he called his EAP that it is a truly confidential service and no one that he works with—not even his employer—would know that he had called. Jerry spoke to an EAP consultant who helped him determine that he would benefit from speaking to a health educator. The counselor also gave Jerry the name of an EAP provider near his home, so that Jerry and his wife could visit with a counselor about the stress and strain in their marriage. The consultant also arranged a phone appointment with a health educator, who began coaching Jerry on weight loss techniques, and helped him develop a daily exercise routine. The health educator recommended that Jerry see his primary care physician about repairing the hernia and getting ongoing follow-up as he lost weight and got himself back into shape.

Jerry had the hernia surgically repaired, and soon afterward began a regimen of weight-loss and exercise. Thanks to their sessions with the EAP counselor, Jerry and his wife began carving out more time in their busy schedules to make time for their relationship and having fun together. Jerry's boss and subordinates have noticed changes, too. "My boss told me he was impressed with the new energy I've been bringing to my work. Losing 15 pounds has put more bounce in my step. I've got 45 more pounds to go, and I know I'll make it."

An Integrated EAP and Work-Life

A work-life survey conducted by William M. Mercer Inc. found that 13 percent of more than 420 responding employers offered integrated EAP and work-life programs, which provide "life cycle resource and referral" services. Mercer expects the percentage of employers offering such integrated programs to rise.[36] The reason these EAP and work-life programs are growing in popularity can be seen in the following example.

- **One worker's story:** Aisha is a 29-year-old administrative assistant who is a first time mom with a one-year-old daughter. She lives with her husband and new baby in a modest two-bedroom apartment. Aisha's husband works hard during the day and is completing a degree in the evenings. When Aisha initially returned to work after her daughter's birth, her mother-in-law took care of the baby. But her mother-in-law recently decided to go back to work, and was no longer able to care for her granddaughter. Aisha debated quitting her job, but financially this was not feasible as long as her husband was in school. Aisha needed to find child care.

- **EAP and work-life meet:** The child care issue was only one aspect of Aisha's problem. Aisha had been staying home alone with her daughter for many nights and began to feel trapped and depressed. In an effort to manage her depression she began drinking. Aisha also began missing work, and her supervisor expressed concern for her future at the company. Aisha's problems seemed to be spiraling out of control when her husband threatened to leave because of her drinking.

- **Solution:** Aisha remembered she had access through work to a confidential program called Ceridian LifeWorks. She also remembered that the program offered a Website with extensive information about child care as well as information on almost any topic she could imagine. Aisha logged onto LifeWorks Online and saw that she could e-mail a consultant to request child care referrals or she could use the child care online locator. Because of her concern about her baby's lactose intolerance, Aisha opted to e-mail a consultant to request child care referrals. Aisha received her child care information in 24 hours and immediately found child care for her daughter.

To her surprise Aisha also saw a self-assessment tool online on substance abuse. She was worried about her marriage and was ashamed that she had gone to work a few times with a hangover. The times she had called in sick because of her problem, she also had to deal with the consequences of not being paid for those sick days. So she decided to take the five-minute test and learned that her drinking may be harmful to her. She was given links to information on alcohol abuse and depression. She noticed she could also take a five-minute depression test. She took that test, too, and learned that she may be depressed. When she finished the depression test she saw the prominently displayed toll free number to her EAP.

Even though it was 9:30 at night, she called them immediately. She was assured that her call would be kept confidential and she spoke to a masters-level counselor. She explained her increasing loneliness and increased drinking and depression. The consultant referred Aisha to an EAP provider that specializes in alcohol abuse. The EAP provider's office was on Aisha's route between home and work. Aisha saw the EAP provider a couple of times and was then referred to Alcoholics Anonymous and ongoing therapy.

"Because I was able to get help for both my problems, my family is still together and I still have my job," Aisha said. My boss recently told me I am doing a good job and put me in for a raise."

Return on Investment

What kind of return can companies typically expect to see from its investment in employee effectiveness services? The answer, of course, depends on the nature and seriousness of the problems addressed.

Because the costs of substance abuse are so great due to higher absenteeism, health problems, workmen's compensation claims, problems with co-workers, etc., addressing alcohol and drug abuse problems generates the highest return. There is a good reason that EAPs grew out of employers' concerns about substance abuse. It is very costly. For every dollar invested in the substance abuse components of an EAP, employers can generally expect to save anywhere from $5 to $16.[37] A study of a major oil company's efforts to address its employees' substance abuse through an EAP showed a return on investment of about 14:1.[38] Ceridian's integrated EAP, work-life, and health and wellness service typically yield a blended return on investment of up to 8:1. The average cost of providing Ceridian's employee effectiveness services is only $2–$4 per month per employee.

The Future of EAPs

As described here, employee assistance programs have been evolving over the last three decades. Ceridian's EAP is a good example. When introduced in the late 1970s, it focused mainly on work-related problems such as substance abuse and depression. Since then, there has been a steady broadening of offerings to include work-life, and health and wellness programs.

There has also been a broadening of methods by which employees can access Ceridian's integrated EAP services—telephone, online, print, and audio recording, seminars and in-person—as well as Ceridian's geographic scope. Ceridian's employee effectiveness services can now be used as a solution for employers with a global work force. Ceridian's multilingual service centers, linked by phone and the Internet to users 24 hours a day, 365 days a year—can make referrals to an extensive network of qualified service providers. The next stage of development will feature the expansion of self-assessment tools and services within a web-enabled technology environment.

Continued integration of employee effectiveness and other employee benefits will drive down administration costs and encourage more cost-efficient management of employee benefit programs.

Employers will achieve greater compensation efficiencies by optimizing the mix of "hard" and "soft" rewards that will have the highest perceived value for employees. There is growing evidence that employers are beginning to use non-monetary compensation—particularly integrated employee assistance programs—as part of their total rewards management strategy. There is great potential for employers to expand the use of financial planning, legal assistance and other voluntary benefits—which have broad-based appeal and are relatively low in cost—to reward high-performing employees and to enhance efforts to attract and retain top talent.

The coming decade will see an expansion of employee benefits of all kinds, as well as greater cost- and risk-sharing between employers and employees. Employees will be steadily encouraged to take greater personal responsibility for their own personal health and welfare, career development, and performance on the job.

As EAPs keep in step with future business models, the challenge will be to maintain the EAP core technology and competences in a competitive marketplace. However, as the one employee benefit that is most directly linked and concerned with the personal issues of greatest importance to employees, EAPs will in some form always be the cornerstone of effective human resources productivity systems.

ENDNOTES

1. *The Economist,* May 9, 2002.
2. *New York Times,* March 7, 2002.
3. *The Economist,* January 31, 2002.
4. Conti, Daniel J. & Burton, Wayne N. "Behavioral Health Disability Management," *The Employee Assistance Handbook,* James M. Oher, Ed., John Wiley & Sons, Inc., 1999, page 320.
5. Human Resource Institute, HRI's TrendWatcher, Issue 77, August 24, 2001.
6. Human Resource Institute, *HRI's TrendWatcher,*
Issue 77, August 24, 2001.
7. *CPA Journal,* April 2000.
8. National Alliance for Caregiving and the American Association of Retired People, *Comparative Analysis of Caregiver Data for Caregivers to the Elderly,* 1997.
9. National Family Caregivers Association, *Random Sample Survey of 1000 Adults,* Summer 2000.
10. National Alliance for Caregiving and the American Association of Retired People, *Comparative Analysis of Caregiver Data for Caregivers to the Elderly,* 1997.

11. Institute for Health and Aging, Univ. of California-San Francisco, for the Robert Wood Johnson Foundation, *Chronic Care in America: A 21st Century Challenge,* 1996.
12. Met Life Mature Market Institute, National Center for Women and Aging at Brandeis University, and the National Alliance for Caregiving, 1999.
13. Family Caregiver Alliance, 1997.
14. Ibid.
15. *Caregiving Across the Life Cycle.* National Family Caregivers Association and Fortis Long Term Care, 1998.
16. www.cch.com/press/news/2001/01absencemain.htm
17. Ibid.
18. National Institute on Aging, *Aging in the United States: Past, Present, and Future,* 1997.
19. Society for Human Resource Management, *Workplace Visions,* No. 1–2000: 2.
20. United States Office of Personnel Management, http://www.opm.gov/ehs/alcohol.asp
21. ALCOWEB, www.alcoweb.com
22. United States Office of Personnel Management, http://www.opm.gov/ehs/alcohol.asp
23. *The Economist,* December 17, 1998.
24. National Institutes of Health, National Institute on Drug Abuse and the National Institute on Alcohol Abuse and Alcoholism, report issued May 13, 1998.
25. National Institutes of Health, National Institute on Drug Abuse and the National Institute on Alcohol Abuse and Alcoholism, report issued May 13, 1998.
26. Pinkerton Consulting & Investigations, press release, June 4, 2002.
27. Workplace Violence Institute, www.noworkviolence.com.
28. Ibid.
29. Van den Bergh, Nan, editor, *Emerging Trends for EAPs in the 21st Century,* The Haworth Press, Inc., 2000.
30. Ibid.
31. Ibid.
32. Ibid.
33. The Harris Poll #19, April 18, 2001. Reproduced in www.louiseharris.com/harris_poll/index.asp
34. Source: Media Metrix & Neilsen/Net Ratings, 2000
35. Psychology Today, March 2001
36. *HRI's TrendWatcher,* Issue 36, October 6, 2000.
37. What Works: Workplaces without Drugs, U.S. Department of Labor, 1990.
38. "Cost/Benefit Analysis Shows EAP's Value to Employer," Association Exchange, Nov/Dec 1998.

Editors' Note: The editors of this Third Edition are deeply appreciative to the professionals at Ceridian who wrote this chapter and requested to remain anonymous and simply have Ceridian take credit for it. They know who they are and we herewith extend our sincerest appreciation to them.

Part III

CLIENT CHARACTERISTICS AND SERVICES

Chapter 8

CASE MANAGEMENT, CASELOAD MANAGEMENT, AND CASE RECORDING AND DOCUMENTATION IN PROFESSIONAL EMPLOYEE ASSISTANCE PROGRAM DELIVERY

WILLIAM G. EMENER and FRED DICKMAN

The continuing emergence and development of employee assistance programs in modern industry has witnessed a growing enhancement and enrichment of the professionalism of employee assistance program service delivery. Contributing to this phenomenon is the fact that more and more professionally educated and trained human service professionals are being employed in employee assistance programs—for example, rehabilitation counselors (Desmond, 1985; Dickman & Emener, 1982) and social workers (Hutchison & Renick, 1985; Maiden & Hardcastle, 1986). Importantly, these human service professionals are being professionally prepared to perform the variety of human service roles and functions that are extremely relevant and necessary for successful employee assistance program service delivery (Dickman & Emener, 1982; Emener, 1986; Emener & Rubin, 1980; Hutchison, 1985). Three categories of professional service delivery, which are critical entities of employee assistance programs, constitute the focus of this chapter: Case Management, Caseload Management, and Case Recording and Documentation. Utilizing relevant information from professional literature (e.g., Cassell & Mulkey, 1981; Henke, Connolly & Cox, 1975; Roessler & Rubin, 1982; Third Institute on Rehabilitation Services, 1965; Thompson, Kite & Bruyere, 1977) and examples and illustrations from their own professional experiences in employee assistance programs, in this chapter the authors: (a) provide a brief overview of important professional attributes critical to case management, caseload management, and case recording and documentation in employee assistance program service delivery; (b) differentially present and discuss case management, caseload management, and case recording and documentation roles and functions in employee assistance program service delivery; and, (c) conclude with a brief discussion of the synergistic relationship among these three categories of EAP professionals' roles and functions.

Important Professional Attributes of the "Case Manager"

In the process of performing the variety of job tasks within the categories of case management, caseload management, and case recording and documentation, it is very important for the practitioner to possess and demonstrate identifiable attributes of a "professional." The primary purpose of the following is to identify, discuss, and illustrate selected important attributes of professionalism. As will be discussed in more detail later in the chapter, there are distinct differences between case management and caseload management. For the moment, however, it is important to acknowledge their differential distinctions: **Case Management** refers to the practitioner's managerial activities that facilitate the individual client's

Note: This chapter is reprinted from *Employee Assistance Programs; A Basic Text* (1988) with permission of the author, the book's editors (Dickman, Emener, & Hutchison, Jr.), and the publisher (Charles C Thomas, Publisher, Ltd.).

progress through the service process; **Caseload Management** refers to the responsibility of the practitioner for the progress of the whole group of clients who constitute the practitioner's caseload. For purposes of expediency, and in view of the fact that the following materials are designed to address generic attributes of professionalism, the following will use the terms practitioner, counselor, social worker, and case manager as generic constructs (viz, they can be considered interchangeable). Understandably, there are numerous important attributes of the professional service provider in an employee assistance program. The following four areas, nonetheless, were determined to be noteworthy of special address in this chapter: (a) community resource awareness, (b) clinical assessment, (c) caseflow expertise, and (d) professional behavior.

COMMUNITY RESOURCE AWARENESS. The effective case manager knows the community–both the "internal community" and the "external community." The internal community is comprised of the company, which the employee assistance program serves and in which the employees are employed. The case manager must know the formal and informal infrastructure of the company. The external community, in effect, is comprised of the community surrounding the company–the community in which the employees live. The case manager has to know the community of available human services. For example, it is commonly known that approximately one-third of the employees who come to a well-run employee assistance program will have some form of alcohol or other substance abuse problem (Dickman, Emener & Hutchison, 1985). Knowing this, knowing that each individual needs individualized assistance and health care, and knowing that the larger the known available array of service centers, facilities, and professionals the higher the probabilities that "the right place or person" can be found for the individual client, case managers should feel compelled to know their community like the backs of their hands. When confronted with an employee with an alcohol or substance abuse problem, it is quite common for case managers to ask themselves questions such as: (a) For this particular client with these particular needs, where can I find

the best professional, center, or facility? (b) Where is the most appropriate inpatient or outpatient, day care or night care, individual or group, and/or AA or NA facility or center? and (c) What are the differential costs of the treatment programs in the community, where are they located, are they available by public transportation, etc? As can be quickly seen, in order to find the right "fit" between the client's needs and the services available, the case manager has to know his or her community. To further illustrate, according to national figures, another one-third will come with marriage and/ or family relationship problems. Some of these clients will have both alcoholism or substance abuse problems and marriage and/or family relationship problems. Again, the questions arise: Where do they treat co-dependents, and/or children of alcoholics, etc. In view of the fact that the remaining approximate one-third of EAP referrals have a wide variety and combination of problems and difficulties, similar concerns also may arise when a client needs legal services, medical assistance, and/or financial services (among others). The bottom line is that when the troubled employee comes to the employee assistance program for help, he or she in many ways is handicapped–not only do they have problems, but they also do not know where to, or how to, get help. It is important for case managers to be sure that they aren't just as handicapped as their clients are!

CLINICAL ASSESSMENT. In order to identify and procure the "best" services in the community for a client, not only does an effective case manager have to know the community, but he or she also has to accurately assess the client's needs and the client's "readiness" for assistance. Employees frequently are defensive, scared, and threatened by the thought of "telling someone the truth" about their problems. Moreover, they can be very reticent about the thought of going somewhere for assistance. Thus, while in the role of a representative of the company and also while having to engage in detailed assessment, the case manager simultaneously has to establish a relationship of openness and trust with the employee so that (a) the assessments are based on accurate information, and (b) when the case manager suggests a treatment strategy and/or makes a referral the client will listen to him or her and follow through. For example, it is not uncommon for an individual who comes to an employee assistance program with a chemical dependency problem to present his or her difficulty as being anything but chemical dependency related–quite often, initial presenting problems are identified by the client as being related to job stress, marital or family difficulties, and/or financial problems. And while the individual indeed may have some real difficulties in these areas, the client with a chemical dependency problem may be very reluctant to discuss the possibility that he or she actually may be chemically dependent. More often than not, the "real problems" are beneath the surface. For reasons such as this, most employee assistance programs allow for three or four evaluation visits so that accurate and thorough assessments and accurate and relevant treatment strategies can be determined. These sessions also allow for the relationship building to take place (e.g., developing openness and trust). In addition to formal clinical assessments of the client (e.g., standardized personality testing), assessment interviews with "significant others" such as family members and supervisors can also be very beneficial to the case manager. Throughout these assessment sessions, however, because of the client's potential fears, denial, and subconscious attempts to mask the real issues, it is imperative for the case manager to communicate compassion, caring, and respect: **to relate not challenge**. Even though the case manager may suspect the existence of a chemical dependency problem early in the first session, it is critical that during the history taking, relating with empathic understanding, and exploring and discussing further what the client is saying, that the case manager not challenge the client–this very easily could threaten the client, enhance their fears and defensiveness, and possibly even run them off. What is being suggested here is that with high level profession clinical and counseling skills, the truth will eventually emerge, and concurrently the client will trust the case manager and the client's "readiness for help" will be such that he or she not only will go for help but also be ready to benefit from it. In view of the critical importance of these clinical assessment issues for the case manager, the

following case example, based on the authors' experiences, is designed to enhance the readers' understanding and appreciation of their magnitude.

A CASE EXAMPLE. A self-referred young couple arrived to see the employee assistance program counselor. They requested to come into the session together. The husband was 30 years old and the wife was 27, they had dated for four years before getting married, and at the time had been married for seven and one-half years and had one child, an eighteen-month-old son. The husband, a college graduate, was working as a junior executive for the company that sponsored the employee assistance program. The wife, who had a two-year junior college degree, was working as a medical secretary. When they sat down to talk with the counselor, they were both very nervous and uncomfortable. Nonetheless, after an atmosphere of trust and acceptance was established and the purpose of the assessment sessions was explained, toward the end of the first session the husband volunteered that he had had an affair. He stated that he felt relieved after he was "found out" (after about three months), but still felt guilty and responsible–responsible not only for his wife's pain and hurt but for the feelings of the other woman as well. The wife explained that she indeed did feel hurt and betrayed, and she also felt very indignant in view of the fact that the other woman was a friend and co-worker in the same medical complex where she was working.

Two days later, each of them came in for individual, one-hour sessions. She revealed that before her husband's affair, she had been feeling down, caught in the trap of work and child care, and possibly not as attentive to herself as she had been previously. He expressed feelings of inadequacy as a provider. He believed that he should have been further along in his career, and generally felt quite frustrated. He also indicated that he had not shared these feelings with his wife (seeing them as his problems). At that juncture, it appeared quite clear to the counselor that in the absence of other possible co-existing and/or confounding problems, they needed to see a marriage counselor to help them learn to communicate with each other more meaningfully, and share with each other their feelings of inadequacy and being trapped. It is important to note that in view of their having had pulled apart from each other and that he had had a three-month affair, a premature and inaccurate assessment that they were having "sexual-boredom problems" could have been determined by the counselor. Had this been the case, inappropriate treatment could have been recommended, and that would have been very unfortunate. Nonetheless, an accurate assessment was gleaned, an appropriate referral was made, and the couple's readiness for help had been established by the counselor.

It was learned through follow-up (with appropriate signed releases for follow-up information), that the couple had seen a marriage therapist, had improved their interpersonal communications, and had regained the meaningfulness from their relationship that they both desired. Moreover, the husband was allowing himself to feel more adequate, and he was becoming more assertive as to his own needs. The wife became aware that she had not been taking care of herself nor being assertive to her own needs, joined an inexpensive spa, began feeling "less down and more attractive," was communicating her needs and feelings to her husband, was receiving more attention from her husband, and importantly was feeling more adequate.

This is somewhat of a typical marital situation case, which an employee assistance program counselor may encounter. With clients who come to an employee assistance program with severe psychiatric problems, mental health concerns, and serious physical problems, the importance of thorough and accurate diagnosis, the appropriate utilization of appropriate medical and paramedical professionals, facilities and centers in the community, and the facilitation of "readiness for help" can be even more demanding of the professional assessment and counseling skills of the case manager.

Case Flow Expertise

From the moment the client appears for EAP assessment until his or her case is closed, the case manager is responsible for knowing what is hap-

pening. The case manager's responsibility includes much more than seeing someone for a few minutes, making an appropriate referral, and then thinking or assuming that his or her job is done. On the contrary, case managers retain responsibility for the client's progress throughout the process. As discussed previously, accurate and thorough clinical assessment (including relationship building) is critical—it is very important that the "real problems" receive appropriate and corrective attention. Two additionally important professional attribute/skill areas extremely relevant to case flow expertise are referral and follow-up.

The process of referring a client to someone else for treatment can be ticklish. Consider, for example, the following scenario. An employee comes to the employee assistance program, usually self-referred, but sometimes supervisor or union referred. He or she is understandably cautious, suspicious, fearful, apprehensive, and nervous. Essentially, he or she is coming to see someone he or she can trust—someone who will genuinely care. During the assessment interviews, the counselor is "real," "genuine," and "open," and the employee's hypothesis that the counselor will be trustworthy and caring is confirmed.

Simultaneously, the client experiences the painful process of revealing himself or herself, sharing personal "secrets" with this caring person he or she trusts, and in effect a closeness, a rapport, develops. Then, just when the client really feels comfortable with this caring and trustable counselor, the client is told that he or she is to be referred to someone else. This is the litmus test of the counselor's art of referring. When handled properly and skillfully, most clients understand the reasons for referring, especially in an EAP setting. Nonetheless, the client can also feel rejected, betrayed, discouraged by the prospect of going through all of that again with someone else, or some other hurtful response. In view of this, the case manager needs to be sensitive to the client's processing and experiencing of the referring process, and compassionately attend to the client's feelings as they emerge. At times, a brief follow-up check with the referred professional is recommended to assure that there aren't any carry over concerns from the referral process that need to be attended to by the case manager.

Follow-up on behalf of the case manager is important, and it is helpful if it is done systematically. Most professionals to whom employee assistance program case managers refer clients, have busy practices and typically are not going to keep the case manager apprised of a referred client's progress (or lack of it). Nonetheless, it is the case manager's responsibility to know what is happening with and for his or her client until the case is closed either by successful resolution, rejection of treatment, improvement, or termination for a variety of reasons. The case manager is also busy, and therefore some systematic method of assuring follow-up is recommended. For example, it can be helpful to place the client's name and telephone number on a "tickler" (like a calendar) and a call can be made periodically (e.g., every month or two) to "see how things are going." With this procedure, it is also recommended that the client be made aware of the "tickler" follow-up call system so that he or she isn't surprised or misinterprets the calls. Likewise, it is a good idea to apprise professionals to whom referrals are made so that they also understand how the case manager will be operationalizing his or her follow-up responsibilities.

PROFESSIONAL BEHAVIOR. Case managers in employee assistance programs must behave like professionals at all times. There is no way, however, that all of the behaviors becoming a "professional" could be addressed in one section of one chapter. There are, nonetheless, some areas of professional behavior on behalf of employee assistance program case managers that deserve special attention. **First**, it is important for case managers to keep in close touch with: (a) professionals in their external professional communities; (b) supervisors, managers, and administrators in the internal communities of their companies; (c) union leaders; and (d) fellow professionals in their employee assistance programs. Maintaining "professional relationships," not being a nuisance, and simultaneously promoting the professional integrity of one's EAP requires skill, tact, constant vigilance of one's own behavior, and awareness of how one's behavior is perceived by others. **Second**, the case manager must remain cognizant

of his or her multiple professional roles and the appropriate professional codes of conduct commensurate with each of them. For example, during the assessment stages of working with a client, the case manager is predominately a representative of the employee assistance program and his or her records are confidential to the EAP. However, if a case manager were to have a client referred to him or her from another case manager for individual treatment (e.g., counseling), he or she would be more in the role of an individual professional practitioner and his or her notes and files would be confidential to his or her own professional domain. In most situations like this latter one, he or she would rely on the code of ethical conduct commensurate with his or her professional preparation (e.g., rehabilitation counseling, social work, counseling psychology) for guidance and direction. **Third**, case managers should make very clear distinctions between their assessment-referral roles and their treatment-practitioner roles. For example, based on their experiences the authors of this chapter strongly recommend that when case managers (who typically are professionally prepared practitioners) conduct an assessment and are ready to recommend treatment, they do not refer the client to themselves. Among the many reasons why this is recommended are the possibilities that: (a) the case manager subconsciously could be less than professionally influenced by self-referral decisions; (b) such decisions may not be as objective as they should be (possible self-serving motives could exist); and (c) even if such decisions were objective and excellent decisions, others may question such processes and ultimately the case manager's perceived level of professionalism could become tarnished.

The bottom line is that **the client always comes first**, and this basic component of the professional's service ethic should guide and drive his or her every action. Moreover, when performing their case management and caseload management roles and functions, employee assistance program professionals are epitomizing the basic integrity of their EAPs for everyone to see. Indeed, they should feel compelled to conduct themselves as professionals at all times.

Case Management, Caseload Management, Case Recording and Documentation Roles and Functions

As discussed earlier in this chapter, professional service delivery in employee assistance programs is predicated upon the existence of numerous "professional" characteristics, attributes, and behaviors on behalf of the service deliverer. Moreover, the service deliverer (e.g., EAP counselor, social worker, case manager) is responsible for what happens to, and for, the client from the time the client enters the assessment session through closure of the case. Knowing what is going on with and for a client, on behalf of the professional, denotes also knowing what he or she is doing and the effects of what he or she is doing. More pointedly, professionals should know: (1) **what** they are doing (throughout all stages and phases of a case); (2) **how** to do what they are doing (with professional skill and expertise); and (3) **why** they are doing what they are doing (viz, knowing the effects of their actions and non-actions). These are three very important guiding challenges for the professional service deliverer. High level knowledge, skill, and expertise in case management, caseload management, and case recording and documentation, however, to a large extent are prerequisites for the professional practitioner committed to successfully responding to these three above guiding challenges. Case management, caseload management, and case recording and documentation are highly interrelated phenomena. For purposes of clarity, understanding, and appreciation, however, the following will present and discuss them separately. (Their synergistic interrelatedness, however, will be discussed and illustrated at the end of the chapter.)

Case Management

Case management refers to the practitioner's managerial activities that facilitate the individual client's progress through the service process.

The social worker, psychologist, or EAP counselor, as a "manager" of the treatment process (es) of the client, is responsible for efficient and effective activity at each step or phase. In the overall carrying out of this responsibility, the case manager typically engages in identifiable job tasks and duties, which collectively constitute the following 10 case management roles and functions:

1. **Case Finding**–activities that facilitate potential clients' awareness of the employee assistance program, as well as their potential utilization of it
2. **Intake**–upon referral, conducting intake interviews with clients and processing their initial contacts with the program
3. **Eligibility Determination**–active engagement in processes and activities designed to determine whether or not an individual is eligible to receive assistance from the program
4. **Assessment**–accurately determining the client's problems and establishing a recommended treatment plan, identifying recommended treatment sources, and determining the client's "readiness" for recommended treatment(s)
5. **Counseling**–providing necessary counseling services commensurate with appropriate assessment and referral services and activities
6. **Plan Development and Implementation**–working with the client in developing and determining a treatment plan
7. **Service Provision and Supervision**–appropriately providing, coordinating, monitoring, and supervising all services provided for and to the client
8. **Monitoring Service Effectiveness**–through systematic follow-up activities, monitoring the efficiency and effectiveness of services being provided to and for the client
9. **Closure Determination**–via contact with the client, relevant professionals providing services, and appropriate others (e.g., the client's family, supervisor, etc.), determining when the case should be closed and the closure status (e.g., successful resolution; incomplete–client refused treatment; etc.)
10. **Post Services Follow-up**–when appropriate, following-up on a client to evaluate the effectiveness of the services the client received, potential needs for additional services, etc.

In the process of performing these case management roles and functions, at times the counselor will be managing the client's treatment relevant activity and at times the counselor will be managing the client's clinical development activity. The following is designed to illustrate the differences between these two distinct categories of the case manager's roles and functions.

The client's **treatment relevant activity** includes those activities on behalf of the client that, by the design of the treatment plan, are directly and indirectly related to resolution of the client's problem(s). For example, in addition to other treatment resolution activities, a client with an alcoholism problem may agree to attend Alcoholics Anonymous meetings. A client with a weight control difficulty may agree to work out at a local gymnasium three times per week. In working with clients such as these, case management activities may include assisting the client in identifying a local AA group or an appropriate gymnasium, and/or keeping in touch with the client to monitor the client's attendance at the AA meetings or the regularity of his or her workouts at the gymnasium. Whatever the treatment-related activities may be for the client, it behooves the case manager to "manage" such activities. Among the many benefits of such management activities is that through activities such as these the counselor demonstrates to the client that the activities are important and that they should be taken seriously.

The client's **clinical development activity** includes a large variety of clinical actions (and nonactions) on behalf of the EAP counselor that are in keeping with the planned clinical development of the individual client. For example, if one of a client's goals is to become more self-directed and/or more independent, then when the client asks the counselor to answer a question such as, "Which gymnasium should I join?" or if the client asks the counselor to tell his supervisor at work that he would like to have a modification made in his job assignment, then the counselor should not answer the question (i.e., make the decision for the client) nor speak to the client's supervisor for him (i.e., to do for the client what he is capable of doing for himself). On the surface, answering a question such as this or talking to a client's supervisor for him could appear to be a helpful thing to do. Unfortunately, however, under circumstances such as those described in this example, actions such as these on behalf of the counselor would actually be counterproductive to the client's problem resolution goals (i.e., to become more self-directed and more independent).

Moreover, this even could be an excellent time for the counselor to process with the client why the client ostensibly is being reluctant to act on his own behalf. With skillful intervention, this could be an advantageous clinical opportunity to work with (e.g., "challenge") the client.

Case management includes a large variety of "managing" job tasks and roles and functions on behalf of the case manager. Of utmost importance, however, is that no matter "What?," "How?," or "Why?" the case manager does them, they should always be by design and they should be guided by what is best for the client.

Caseload Management

Caseload management refers to the responsibility of the practitioner for the progress of the whole group of clients who constitute the practitioner's caseload. Obviously, the most outstanding difference between case management and caseload management is that the former focuses the case manager's management energies on the individual client, and the latter focuses the case manager's energies on the aggregate group of clients with whom he or she is working. The understandable overlap between these two sets of "management activities" as well as this obvious distinguishing feature which separates them, are contained in Cassell and Mulkey's (1981) Functional Definitions of Caseload Management:

- the process of analyzing, planning, supervising, and administering the smooth flow of rehabilitation services to the number of clients for which you have responsibility and the coordination of other professionals and resources utilized.

- to effectively coordinate a system whereby the individual clients are provided services toward eventual rehabilitation by predicting through evaluation, setting objectives, processing, coordinating, and maintaining an equitable and just flow of clients toward individual goals.

- the ability to organize, coordinate, and effect the smooth flow of cases and services with maximum return from the services, to be utilized in returning clientele to the most independent status of which he is capable (p. 9).

As can be easily discerned from these above functional definitions, effective caseload management on behalf of EAP counselors maximizes the probabilities that smooth, equitable, efficient, and efficacious services will be provided to all clients served by the program. The number of specific job tasks and roles and functions under the rubric of caseload management is too large to receive presentation in this one section of one chapter. Nonetheless, the experiences of the authors repeatedly have indicated the following three to be paramount, and therefore worthy of address and discussion.

ACCURATE ASSESSMENT OF CASELOAD SERVICE DEMANDS. It is critical for the caseload manager to accurately assess the demands of providing services (especially caseload services) to each individual client as well as to the aggregate of all the clients on his or her caseload. In order to effectively plan, organize, coordinate, and manage one's work, the individual must be able to accurately assess and predict "what it will take" and "how long it will take" to do what needs to be done.

PLANNING, ORGANIZING, AND COORDINATING WORK TASKS. The effective case manager simply cannot wait until things need to be done before doing them. An approach such as this eventually would turn into nothing more than a minimally effective, crisis-oriented work life. The effective case manager plans, organizes, and coordinates his or her work tasks, such as, for example: (a) plant visitations and "walk-throughs" (when supervisors, managers, and union officials are visited); (b) community contacts and visitations; (c) staff meetings and professional consultations; (d) paperwork; and (e) the scheduling of appointments with clients and times for intake assessment sessions. As one EAP case manager stated to one of the authors of this chapter: "I simply cannot be effective if I fly by the seat of my pants."

TIME MANAGEMENT. The case manager's "time" could be considered his or her most precious commodity. It is a finite variable. And by planning, organizing, and coordinating their time, on a daily, weekly, monthly, and annual basis, case managers can maximize the potential benefits resulting from efficient use of their time.

Accurate assessments of caseload service demands, good planning, organizing, and coordinating, and efficient and effective use of time on behalf of case managers in employee assistance programs, produce numerous benefits. For example, it is important that clients receive services when they need them; unnecessary delays in service provision can be detrimental. Employee assistance programs are charged with the responsibility of efficiently and effectively utilizing their resources; the professional case manager is one of an EAP's most valuable resources. Moreover, effective caseload management also can minimize job stress and professional burnout on behalf of professional human service practitioners (Emener, 1979; Emener, Luck & Gohs, 1982; Krucoff, 1980; Maslach, 1976). These are just a few of the many reasons why caseload management constitutes an extremely important part of the effective EAP counselor's professional skills and expertise.

CASE RECORDING AND DOCUMENTATION. From a global perspective, case recording and documentation involves three sets of professional activities on behalf of the case manager: (1) keeping client records; (2) reporting on client progress to appropriate persons within the employee assistance program, the company, the union, and within the community of professionals providing client services; and (3) preparing summary reports to describe aspects of a client's progress to professionals involved in a client's treatment. The specific job tasks on behalf of the case manager involved in these three sets of activities, constitute an exhaustive list. Nonetheless, the experiences of the authors repeatedly have demonstrated that among the extensive list there are three critical areas of job task functions worthy of presentation and discussion in this chapter: (a) recording and reporting; (b) case documentation and report writing; and (c) the use of forms.

RECORDING AND REPORTING. Among the variety of recording and reporting functions of professional case managers, the following five are especially relevant in an employee assistance program setting (with appropriate signed releases when necessary):

1. completing assessment and evaluation summaries, and forwarding them to one's supervisor for review and approval (especially during the case manager's training and/or probationary period).

2. recording the steps in a recommended treatment plan, as developed with the client, and forwarding them to one's supervisor for review and approval (especially during the case manager's training and/or probationary period).

3. preparing summary reports and letters regarding clients for cooperating professionals, facilities, agencies or centers.

4. reporting verbally and in writing on a client's progress to a treatment team or selected group of professionals.

5. writing case notes, and interim and summary reports (including analyses, reasoning, and comments) so that others clearly can understand the client's progress and experiences.

In the process of carrying out these above job functions, it is important for the case manager to have high level cognitive and organizational thinking abilities. Moreover, it is very important for the case manager to be able to write thoroughly, clearly, cogently, and with detail and accurate expression.

CASE DOCUMENTATION AND REPORT WRITING. There are many instances when the case manager has to record, document, and report specific aspects of a client's case. Individual employee assistance programs usually develop specific forms for such occasions in order to facilitate and systematize such activities (the use(s) of forms will be addressed in the next section of this chapter). In the process of working with a client, nonetheless, there are four typical instances when a case manager will have to prepare a written record: (1) Intake Interviewing; (2) Services Planning; (3) Routine Contacts; and (4) Case Closure. For each of these four typical instances, the following provides a list of content, which may be relevant to a client's case. (Each client's case obviously is

unique, and as such, the specific content of each report will be different and unique to the individual client under consideration.)

1. Intake Interview

1. identification information on the referral, EAP counselor, and date
2. reason(s) why the referral came to the EAP (also, type of referral: self-, supervisor-, etc.)
3. description of the counselor's perception of the referral (noting that it is the counselor's perception)
4. an indication and discussion of the referral's assets, liabilities, problems, concerns, and difficulties
5. indications of the referral's experiences and perceptions of his or her problem(s)
6. an indication that the referral understands the employee assistance program (its policies, operations, services, etc.)
7. discussion of the referral's current circumstances (including family situation)
8. an indication of the referral's background, specifically: education, employment, and previous incidences with the problem(s) which brought the referral to the EAP
9. indications of the referral's social or leisure activities
10. justification(s) for accepting (opening) the case and providing services to the referral (and/or denying the referral)
11. indications of the referral's financial resources and ability to pay for services (if appropriate)
12. a list of the types of evaluations necessary to determine the individual's capacities, limitations and treatment needs
13. recommended action steps

2. Services Planning

1. identification of the client, counselor and date
2. review of the client's problem(s)
3. discussion of the client's "readiness" for services and treatment
4. justification, identification, and discussion of recommended treatment services (including availability and sources)

5. indication of the client's involvement in the planning process(es)
6. identification and justification of selected professionals, facilities or centers to which client will be referred
7. notation that all official releases and other appropriate forms have been signed by the client
8. a statement as to the client's prognosis for success (upon receipt of recommended treatment services)

3. Routine Contact

1. identification of the client, counselor and date
2. identification of the person(s), facility and/or center contacted
3. explanation of the reason(s) for the contact
4. discussion of what was accomplished 5. recommended action steps

4. Case Closure

1. identification of the client, counselor, and date
2. detailed description of services received by the client (types, sources, duration, etc.)
3. behavioral and emotive indications of the status of the client's resolution of his or her problems and difficulties (including appropriate information from others, e.g., family members, supervisor, etc.)
4. statement(s) as to why the case is being closed
5. an indication of recommended future follow-up (and with whom)

The actual format that case managers use for their report writing is typically contingent upon a combination of the individual policies and procedures of the employee assistance programs in which they are working and their own individual style. For some aspects of documentation, recording and reporting, however, the use of standardized forms can be very helpful in the overall operations of an employee assistance program.

USE OF FORMS. If an employee assistance program is going to use standardized forms for specific case services functions, it is highly recommended that all members of the staff of the EAP understand the forms, know how to use them, and know why they are important and related to the goals of the program. The following discusses three of the numerous benefits that can be derived from their effective use.

1. Assessment and Planning. The assessment and planning phases of EAP service delivery are highly reliant on the gathering and processing of data and information on clients. The intake assessment process and the effective use of the case manager's time can be facilitated if the referral completes a standardized Information Sheet (see Fig. 8-1) and a Health Statement (see Fig. 8-2) prior to entering the initial assessment session. Not only can this information be kept in the client's file for future reference, but the case manager can use the information from the forms as stimulus exploration sources for intake counseling with the client.

2. Legal Protection. Federal confidentiality laws prohibit the release of information on individuals without their written permission. In the event that the treatment plan for a client will necessitate the release of information, an advantageous time to have an Authorization of Release of Information Form (see Fig. 8-3) signed by the referral is during the initial assessment session (or even prior to it). Another important authorization to obtain from a referral is his or her signed Consent for Services (see Fig. 8-4). In most employee assistance program settings, clients are aware of the need for such forms and written releases and are quite willing to complete them.

3. Program Evaluation and Documentation. For a variety of reasons, as discussed in Chapter 26, employee assistance programs are compelled to document and evaluate their efficiency and effectiveness. Accurate and systematic case recording and documentation plays a critical role in an EAP's impact—not only in terms of being pivotal to its program evaluation efforts, but in the many ways it enhances the efficiency and effectiveness of the services provided by the program's professional practitioners.

Case recording and documentation unfortunately is perceived by some practitioners as a "necessary evil." On the contrary, case recording and documentation, when used effectively by the professional practitioner, not only enhances the overall efficiency and effectiveness of the employee assistance program, but it also plays a vital role in the quality and quantity of clinical treatment services provided to and for the program's clients.

PLEASE TAKE A FEW MOMENTS TO COMPLETE THIS INFORMATION SHEET

Client Name: _____ Spouse Name: _____

Address:_____ Spouse Address: _____

_____ Zip _____ Zip

Phone: (Home)_____ Birth Date: _____

    (Work)_____

Place of Employment: Client_____

        Spouse_____

Social Security Number: Client_____ Spouse_____

Who can we notify in an emergency?

Name:_____ Phone:_____

Family Physician: _____

Do you have any medical condition(s) we should know about? If so, explain: _____
_____

If currently taking any prescription medication, list here: _____
_____

Have you ever had psychological testing? If so, state where and when: _____
_____

Do you have medical insurance?_____ Policy Holder: _____

Name of company, address, and policy number: _____
_____

How di you hear about us? _____

PLEASE NOTE:

The above information as well as all information pertaining to your treatment is considered strictly confidential.

A fee may be charged for appointments not cancelled within 24 hours.

_____ _____
   Client's Signature   Date

Figure 8-1.

HEALTH STATEMENT

NAME_____ DATE OF BIRTH _____ SEX ____

	YES	NO	REMARKS (re "YES" responses)

Have you ever applied for or received disability benefits, compensation or pensions for illness or injury? _____ _____

Were you ever rejected, deferred or released for physical or mental reasons? _____ _____

To the best of your knowledge and belief, have you suffered from or ever been treated for:

a. Epilepsy, fainting spells, nervous or mental disorder? _____ _____

b. Tuberculosis, asthma, pneumonia? _____ _____

c. Heart disease or murmur, high or low blood pressure? _____ _____

d. Stomach or duodenal ulcer, gall bladder, liver disease, colitis? _____ _____

e. Kidney or prostatic problems, or albumin or blood in the urine? _____ _____

f. Diabetes, sugar in urine? _____ _____

g. Rheumatic fever, arthritis, gout, bone or joint disorder? _____ _____

h. Cancer, tumor, polyp, goiter? _____ _____

i. Hernia, hemorroids, varicose veins, appendicitis? _____ _____

j. Venereal disease, blood or skin disorder? _____ _____

To the best of your knowledge and beliefs:

a. Do you have any eye, ear, nose, or throat problems? _____ _____

b. Have you ever had chest pains, shortness of breath, or palpitation of the heart? _____ _____

c. Have you ever had back strain or back injury? _____ _____

d. Have you ever had any physical examinations, x-rays, or EKG within past 5 years? _____ _____

e. Are you addicted to or ever been treated for alcoholism or drug addiction? _____ _____

f. Have you ever undergone or been advised to have surgical operation not included in above questions? _____ _____

g. Any illness or injury requiring medical treatment or hospitalization within past 5 years? _____ _____

h. Are you now taking any medications? _____ _____

i. Any physical or mental impairments or any reason you think you are not in good health? _____ _____

j. Were you absent from work (school) during past year? _____ _____

k. Any of the following diseases:
     smallpox, diphtheria, scarlet fever, whooping cough,
     typhoid fever, influenza? _____ _____

I hereby declare that to the best of my knowledge the statements and answers above are full, complete, and true.

Date_____ Signature_____

Figure 8-2. Example of Health Statement used at intake.

THE SYNERGISTIC RELATIONSHIP AMONG CASE MANAGEMENT, CASE-LOAD MANAGEMENT, AND CASE RECORDING AND DOCUMENTATION

Professional EAP counselors' working lives are typically very rapid-paced and hectic ones. They have many, many responsibilities, perform numerous important roles and functions, and are in very important positions in the lives of employees and clients who have a wide variety of problems, difficulties, and concerns. In addition to counseling with clients, they also coordinate and "manage" a variety of other professionals' services provided to their clients. Tantamount to their suc-cessfulness is their ability to be in control. **They have to know what's going on**–in the various treatment services being provided to their clients, in their relationships with their clients, in their client's experiences with what is happening to them, and in their own professional working lives. Furthermore, **professional EAP counselors have to influence what's going on, know how they impact such influences, and be able to predict and measure the impact of their influ-**

AUTHORIZATION OF RELEASE OF INFORMATION

I, the undersigned, hereby authorize _____
(name of agency)

_____
(address)

to disclose to_____
(name of person/agency to receive information)

the following information from records in its possession:

____ Treatment and Discharge Summary   ____ Laboratory Reports
____ Psychological Testing & Evaluation   ____ School Transcripts & Grades
____ Medical History & Physical   ____ Other (specify)

The purpose or need for such disclosure is _____

This authorization to disclose information may be revoked by me at any time except to the extent that action has been taken in reliance thereon.

This authorization shall expire upon: _____

(specify date, event, or condition upon which it will expire)

_____   _____
Signature of Client   Date

_____   _____
Signature of Legal Guardian   Date

_____   _____
Signature of Witness   Date

NOTICE TO WHOMEVER DISCLOSURE IS MADE: This information has been disclosed to you from records whose confidentiality is protected by FEDERAL LAW. Federal regulations (42 CFR part 2) prohibits you from making any further disclosure of this information without the specific written consent of the person to whom it pertains, or as otherwise permitted by such regulations. A general authorization for the release of medical or other information is NOT sufficient for this purpose.l

---

Figure 8-3. Example of Authorization of Release of Information form to be completed at intake.

ences. From a macro or gestalt perspective, effective EAP counselors understand and appreciate the individual events in the clinical services and processes that their clients are experiencing, and also understand and appreciate the aggregate, collective, and overall impact of the individual events. Thus, the highly synergistic and interrelated relationships among effective EAP 'counselors' case management, case load management, and case recording and documentation roles and func-

tions become glaringly evident. For the ultimate benefits of their clients, their employee assistance programs, and their own professional working lives, EAP counselors should give these roles and functions their utmost attention and constantly strive to improve them through continuous self-evaluation and professional continuing education and training. In doing so, they validate and verify the essence of their existence as "professionals."

CONSENT FOR SERVICES

Signed Consent is required before services can be rendered.

I, _____ hereby authorize and give
　　　　　　　　　　　　　　　　　(client's name)

consent to _____ to provide
　　　　　　　　　　　　(name of program providing services)

family therapy services. These services may consist of evaluation, counseling, individual and/or group therapy, and such other services as the _____
　　　　　　　　　　　　　　　　　　　　　(program)

believes are necessary and to which I agree.

I agree to pay for services received according to the _____
　　　　　　　　　　　　　　　　　　　　　(program)

approved fee structure. I understand I may be charged a fee for appointments not cancelled withint 24 hours.

In the event that I become ill or am injured while on the premises, I a;uthorize

_____ to provide or obtain emergency medical services
　　　　　　　　　　　　(program)

(i.e., call an ambulance).

_____　　　　_____
Witness　　　　　　　　　　　　　　　　　　Signature of Client

_____　　　　_____
Date　　　　　　　　　　　　　　　　　　　　Signature of Parent/Guardian

　　　　　　　　　　　　　　　　　　　　　_____
　　　　　　　　　　　　　　　　　　　　　(Relationship)

　　　　　　　　　　　　　　　　　　　　　_____
　　　　　　　　　　　　　　　　　　　　　Date

Figure 8-4. Example of Consent for Services form to be completed at intake.

Acknowledgment. Sincerest appreciation is extended to the Seminole Heights Counseling Center. Tampa. Florida for granting permission to reproduce (with minor modifications) the four examples of forms published in this chapter (Figures 8-1 to 8-4).

REFERENCES

Cassell, J. L., & Mulkey, S. W. (1981). *Rehabilitation caseload management: Concepts and practice.* Austin: PRO-ED.

Desmond, R. .E. (1985). Careers in employee assistance programs. *Journal of Applied Rehabilitation Counseling, 16* (2), 26–30.

Dickman, F., & Emener, W. G. (1982). Employee assistance programs: An emerging vista for rehabilitation counseling. *Journal of Applied Rehabilitation Counseling, 13* (3), 18–20.

Emener, W. G. (1979). Professional burnout: Rehabilitation's hidden handicap. *Journal of Rehabilitation, 45* (1), 55–58.

Emener, W. G., Luck, R. S., & Gohs, F. X. (1982). A theoretical investigation of the construct burnout. *Journal of Rehabilitation Administration, 6* (4), 188–196.

Emener, W. G., & Rubin, S. E. (1980). Rehabilitation counselor roles and functions and sources, of role strain. *Journal of Applied Rehabilitation Counseling, 11* (2), 57–69.

Hastings, M.A. (1984). Employee assistance programs: A place for rehabilitation counselors? *Journal of Applied Rehabilitation Counseling, 15* (4), 29–30, 56.

Henke, R. O., Connolly, S. G., & Cox, J. G. (1975). Caseload management: The key to effectiveness. *Journal of Applied Rehabilitation Counseling, 6,* 217–227.

Hutchison, Jr., W. S. (1985). Personal and family problems in living: Implications for EAP service delivery. In J. F. Dickman, W. G. Emener & W. S. Hutchison, Jr. (Eds.), *Counseling the troubled person in industry.* Springfield, IL: Charles C Thomas, Publisher, Ltd.

Hutchison, Jr., W. S., & Renick, J. C. (1985). Social work in an industrial setting: An idea whose time has finally come. In J .F. Dickman, W. G. Emener & W. S. Hutchison, Jr. (Eds.), *Counseling the troubled person in industry.* Springfield, IL: Charles C Thomas, Publisher, Ltd.

Kaplan, H. I., & Sadock, B. J. (1981). *Modern synopsis of comprehensive textbooks of psychiatry III* (3rd ed). Baltimore: Williams & Wilkins.

Krucoff, C. (1980). Careers: Confronting on-the-job burnout. *Washington Post,* August 5, B–5.

Maiden, R. P., & Hardcastle, D. A. (1986). Social work education: Professionalizing EAPs. *EAP Digest,* November/December, 63–66.

Maslach, C. (1976). Burn-out. *Human Behavior, 5,* 16–22.

Roessler, R. T., & Rubin, S. E. (1982). *Case management and rehabilitation counseling: Procedures and techniques.* Baltimore: University Park Press.

Third Institute on Rehabilitation Services. (1965). Training Guides in Caseload Management for Vocational Rehabilitation. Vocational Rehabilitation Administration, DHEW, Washington, DC.

Thompson, J. K., Kite, J. L., & Bruyere, S. M. (1977). Caseload management: Content and training perspective. Paper presented at the American Personnel and Guidance Association.

Chapter 9

ALCOHOLISM AND EMPLOYEE ASSISTANCE PROGRAMS: ASSESSMENT AND TREATMENT

FRED DICKMAN

Alcoholism, alcohol-related problems (co-dependency), and alcohol and drug abuse (polydrug addiction) encompass a category of problems, which comprise 30 to 40 percent of the cases entering an Employee Assistance Program for assessment, assistance, and follow-up. Consequently, it is imperative that EAP coordinators, contractors, and assessors are thoroughly competent in the identification of alcoholism, its ramifications, and its treatment. To follow is a general discussion on alcoholism, its pervasiveness, its definition, alcoholism as a disease, signs and symptoms, principles of intervention, treatment options, and implications for EAP practitioners.

Alcoholism has been universally recognized as at least the third leading health problem and disabling condition in the United States (National Center for Alcohol Education, 1978; U.S. Department of Health, Education, and Welfare, 1981). In addition to its status as the third most serious primary disabling condition, it is known to impact on and exacerbate many other disabling conditions–including some forms of heart disease and cancer, first and second in fatality causation respectively (American Medical Association, 1973; U.S. Department of Health, Education, and Welfare, 1981).

Conditions affected by alcohol abuse and alcoholism frequently encountered in Employee Assistance Programs are:

Pervasiveness

1. **Mental Illness.** It is estimated that up to 40 percent of persons diagnosed as mentally ill may be dually afflicted by alcoholism (Bachrach, 1976; Cotton, 1979; Leiber, 1982).

2. **Heart Disease.** Researchers contend that alcohol has a detrimental effect on the heart muscle and is significantly correlated with cardiomyopathy (Hamby, 1970; Schwartz, Sample & Wegle, 1975). Heart patients no longer are advised to have "a little glass of wine" (Schneider, 1980).

3. **Cancer.** While the research results on cancer are far from being conclusive, evidence is emerging to allow an inference of higher risk associated with alcoholism, alcohol abuse, and mere alcohol intake and some forms of cancer (Williams & Horn, 1977; Wynder, 1978; Wynder, Bross, & Feldman, 1957).

4. **Orthopedic Impairments and Amputations.** Since 40–60 percent of all accidents are reported to be alcohol-related (U.S. Department of Health, Education, and Welfare, 1981), an as yet untested hypothesis is that alcoholism may impede the rehabilitation progress of the victim.

5. **Birth Defects.** There is an abundance of new research available on fetal alcohol syndrome (FAS). FAS is the third leading cause of birth

Note: This chapter is reprinted from *Employee Assistance Programs: A Basic Text* (1988) with permission of the author, the book's editors (Dickman, Emener, & Hutchison, Jr.), and the publisher (Charles C Thomas, Publisher, Ltd.).

defective persons, which adds significantly to the population of mentally retarded individuals (Clarren & Smith, 1978; Streissguth, Little, Herman, & Woodell, 1979).

6. **Other Disorders.** Characteristic disorders of rehabilitation populations related to alcohol abuse and alcoholism are gastrointestinal disorders (Leiber, 1982), genitourinary disorders (Fort, 1973), liver problems and disease (Leiber, 1982), diabetes (Kissin & Begleiter, 1977), and central nervous system problems (Parsons & Farr, 1981; Smith, 1977).

While the above disabilities tend to be most frequently encountered in public rehabilitation programs (Wright, 1980), the private sector rehabilitation focuses on workers' compensation cases (Rasch, in press). Many industrial accidents, which are associated with a significant percent of these conditions, are clearly alcohol-related (Manello & Seaman, 1979; Wolkenberg, Gold, & Tichauer, 1975). Other accidents covered by insurance, such as auto accidents and domestic falls, (Haberman & Baden, 1978) are highly related to drinking alcohol.

When other rehabilitation issues and populations are addressed, i.e., divorce, spouse abuse, child abuse, runaways, school dropouts, suicide, and public offenders (Emerson, 1979; Hindman, 1977; Julian & Mohr, 1980; Kempe & Heller, 1972), and the clear relationship these have to alcoholism is noted, the magnitude of the problem is brought into focus. These stress only alcohol relatedness. When the identified alcohol client population is considered, the problem for rehabilitation is formidable. Clearly, the rehabilitation counselor requires tools for diagnosis (early and late) and state-of-the-art methods of treatment (Dickman & Phillips, 1985).

Alcoholism—A Definition

In general, treatment experts and scholars vary only minimally in defining alcoholism. E. M. Jellinek (1960) defined alcoholism as any use of alcoholic beverages that causes any damage to the individual or to society or both.

The Alcoholism Subcommittee of the World Health Organization (1952) defined alcoholism as any form of drinking which in extent goes beyond the traditional and customary "dietary" use, or the ordinary compliance with the social drinking customs of the community concerned, irrespective of etiological factors leading to such behavior, and irrespective also of the extent to which such etiological factors are dependent upon heredity, constitution, or acquired physiopathological and metabolic influences.

The following definition is from the American Medical Association (1973, p. 11):

Alcoholism is an illness characterized by preoccupation with alcohol and loss of control over its consumption such as to lead usually to intoxication if drinking is begun; by chronicity; by progression; and by tendency toward relapse. It is typically associated with physical disability and impaired emotional, occupational, and/or social adjustments as a direct consequence of persistent and excessive use of alcohol.

The National Council on Alcoholism defined alcoholism as a chronic, progressive, and potentially fatal disease. It is characterized by tolerance and physical dependency, pathologic organ changes, or both, all of which are the direct consequences of the alcohol ingested.

Finally, Marty Mann, founder of the National Council on Alcoholism, defined the alcoholic as "a very sick person, victim of an insidious progressive disease, which all too often ends fatally. An alcoholic can be recognized, diagnosed, and treated successfully" (Mann, 1958, p. 17).

The diagnostic criteria for alcohol abuse published by the American Psychiatric Association (1980, p. 169) specifically addresses:

a. pattern of pathological alcohol use;
b. impairment in social or occupational functioning due to alcohol use; and
c. duration of disturbance of at least one month.

The diagnostic criteria for alcohol abuse published by the American Psychiatric Association (1980, p. 170) are:

a. either a pattern of pathological alcohol use

of impairment in social or occupational functioning due to alcohol use; and

b. either tolerance or withdrawal.

These definitions, a few among a myriad in the alcoholism literature, have a common theme, which leads the author to define alcoholism as a phenomenon with three criteria:

a. a drinking pattern;
b. a loss of control due to the drinking pattern;
c. a serious interference with one or more major areas of the drinking person's life, i.e., marriage and family, vocational, legal, financial, physical/medical, social, and intrapersonal areas.

Alcoholism–The Disease Concept

In addition to a growing consensus on the definition of alcoholism, the rapidly growing alcoholism treatment community is gaining agreement on the notion of alcoholism as a disease (American Medical Association, 1973; Blum & Blum, 1972; Forrest, 1978; Gitlow, 1973; Hunter, 1982; Jellenik, 1959; Johnson, 1980; King, Bissell, & O'Brien, 1979).

Inherent to the disease concept are the following:

1. **Chronicity.** Alcoholism once contracted is contracted unto death (Martin, 1972). This is the belief that alcoholism is incurable. This incurableness, however, had led many researchers (Armor, Polich, & Stambul, 1976; Sobell & Sobell, 1978) to hypothesize the opposite. Interestingly, to date no one has been able to prove that alcoholism recovery can be obtained with any treatment goal short of total abstinence (Fewell & Bissell, 1978; Gitlow, 1973; Johnson, 1980; Milam & Ketcham, 1981).
2. **Progressiveness.** Like any other disease, alcoholism has been thought of as having a "course" with definite, identifiable symptoms (Forrest, 1978; Jellinek, 1960; Johnson, 1980). This consideration is crucial to the rehabilitation counselor in that early identification is vital to successful intervention (Catanzaro, 1974; Johnson, 1980; Kinney & Leaton, 1978).

3. **Predictability.** Consequences of alcoholism are foreseeable, and as the progression of addiction continues, what is in the beginning a disparate and uniquely individual population (Catanzaro, 1974; Jellinek, 1960; Johnson, 1980).
4. **Primariness.** Alcoholism is a disease in and of itself and not a symptom of other more underlying disorders. In other words, alcoholism causes symptomatology–symptomatology does not cause alcoholism (American Medical Association, 1973; American Psychiatric Association, 1980; Estes, Smith-Dejulio & Heinemann, 1980; Forrest, 1978; Johnson, 1980; Milam & Ketcham, 1981; Murphy, 1980).
5. **Fatality.** Undiagnosed, untreated alcoholism results in early fatality estimated between 12 and 15 years off the average expected lifespan (American Medical Association, 1973; Kissin & Begleiter, 1972).
6. **Arrestableness.** Alcoholism is paradoxical in nature. It is the most destructive, pervasive, costly, and debilitative of the diseases; yet it is one of the most rehabilitative. Left alone, it is always fatal; diagnosed and successfully treated, the recovery is the most complete of all the diseases (Forrest, 1978; Glatt, 1974; Goldenson, Dunham, & Dunham, 1978; Milam & Ketcham, 1981).

Ironically, rehabilitation counselors, social workers, and other health professionals view the alcoholic as the least attractive, least acceptable client (Fewell & Bissell, 1978; Milam & Ketcham, 1981; Wechsler & Rohman, 1982).

A Model of Alcoholism: Diagnosis, Intervention, and Treatment

Figure 9-1 illustrates a theory of the alcohol addictive progression and its predictable consequences, the intervention process, and signs of recovery. This model provides the counselor with state-of-the-art knowledge of alcoholism and its symptomatology with implications for intervention and rehabilitation planning. The model reproduces signs of alcoholism from early to late stages in that alcoholism, like most other diseases, is treatable in proportion to its early identification.

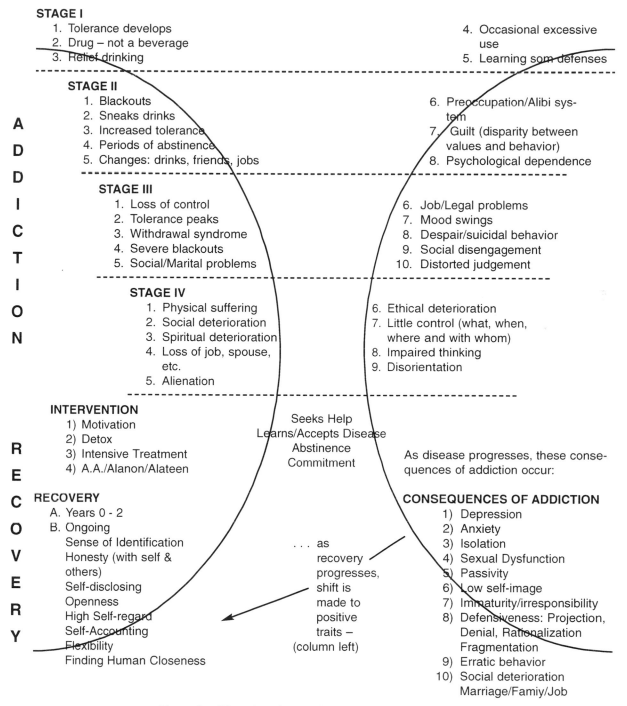

STAGE I
1. Tolerance develops
2. Drug – not a beverage
3. Relief drinking
4. Occasional excessive use
5. Learning some defenses

STAGE II
1. Blackouts
2. Sneaks drinks
3. Increased tolerance
4. Periods of abstinence
5. Changes: drinks, friends, jobs
6. Preoccupation/Alibi system
7. Guilt (disparity between values and behavior)
8. Psychological dependence

STAGE III
1. Loss of control
2. Tolerance peaks
3. Withdrawal syndrome
4. Severe blackouts
5. Social/Marital problems
6. Job/Legal problems
7. Mood swings
8. Despair/suicidal behavior
9. Social disengagement
10. Distorted judgement

STAGE IV
1. Physical suffering
2. Social deterioration
3. Spiritual deterioration
4. Loss of job, spouse, etc.
5. Alienation
6. Ethical deterioration
7. Little control (what, when, where and with whom)
8. Impaired thinking
9. Disorientation

INTERVENTION
1) Motivation
2) Detox
3) Intensive Treatment
4) A.A./Alanon/Alateen

Seeks Help
Learns/Accepts Disease
Abstinence
Commitment

As disease progresses, these consequences of addiction occur:

RECOVERY
A. Years 0 - 2
B. Ongoing
Sense of Identification
Honesty (with self & others)
Self-disclosing
Openness
High Self-regard
Self-Accounting
Flexibility
Finding Human Closeness

. . . as recovery progresses, shift is made to positive traits – (column left)

CONSEQUENCES OF ADDICTION
1) Depression
2) Anxiety
3) Isolation
4) Sexual Dysfunction
5) Passivity
6) Low self-image
7) Immaturity/irresponsibility
8) Defensiveness: Projection, Denial, Rationalization Fragmentation
9) Erratic behavior
10) Social deterioration Marriage/Famiy/Job

A D D I C T I O N

R E C O V E R Y

Figure 9-1. Hourglass theory of addiction and recovery.

Symptoms Critical to Early Identification

The scope of this paper precludes a thorough discussion of all symptoms depicted in Figure 9-1, but following are the more common ways the EAP assessor/counselor can identify alcoholism early on in the progression.

1. **Has there been an increase in tolerance?** The concept of tolerance is considered a major indicator of addiction (American Psychiatric Association, 1980; Forrest, 1978; Jellenik, 1960; Kinney & Leaton, 1978). In the early stages tolerance increases and often is a source of pride for the progressing alcoholic. Yet increasing tolerance is indicative of heavy consumption as the "budding" alcoholic is adding acquired and metabolic tolerance to innate individual capacities. For example, a high blood alcohol content (BAC) has emerged from Driving While Intoxicated (DWI) Counterattack studies as a major early identifier.

2. **Has there been an arrest record, especially a DWI or driving while under the influence (DUI) charge?** U.S. Department of Transportation studies (1974) suggest that of those persons with one arrest, 60% are in some stage of alcoholism. Those with two or more arrests are within a 900;0 certainty of being alcoholic.

3. **Has the client experienced periods of forgetting events or blocks of time, even though not asleep, while drinking?** While blackouts occur all through many alcoholic individuals' drinking lives, in varying degrees, they definitely are a sign of neurological disturbance due to alcohol ingestion (Fort, 1973; Kissin & Begleiter, 1972; Milam & Ketcham, 1981).

4. **Has the client experienced signs of physical withdrawal indicative of some phase of physical addiction?** Butterflies in the stomach, shakiness, insomnia, and irritability are all signs of alcohol withdrawal in some phase. Signs can be less severe to severe, such as delirium tremens, convulsions, hallucinations (Fort, 1973).

5. **Does the client become defensive when asked about his drinking pattern?** Treatment personnel agree alcoholic persons build a predictable wall of defenses to protect their drinking. They tend to rationalize, deny, project, and repress their drinking-involved behavior, probably to protect a declining self-image (Fewell & Bissell, 1978; Forrest, 1978; Johnson, 1980; Murphy, 1980).

6. **What exists in the client's medical history with a probable relationship to an abusive drinking pattern?** Liver functioning, the gastrointestinal system, the pancreatic system (especially adult diabetes), and cardiomyopathy are particularly affected by alcohol abuse (Estes, et al., 1980; Hamby, 1980; Schneider, 1980).

7. **What in the client's marital and family history and present situation may point to alcoholism?** Has there been child or spouse abuse reported? Is there alcoholism in their history/Have they been involved in frequent divorce? Each of these has been correlated with alcohol abuse and alcoholism (Emerson, 1979; Filstead, 1977; Hindman, 1977; Krimmel, 1973).

8. **Is there any sign of loss-of-control drinking?** Progressing alcoholic persons cannot always predict how much they will drink, on which occasions they will drink, with whom they will drink, or what they will do when they drink. The insidiousness of this phenomenon is that often they can predict, but there are many times they cannot. This adds to their increasing fear, which they attempt to build a defense against (Forrest, 1978; Jellinek, 1960; Johnson, 1980; Kissin & Begleiter, 1977).

9. **Do they project frequently rather than take responsibility for their behavior?** Progressing alcoholic persons quickly learn to defend a weakening ego by blaming their troubles on the outside world (Fewell & Bissell, 1978). The skilled rehabilitation counselor can typically recognize this in the initial interview.

10. **Have any of the problems presented to the counselor been accompanied by drinking or other drug use?** Often an aware

and sensitive intake counselor can identify a problem with drinking by asking the client or significant others the appropriate questions about presenting problems, i.e., a family fight, trouble with a child, marital problems, problems with an employer, etc. (Dahlhauser, Dickman, Emener, & Lewis, 1982).

Intervention Strategy

A myth exists that implies alcoholic individuals have to "hit bottom" before they will seek help or be receptive to treatment. Quite often, they are unable to do this. Their defense system is too strong. They must be confronted before they can perceive the need for treatment (Catanzaro, 1974; Fewell & Bissell, 1978; Forrest, 1978; Johnson, 1980). Essential to intervention strategy are: (1) significant others, (2) caring confrontation, and (3) a treatment plan.

Significant Others

People close to defended alcoholic individuals can penetrate their defense system so that they can see enough reality to enter treatment. Research indicates that well-trained confronters can increase the probability of entering treatment from 15 percent up to 70 percent (Dickman & Emener, 1982b; Emener & Dickman, 1983; Johnson, 1980). Also, research indicates that the best confronters are employers, spouse, other family members, and friends, in that order (Johnson, 1980).

The counselor is invaluable in this process in that they train the interveners to make successful confrontation on the basis of proven principles.

Caring Confrontation

The following principles of caring confrontation are generally recommended:

1. The goal is to get the alcoholic into treatment; to take a first step toward recovery. The goal is not to get him to see all the ramifications of his or her disease at once.
2. Significant others have to be involved. Only

those who see the seriousness of the problem and have first-hand, observed data as to the addicted person's use can be helpful.

3. The significant others need to be trained:

   a. To present facts as to what they have seen and how they felt about what they saw.
   b. To present facts nonjudgmentally and with a minimum of emotion.
   c. To present facts as specifically as possible.
   d. To present data only related to drinking or use.
   e. To learn to feel comfortable about what they are doing; that they are trying to help the addicted person, not condemn him or her.
   f. To see that they too will be personally involved in a program of recovery, i.e., co-dependency, ACOA, and enhanced family/employer/employee communication.
   g. To agree upon appropriate treatment modalities.

4. Present available, appropriate choices to the alcoholic (Johnson, 1980).

Treatment Plan

Treatment choice depends upon how far the addicted client has progressed. If they are clearly and well into Stages III or IV (see Fig. 9-1), they probably need medical attention and should be referred to an intensive, inpatient (usually 28-day) program. For this purpose, the practicing EAP assessor/counselor should have a directory of resources and treatment facilities. While the client is in his program, it is recommended that the EAP assessor/counselor:

1. Visit the client to secure the relationship as a caring one.
2. Arrange for outpatient follow-up.
3. Arrange for members of Alcoholics Anonymous to meet the client to secure a continuing program after inpatient treatment.
4. Arrange an appointment for weekly follow-up counseling with alcoholism specialists for the client and his/her family.
5. Continue frequent follow-up to check the progress of the client's recovery.

6. Make sure to provide needed family therapy.
7. Contact ACOA specialist counselors for an appointment with the family including small children.

If intervention is early enough, inpatient treatment may not be necessary. For instance, it was found that a good employee assistance program intervenes early enough so that 7 out of 10 alcoholic employees can recover without inpatient treatment (Dickman & Emener, 1982a). If such is the case, all the above recommendations hold with the addition of:

a. an immediate physical;
b. antabuse treatment (if medically feasible); and,
c. an intensive outpatient program to include individual, group, and family counseling.

Signs of Recovery

Commensurate with the progression of the disease, the process of recovery offers predictable indicators for the rehabilitation counselor. Although abstinence is critical to recovery (Gitlow, 1973; Milam & Ketcham, 1981), it must be considered as a first step on a journey of recovery along with other emotional and behavioral signs. Indeed, to get sober, the alcoholic individual cannot drink; to stay sober, alcoholic clients need to make changes in their lives. The process of recovery reverses the consequences of addiction (see Fig. 9-1).

The following are signs to look for, and to counsel toward, in following up the recovery of an alcoholic individual:

1. **Hope replaces despair.** Does the client believe the circumstances can change? Do they believe their lives can become more meaningful? Are they willing to take steps to effect these changes?
2. **Acceptance of alcoholism.** Has the client stopped blaming others for the drinking behaviors? Do they understand it was not outside circumstances and people that caused them to drink? The clients grow to accept their alcoholism and incorporate it as part of their self-image.
3. **Attendance at Alcoholics Anonymous meetings.** Is client attending AA meetings regularly and willingly? This can be vital to recovery, increasing chances for a successful recovery by as much as 75 percent by attending AA meetings (Gellman, 1964). Does the client go to a particular group on a regular basis? Has the client obtained a sponsor?
4. **General appearance.** The counselor may notice early on the alcoholic client's recovery a "glow" of health, i.e., improved personal appearance, with clients taking an interest in how they look. They begin to like the person they see in the mirror in the morning. For example, the rehabilitation counselor will notice improved eye contact and more open-body language.
5. **Responsibility.** Are the clients taking responsibility for themselves in all areas of their lives? Are they going to work regularly and arriving on time? Are they fulfilling obligations and commitments to family and friends?
6. **Communication.** Is the client communicating more freely with significant persons, i.e., employer, family, counselor? Is the client more willing to share feelings and risk self-disclosure? In this sense, the rehabilitation counselor will note increasing congruency in what the client feels and says, with appropriate voice tone and cadence.
7. **New interests.** To replace the time spent drinking, the client will develop interests in leisure activities, i.e., sports, hobbies, and social situations that do not involve drinking alcohol. They will become less and less threatened by new experiences. Is the client experiencing socialization and integration in the community?
8. **Present-centeredness.** Is the client focusing on the here and how and on what is, rather than what has been or what might be? With increased self-worth and resultant self-acceptance, the recovering alcoholic client will experience "living in the here and now" more and more fully.
9. **Goal-directedness.** Has the client's life become purposeful? Does the client have short and long-term goals that are realistic? With increasing self-worth, the client can func-

tion more freely and work in the direction of fulfilling personal potentials.

10. **Spirituality.** On a continuing journey of recovery, the alcoholic individual gains a sense of identification, of oneness, a feeling of being a part of rather than apart from. A sense of alienation and loneliness is replaced with a sense of belonging and purposefulness; and the client grows to accept and believe in a power greater than self. Fears are replaced with a faith, and an attitude of trust develops that things will work out as they should, not necessarily as the client wants them to be.

11. **Family growth.**

12. **Children's growth.**

The process of recovery is lifelong, beginning with abstinence, maintained by a support system of which Alcoholics Anonymous is crucial and of which the EAP assessor/counselor can be a powerful part.

Follow-up and Reentry

Follow-up by way of telephone calls, plant visitation or sessions every month or so is crucial. Is the recovering person active in AA/NA treatment center follow-up groups, other group counseling, and private alcoholism counseling designed for continuing recovery? Is he relating at work? Are supervisors aware of his reentry problems? If the absence for treatment (in the case of inpatient) were known by supervisors were they involved in the intervention and how can they help in the client's reentry? Are the family members in Alanon/Narcanon, ACOA, Alateen and other forms of recovery treatment? These are important questions to be answered by the assessor/coordinator/counselor in charge of overall case management (see Chapter 8).

SUMMARY, CONCLUSIONS, RECOMMENDATIONS

The following conclusions and recommendations are offered.

1. Alcoholism is a hidden, serious factor in many other disabled populations and can easily sabotage the rehabilitation process if not detected.

2. Alcoholism is one of the most treatable of the major rehabilitation disabilities.

3. The stigma surrounding alcoholism still is the major barrier to treatment and rehabilitation of alcoholic persons and their families. Rehabilitation counselors themselves need more alcoholism awareness training to make sure that their own attitudes are nonjudgmental. Alcoholism education and awareness help in this regard.

4. Alcoholism is a disease in the most practical sense of the concept. Whether alcoholic individuals can learn to drink again or not is a major research issue. However, state-of-the-art treatment practice would dictate a program aimed at cessation of drinking and a definite

recovery program.

5. Family involvement in alcoholism counseling and treatment is critically important.

6. Counselor education programs need to offer more courses and training in alcoholism and alcoholism counseling.

7. Counselor education needs to focus more on family counseling theory and practice or, at least, help the assessor/counselor become aware of these services in the community.

8. Alcoholic individuals, fully recovering, are among the most productive workers in industry (Dickman & Emener, 1982b).

No one doubts that alcoholism is a major disabling condition. Nor is there doubt that alcoholism seriously affects the rehabilitation process in many cases involving other disabilities. Therefore, the profession of counseling and EAP should feel compelled to consider the pervasiveness of alcoholism and all of its ramifications.

RESOURCES FOR THE REHABILITATION COUNSELOR
ON ALCOHOLISM INFORMATION

Alcoholics Anonymous
P.O. Box 459, Grand Central Station
New York, NY 10017
(212) 686-1100

Al-Anon Family Groups
P.O. Box 182, Dept. G
Madison Square Garden Station
New York, NY 10010
(212) 475-6110

National Council on Alcoholism
733 Third Avenue
New York, NY 10017

**National Institute on
Alcohol Abuse & Alcoholism**
Division of Resource Development
5600 Fishers Lane
Rockville, MD 20857
(301) 443-2570

**National Clearinghouse
for Alcohol Information**
P.O. Box 2345
Rockville, MD 20852
(301) 948-4450

REFERENCES

American Medical Association. Manual on Alcoholism (Rev.). Chicago: Author, 1973.

American Psychiatric Association. *Diagnostic and statistical manual of mental disorders* (3rd ed.). Author, 1980.

Armor, D. J., Polich, J .M., & Stambul, H. B. (1976). *Alcoholism and treatment.* Report R–1739–NIAAA, Santa Monica, CA: Rand Corporation.

Bacharach, L. Characteristics of diagnosed and missed alcoholic male admissions to State and County mental hospitals in 1972. *Mental Health Statistical Note No. 124.* National Institute of Mental Health, 1976.

Blum, E., & Blum, R. (1972). *Alcoholism: Modem psychological approaches to treatment.* San Francisco: Jossey-Bass Publishers.

Catanzaro, R. J. (1974). The disease: Alcoholism. In R. J. Catanzaro (Ed.), *Alcoholism: The total treatment approach* (3rd printing). Springfield, IL: Charles C Thomas.

Clarren, S. K., & Smith, D. W. (1978). The fetal alcohol syndrome. *New England Journal of Medicine, 298,* 1063–1067.

Cotton, N. S. (1979). The familial incidence of alcoholism: A review. *Journal of Studies on Alcohol, 40* (1), 89–116.

Dahlhauser, H. F., Dickman, F., Emener, W. G., & Lewis, G. Y. (1982). *Alcohol and drug abuse awareness: Implications for intake interviewing.* Manuscript submitted for publication.

Dickman, F., & Emener, W. G. (1982). Employee assistance programs: An emerging vista for rehabilitation counseling. *Journal of Applied Rehabilitation, 13* (3), 18–20.

Dickman, F., & Phillips, I. A. Alcoholism: A pervasive rehabilitation counseling issue. *Journal of Applied Rehabilitation Counseling,* 1985.

Emener, W. G., & Dickman, F. (1983). Corporate caring. *Management World, 12* (1), 36–38.

Emerson, C. D. (1979). Family violence: A study by the Los Angeles County Sheriffs Department. *Police Chief, 46,* 48–50.

Estes, N. J., Smith-Dejulio, J., & Heinemann, M. E. (1980). *Nursing diagnosis of the alcoholic person.* St. Louis: C. V. Mosby.

Fewell, C. H., & Bissell, L. (1978). The alcoholic denial syndrome: An alcohol-focused approach. *Social Casework, 59* (1), 6–13.

Filstead, W. (1977). The family, alcohol misuse and alcoholism: Priorities and proposals for intervention. *Journal of Studies on Alcohol, 38,* 1447–1454.

Forrest, G. C. (1978). *The diagnosis and treatment of alcoholism* (2nd ed.). Springfield, IL: Charles C Thomas, Publisher, Ltd.

Fort, J. (1973). *Alcohol: Our biggest drug problem.* New York: McGraw-Hill.

Gellman, I. P. (1964). *The sober alcoholic: An organizational analysis of Alcoholics Anonymous.* New Haven: College and University Press.

Gitlow, S. E. (1973). Alcoholism: A disease. In P. G.

Bourne & R. Fox (Eds.). *Alcoholism progress in research and treatment.* New York: Academic Press.

Glatt, M. M. (1978). *A guide to addiction and its treatment.* New York: John Wiley & Sons, 1974.

Goldenson, R. M., Dunham, J. R., & Dunham, C. S. (Eds.). *Disability and rehabilitation handbook.* New York: McGraw-Hill.

Haberman, P. W., & Baden, M. M. (1978). *Alcohol, other drugs, and violent death.* New York: Oxford University Press.

Hamby, R. I. (1970). Primary myocardial disease. *Medicine, 49,* 55–78.

Hindman, M. (1977). Child abuse and neglect: The alcohol connection. *Alcohol Health and Research World,* 2–7.

Hunter, C. W., Jr. (1982). Freestanding alcohol treatment centers–a new approach to an old problem. *Psychiatric Annals, 12* (4), 396–408.

Jellinek, E. M. (1959). Recent trends in alcoholism and in alcohol consumption. *Quarterly Journal Studies on Alcoholism, 20,* 261–269.

Jellinek, E. M. (1960). *The disease concept of alcoholism.* New Haven, CT: Hill House Press.

Johnson, V. W. (1980). *I'll quit tomorrow* (Rev. Ed.). San Francisco: Harper & Row.

Julian, V., & Mohr, C. Father-daughter incest–profile of the offender. *Denver National Study on Child Neglect and Abuse Reporting,* 1980.

Kempe, H., & Heller, R. E. (1972). *Helping the battered child and his family.* New York: Lippincott.

King, B. K., Bissell, L., & O'Brien, P. (1974). AA, alcoholism counseling and social work treatment. *Health and Social Work, 4* (4), 181–198.

Kinney, J., & Leaton, G. (1978). *Loosening the grip: A handbook of alcohol information.* St. Louis: C. V. Mosby.

Kissin, B., & Begleiter, H. (1972). *The biology of alcoholism.* New York: Plenum Press.

Krimmel, H. E. (1973). The alcoholic and his family. In P. G. Bourne & R. Fox (Eds.), *Alcoholism progress in research and treatment.* New York: Academic Press.

Leiber, C. S. (1982). Medical issues: The disease of alcoholism. In E. L. Gomberg, H. R. White, & J. A. Carpenter (Eds.), Alcohol science, and society revisited. New Brunswick: Rutgers Center of Alcohol Studies, and Ann Arbor, MI: University Press of Michigan.

Manello, T. A., & Seaman, F. J. (1979). *Prevalence, costs, and handling of drinking problems on seven railroads.* U.S. Department of Transportation Federal Railroad Administration. Washington, D.C.: University Research Corporation.

Mann, M. (1958). *New primer on alcoholism: how people drink, how to recognize alcoholics, and what to do about them.* New York: Holt, Rinehart & Winston.

Martin, J. Chalk talk on alcoholism. National Audiovisual Center. Washington, D.C.: General Services Administration, 1972.

Milam, J. R., & Ketcham, K. (1981). *Under the influence.* Seattle: Madrona Publishers.

Murphy, H. B. M. (1980). Hidden barriers to the diagnosis and treatment of alcoholism and other alcohol misuse. *Journal of Studies on Alcohol, 40* (5).

National Center for Alcohol Education. *The community health nurse and alcohol-related problems.* Rockville, MD: National Institute on Alcohol Abuse and Alcoholism, 1978.

Parsons, O. A., & Farr, S. P. (1981). The neuropsychology of alcohol and drug use. In S. B. Filskov & T. J. Boll (Eds.), *Handbook of clinical neuropsychology.* New York: John Wiley & Sons.

Rasch, J. D. (1985). *Rehabilitation of workers' compensation and other insurance claimants: Case management, forensic and business aspects.* Springfield, IL: Charles C Thomas, Publisher, Ltd.

Schneider, M.A. Some medical aspects of alcohol and other drugs of abuse. (Film narrative), Rev. 1980.

Schwartz, L., Sample, K. A., & Wegle, E. D. (1975). Severe alcoholic cardiomyopathy reversed with abstention from alcohol. *American Journal of Cardiology, 36* (12), 963–966.

Smith, J. W. (1977). Neurological disorders in alcoholism. In N.J. Estes, & M. E. Heinemann (Eds.), *Alcoholism.* St. Louis: C.V. Mosby.

Sobell, M. B., & Sobell, L. C. (1978). *Behavioral treatment of alcohol problems: Individualized therapy and controlled drinking.* New York: Plenum Press.

Streissguth, A. P., Little, R. E., Herman, C. S., & Woodell, S. (1979). IQ in children of recovered alcoholic mothers compared to matched controls. *Alcoholism: Clinical and Experimental Research, 3* (2), 197.

U.S. Department of Health, Education, & Welfare. *Fourth special report to the US. Congress on alcohol and health from the Secretary of Health and Human Services.* January 1981. National Institute on Alcohol Abuse and Alcoholism. Washington, D.C.: U.S. Government Printing Office, 1981.

U.S. Department of Transportation. *Alcohol safety action projects: Evaluation of 1972 operations.* Vol. 1 NHTSA Technical Report. Washington, DC: The Department: 1974.

Wechsler, H., & Rohman, M. (1982). Future caregivers' views on alcoholism treatment–a poor prognosis. *Journal of Studies on Alcohol, 43* (9), 939–955.

Williams, R. R., & Horn, J. W. (1977). Association of cancer sites with tobacco and alcohol consumption and socioeconomic status of patients; interview study from the Third National Cancer Survey. *Journal of National Cancer Institute, 58* (3), 525–547.

Wolkenberg, R. C., Gold, C., & Tichauer, E. R. (1975). Delayed effects of acute alcoholic intoxication of performance with reference to work safety. *Journal of Safety Research, 7,* 104.

World Health Organization, Expert Committee on Mental Health (1952). *Alcohol Subcommittee Second report.* WHO. Technical Report Series, No. 48.

Wright, G. N. (1980). *Total rehabilitation.* Boston: Little, Brown.

Wynder, E L. (1978). Epidemiology of cancers of the upper alimentary and upper respiratory tracts. *Laryngoscope, 88* (1), 50–51.

Wynder, E. L., Bross, I. J., & Feldman, R. M. (1957). A study of the etiological factors in cancer of the mouth. *Cancer, 10,* 1300–1323.

Chapter 10

WORKING WITH FAMIIES THROUGH EMPLOYEE ASSISTANCE AND WELLNESS PROGRAMS

WILLIAM S. HUTCHISON, JR.

Prevention of illness and promotion of health have become major values for America (Weiss, 1991). Two problems contributing to this development are increased longevity and the increasing costs of treating illness (Weiss, 1991). Employee assistance professionals have contributed approaches to these problems by emphasizing early treatment for human problems identified in the workplace as well as expanding health promotion programs in the workplace such as stress management and financial and retirement planning (Opatz, 1994).

In addition, Employee Assistance programs recognize a dual perspective, that a healthy workplace promotes healthy family and community living and conversely, healthy family living promotes healthier workplace performance (Keita, 1994). This article describes a theoretical framework to analyze selected wellness/health promotion programs and to draw implications for continued development of employee assistance and wellness programs.

The first part of this framework draws from the concept of family socialization, e.g., the fact that families are the primary teachers of health attitudes and behaviors (Anspaugh, 1994).

From the field of health come the concepts of health, wellness, and health promotion. Originally, health meant that the individual had no disease. However, in 1940, the World Health Organization proposed that health was "a state of physical, mental and social well-being and not merely the absence of disease" (Anspaugh, 1994). This definition has stimulated the development of the concept of wellness as engaging in attitudes and behaviors that enhance quality of life and maximize personal potential (Anspaugh, 1994). Health promotion consists of efforts that help people change their lifestyles and thereby move toward a higher state of wellness (Anspaugh, 1994).

Health promotion methods include education, treatment, and related organizations, and economic or political interventions designed to facilitate behavioral and environmental changes conducive to health (Klarreich, 1987).

Elements of a comprehensive health promotion program would include (Chenoweth, 1987):

Healthy Lifestyle Education

- Drug and alcohol awareness
- Exercise and physical fitness
- Lifting properly—body mechanics
- Nutrition
- Smoking cessation
- Stress management
- Weight control
- Sexuality

Screening, Monitoring, and Follow-Up

- Cancer screening (breast self-examination, testicular self-examination, colorectal screening)

Note: This chapter is reprinted from *Employee Assistance Programs; A Basic Text,* Second Edition (1997) with permission of the author, the book's editors (W.S. Hutchison, Jr. & W.G. Emener) and the publisher (Charles C Thomas, Publisher, Ltd.).

- Diabetes, glaucoma, sickle cell anemia
- Heart disease risk
- Hypertension screening
- Immunization (tetanus, measles for example)

Safety Promotion and Accident Prevention

- Cardiopulmonary resuscitation (CPR)
- Choke-saving techniques
- Emergency medical treatment and first-aid
- On-the-job safety
- Right to know education (potentially hazardous substances)
- Seat belt/shoulder strap usage

Employee Assistance Programs (EAP)

- Family Health Promotions
- Domestic counseling (families, marriage and family problems)
- Preparation for retirement
- Psychological counseling

There are a number of methods and techniques available to deliver the program. These include:

PRINT MATERIALS: Two general categories of print materials exist for use in health promotion: Externally produced print materials such as posters, pamphlets, payroll stuffers, calendars, newsletters, magazines, and booklets on specific or general health issues; and internally produced publicity that can include but not be limited to, announcements or program summaries appearing in the form of flyers, posters, newsletter announcements, or newspaper articles.

AUDIO-VISUAL MATERIALS: Due to the rise in popularity of "wellness," the production of audio-visual materials on various health themes has expanded. Films, videos, and slide/tape presentations are available in a wide variety of topics.

MANAGEMENT AND AUTHORITY: The authority figures in the workplace convey a tremendous message to the employee population, both directly in what they say, and indirectly in what they do not say, and how they behave. Therefore, the program can be given a marvelous boost by managers who make a personal commitment to the programs goals.

COMMITTEES: Committees are made up of carefully appointed representative employee groups that are given a serious mandate to investigate, problem-solve, monitor, and/or plan in areas that may affect employee health. The use of employee committees in overall workplace intervention can be a powerful way to expand the legitimacy of employee health concern in areas beyond the traditional individual behavior change strategies.

MICROCOMPUTER SOFTWARE: New software products are being developed continually for the health promotion market. Interactive programs are available for almost any behavior change strategy from psychotherapy to weight loss and quitting smoking.

HEALTH PROMOTION EVENTS: An excellent way to increase the visibility of the health promotion program in an organization is through the sponsorship of large, widely publicized events. Because the objective here is cultural change, not health behavior change, they are ideal for launching a new program. .

LECTURES/TALKS: There are two types of talks or lectures that are important in a workplace health promotion program; (1) a promotional talk in which staff members speak to internal groups about the program itself, and (2) a lecture by an expert on specific health or program-related topics.

WORKSHOPS/SKILLS TRAINING: In a workplace health promotion program, the purpose of any skills training intervention essentially is to teach people the skills they need to reach the goal of physical and psychological well being. Areas where workshops and training programs are beneficial include, but are not limited to, weight control, exercise, stress management, smoking cessation, blood pressure control, nutrition, cancer detection and prevention, cardiovascular fitness, communications, management, decision making, and interpersonal skills.

ONGOING PROGRAMS: Facilitate the organization of all kinds of fitness activities, such as walking during lunch hour, running, biking, swimming, or aerobics. Set up a nutrition awareness in the company cafeteria, lunchroom, or vending machine to assist in food-choice and decision-making by employees. Organize regularly scheduled public meetings to discuss a particular work-related topic with an expert.

SELF-HELP/SUPPORT GROUPS: Self-help groups are extremely helpful in providing socioemotional support for health-related topics, addiction problems, and family issues.

REFERRAL: Because no workplace will ever be able to serve all of the health and psychosocial needs of every employee, it is imperative that the health promotion program provide a source of referrals to community groups and agencies.

HEALTH RISK APPRAISALS: (HRA) A HRA is a general questionnaire that compares individual personal characteristics and behavior patterns with factors believed to increase the risk of disease, injury, or death. HRAs are used in three ways (1) to identify clusters of risk-producing behaviors in large populations, (2) to evaluate health promotion activities through administration at fixed intervals over time, and (3) to educate participants about the relationship between their behavior and health risks, thereby motivating behavior change.

It is important to remember, whatever the organization does, it needs to make certain that it has selected as wide a variety of tools as possible. In addition, it needs to recognize that the use of these tools has at least two purposes: (1) to encourage awareness of the health promotion program and participation in it, and (2) to promote incremental changes in the organizations norms regarding health.

Further research regarding this topic, produced numerous companies that have incorporated wellness in their EAPs. Some are: (1) Johnson and Johnson, (2) Control Data, (3) AT & T, (4) Speedcall Corp., (5) New York Telephone, (6) Great Salt Lake Minerals, (7) Volvo, (8) Union Carbide, (9) Tel-Med Program, (10) Robert Mason, (11) Lord Corp., and (12) Quaker Oats (Weiss, 1991; Sloan, 1987; Klarreich, 1987; Opatz, 1994). A more detailed look at Johnson & Johnson, Control Data, A T & T, and Union Carbide follows.

JOHNSON AND JOHNSON: The name of the program this company established is "Live for Life." The principal goals of this program are to provide the opportunity and encouragement for Johnson

and Johnson employees to become the healthiest in the world and to control the corporate costs of employee ill health. It is a comprehensive effort aimed at helping all employees at a work site to improve and maintain their health by establishing good health habits. Standard components include: (1) a health screening, (2) communications programs, (3) a lifestyle seminar, and (4) a variety of behavior-change-oriented action programs on numerous topics (Weiss, 1991).

Our objectives (Johnson and Johnson) include measurable, sustained lifestyle improvement among the greatest number of employees possible in regular exercise, smoking cessation, weight control, stress management, health knowledge, and awareness of medical intervention programs. (Sloan, 1987, p. 105–6)

CONTROL DATA: The name of the program this company established is "Stay Well." It is a comprehensive health promotion program designed to manage health care costs and improve productivity by reducing the level of lifestyle risk among employees and their families. StayWell was initially developed for Control Data's employees, however today, it is available to other organizations through a nationwide network of over 50 authorized distributors. The StayWell program is organized around the four key phases of the health-promotion process:

1. **awareness**,
2. **assessment**,
3. **behavior change**, and
4. **maintenance**

The StayWell program objectives fall into four broad categories:

1. To assess risk status in the eligible employee population initially subsequent time periods.
2. To evaluate StayWell components and the overall program to support further development and refinement, including;
   - participation rates and patterns;
   - participation reactions to program activities; and
   - changes in participant knowledge, attitudes, skills, and behaviors.

3. To assess the effect of the StayWell program on long-term risk reduction.
4. To determine the impact of the StayWell program on healthcare costs and productivity (e.g., absenteeism) (Weiss, 1991, p. 50).

The major components of the Stay Well program include:

1. An Employee Health Survey (EHS) that provides a corporate-wide description of health risk status.
2. An orientation to the program for all employees, on company time.
3. The Health Risk Profile and screening, with interpretations of results in group sessions.
4. Availability of lifestyle change courses in the areas of fitness, weight control, smoking cessation, nutrition, back care, and stress management.
5. Action teams, employee-led groups that concentrate on specific activities and goals, such as work site changes or lifestyle changes.
6. Special events such as health fairs or hypertension screenings (Klarreich, 1987, p. 115).

The premise of Stay Well is that if people know how to reduce preventable risks and then choose to do something about these risks, health care costs can be reduced and people can live longer, healthier, and more productive lives (Klarreich, 1987).

AT&T: The name of this company's program is "Total Life Concept." AT&T communications conducts one of the most extensive and thoroughly evaluated workplace health promotion programs. Total Life Concept was initially proposed as a way of helping employees cope with the disruption caused by massive reorganization of their work environment (Sloan, 1987).

The planning stage of AT&T's "Total Life Concept" included the following:

• Formulation of mission goals
• Objective setting
• Hypothesis development
• Analysis of health care costs
• Assessment of corporate culture and norms and

their impact on employees health (Weiss, 1991, p. 33).

The core components of Total Life Concept are as follows:

• Exercise
• Back care
• Weight management
• Smoking cessation
• Blood pressure control
• Cholesterol/nutrition monitoring
• Cancer screening/awareness
• Stress management
• Interpersonal communications (Weiss, 1991, p. 34).

Evaluation variables selected for Total Life Concept were:

• Health and job attitudes
• Health risks
• Health behaviors
• Program process (participation)
• Cost-benefit analysis (Weiss, 1991, p. 34).

The mission statement from AT&T regarding their Total Life Concept program is: "To create a corporate culture that is supportive of a healthy lifestyle" (Sloan, 1987, p. 105).

UNION CARBIDE: "Health Plus" is Union Carbide Corporations comprehensive health promotion and fitness program. This program includes the "Health Plus Fitness Program" and the "Health Plus Learning Center." The "Health Plus" program is designed to have a positive influence on individuals, the organization, and the work environment. This program provides its participants with the tools to manage their own health with an emphasis on understanding the dynamics of personal change and the environmental/organizational changes that support these changes (Klarreich, 1987).

The objectives of "Health Plus" stem from the program philosophy that endorses the prevention of health problems in a comprehensive fashion, addressing the entire persons health needs and habits in programs that contribute to Union

Carbides business objective and enhance personal quality of life and productivity (Klarreich, 1987).

The objectives relating to individuals are:

Prevention of cardiovascular disease (specifically heart attacks and strokes) through prevention and reduction of cardiovascular risk factors (tobacco smoking, elevated cholesterol, high blood pressure, physical inactivity, excessive stress, diabetes, obesity); prevention and early detection of cancer; prevention and rehabilitation of lower back pain; and the prevention of other health problems through programs that impart personal lifestyle management skills, actively involve participants in changing their lifestyles, and provide health self-management information.

Enhancement of personal effectiveness and quality of life through the development of health as defined by dynamic health rather than lack of symptoms. The objectives that support organizational business objectives are:

Economic: management and reduction of health care costs and costs resulting from disability, workman's compensation, and absenteeism as they relate to preventable, lifestyle-related causes.

Subjective employee relations parameters: recruiting and retaining high quality personnel and enhancing employee morale.

Promotion of a healthy work environment. Promotion of organizational and personal changes to promote greater productivity.

Management of occupational health issues as they relate to lifestyle (Klarreich, 1987, p. 126).

Each of these programs provides core services designed to prevent illness, increase health and promote wellness. The attainment of these program goals will reduce health care costs and keep American companies competitive in the global economy (Opatz, 1994). As these programs continue their impact, family wellness and health will be a rich area for research. In addition, program elements that are made available to nonemployee family members will allow further exploration of the potential interactive effects of family functioning and employee work performance measurers such as absenteeism, production quality and quantity, and accident rates. There is promising evidence now that Employee Assistance Programs, and health prevention and wellness programs are increasing health in the American work force (Keita, 1994). The potential for expanding the availability of these programs to employee families is an exciting opportunity.

REFERENCES

Anspaugh, D. J., Hamrick, M. H., & Rosato, F. D. (1994). *Wellness.* St. Louis: Mosby-Year Book, Inc.

Chenoweth, D. H. (1987). *Planning health promotion at the worksite.* Indianapolis, IN: Benchmark Press, Inc.

Jensen, D. W. (1987). *Worksite wellness.* Paramus, NJ: Prentice Hall Information Services.

Keita, G., and Hurrell, J. J. (1994). *Job stress in a changing workforce.* Washington, DC: American Psychological Association.

Keita, G. P., & Sauter, S. L. (Eds.) (1992). *Work and well-being.* Washington, DC: American Psychological Association.

Klarreich, S. H. (1987). *Health and fitness in the workplace: Health education in business organizations.* New York: Praeger Publishers.

Opatz, J. P. (1994). *Economic impact of worksite health promotion.* Champaign, IL: Human Kinetics Publishers.

Sloan, R. P. (1987). Investing in employee health. San Francisco: Jossey-Bass Publishers.

Weiss, S. M. (1991). *Perspectives in behavioral medicine.* Hillsdale, NJ: Lawrence Erlbaum Associates, Inc.

Chapter 11

THE MENTAL HEALTH COMPONENT OF EMPLOYEE ASSISTANCE PROGRAMS

WILLIAM S. HUTCHISON, JR. and KEELY SPRUILL

The mental health component of Employee Assistance Programs has emerged as the major area of direct concern to society, employers, and employees (Goin, 2002). From society's standpoint, mental disorders are estimated to cost 500 billion dollars a year in direct treatment costs, disability and unemployment benefits, and other entitlement program costs (Sederer, 2001). Employers incur costs for absenteeism, lowered productivity, increased health insurance premiums, extended sick and long-term disability reimbursement. It is estimated that employees suffering from depression cost employers 50 billion dollars in 2001. In addition, employees impaired by substance use disorders cost companies some 150 billion in 2001. An overall estimate for other combined mental disorders is a cost of another 150 billion per year (Sederer, 2002).

Looking at mental disorders from the standpoint of children, both preschool and school age through adolescence is another aspect of the broadening importance of mental health and EAPs. It is now recognized that a portion of employee absenteeism is a result of employees who are parents taking care of, obtaining treatment and educational assistance for their children who have mental disorders. There has been a fairly recent new development in the Student Assistance Program (SAP) movement regarding public school systems K–12. SAP's view school settings for children as identical for work settings for adults and by analogy children presenting with performance problems are offered interventions immediately in an effort to prevent the development of more serious and potentially disabling conditions (Alexander, 1999).

Combined, the personal impact of mental disorders on adult employees, their families/primary relationships and children in school is immense in human costs. The suffering of families who have lost a loved one to suicide, families split by divorce caused by the barriers created by symptoms of mental disorders including self blame, affectional inability, decreased self care, and children who suffer severely lowered self-esteem, generally lowered academic performance and frequently dropping out of school with the accompanying lowered economic potential, are prime examples.

In view of the increased need for prevention and treatment of mental disorders, there are challenges and new developments as they relate to EAPs and mental health. One of the more significant challenges is integrating EAP work with managed mental health care which emphasizes brief and time limited treatment and cost containment strategies not always congruent with the severity and treatment needs of the patient (Goins, 2002). EAP professionals are well advised to consult protocols for best practices for treatment of the mental disorders explicated in the Synopsis of Psychiatry (Kaplan & Sadock, 2002). This will assist them to advise clients they have assessed as to general expectations as well as to guide their own case management activities with clients. On the positive side, there have been several important developments which are having a positive impact on the successful treatment of mental disorders. From the biological point of view, the development of more sophisticated medications that help to restore normal functioning of specific neurotransmitter sites in the brain have greatly improved treatment outcomes of mood, anxiety, psychotic, attention deficit and hyperactivity, obsessive compulsive disorder, Tourette's and co-morbid disorders with substance use disorders. In addition, the emphasis of managed care on empirically verifiable treatment approaches has produced a number of new and effective therapy methods including: EMDR, NLP, Brief Therapy, Cognitive Behavioral Therapy and Solution Focused Therapy. Further, the research has elaborated on the combinations of medication, types of therapy, psychoeducation of family and other interventions, e.g., multisensory teaching for children with math or reading disorder, that produce improved treatment outcomes for patients (Sadock & Kaplan).

The remainder of this chapter is divided into three sections: in the first, information is presented regarding disorders and their treatment that typically begin in childhood or adolescence. This includes the involvement of family and school and concludes with approaches to prevention through the development of resiliency. The second section parallels the preceding but presents information on disorders that most frequently develop in adulthood, their treatment, the involvement of family and the workplace and concludes with approaches to prevention through an emphasis on health, wellness and stress management. The third and final section summarizes the chapter and notes directions for the future. Of particular note is the reference section that provides a comprehensive list of resources including web sites for additional research information on treatment and support services for each of these disorders.

Children and Adolescents

Mental Disorders

The diagnosis of children and adolescents with mental disorders provides unique challenges. Although mental health providers must always consider what is developmentally appropriate behavior when diagnosing a client of any age, this issue becomes critical when working with children and adolescents. Other factors also complicate the diagnosis and treatment of children and adolescents with mental disorders. The individual often does not refer themselves for treatment and may not perceive their behavior as unusual or maladaptive. As young children have limited language facility compared to older individuals, therapists may have to rely on reports from others about the child's behaviors, assessment results are usually less reliable, and children and adolescents typically have limited control of their environments.

The DSM-IV-TR (2000) provides a separate section describing disorders usually first diagnosed in infancy, childhood, or adolescence. The authors note the dual caveat that the disorders detailed in that section may not be diagnosed until later in the lifespan, and that disorders found elsewhere in the DSM-IV-TR may be diagnosed in children and adolescents. For the purposes of this chapter, the separate description of disorders typically diagnosed in childhood and adolescents provides an appropriate and useful dichotomy. Following are summaries of and commonly employed treatment techniques for each class of disorder specified by the DSM-IV-TR as usually first diagnosed in infancy, childhood, or adolescence.

Mental Retardation. A diagnosis of mental retardation requires below average cognitive ability and deficient adaptive functioning. Mental retardation is classified into the four categories of mild, moderate, severe, and profound based on the severity of the intellectual deficit. Treatment interventions include academic, vocational, adaptive skills training, and behavioral interventions to reduce other interfering behavior. School-age individuals with mental retardation typically qualify for special education services provided by the schools, which will be discussed later in this section.

Learning Disorders. A learning disorder is characterized by achievement levels significantly lower than expected based on an individual's intellectual ability, age, and educational history. The category of learning disorders includes Reading Disorder, Mathematics Disorder, and Disorder of Written Expression.

Treatment of children with learning disorders includes academic training to address specific skills deficits and cognitive strategy instruction to help increase the efficiency of information processing (Torgesen, 1980). In addition, children with learning disorders often experience associated demoralization and deficits in social skills (DSM-IV-TR). These difficulties may be addressed through parent and teacher education and direct therapy with the child.

Motor Skills Disorder. Developmental Coordination Disorder is diagnosed when a child's development of motor coordination is markedly impaired. Depending on the severity of the problem, deficits in motor coordination may require occupational and/or physical therapy.

Communication Disorders. The category of communication disorders includes two disorders affecting the ability of an individual to understand language (receptive language) and express ideas through language (expressive language), and two disorders affecting the production of speech sounds. The disorders in the former group include Expressive Language Disorder and Mixed Receptive-Expressive Language Disorder. In the latter group are Phonological Disorder wherein the child is unable to produce certain speech sounds expected for her age, and Stuttering which is characterized by disruption in speech fluency and unusual time patterning of speech. Depending on the severity of the disorder, treatment of communication disorders generally requires speech and language Therapy. Individual counseling may be indicated to address issues of self-esteem, and parent and teacher education may also be necessary to help foster understanding and introduce strategies for aiding communication.

Pervasive Developmental Disorders. Individuals with pervasive developmental disorders exhibit severe impairments in the development of normal social interaction, communication, activities, and interests. Children with Autistic Disorder display impairments in social interaction, impairments in communication, and restricted repetitive and stereotyped patterns of behavior. The other disorders in this category share these symptoms with certain differentiating features: Asperger's Disorder lacks the delays in language development, Rett's Disorder is found only in females and is characterized by a short period (5 to 8 months) of normal development after birth and Childhood Disintegrative Disorder is typified by a normal

development for the first two years of life followed by rapid loss of social interaction, language, and motor skills.

Treatment for these disorders may include neuroleptic medication to control aggression and self-injurious behavior, antianxiolytics to increase social interaction, behavioral methods including positive reinforcement and mild punishment, academic, self-care, socialization, and vocational training, and parent training and support (Schopler & Mesibov, 1986; Schopler, Reichler & Lansing, 1980).

Attention Deficit and Disruptive Behavior Disorders. Attention Deficit/Hyperactivity Disorder, Conduct Disorder, and Oppositional Defiant Disorder are the three disorders described in this section. Attention Deficit/Hyperactivity Disorder is typified by inattentiveness, hyperactivity, and impulsivity, but may present with only inattentiveness or only hyperactivity and impulsivity. Attention Deficit/Hyperactivity Disorder is often treated with stimulant medication, teacher and parent education and training, behavior management programs in the school and home including incentive systems and time-out procedures, self-monitoring programs, and psychotherapy for co-morbid depression and anxiety. A child diagnosed with Oppositional Defiant Disorder exhibits a pattern of negative, hostile, and defiant behavior which may be a precursor to Conduct Disorder. Treatment for Oppositional Defiant Disorder is primarily behavioral and includes the manipulation of behavioral antecedents, emphasizing consistent reinforcement, and the use of time out and response cost procedures. Parent and teacher training is critical to maintain the consistency of the implementation of behavioral interventions across settings. Conduct Disorder is similar to Oppositional Defiant Disorder but includes a pattern of violation of social conventions and the basic rights of others. Treatment of Conduct Disorder is similar to that of Attention Deficit/Hyperactivity Disorder and Oppositional Defiant Disorder in terms of behavioral techniques and parent and teacher training. In addition, anger management interventions may also be utilized.

Feeding and Eating Disorders of Infancy or Early Childhood. The disorders included in this section include Pica, Rumination Disorder, and Feeding Disorder of Infancy or Early Childhood. Although the three disorders are characterized by some disruption of typical food intake, the three disorders are distinct in symptomatology and treatment approach. Pica is characterized by eating nonnutritive items. Pica is usually treated though behavioral interventions such as mild punishment, overcorrection, and differential reinforcement. Rumination Disorder is a relatively rare condition in which food is repeatedly regurgitated and re-chewed. The age of onset is typically in the first year of life, so treatment usually includes parent education and promotion of healthy attachment. In Feeding Disorder of Infancy or Early Childhood the individual fails to eat adequately or gain weight. Depending on the severity of the resulting malnutrition, the first step in treatment is medical intervention to address the physical health of the child. Where parental psychopathology or neglect is suspected, child protective services may need to be involved, and parent education is critical. Direct behavioral interventions with the child may also be employed.

In addition to these disorders, the eating disorders of Anorexia Nervosa and Bulimia Nervosa often have onset in adolescence. These disorders will be discussed elsewhere in this chapter.

Tic Disorders. The DSM-IV defines a tic as "a sudden, rapid, recurrent, nonrhythmic, stereotyped motor movement or vocalization." They further state that although the individual may perceive a tic as irresistible, a tic can be suppressed for finite periods. Tic Disorders include Tourette's Disorder, Chronic Motor or Vocal Tic Disorder, Transient Tic Disorder, and Tic Disorder Not Otherwise Specified. Tourette's Disorder is characterized by individuals with both motor and vocal tics as opposed to Chronic Motor or Vocal Tic Disorder wherein both are not present. An individual diagnosed with Transient Tic Disorder experiences both motor and vocal tics over a shorter duration than in Tourette's Disorder.

The treatment of Tic Disorders may include neuroleptic medication in severe cases, and addressing the academic and social problems resulting from the tics. Education and promotion of tolerance in the environment (among teachers, peers, and family members), is also an important part of treatment to help alleviate the deleterious effects these disorders can have on the child's self-esteem. Treatment may also include addressing possible co-morbid disorders including Mood Disorders, Obsessive-Compulsive Disorder, Anxiety Disorders, Learning Disorders, and Attention Deficit/Hyperactivity Disorder.

Elimination Disorders. Elimination Disorders include Encopresis, the passage of feces into places not appropriate, and Enuresis, or urination into bed or clothing. The diagnosis of either disorder is made regardless of whether the behavior is involuntary or intentional. When treating Encopresis where withholding of feces has been involved, medical intervention may first be necessary to remove fecal impaction, and dietary changes may be indicated. Treatment interventions also include behavioral therapy and parent education to decrease use of punitive measures. Enuresis is most common at night during sleep, and may be treated with medications such as imiprimine or tofranil. Behavioral techniques for nocturnal enuresis also include the use of equipment such as a moisture-sensitive pad on the bed that triggers a bell when the child urinates. For diurnal enuresis, retention control training may also be employed.

Other Disorders of Infancy, Childhood, or Adolescence. This final section includes the miscellaneous grouping of Separation Anxiety Disorder, Selective Mutism, Reactive Attachment Disorder, and Stereotypic Movement Disorder. Children experiencing Separation Anxiety Disorder exhibit extreme anxiety when separated from home or people to whom they are attached. Treatment typically involves cognitive behavioral approaches with the child and family members. In Selective Mutism, children fail to speak in certain social situations, yet converse freely in other settings. Selective Serotonin Reuptake Inhibitors (SSRI's) are sometimes employed as a part of treatment. In addition, behavioral approaches such as contingency management, stimulus fading, and self-modeling are also considered effective (Sadock & Kaplan). Reactive Attachment Disorder is an apparently uncommon disorder in which a child displays disturbed social relatedness. As this disorder is usually presumed to arise from patho-genic care, treatment involves parent education and possible intervention of social services. Children with Stereotypic Movement Disorder exhibit the repetitive, nonfunctional behavior patterns typical in children with Autistic and other Pervasive Developmental Disorders; however, the other criteria for those disorders are not met. Although limited information is available regarding this condition, these children may be candidates for pharmacological treatment, especially if their behavior is self-injurious.

Collaboration with the Schools and Family

As noted previously, mental health interventions with children and adolescents can be complicated by the fact that the client often has little or no control over his or her environment. In addition, behavioral interventions are often more successful than individual therapy, particularly with children (Weitz et al., 1999). Given these factors, collaboration and consultation with teachers and caregivers is an essential component of working with children and adolescents.

Consultation. In consultation, a therapist works directly with teachers and caregivers on identifying areas of difficulty for the client and developing intervention strategies to address these areas of need. The consultee then directly implements the strategies discussed and continues to meet with the consultant to modify the strategies as needed. For example, in behavioral consultation with the child's teacher, a mental health professional would first attempt to talk with the teacher and narrow down her complaints into one to three "target behaviors." These behaviors would be clearly defined in operational terms by the teacher and consultant so that progress can be objectively measured. The consultant would then work with the teacher on interventions for the teacher to implement to specifically address the target behaviors.

Special Education. Many, although not all, children who are diagnosed with a disorder based on the criteria described in the DSM-IV will also qualify for special services in the schools.

Depending on the type of disorder, and the degree to which it impairs the child's ability to function in the school environment, a child with a disability may receive services mandated under the Individuals with Disabilities Education Act (IDEA) or Section 504 of the Rehabilitation Act of 1973.

An in-depth discussion of the differences between IDEA and Section 504 is beyond the scope of this chapter. Briefly, IDEA is a Federal statute that provides funding to states to ensure adequate and appropriate services for school-age children who qualify in one or more of 13 specific areas of disabilities. Section 504 is civil rights legislation providing equal access to schools receiving federal funding of school-age children who meet the definition of a handicapped person. All students who qualify for services under IDEA are also afforded protection under Section 504; however, many students protected under Section 504 do not meet the criteria for services under IDEA.

Both IDEA and Section 504 require a group of individuals who are knowledgeable about the child to determine eligibility and write a plan for the student that allows for the provision of a free and appropriate public education. These multidisciplinary team meetings offer excellent opportunities for consultation with school staff and parents.

Approaches to Primary Prevention

Risk and Resiliency. Garmezy (1982) defined resilience as coping and adapting well in the face of major, enduring life stress. The study of risk and resiliency seeks to identify why some individuals adapt and succeed in the face of circumstances that contribute to negative outcomes in most individuals. The information provided in the study of effective adaptation in children considered to be at risk is important in considering effective preventive interventions (Masten, 1989). In a review of research, Garmezy (1985) identified three categories of protective factors: dispositional attributes of the child, family warmth, security, cohesion, and availability of supports outside of the family.

Primary Prevention Programs. Primary prevention in mental health is a type of early intervention targeted to normal and at-risk populations who have not yet developed a mental disorder or other difficulty. These interventions are oriented to a group, rather than the individual. For example, programs such as DARE (Drug Abuse Resistance Education) in school settings attempt to prevent alcohol and drug abuse through awareness and education programs for pre-teen students. In addition to awareness programs targeted to children and adolescents, primary prevention may also include programs for the promotion of competency in parents and teachers, environmental and systems change, and identifying at-risk individuals (Reinherz, 1979). Programs for primary prevention in youth target such diverse areas as eating disorders, gang involvement, suicide, and emotional disorders (Esbensen, 2000; Sandoval et al., 1987).

Additional Disorders

The DSM-IV-TR notes that the division of disorders by the age of presentation is for convenience and also because some disorders are exclusive to an age. Further, "clinicians" should be familiar with the entire classification due to this consideration (DSM-IV-TR).

Cognitive Disorders. The primary symptom common to these disorders is memory loss. The disorders include dementia of the alzheimer's type, multi-infart dementia, amnestic disorder, dementia due to general medical condition and dementia due to effect of substance use. Treatment is based on an accurate diagnosis of the underlying etiology and requires a complete medical evaluation. Treatment almost always requires medication and a combination of supervised activities of daily living along with adequate sleep, nutrition, physical and social activity. Cognitive behavioral psychotherapy for the patient along with psychoeducational counseling with family and community caregivers provide a comprehensive and empirically verified combination of interventions that enhance treatment outcomes.

Schizophrenia and other Psychotic Disorders

The most prominent feature of this group of disorders is psychotic symptoms (delusion and/or hallucinations). Five specific disorders are identified: (1) Schizophrenia; (2) Schizophreniform; (3) Delusional; (4) Brief Psychotic; and (5) Shared Psychotic. Differential diagnosis requires medical evaluation to ascertain if an underlying condition is causing the psychotic symptoms (lead poisoning stroke). Antipsychotic mediation is almost always the treatment of choice. Supportive and structured psychotherapy emphasizing activities of daily living and assuring the meeting of basic physical needs and hospitalization are essential during the acute phases. During the remission phases structured living arrangements with caregivers and ongoing psychosocial treatment focusing again on ADLS and medication monitoring are ideal.

Work with family is important specifically to educate them on known etiology, medication, communication with patient, signs of decompensation, and assistance with financial matters including health insurance, medical care, social security disability, or supplemental security income, and housing assistance.

Mood Disorders

Depressed mood is the common symptom of each of the five disorders in this category. However, manic and hypomanic moods are also present in Bipolar I and II as well as Cyclothymia. Major Depression and Dysthymia are the other two mood disorders. As with all other disorders, underlying medical conditions may cause these disorders and the patient should be examined to determine if such is the case. Treatment of choice is first a consideration of antidepressant medication combined with cognitive behavioral therapy that focuses on logical self talk and developing a prescribed daily regimen of physical and social activities appropriate to the patients' level of physical and mental ability.

Working with the family focuses on allowing them to express feelings (usually without the patient present, but with permission). Frequently they are frustrated that the patient is doing so little. Explaining the nature of these illnesses in terms of chemical imbalances and affirming the normalcy of the feeling the family is experiencing, typically lead to more constructive communication between the patient and family. Likewise, letting everyone in on treatment (with patient's permission) enhances treatment compliance.

Anxiety Disorders

Anxiety is the common symptom of eight disorders which include: (1) Panic Disorder without Agoraphobia; (2) Panic Disorder with Agoraphobia: (3) Specific Phobia, (4) Social Phobia; (5) Obsessive-Compulsive Disorder; (6) Posttraumatic Stress Disorder, (7) Acute Stress Disorder; and (8) Generalized Anxiety Disorder. Once underlying medical conditions, e.g., hyperthyroidism, cardiovascular disease have been ruled out etiologically treatment of choice becomes antianxiety medication (xanax, valium, etc.) or the more sedating antidepressant (paxil, zoloft) combined with cognitive behavioral procedures (Sadock & Kaplan, 1998). Thought stopping, rational self-talk, covert and envivo desensitization, EMDR, NLP, and systematic desensitization coupled with psychoeducation regarding the disorder have proven successful. Family work includes psychoeducation and communication between the family and patient regarding the disorder and treatment so that a mutual support system can be built.

Somatoform Disorders

The common symptoms of these disorders are physical symptoms without a biological etiology (e.g., medical condition or substance induced). The disorders are: (1) Somatization Disorder; (2) Undifferentiated Somatoform Disorder; (3) Conversion Disorder: (4) Pain Disorder; (5) Hypochondriasis; and (6) Body Dysmorphic Disorder. Ruling out biological etiology is the first order of diagnostic procedure. (Only medications that reduce or eliminate the physical symptoms have proved effective in treating these disorders. Biofeedback, hypnosis, relaxation training and psychodynamic psychotherapy have proven useful.) Discounting the physical symptom, as "psychological" or "all in your head" has proven ineffective (fortunately most patients with these disorders have strong enough ego defenses to ward off these

clumsy approaches). Family reframing to work with the patient in recovering from the disorder is helpful to use secondary gain in the recovery goal.

Dissociative Disorders

Suspension of consciousness, memory, identity or perception manifest in the following four disorders: (1) Dissociative Amnesia: (2) Dissociative Fugue; (3) Dissociative Identity Disorder; and (4) Depersonalization Disorder. When assessment confirms any of the first three of these diagnoses then a discussion with the patient about the use of insight-oriented procedures including hypnotherapy, amytal interview and ultimately the integration of the dissociated trauma into an acceptable part of the patient's self-concept is discussed. It is critical to establish this therapeutic alliance so that the patient feels in control as he/she works to confront painful memories and gain empowerment through her/his courageous encounters (Nichols & Schwartz, 1998). Therapeutic contracts for safety are essential along with family education. Family members who have perpetrated patient trauma should not be included. Abuse reports may be required in the case of children with disorder and assisting adult client to decide if and how they wish to proceed in confronting abusers.

Sexual and Gender Identity Disorders

The three subcategories in this class are: (1) Sexual Dysfunctions are disturbances in normal sexual functioning; (2) Paraphillias are sexual behaviors that cause distress or impairment in important areas of social functioning and frequently lead to illegal acts (pedophilia, necrophilia, exhibitionism . . .); and (3) Gender Identity Disorder in which there is strong cross gender identification and consistent discontent with the individual's biological sex. Treatment for each of these subcategories varies substantially. Sexual dysfunctions require differential diagnosis to rule out physical etiologies. Treatment includes psychoeducation, sex therapy (including couples therapy when possible) by certified and licensed sex therapists. Treatment for these disorders is primarily based on extensive research conducted by

Masters and Johnson and their associates over the last 25 years (Sadock & Kaplan). Treatment of the pedophilias includes behavioral approaches along with support groups and the 12-step models. Frequently the legal system is involved with individuals having these disorders. Finally, individuals with gender identity disorder may suffer so strongly that they seek to biologically alter their assigned gender through surgery and hormonal therapy. Only specially certified sex therapists and physicians should work with individuals with this disorder due to the very specific legal/medical and psychological issues involved (Sadock & Kaplan).

Eating Disorder

Anorexia Nervosa and Bulimia Nervosa are the two disorders in this group and abnormal eating behaviors are the common symptom in each. With anorexia there is a refusal to maintain normal body weight (85% of weight for the person's age and height–usually pediatric growth charts or Metropolitan Life Insurance tables). Binge eating followed by self-induced vomiting, laxative and diuretic use, fasting or excessive exercise are disturbances seen with Bulimia. Treatment begins by assuring the medical safety of the patient and proceeds to a systematic combination of structured and balanced nutrition; individual cognitive-behavioral psychotherapy and a long-term supportive relationship approach are treatments of choice.

Medication to treat the frequently co-occurring conditions of anxiety and depression is essential when present. Family therapy to reframe secondary gain issues of being special because of the disorder is helpful such as seeking to attain education or career success while despite the disorder.

Sleep Disorders

A disturbance of the normal sleep pattern that interferes with an individual's social functioning is the common feature of the four subcategories of this disorder. Primary Sleep Disorder is believed to arise from endogenous abnormalities in sleep-wake mechanisms. Sleep disorders related to another mental disorder result from the disturbed physiology caused by the mental disorder and is severe enough to require separate treatment. The third condition is Sleep Disorders due to a General Medical Condition such as severe pain caused by orthopedic conditions, cancer, etc. Finally, there are Substance-Induced Sleep Disorders caused by the use of and then discontinuance of substances, e.g., cocaine use and withdrawal from alcohol, etc.

Sleep clinics are an excellent source of specialized diagnosis and treatment for these disorders. Medical treatment is the first treatment of choice and depending on the condition, offers a variety of useful treatments from c-pap oxygen machines for sleep apnea, sleep medication, biofeedback. Additional cognitive-behavioral approaches including systematic sleep protocol, relaxation training, hypnosis, and NLP are useful. Psychoeducation for the family is important since sleep disorder can interrupt the family members sleep (particularly spouses), cause lethargy, decreased functional ability and job loss. Vocational rehabilitation is frequently a useful part of a patient's return to full functioning.

Impulse Control Disorders

Failure to resist an impulse and to act in a way that is harmful to the person or to others is the common symptom of this group of disorders. Trichotillomania means a person pulls out their hair for pleasure or relief of tensions resulting in noticeable hair loss. Pathological gambling results in financial, social, and sometime physical injury to the individual. Setting fires for pleasure or tension reduction are symptoms of Pyromania while stealing objects not needed for personal use or gain is a symptom of Kleptomania. Serious assaults and destruction of property by not resisting aggressive impulses are symptoms of Intermittent Explosive Disorder. Treatment of each of these disorders is distinctly unique and the reader is referred to Sadock and Kaplan (1998) for an excellent summary of treatments for this category.

Adjustment Disorders

These five disorders have in common emotional or behavioral symptoms that appear in response to an identifiable stressor within three months of the stressors appearance. The disorders do not meet the criteria for any other mental disorder and include Adjustment Disorder with: (1) depressed mood; (2) anxiety; (3) mixed anxiety and depression; (4) disturbance of conduct; and, (5) disturbance of emotions and conduct. Treatment includes cognitive behavioral procedures that reduce symptoms through rational self-talk, relaxation-training removal of stressor (e.g., finding a new job if stressor was job loss), grief work and supporting person's strengths. Family work includes psychoeducation as to the nature of persons' reactions to stressors and problem-solving approaches to find resolution.

Personality Disorder

These 10 disorders are characterized by traits and behaviors that are pervasive and deviate from cultural norms. Individuals with these disorders frequently do not recognize the impact of their deviance on others and typically they do not seek treatment on their own but come to treatment under duress (legal, spousal, parents, threatened job loss). The ten personality disorders are: (1) Paranoid; (2) Schizoid; (3) Schizotypal; (4) Antisocial; (5) Borderline; (6) Histrionic; (7) Narcissistic: (8) Avoidant; (9) Dependent; and (10) Obsessive-Compulsive. Treatment of these disorders is idiosyncratic to each disorder and again the readers are referred to Sadock and Kaplan (1998) as well as the reference section of this article. It is important to note that since the main feature of all but one of these disorders is denial of the disorder (unconscious ego defense) that clinicians and social policy has thought of these conditions as untreatable. However, it is becoming clearer that clinicians who are patient and adept at discovering hidden motivations within the patient (ego ideal—who the person wishes they were or simply to avoid the negative consequences of nonconforming behavior) are examples of this approach. Family work when indicated includes psychoeducation and communicative problem solving (Nichols & Schwartz, 1998).

The Family and the Workplace

It has been suggested there is a dual and reciprocal relationship between the family and individuals' family members workplace, (Hutchison, 1997). Thus, positive and negative variables from each setting are exported to the alternate setting. For instance, an employee may receive a raise and share by taking the family to dinner. Likewise, an employee could come to work sharing smiles and compliments to co-workers after the children make the academic honor roll. Most of us have heard of the converse situation where an employee abates family members after being criticized by the supervisor as well as the employee who is sullen and silent at work after a heated argument at home occurring as they left for work. These are simple examples of stressors affecting individuals and it is well documented that the type and number of stressors increase within a 12-month time period. The resulting stress syndrome produces physical and mental illness or both (Sadock & Kaplan).

Employees assistance programs can assist in both primary and secondary prevention in a number of ways:

1. Education
2. Teaching communication skills
3. Consulting in the development of work place policies and procedures

Programs that provide information on the sign and symptoms of stress syndromes, mental and physical disorders have been delivered at the work place through newsletters, web sites, videos and other media tools (Hutchison, 1997). It is particularly important that education emphasize appropriate communication skills, including how to assess the problem, develop a plan of approach and carry out the plan (OPTUM, 2002).

Workplace policies and procedures need to address performance problems to determine if the workplace is iatrogenic and when it is, to develop policies to correct the situation. Likewise, when this is not the case, employees should be encouraged (and in certain situations mandated) to seek EAP assistance.

Primary Prevention

There is a large body of research on the genetic bases of mental disorders (Dobberfuhl, 2002). EAP professionals can stay apprized of this information through web sites and reading so that they can provide education to employees and organization they serve. Likewise, psychological/physical approaches to primary prevention are being delivered through health promotion and wellness programs through the EAP. These approaches include stress management, nutrition counseling, sleep training, physical fitness programs, smoking cessation, and spiritual awareness (clarity of life meaning for the person), mediation, relaxation training, financial planning, parenting skills, marital communication, and dealing successfully with change (Hutchison, 2002).

CONCLUSION

We have outlined the essential knowledge needed for employee assistance professionals to deliver services in the area of mental health. Brief information regarding signs, symptoms, and treatment for disorders of childhood and adulthood were presented. Methods of working with families and schools as well as families in the workplace have been described. Approaches to the prevention of mental illness were outlined and referenced. References follow to a wide variety of web sites and organizations which can provide information and support to the professional in the field of mental health.

REFERENCES

Alexander, W. (1999). Personal communication regarding student assistance programs. (SAP).

American Psychiatric Association. (1998). *DSM-IV-TR* (4th Edition).

Darling, H. (2002). Rising health care cost in *EAP Digest,* 32.2.

Dobberfuhl, A. M. (2002). Personal communication regarding the genetics of mental health.

Esbensen, F., & Osgood, D. W. (1999). Grand resistance education and training: Results from the national evaluation. *Journal of Research in Crime and Delinquency, 36* (2), 194–225.

Goins, M. (2002). Raising the profile of workplace mental health in *EAP Digest,* 32, 4.

Garmezy, N. (1982). Foreword in E. E. Werner & R. S. Smith, *Vulnerable but invincible: A study of resilient children.* (pp. xiii–xix). New York: McGraw-Hill.

Garmezy, N. (1985). Stress Resistant Children: The Search for Protective Factors. In J.E. Stevenson (Ed.), *Recent research in developmental psychopathology* (pp. 313–233). Oxford Pergamon Press.

Hutchison, W. (1997). Family Wellness in Employee Assistance Programs. In W.S. Hutchison & W.G. Emener (Eds.). *Employee assistance programs: A basic text* (2nd Edition) Springfield, IL: Charles C. Thomas, Publisher, Ltd.

Kaplan, H., & Sadock, B. (1998). *Synopsis of psychiatry* (8th Edition). John Wiley and Sons.

Nichols, M., & Schwartz, R. (1998). *Family therapy: Concepts and methods* (5th Edition). Allyn and Bacon.

Masten, A. S. (1989). Resilience in development. Implications of the successful adaptation for developmental psychopathology. In Cicchetti (ed.), Rochester Symposium on Developmental Psychopathology. Hillsdale, NJ: Erlbaum.

OPTUM (2002). Optum Trainer Performance Expectations, Golden Valley, MN.

Reinherz, H. Z. (1979). Primary prevention of emotional disorders of children: Mirage or reality. (ERIC Documentation Reproduction Services No. Ed170969).

Sederer, L. (2001). The business case for quality mental health services: Why employees should care about the mental health and well being of their employees. *Journal of Occupational and Environmental Medicine.*

Schopler, E., Reichler, R. J., & Lansing, M. (1980). *Individualized assessment and treatment for developmentally disabled children.* Austin, TX: Pro-Ed.

Schopler, E., & Mesbov, G. B. (1986). *Social behavior in autism.* New York: Plenum Press.

Segal, E., & Brzuzy, S. (1998). *Social welfare policy. Program practice.* Ithasca, IL: F.E. Peacock.

Torgesen, J. K. I. (1980). Conceptual and educational implications of the use of efficient task strategies by learning disabled children. *Journal of Learning Disabilities, 13* (7), 364, 371

Weiss, B., & Weosz, K. R. (1995) Relative effectiveness of behavioral versus non-behavioral child psychotherapy. *Journal of Consulting and Clinical Psychology, 63* (2), 317–320.

WEB SITES

AD/HD and Disruptive Behavior Disorders
   http://www.chadd.org
   http://www.conductdisorders.com
Anxiety Disorders
   http://www.adaa.org
Communication Disorders
   http://www.asha.org
Dissociative Disorders
   http://www.issd.org
Eating Disorders
   http://www.anred.com
   http://www.nationaleatingdisorders.org
General Mental Health Resources
   http://www.mentalhelp.net
   http://www.mentalheath.com
   http://www.nimh.nih.gov
   http://www.psycho.org/public info

Learning Disorders
   http://www.allkindsofminds.org
   http://www.Idonline.org
Mental Retardation
   http://www.aamr.org
   http://www.thearc.org
Mood Disorders
   http://www.ndmda.org
   http://www.depression.org
Pervasive Developmental Disorders
   http://www.teacch.com
   http://www.asperger.org
Special Education
   http://www.ideapractices.org
   http://www.cec.sped.org
Schizophrenia/Psychotic Disorders
   http://www.schizophrenia.com
Tic Disorders
   http://www.tourette-syndrome.com

Part IV

PROGRAM PLANNING AND EVALUATION

Chapter 12

PROGRAM PLANNING AND EVALUATION OF EMPLOYEE ASSISTANCE PROGRAMS: FOUNDATIONS AND CONCEPTS

WILLIAM G. EMENER and BONNIE L. YEGIDIS

The concept of evaluation can easily have different meanings to people. "Evaluation" includes a determination of the relative importance of something, an extent to which a predetermined goal or expectation has been attained, and the relative effectiveness or efficiency of specific activities or sets of activities. When individuals plan a program, they typically consider some entity (e.g., events, people, activities) to be important, they have some preconceived goals or expectations in mind, and they have relative expectations regarding the activities and outcomes of the activities under consideration. For reasons such as these, program planning and program evaluation are interrelated and their relationship to one another is, at times, equally or more important than they are by themselves. Program evaluation and program planning of any quality, must include a relationship factor–consider, for example, Trantow's (1970) definition of program evaluation:

> Evaluation is essentially an effort to determine what changes occur as the result of a planned program by comparing actual changes (results) with desired changes (stated goals) and by identifying the degree to which the activity (planned program) is responsible for the changes. (p. 3)

With some Aristotelian logic, the following "If–Then" argument concretizes the importance of the relationship between program planning and program evaluation:

- **If** when people plan a program they do not have specific outcomes or outcome effects in mind (results);
- **If** they do not consider their expected outcomes to be important (stated goals);
- **If** the outcomes or outcome effects are not discernible (observable or measurable);
- **Then** why have the program in the first place? Thus, assuming that there are valid answers to this latter question, there are some general reasons for conducting program evaluations; for example:

1. **Vindication.** At times, it is important to collect facts (data) to illustrate and demonstrate that a program is worthwhile. Justifying a program's existence and its continuance can be a very important function (especially if resources are scarce or threatened).

2. **Salesmanship.** It may be desirable to expand or extend parts of a program into new areas. Activities such as these frequently require the convincing of others that expansion or extension is worthwhile, and program evaluation facts (data) can be very useful.

3. **Verification.** In an era of "high accountability," it is not uncommon for people to say, "It's not that I don't trust you, but could you show me some evidence. . . ." Verifying worth and impact is important to a program's survival.

4. **Improvement.** In order to improve a program, program leaders typically attempt to minimize a program's weaknesses and maximize a pro-

Note: This chapter is reprinted from *Employee Assistance Programs: A Basic Text* (1988) with permission of the author, the book's editors (Dickman, Emener, &: Hutchison, Jr.), and the publisher (Charles C Thomas, Publisher, Ltd.).

gram's strengths. Analyzing facts about a program can not only specify strengths and weaknesses, but also suggest their magnitude and overall impact on program outcomes (results and effects).

5. **Understanding.** Program improvement requires knowledge and understanding of how a program works and why a program works. Program evaluation activities cannot always totally answer questions such as these, but indeed it can enhance one's understanding of the how? and why? aspects of a program.

6. **Accountability.** Beyond the genuine commitment to excellence on behalf of a program's leaders, programs are frequently under much pressure to demonstrate effectiveness, "results that show a difference–an impact." Direct funding sources (e.g., governmental bodies, grant agencies) and indirect funders (e.g., taxpayers, insurance companies' premium-paying constituents), insist on holding programs accountable for producing results. This funding source reality can be responded to in an effective manner if a strong program evaluation component is part of the infrastructure of a program.

There are numerous programmatic interaction effects that also deserve recognition. For example, high quality program planning includes important attributes such as specificity, objectivity, awareness of detail, reality factors, and tempered (realistic) goal setting. Program evaluation facilitates program planners' attention to attributes such as these, and this aspect of program planning has been found to be critical to high quality programs.

Beyond Planning and Evaluation

Good, high quality, efficient and effective programs operationalize the tenet: "Every program should be continually striving for improvement." From a philosophical point of view, it is suggested that while ultimate program improvement is an important aspect of a program, the process of "continuous striving for program improvement" is an important aspect of a program in and of itself. Programs that are remedial, restorative, preventative and/or curative in nature (e.g., rehabilitation programs, employee assistance programs), occa-

sionally suggest that in view of their preventative mission(s), their ultimate goal is to go out of business–viz, to ultimately establish a condition in which there is no longer a need for the program. It is important for such programs to remain cognizant of their "ultimate" goals, and utilize their program evaluation components to drive their program initiatives closer and closer toward their "ultimate" goals.

The Program Planning and Program Evaluation Cycle

There are alternative models of program evaluation. For example, there is the **goal attainment model** which focuses on measuring the extent to which a program achieves the objectives which it set out to achieve; also, there is the **systems analysis approach** which focuses on the extent to which a program's functional organizational units demonstrate their worth in accomplishing the program's objectives. (These two approaches typically are not mutually exclusive–most program evaluation systems designed for a specific program are composed of components of more than one program evaluation model or approach.) Nonetheless, no matter which model or approach, or combinations of models or approaches, is best for a given evaluation program, the assessment procedures must be linked to the program planning. The missions, goals, and objectives of a program are often a result of personal, subjective, philosophical, and/or political initiatives. It is usually the case, however, that as program planners translate ambiguous mission, goal and objective statements into functional, operationally defined, and evaluative/measurable entities, resulting program plans gain greater potentials for success. The program planning and program evaluation processes typically follow a pattern of development, and a movement "from the general to the specific."

Program Mission. This is generally a nonspecific yet comprehensive statement regarding the purpose and rationale for the developing and continuing existence of a program. In effect, the program's mission is its **raison d'etre**–an indirect response to the "why?" question of the program's existence.

Program Goals. From the program's mission(s) emerge action statements related to the program's client-, customer-, and/or consumer-related activities. While program goals have some attributes similar to a program's mission(s), for example they tend to be related to the program's intentions, they suggest directionality and are not time bound, they are dissimilar in that they can change and usually are responsive to changing program priorities.

Program Objectives. Pivotal to program planning is the determination of program objectives which clearly specify the specific "how's?" and "when's?" of program goal(s) attainment. As opposed to missions and goals, program objectives are specific, concrete, and time-limited. By their nature and character, program objectives are assessment related. Three key attributes of a program's objectives must exist–they must be **observable**, within or over a specific **time frame**, and they must be identified in **measurable** ways.

Overall, a program's mission statement(s), goals and objectives: (a) define the purpose of the program; (b) define the reason for the program's existence; and, (c) indicate how and by when the program's goals will be attained. The next logical part of this consideration of a program is program

evaluation.

Program Evaluation. Later in this chapter, some of the alternative ways program evaluation responds to questions regarding a program's mission(s), goals and objectives, will be presented. Importantly, the program evaluation component responds to questions such as: "Is the program doing what it is supposed to be doing?" "Is the program having the effect it is supposed to have?" "Is the program doing what it is doing efficiently and effectively?" With reliable, valid, and objective responses to questions such as these, program planners can then engage in program review, program refinement, and program modification activities.

Thus, the program planning and program evaluation cycle continues–hopefully, it continues in such a way that as time goes on the program continues to improve. This cyclical process is displayed in Figure 12-1. A fuller and richer appreciation of the importance of program evaluation and its important influences on program planning and program refinement can be enhanced by understanding the essential questions to be addressed by an evaluation. According to Mayer (1985) these are:

Phase I.   Phase II.

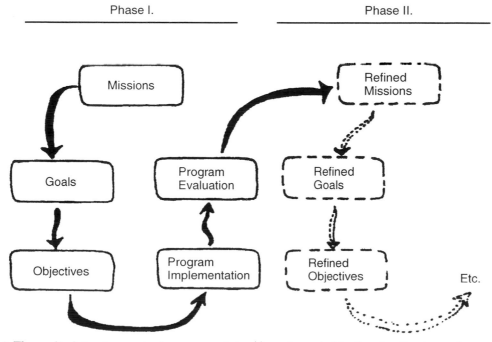

Figure 12-1. The cyclical development of program mission(s), goals, and objectives leading toward program refinement.

1. Was the program implemented as intended?
2. Were the program objectives achieved?
3. Was the program effective?
4. Was the program efficient?

Was the Program Implemented as Intended? This component of evaluation assesses whether a program was implemented according to plan. This is important because a given operational program may function very differently than how it was intended to, and similarly may bring about different outcomes than were planned. Therefore, an analysis that examines the degree of consistency between program plans and actual program activities is crucial. Evaluating these program plans, inputs, and activities is frequently termed process evaluation. Process evaluation involves monitoring program inputs, resources, efforts, and activities.

Were the Program Objectives Achieved? Key to a program evaluation is the determination of whether specified program objectives were actually achieved. A program may affect unintended consequences, but it is the intended outcomes (objectives) that are of primary interest. This kind of evaluation is known as outcome or product evaluation. In order to determine whether program objectives were achieved, evaluators must develop or locate measures that will tap the program objectives. Suchman (1967) stated that the kinds of outcomes that may be measured include knowledge, attitudes, skills, and behaviors.

Perhaps the most direct method of determining whether program objectives were achieved is to compare before program measures with after program measures on specific objectives. If the after program measures reflect a change in the desired direction from the before program measures, then it could be concluded that the program objectives have been met.

Was the Program Effective? One way to address whether or not a program was effective is to conceptualize a model of the processes and results of the program (Van Maaren, 1978). Thus, measuring the objectives of a program (as previously discussed) also provides an assessment of program effectiveness. This is so because if program objectives were achieved, then it can be inferred that the program activities brought about the desired change in the measurement of objectives. This is tantamount to concluding that the intervention caused the desired change.

In evaluation, we typically determine program effectiveness through implementing some type of experimental design. The logic of experimental design enables the evaluator to make the kind of conclusions about the program's effectiveness in which we are most interested. (For a more indepth discussion of experimental designs, the reader may consult nearly any standard social science research text.)

Was the Program Efficient? The aspect of efficiency taps the relationship of outcome to efforts. Assessing program efficiency requires determining the costs of the program in terms of time, energy, and resources and relating these costs to the program's effects. Essentially, program efficiency is evaluated by cost-benefit or cost-effectiveness analyses, depending upon what types of objectives are the subject of evaluation.

Utilization of Evaluation Results

The Benefits of Program Evaluation

As outlined in an earlier section of this chapter, securing and disseminating evaluation findings is critical for the program planner/evaluator. Evaluation data enable one to demonstrate empirically what the program activities were (verification), what outcomes were achieved and at what costs (accountability). Appropriate utilization of evaluation findings allows one to tune up or modify program activities to improve and enhance program outcomes. Moreover, evaluation data permit planners and administrators to justify continued or enhanced program funding.

The Political Context of Evaluation

There is a political reality to program evaluation, though, that must be understood by planners and researchers. Part of this political context is determined by the nature of the decisions that may be made as a result of the evaluation. Such decisions are basically either: (a) to continue operating the program as planned and implemented; (b) to modify the program or some component of the program; or (c) to terminate the program or one or more of its components. The reality of these alternative decisions may create difficulties among staff members and administrators (the decision makers), and between the evaluator and various constituent groups.

Additionally, there may be other political issues that the EAP evaluator is not even aware of–for example, the careers and egos of various personnel involved in, or affected by, the evaluation. While there are no cookbook responses on how to deal with these real and potential political issues, they are important considerations for the evaluator. The role of the evaluator, nonetheless, requires one to conduct him/herself in a professional and ethically responsible fashion.

CONCLUDING COMMENT

Programs, typically, are designed, developed, and implemented as a result of individuals' operationalized concern for the common good–for improving the existence and the essence of life for a targeted constituency group. For example, one of the primary reasons why companies and employers will institute employee assistance programs in their organizations and businesses is because they care about their employees and the quality of their lives. They want to be helpful to them. Assuring that program evaluation is an integral part of their programs, from the beginning and throughout, is an excellent way of assuring that their caring about their employees, viz helping them with their problems and difficulties, is what the program is doing. Reasons such as this should compel us to be sure that our program evaluation components of our EAPs are the best they can be–that way, our EAPs can be the best they can be!

REFERENCES

Mayer, R. R. (1985). *Policy and program planning.* A developmental perspective. Englewood Cliffs, NJ: Prentice Hall, Inc.

Suchman, E. A. (1967). *Evaluative research.* New York: Russell Sage Foundation.

Trantow, D. (1970). An introduction to evaluation: Program effectiveness and community needs. *Rehabilitation Literature, 31,* 2–9.

Van Maaren, J. (1978). The process of program evaluation. Washington, D.C. National training and development service. *The Grantmanship News.* Jan.-Feb.

Chapter 13

PROGRAM PLANNING AND EVALUATION OF EMPLOYEE ASSISTANCE PROGRAMS: RATIONALE, TYPES, AND UTILIZATION

JASON LIGON and BONNIE L. YEGIDIS

It has been reported that since the early 1990s, about 80 percent of organizations having over 250 workers offer employee assistance programs (White, McDuff, Schwartz, Tiegel & Judge, 1996) while 45 percent of all of those employed full-time have access to programs (French, Zarkin & Bray, 1995). Services offered by employee assistance programs (EAP) have greatly expanded from a focus on alcohol problems in the 1950s to providing services for financial problems, wellness programs, and stress management seminars (White et al., 1996).

At the same time, organizations have increasingly moved to managed care models to control and reduce their expenditures on behavioral health care services. In some programs, the EAP now functions as the gatekeeper to other mental health and substance abuse services (White et al., 1996) and large national service providers market both EAP and managed care products (Winegar, 1993). While more expansive information concerning managed behavioral health care is available elsewhere (Corcoran & Vandiver, 1996; Hoyt, 1995), increasing pressures to evaluate both practice (Corcoran & Vandiver, 1996) and programs (Chartier, 1995; Winegar, 1993) prevail.

While the intent of research is primarily to test hypotheses and develop new knowledge, program evaluation has a very different purpose. Program evaluations are charged with determining the worth or value of a program by assessing whether the program was effective or ineffective in reaching "a given action, process, or product" (Isaac & Michael, 1982, p. 2). Evaluations seek to determine if the target population was reached, whether or not the program was effective, and at what cost (Rossi & Freeman, 1993).

Reasons for Evaluating EAPs

1. **Vindication.** It is increasingly important to obtain data which will demonstrate that the EAP is 'worthwhile. Justifying a program's existence is essential to its continuance.
2. **Marketing.** As EAPs continue to broaden their services, it is important to be able to market the need for expansion in a persuasive and convincing manner.
3. **Verification.** EAPs cannot survive simply on faith that the services are beneficial. Instead, organizations are "calling for cold, hard data" (Landers, 1993, p. 3) to support the need for expending resources for EAPs.
4. **Improvement.** EAPs are subject to "the changing moods of the times" (Rossi & Freeman, 1993, p. 23) so it is important to understand the strengths and weaknesses of the EAP over time. Program evaluations provide input that is useful in modifying services on an ongoing basis.
5. **Understanding.** Evaluations help to provide a better understanding of how and why a program is working and this information may be invaluable when incorporating changes.

Note: This chapter is reprinted from *Employee Assistance Programs: A Basic Text*, Second Edition (1997) with permission of the author, the book's editors (W.S. Hutchison, Jr. & W.G. Emener) and the publisher (Charles C Thomas, Publisher, Ltd.).

6. **Accountability.** Beyond a commitment to excellence on behalf of program leaders, funding sources hold programs accountable for producing results; evaluations can provide that accountability.

Steps in Planning the EAP

EAP planning and program development should begin with a *needs assessment* in order "to identify the requirements of the work force prior to actually developing and implementing a program" (Csiernik, 1995, p. 26). Csiernik (1995) recommended several sources of information including personal interviews, surveys, and focus groups. Ideally, evaluation consultants should be included in this process unless this expertise is available in-house. It is important to assess all levels and functions of the organization in order that a thorough needs assessment is accomplished.

Next, a comprehensive *mission statement* is written to explicate the purpose and rationale for the development or continuation of the EAP followed by clearly formulating "a detailed and explicit statement of all program *goals* and *objectives* [emphasis added]" in order to "understand the nature of the phenomenon to be evaluated" (Albert, Smythe & Brook, 1985, p. 179). Therefore, from the mission will develop *goals* or action statements related to the EAP's activities followed by objectives that specify how the goals will be obtained. Program *objectives* should be specific, concrete, time-limited, and attainable. It is important that each objective can be observed and measured, and can occur within a specific period of time.

Finally, both the costs and outcome variables of the EAP are identified. French, Zarkin and Bray (1995) noted that both direct costs (personnel, supplies, contractors' fees, and office expenses) and indirect costs (office space and shared facilities or equipment) must be included to determine true costs of the EAP program. While EAP programs differ greatly, the authors identify a number of outcome variables that are frequently used including absenteeism, health care costs, workplace accidents, job performance, and numbers of grievances. Yamatani (1993) stressed the desirability to also include such intangible benefits as changes in worker attitudes

and interpersonal relationships at work and home. It is important to secure both the sources of needed data and the support of those involved in providing the data prior to the EAPs implementation.

Types of EAP Evaluations

Because EAP evaluations will vary as much as the programs themselves, evaluators and program administrators may select from a combination of evaluation methods (Csiernik, 1995; French et al., 1995; Yamatani, 1993). The following examples, while not exhaustive, describe several approaches while potential obstacles are also noted which may be helpful in planning evaluations that will avoid the barriers indicated.

1. **Input evaluations** have been described by Csiernik (1995) as an internal method "that is of value in charting the evolution and development of an EAP" (p. 30) and consists of a simple audit "that takes an inventory of resources an EAP was intended to have and compares the list with those features the program actually has" (p. 28). This method is helpful in providing early information and no barriers are indicated.

2. **Utilization evaluations** provide programs with data concerning who is using what services and to what extent. For example, White, et al. (1996) found that their EAP utilization rate increased from five percent to 12 percent in two years following the addition of staff, outreach efforts, and an off-site location. Such data are also helpful in determining if the target populations of the program have been reached and whether different aspects of the EAP are over or underutilized. A potential barrier is lack of access to data due to employee confidentiality, which is easily remedied, by coding data to eliminate any identifying information.

3. **Satisfaction evaluations** go beyond which services were utilized to a determination of the level of satisfaction employees have with the services received. The Client Satisfaction Questionnaire (Larsen, Atkisson, Hargreaves & Nguyen, 1979) is a brief, well-established instrument, which has been used to measure satisfaction with EAP services (Ligon, 1996). There are other relevant short review instruments avail-

able to measure client satisfaction as well. Difficulty obtaining completed instruments is a potential barrier and can be addressed through the assurance of anonymity, by eliminating any personal identification, and by providing a secure method of collection such as a reply envelope mailed to an off-site address.

4. **Outcome evaluations** assess to what degree the EAP impacted the outcome variables identified at the onset of the program such as the level of absenteeism, the number of grievances filed and the number of workplace accidents. The primary obstacle to conducting outcome evaluations is the inability to obtain data, which often crosses numerous organizational units, as well as securing data from external resources (such as health insurance providers).

5. **Cost-benefit evaluations** are the most commonly published studies concerning EAPs (Csiernik, 1995; French, Zarkin & Bray, 1995; Yamatani, 1993) and involve summing the program's cost, determining savings to the organization on all outcome measures, then calculating a ratio of the costs to the benefits to reflect the "costworthiness" (Chartier, 1995, p. 18) of the program. Barriers to cost-benefit analyses include difficulty in determining costs and savings. Also, these studies often cover a relatively short time frame while savings from some costs, such as health care, may not be evident for a longer period of time.

Utilization of Evaluation Results

The Benefits of Program Evaluation

As addressed earlier in this chapter, securing and disseminating evaluation findings is critical for the program planners and administrators. The obtained data can enable one to demonstrate empirically what the program activities were (verification), what outcomes were achieved and at what costs (accountability) to various stakeholders. Evaluation findings provide valuable input for use in the modification of program activities to improve and enhance the EAP. Moreover, evaluation data permit planners and administrators to justify continued or enhanced program funding.

The Political Context of EAP Evaluation

There is a political reality to EAP evaluation, which must be recognized by both evaluators and administrators. EAPs involve many stakeholders within an organization (administration, finance, human resources, EAP staff, employees, etc.) and conflicting agendas are common. While Csiernik (1995) acknowledged that EAPs "actually do save companies some unspecified dollar amounts" (p. 32), French et al. (1995) noted that "many EAP evaluations tend to be in-house promotional efforts" (p. 453).

Albert et al. (1985) offered several suggestions that may facilitate the planning and evaluation of EAPs despite the complex political and organizational influences. First, "all of the different interest groups upon whom EAP activities may impinge" (p. 180) should be involved in determining program outcomes. Second, it is essential, during the planning and implementation stages, that goals and objectives are clear, specific, and realistic. Finally, evaluations should incorporate a team approach with all stakeholder groups to assure that "all of these relevant perspectives are employed" (p. 180).

CONCLUSION

Organizations implement employee assistance programs because they care about their employees and the quality of their lives. Employers are compelled to be sure that their EAPs are the best they can be and program evaluations play a critical role in making this determination. As EAPs continue to expand and broaden their scope, the demand by organizations for solid program evaluations will no doubt continue to increase.

While the future of EAPs looks very bright, there is no greater assurance of their continued value than the ongoing evaluation, modification, and improvement of programs.

REFERENCES

Albert, W. C., Smythe, P.C., & Brook, R. C. (1985). An evaluator's perspective on employee assistance programs. *Evaluation and Program Planning, 8,* 175–182.

Chartier, B. (1995). EAP 2000: Leaders look at factors influencing EAPs in the year 2000 and beyond. *EAP Digest, 16* (1), 16–21.

Corcoran, K., & Vandiver, V. (1996). *Maneuvering the maze of managed care.* New York: Free Press.

Csiernik, R. (1995). A review of research methods used to examine employee assistance program delivery options. *Evaluation and Program Planning, 18,* 25–36.

French, M. T., Zarkin, G. A., & Bray, J. W. (1995). A methodology for evaluating the costs and benefits of employee assistance programs. *Journal of Drug Issues, 25,* 451–470.

Hoyt, M. F. (1995). *Brief therapy and managed care.* San Francisco: Jossey-Bass.

Isaac, S., & Michael, M. B. (1982). *Handbook in research and evaluation.* San Diego: Edits.

Landers, S. (1994). Managed care's challenge: 'Show me!' *NASW News,* September, 1994. Washington, DC: National Association of Social Workers.

Larsen, D .L., Atkisson, C. C., Hargreaves, W. A., & Nguyen, T .D. (1979). Assessment of client/patient satisfaction: Development of a general scale. *Evaluation and Program Planning, 6,* 211–236.

Ligon, J. (1996). Client satisfaction with brief therapy. *EAP Digest, 16* (5), 30–31.

Rossi, P. H., & Freeman, H. E. (1993). *Evaluation: A systematic approach* (5th ed.). Newbury Park, CA: Sage.

White, R. K., McDuff, D. R., Schwartz, R. P., Tiegel, S. A., & Judge, C .P. (1996). New developments in employee assistance programs. *Psychiatric Services, 47,* 387–391.

Winegar, N. (1993). Managed mental health care: Implications for administrators and managers of community-based agencies. *Families in Society, 74,* 171–177.

Yamatani, H. (1993). Suggested top ten evaluations for employee assistance programs: An overview. *Employee Assistance Quarterly, 9,* 65–82.

Chapter 14

EMPLOYEE ASSISTANCE PROGRAMS:
BASIC CONCEPTS, ATTRIBUTES, AND AN EVALUATION

FRED DICKMAN and WILLIAM G. EMENER

Responding to Employee Problems and Their Effects on Industry

Over the past decade, Employee Assistance Programs (EAPs) in the United States have increased significantly in their quantity and importance to major industries. For example, Land[1] recently stated, "There are over 4,000 employee assistance programs in the U.S." Over half of the largest 500 industries in the United States currently have EAPs, over 5,500 American industries have EAPs and the Association of Labor and Management Administrators and Consultants (ALMACA) currently has 2,200 members.[2,3] Thus, it would appear that American industries are positively responding to their employees' problems and the effects these problems have on industry.

The EAP concept is rapidly expanding from an occupational alcoholism program concept to an EAP concept, which includes response to other problems of employees–including both psychological and physical difficulties known to impede overall productivity and hinder human well-being. Most EAPs today offer a variety of services for everything from marital problems to financial difficulties. The core of the current movement, as well as the largest part of the daily casework, is rooted in problem identification, intervention, treatment, and recovery.

Specific problems dealt with include depression, substance abuse, anxiety, domestic trauma, financial problems, and psychiatric/medical problems. EAPs take into account the financial effects these problems can have on the company, plus "human cost factors" (loss of job, dignity, family, and sense of worth). Thus, it is not surprising that the EAP philosophy being adopted by industry embraces the tenet that workers, families, and the company all benefit by early identification and remediation of problems.

Vital Elements

The critical attributes of an EAP are central to its programmatic philosophy, which was articulated by Busch: "An employee's personal problems are private unless they cause the employee's job performance to decline and deteriorate. When that happens, the personal problems become a matter of concern for the company. A trained employee is valuable and represents an asset to be protected if possible."[4]

Recent literature describing EAPs has addressed the key ingredients of a successful EAP. For example: "The most common ingredients, characterizing more than 75 percent of the programs in 1979, were assurance of confidentiality, written policy, written procedures and health insurance coverage for both inpatient and outpatient treatment of alcohol problems. A second set of ingredients was found in about 60 percent of the programs: management orientation, supervisory training, employee education and at least one full-time staff member."[5]

Note: This chapter is reprinted from *Counseling the Troubled Person in Industry* (1985) with permission of the author, the book's editors (Dickman, Emener, and Hutchison, Jr.), and the publisher (Charles C Thomas, Publisher, Ltd.).

A General Motors study concluded that a program should have at least one full-time professional. Programs with such a person(s) "saw more clients with a greater variety of problems, dealt with more of the problems themselves, and made more contacts relevant to the program than did programs with part-time staff only."[5] A review of related literature and the authors' experience strongly indicates 10 attributes of an EAP are critical for success:

1. **Management backing:** without it at the highest level, key ingredients and overall effect are seriously limited.
2. **Labor support:** the EAP cannot be meaningful if it is not backed by the employees' labor unit.
3. **Confidentiality:** anonymity and trust are crucial if employees are to use an EAP.
4. **Easy access:** for maximum use and benefit.
5. **Supervisor training:** is crucial to employees needing understanding and support during receipt of assistance.
6. **Labor steward training:** occasionally assistance alternatives are costly and insurance support is a must.
7. **Insurance involvement:** occasionally assistance alternatives are costly and insurance support is a must.
8. **Breadth of service components:** availability of assistance for a wide variety of problems (e.g., alcohol, family, personal, financial, grief, medical, etc.).
9. **Professional leadership:** from a skilled professional with expertise in helping. This person must have credibility in the eyes of the employee.
10. **Follow-up and evaluation:** to measure program effectiveness and overall improvement.

The specific importance of these 10 critical attributes as well as others, was experienced in the development and conduct of the EAP at Anheuser-Busch in Tampa, Florida.

EAP in Practice

In March 1979, Anheuser-Busch contracted with the Tampa Bay Neuropsychiatric Institute (then South Florida Mental Health Associates) to coordinate and implement its EAP in Tampa, Florida. EAP service was extended to all employees of the Tampa Brewery (about 350 employees), regular employees of Busch Gardens (about 350 employees) and their families.

The Tampa EAP office is not staffed with Anheuser-Busch employees, but is separate from both corporate management and labor. Moreover, a specific EAP coordinator and a medical director were designated to facilitate communication between the EAP, the company, and labor officials. Managerial supervision of the Tampa EAP office comes from the corporate EAP office in St. Louis through the Newark, NJ, Anheuser-Busch EAP. In essence, Anheuser-Busch uses corporate EAP professionals and contracted noncorporate EAP professionals to manage and supervise the entire corporate EAP program (52 sites).

The Tampa EAP office includes a variety of professionals: five psychiatrists, two clinical psychologists, two counseling psychologists, two clinical social workers, three rehabilitation counselors, two psychiatric nurses and support personnel. In addition, it has a 20-bed alcoholism treatment unit with accompanying qualified personnel. These trained professionals are of both genders. They include recovering alcoholics with long-term sobriety; generalists; and specialists in various aspects of alcoholism, marriage and family counseling, pain rehabilitation, child and adolescent therapy, etc. The professionals provide a vast resource for EAP referrals, since the Anheuser-Busch Program is "broad-brush." Thus, the coordinator has the option to refer within or without the Tampa EAP office.

In addition to counseling and rehabilitative responsibility, the Tampa EAP coordinator consults with managers, supervisors, labor authorities and labor stewards. He participates in supervisor training and has free access to the company premises to make contacts and make presentations on the EAP. He enjoys the enthusiastic support of corporate and local management and labor leadership, all of which publicize the program throughout the workplace and in employees' homes via mailouts. This three-way cooperation between management, labor and the EAP office seems to ensure full participation; at the same time, absolute confidentiality is maintained.

Participation is encouraged by liberal company financial support. The first three diagnostic/evaluative visits are paid for by the company, then the company health insurance covers 80 percent of all outpatient costs and most hospital expenses. Separate colored insurance forms are sent directly to the insurance company so that no local insurance clerks can know who participates, thus safeguarding confidentiality.

In general, the Anheuser-Busch EAP vigorously attempts to uphold all principles known to be vital to successful company programs, both corporately and locally. With this overall mission in mind, the following evaluation was conducted.

Evaluating the Program

Satisfaction estimates were determined by an ex post facto survey of the Anheuser-Busch, Tampa EAP participants who participated in the program over a 26-month period (March 1979 through May 1981). Endorsements of the survey were obtained from the company and the EAP staff. In August 1981, each of the 148 participants who participated in the program during the 26-month period was sent a cover letter confidentially soliciting their participation: a specifically-designed employee assistance program follow-up questionnaire; and a postage-paid self-addressed envelope. Of the 148 mailouts, 13 were returned "address unknown"; of the remaining 135, 45 usable returns were received for a 33.3 percent return rate. Frequencies, percentages, and measure of central tendency on the questionnaire data are displayed in Figure 14-1.

Results: As can be seen in Figure 14-1, analyses of the respondents' reported demographics reveal:

Part I. Demographic

1. *Age:* R = 11 – 57; x = 38.48; sd = 12.34

2. *Highest grade in school completed:*	f	%
1. elementary school	1	2
2. junior high school	–	–
3. some high school	4	9
4. high school graduate	14	31
5. some college	15	33
6. college graduate	8	18
7. graduate school	2	4
missing information	1	2
Total	45	99

3. *Sex:*		
1. male	17	38
2. female	28	62
Total	45	100

4. Were you working at the time you came to the Employee Assistance Program?		
1. yes	39	87
2. no	6	13
Total	45	100

5. If yes, what was your job title: _____

6. For what reason(s) did you seek assistance from the Employee Assistance Program—that is, what problem(s) or difficulty(s) did you have?	f	%
1. personal problem (e.g., depressed, nervous)	20	35
2. alcoholism (e.g., excessive drinking)	6	11
3. family or marital problem	24	43
4. other	6	11
Total	56	100

*seven responded with more than one answer indicating multiple reasons . . .

Figure 14-1. Participants' (N = 45) Evaluations of an Employee Assistance Program.

7. In your own words, how would you describe what your problem or difficulty was?

_____

8. Was your problem or difficulty affecting your job (your ability to do your job)?

	1	2	3	4	5	missing info	Total
	no	probably no	maybe yes maybe no not sure	probably yes	yes		
f	11	5	7	9	11	2	45
%	24%	11%	16%	20%	24%	4%	99%

9. What services did you receive from the Employee Assistance Program?

	f	%
1. medical evaluation	3	4
2. medical treatment	4	5
3. psychological evaluation (testing)	16	21
4. individual counseling	38	50
5. group counseling	9	12
6. referral to another program or service	–	–
7. other (explain)	1	1
Total	76	99

*seventeen responded with more than one answer indicating multiple services.

Part II. Evaluation

Scale used for items 10–13:

	1	2	3	4	5	missing info	Total
	no	probably no	maybe yes maybe no not sure	probably yes	yes		

10. Did you find the people you saw (doctors, psychologists) helpful to you?

	1	2	3	4	5	missing info	Total
f	1	2	3	8	31		45
%	2%	4%	7%	18%	69%		100%

11. In terms of confidentiality, did you feel that you could trust the people you saw?

	1	2	3	4	5	missing info	Total
f	1	–	2	4	37	1	45
%	2%	–	4%	9%	62%	2%	99%

12. If there had been no Employee Assistance Program like your company's, would you have sought assistance on your own?

	1	2	3	4	5	missing info	Total
f	7	14	12	5	7		45
%	15%	31%	27%	11%	15%		99%

13. If you knew of someone else (e.g., a fellow employee) who was having a problem or difficulty, would you recommend that they seek help from the Employee Assistance Program?

	1	2	3	4	5	missing info	Total
f	1	–	–	6	38		45
%	2%	–	–	13%	84%		99%

Figure 14-1–*Continued.*

(1) they ranged in age from 11 to 57; (b) 31 percent were high school graduates, 33 percent attended some college and 18 percent were college graduates; (c) there were more females (62%) than males (38%); (d) 87 percent were working when they sought assistance from EAP; (e) they sought assistance mostly for family or marital (43%) or personal (35%) problems; (f) 44 percent indicated their problems or difficulties were affecting their job; and (g) they received individual counseling (50%), psychological evaluation (21%) and/or group counseling (12%).

The respondents' reported evaluations of the EAP indicated that: 87 percent found the people they saw (doctors, psychologists) helpful; 91 percent felt they could trust the people they saw; almost half (46%) would not have or probably would not have sought assistance on their own if there hadn't been an EAP; and if they knew a fellow employee with a problem or difficulty, 84 percent would or probably would (13%) recommend that they seek help from the EAP.

An estimate on how satisfactory the programs were was determined by conducting interviews with four individuals directly involved in the conduct and support of the Anheuser-Busch, Tampa, EAP. Their testimonial statements, in response to the question, "What is your evaluation of the EAP?" were as follows:

1. Frank R. Logan; Director of Personnel, Busch Gardens. "I feel the EAP offers the employee a new option to solving both work problems and personal problems that affect the job. In today's work, environment stress is more prevalent than ever. The EAP helps us solve some of the employees' problems that we as employers helped to create."
2. William C. Bennett, Assistant Industrial Relations Manager, Plant Personnel Supervisor, Director of Plant Safety. "I've been able to witness some marked improvement in work performance in several persons known to be in the program. I've seen a change in the character and work performance of the many people I know who have used the EAP. It (the program) is a great benefit to the employees and the company in my opinion."

3. Fred J. Tarza, Plant Manager, Anheuser-Busch Brewery. "The EAP is a very valuable option in handling cases where job performance is involved. I've heard employees say it is the most valuable benefit the company offers."
4. Jimmy Dunlap, Business Agent, Teamsters and Brewer's Local No. 338. "At first some of our members were cautious but now the union is totally behind the program. A lot of our people and their families have been helped."

Overall Success

The responding participants seemed satisfied with the assistance they received. While it was hoped that a larger return rate would have been received, the extent to which the indices of satisfaction as indicated by the respondents was representative of the nonrespondents' is unknown. Nonetheless, the respondents' evaluations endorsed the key ingredients of an EAP:

1. **Confidentiality.** The respondents indicated satisfaction with this factor of the EAP. No EAP can expect to be worthwhile unless the individual anonymity of each participant and his family is protected.
2. **Referral.** It is crucial to an EAP that participants are willing to refer fellow employees when assistance is needed. Fellow employees are the best advocates of an EAP.
3. **Early Intervention.** The participants' evaluations validated the hypothesis that an industrial milieu is most suitable for each intervention into employees' mental, social, emotional, and substance abuse problems (among others).
4. **Effects on Job Performance.** The participants' responses strongly suggested employees are aware of the extent to which personal/social problems affect their job performance. Thus, the philosophical tenets of an EAP are substantiated—vis, when an industry helps its employees with their "personal" problems, the industry is ultimately helping itself.
5. **Problem Resolution.** It was refreshing to see that the EAP, designed and operated as described herein with the discussed critical attributes, was helpful to the participants and it actually assisted them in resolving their problems.

The indices of satisfactoriness demonstrated that if an EAP is designed and conducted properly, mutual benefits are realized by management (company officials) and labor (e.g., union officials). The importance of company and labor support is obvious.

Recommendations

Based on the outcomes of this project, it is recommended that the continuing development of EAPs in American industries would be enriched by:

1. Continuing evaluation components such as the areas in this project (e.g., measures of satisfaction).
2. An expansion of research methodologies to include pretest and postmeasures and other indices of effectiveness (e.g., supervisory ratings, absenteeism, safety records, productivity, etc.).
3. Differential evaluations of the critical attributes of an EAP to further document their importance.

In conclusion, it would seem fitting to assume that this study documented the importance, value and effectiveness of an employee assistance program. It could be suggested that everyone wins–the employee, the company and labor (e.g., the union). The essence of this conclusion is captured in an evaluative testimonial solicited from William H. Bohlinger, Director of Industrial Relations, Owens-Illinois, Inc., Glass Container Division, Lakeland, FL: "The EAP gives us more flexibility in dealing with problems which I believe industry used to cover up. People in industry have problems like everyone else and this new option is welcomed."

REFERENCES

1. Land, T. (1981). Global strategy: Confronting alcoholism at the workplace. *Alcoholism, 1* (6), 41–42.
2. Roman, P. M. (1981a). From employee alcoholism to employee assistance. *Journal of Studies on Alcohol, 42* (3), 244–272.
3. Land's (1981) estimation that there are over 4,000 Employee Assistance Programs and Roman's (1981a) estimation that over 5,500 American industries currently have an EAP, is accountable by the fact that some EAP's serve more than one industry.
4. Busch, E. J. (1981). Developing an employee assistance program. *Personnel Journal, 60* (9), 708–711.
5. Roman, P. M. (1981b). Corporate pacesetters making EAP progress. *Alcoholism, 1* (4), 37–41.

Acknowledgment: The authors thank Anheuser-Busch, Tampa EAP participants who returned the satisfaction questionnaires. Furthermore, the assistance and support from Frank Logan, Bill Bennett, Fred Tarza, Jimmy Dunlap and Bill Bohlinger was crucial to the conduct and outcome of this study. Also acknowledged is Thomas L. Porter, professor at

Chapter 15

EMPLOYEE ASSISTANCE PROGRAM UTILIZATION EVALUATION: AN EXCELLENT MANAGEMENT TOOL

WILLIAM G. EMENER

In Chapters 12, 13 and 14, the rationale, importance and utilization of program evaluation in employee assistance programs (EAPs) is clearly articulated and demonstrated. In the past few years, moreover, program evaluation (a) has come to be considered a core component of any valued, ongoing EAP (Beard, 2000; Elliott, 1999), (b) continues to have a focus on client satisfaction (e.g., Haines, Petit & Lefrancois, 1999; Shumway, Dersch, Harris & Arredondo, 2001), and (c) indeed is central to marketing strategies for EAPs (e.g., Beidel, 1999). These phenomena essentially have been driven by the Zeitgeist of modern industry–as Amaral (1999) aptly stated, "Total quality management, continuous quality improvement, and other quality initiatives have become a visual part of the American business and industry landscape" (p 161).

Sciegaj, Garnick, Horgan, Merrick, Goldin, Urato and Hodgkin (2001) investigated the status of employee assistance programs (EAPs) in 1997. Representatives of 336 firms listed among the Fortune 500 completed questionnaires concerning EAP services and procedures. Results showed that "92 percent of firms offered EAPs in 1997 and of those, 90 percent reported that the EAPs provided some mental health and substance abuse services which were not counted against employee health insurance benefit limits . . . [and] findings suggest that the use of EAPs are at a historic high" (p. 25). Pointedly, *benchmarking* has emerged as an essential component of these quality initiatives.

Among other things, benchmarking "involves isolating key metrics in specific functions and comparing one's own practices with those of organizations that have established themselves as leaders or innovators in that specific business function" (Amaral, 1999, p. 161). In the process of evaluating EAPs, Amaral (1999) demonstrated how EAPs can "track core activities of employee assistance work, be easily calculated, can be derived from process data that are readily available to most EAPs, are easy to standardize, and they are applicable to a wide variety of organizations and programs" (p.161). Businesses and industries not only are concerned about quality, but also about costs. Thus it is important to note, for example, that in their national survey of the costs of internal versus external EAPs, French, Zarkin, Bray and Hartwell (1999) concluded that "internal EAPs generally were more expensive than external EAPs" (p. 95).

Van Den Bergh (2000), in discussing the changing practices within the employee assistance program field, concluded that "a strengths-based, solution-focused, empowerment-oriented, ecological program model is more relevant for the diverse needs of employees" (p. 1). Successful and highly valued EAPs have become thought of as *enhanced*, meaning that they are actively (as opposed to reactively) responsive to the needs of employees. In their recent article in which they reported program evaluation findings pertinent to an "enhanced employee assistance program," Zarkin, Bray, Karuntzos and Demiralp (2001) concluded, "This study shows that, for a modest cost, the enhanced EAP intervention successfully increased utilization of the EAP by all employees, especially utilization by women and minority employees" (p. 351).

Employers frequently ask two pertinent questions (among others): (1) How many of our employees are utilizing the EAP? and (2) In what ways are they using the EAP (e.g., on-site or off-site)? Essentially, these questions are addressing an EAP's *utilization rate(s)*. The primary purpose of the following is to demonstrate how the author of this chapter was able to use monthly billing data over a two-year period to demonstrate an EAP's utilization rates.

Background

Eva-Tone, Inc., a family-owned manufacturing business, started in 1925 in Deerfield, Illinois. When the company moved to Clearwater, Florida in 1979, approximately 80 of the company's employees moved with the company, and, understandably, many were experiencing numerous adjustment difficulties. Fittingly, an employee assistance program was developed with and for Eva-Tone by a nearby psychological services company, Professional Psychological Services (PPS). In 1996, Dr. William G. Emener, a licensed psychologist who was working part-time for PPS, took over and ran Eva-Tone's EAP on a contract-for-services basis. In April, 2000 when PPS was sold to another health care company and Dr. Emener then opened his own private practice, he was allowed to bid for the EAP. Thus, while Dr. Emener has been coordinating Eva-Tone's EAP for the past six years, since April, 2000 he has been coordinating it on his own.

Data Sources

Part of Dr. Emener's contractual arrangement includes submitting monthly, categorized billing statements to the company's Vice-President of Human Resources. These monthly billing categories include the number of billable hours for: (1) **"Walk-Throughs":** one day per week Dr. Emener goes to the plant to counsel employees with whom he has scheduled appointments, and walks through the plant to talk with supervisors and any employees wanting to talk with him; (2) **Employee Evaluations:** when he meets with a referred employee for the first time (for counsel-

ing), self-referred or supervisor-referred, he conducts an "evaluation"; (3) **Supervisory Training:** formally scheduled on-site supervisory training (for a variety of reasons and including a array of topics such as "How to Make a Referral to the EAP" and "Interpersonal Communications Skills for Supervisors"); (4) **Off-Site Counseling and Psychotherapy:** billable hours for seeing an employee or an immediate family member at his office; (5) **Management Consultation:** in the first year, there was a 16-hour, off-site Team Building Workshop for the company's Executive Management Group, and two, one-hour debriefing sessions with a total of 23 employees to facilitate their grieving process regarding the cancer/death of a popular and well-liked employee. In the second year, there was one, one-hour stress management workshop (for 14 employees from one unit of the company) and one, four-hour afternoon which included two Grief Workshops and individual counseling for employees struggling with the sudden death of a popular employee killed while crossing a street adjacent to the plant; and (6) **Other:** e.g., for each of the two years, Dr. Emener wrote the "Wellness . . ." article for the company's quarterly newsletter, the *Eva-Tone Hotline*.

Discussion of the Data

The two-year periods of the categorical data, compiled from the 24 monthly billing statements (April 1, 2000 thru March 31, 2001), are displayed in Table 15-1.

Categorical Observations

Observations of two-year period of time data include:
1. **Month:** In some months there were five (5) walk-through weeks (noted by an asterisk *). The average hours per week, however, were relatively consistent (ranging from 19–24 hours per month).
2. **Walk-Throughs:** With a total average of 255 hours for Walk-Throughs, this averaged 4.90 hours per week.
3. **Employee Evaluations:** There was an average of 30.5 hours of Employee Evaluations for the

Table 15-1.
TWO-YEAR REVIEW OF UTILIZATION RATE: APRIL 1, 2000 THROUGH MARCH 31, 2002

Category:	Walk-Throughs	Employee Evaluations	Supervisory Training	Off-Site Co. & Psych.	Management Consultation	Other Pro. Services	TOTAL HOURS
April 1, 2000 – March 31, 2001							
Month:							
April, 00	20	3		3		1	27
*May, 00	21	3		2	2		28
June, 00	21	2		3			25
*July, 00	24	4		3		1	32
Aug., 00	20	4		4			28
Sept., 00	22	2		1			25
Oct., 00	21	3	8	3		1	36
*Nov., 00	24	4	4	1			33
Dec., 00	20	3	4	1			28
Jan., 01	19	2		2		1	24
Feb., 01	20	3					23
*Mar., 01	24	1		2			27
SUB:	256	33	16	25	2	4	336
April 1, 2001 – March 31, 2002							
Month:							
April, 01	20	2		2		1	25
*May, 01	23	3		9			35
June, 01	19	3		4			26
*July, 01	24	4		5		1	34
Aug., 01	20	2		4			26
Sept., 01	20	3		2			25
Oct., 01	20	2		1		1	24
*Nov., 01	25	3					28
Dec., 01	19	1		2	1		23
*Jan., 02	25	1		4		1	31
Feb., 02	19	1		1			21
*Mar., 02	20	3		1	4		28
SUB:	254	28		35	5	4	326
AVERAGES:	255	30.5	8	30	3.5	4	331

two 52-week periods, thus averaging 0.50 hours per week (or about one every other week).

4. **Supervisory Training:** In the first year, this was the 16-hour Team Building Workshop for the Executive Committee (October-December, 2000); in the second year, there were no supervisory training sessions.

5. **Off-Site Counseling and Psychotherapy:** The average total of 30 hours of off-site Counseling and Psychotherapy for the two 52-week periods averaged 0.57 per week (or about one session every two weeks). Inspection of Dr. Emener's monthly invoices, moreover, revealed that a total of 13 different employees

were seen in the first year (ranging from 1–3 hours each) and a total of 17 different employees seen in the second year (also ranging from 1–3 hours each).

6. **Management Consultation:** These hours were spent in performing the tasks associated with the activities discussed earlier (in Data Sources).

7. Other: For each of the two years, four (4) hours for writing the "Wellness . . ." article for the company's quarterly newsletter, the Eva-Tone Hotline.

Penetration Rate(s)

There are two kinds of Penetration Rates, both of which account for scheduled sessions/meetings with employees during weekly Walk-Throughs:

Employee Census Rates: Analyses of employee census data provided by Eva-Tone's Human Resources Department revealed the following census rates for the two, one-year time frames:

April 1, 2000 thru March 31, 2001: Range: 433–454
Average: 445.33
April 1, 2001 thru March 31, 2002: Range: 400–456
Average: 430.50
Two-year Averages: Range: 400–454
Average: 437.90

1. **New Employee Contacts:** The nation-wide "New Employee Penetration Rate" is 5–7 percent. For these two, one-year time frames the "new employee contacts" were:

April 1, 2000 thru March 31, 2001 Total: 33
Penetration Rate: 7.41%
April 1, 2001 thru March 31, 2002 Total: 28
Penetration Rate: 6.50%
Two-year Average: 30.5
Penetration Rate: 6.96%

Thus, the "new employee penetration rate": (1) for the first, one-year time frame exceeded the national average; (2) for the second, one-year time frame was within the national average; and (3) for the overall two-year period was at

the upper limit of the national average.

2. **Total Penetration Rate:** The nation-wide "Total Employee Penetration Rate" is 8–10 percent. In the first year, there were 12 continuing employees being officially seen at the beginning of the review date (April 1, 2000), and with the total of 33 new employees being seen the total would be 45 employees officially seen for scheduled sessions during that 52-week period. In the second year, there were 14 continuing employees being officially seen at the beginning of the review date (April 1, 2001), and with the total of 28 new employees being seen the total would be 42 employees officially seen for scheduled sessions during that 52-week period. For these two, one-year time frames the "total employee contacts" were:

April 1, 2000 thru March 31, 2001 Total: 45
Penetration Rate: 10.10%
April 1, 2001 thru March 31, 2002 Total: 42
Penetration Rate: 9.75%
Two-year Average: 43.5
Penetration Rate: 9.93%

Thus, the "total employee penetration rate": (1) for the first, one-year time frame slightly exceeded the national average; (2) for the second, one-year time frame was at the upper limit of the national average; and (3) for the overall two-year period was at the upper limit of the national average.

Management Evaluation and Planning

Every year, mid-April, Dr. Emener, the company's EAP Coordinator, and Mr. Tim Crouch, Vice-President for Human Resources, jointly review the Annual Review of Utilization Data (consult Table 1.). Together they are able to appreciate indices of the overall impact of the EAP on the company, and discuss and plan modifications for the upcoming year. During their mid-April, 2002 review of the data in Table 1, for example, they discussed the possible addition of another Team Building Workshop for the Executive

Committee and another series of Supervisory Training activities for 2002–2003. During their 2002 review of the 2000–2002 data (Table 1.), Mr. Crouch said, "My early HR assignments at (a large, family-owned corporation known for its fair treatment of employees) were in Compensation, Policy and Procedure, and Benefits; therefore, I am more analytical and quantitative than the typical personal heading an HR function. I find this kind of data and analyses helpful to me and to the organization's other executives who also tend to be analytical and quantitative" (Personal Communication, May 28, 2002).

CONCLUDING COMMENT

As stated earlier, it is important for an EAP to be an all-inclusive, enhanced entity within a company. It also is important for the coordinator of an EAP to work cooperatively with the company's Department of Human Resources to periodically evaluate and modify the EAP. I asked Mr. Crouch to review an initial draft of this chapter, and in addition to offering helpful literary suggestions he offered a very complimentary statement pertinent to the overall roles and functions of an EAP coordinator, "While these data are helpful, the key to our EAP's success is having an EAP Coordinator who knows us–our culture, our people, and our goals. Dr. Emener also enjoys the respect and trust of the people he helps and the Management team" (Personal Communication, June 7, 2002).

The Eva-Tone experience, including the data presented herein effectively demonstrates the specific and overall managerial benefits of the collection, review and discussion of an EAP's Annual Review of Utilization Data. As Van Den Bergh fittingly stated, "EAPs need to be involved in multiple aspects of an organization's work culture" (p. 1).

REFERENCES

Amaral, T. M. (1999). Benchmarks and performance measures for employee assistance programs. In Oher, James M. (Ed), *The employee assistance handbook.* (pp. 161–178). New York, NY: John Wiley & Sons, Inc.

Beard, M. (2000). Organizational development: An EAP approach. *Employee Assistance Quarterly, 16* (1–2), 117–140.

Beidel, B. E. (1999). Internal marketing strategies to maximize EAP visibility and effectiveness. In Oher, James M. (Ed), *The employee assistance handbook.* (pp. 91–115). New York, NY: John Wiley & Sons, Inc.

Elliott, T. J. (1999). EAPs and the future of work. In Oher, James M. (Ed). (1999). *The employee assistance handbook.* (pp. 267–288). New York, NY: John Wiley & Sons, Inc.

French, M. T, Zarkin, G. A, Bray, J. W., & Hartwell, T. D. (1999). Cost of employee assistance programs: Comparison of national estimates from 1993 and 1995. *Journal of Behavioral Health Services & Research, 26* (1), 95–103.

Haines, Victor, Y., Petit, A., & Lefrancois, S. (1999). Explaining client satisfaction with an employee assistance program. *Employee Assistance Quarterly, 14* (4), 65–78.

Sciegaj, M. G., Garnick, D. W., Horgan, C. M., Merrick, E. L., Goldin, D., Urato, M., & Hodgkin, D. (2001). Employee assistance programs among Fortune 500 firms. *Employee Assistance Quarterly, 16* (3), 25–35.

Shumway, S. T., Dersch, C. A., Harris, S. M., & Arredondo, R. (2001). Two outcome measures of EAP satisfaction: A factor analysis. *Employee Assistance Quarterly, 16* (4), 71–79.

Van Den Bergh, N. (2000). Where have we been? . . . Where are we going?: Employee assistance practice in the 21st century. *Employee Assistance Quarterly, 16*

Acknowledgement: Sincerest appreciation is extended to Mr. Tim Crouch, Vice-President for Human Resources, and Eva-Tone, Inc., Clearwater, Florida, for allowing Dr. Emener to use the utilization data for their Employee Assistance Program in this chapter.

(1–2), 1–13.

Zarkin, G. A., Bray, J. W., Karuntzos, G. T., & Demiralp, B. (2001). The effect of an enhanced employee assistance program (EAP) intervention on EAP utilization. *Journal of Studies on Alcohol, 62* (3), 351–358.

Part V

PROFESSIONAL TRAINING AND DEVELOPMENT

Chapter 16

HUMAN RESOURCES: BASIC DEFINITIONS AND CONCEPTS FOR EMPLOYEE ASSISTANCE PROFESSIONALS

FRED DICKMAN

INTRODUCTION

The purpose of this chapter is to present basic human resources definitions and concepts to the EAP professional. There is no attempt to cover the vast array of knowledge pertaining to the complexity of human resources. As a matter of fact, such would be not only a volume, but also volumes, in itself. Neither does the chapter attempt to acquaint the EAP professional with personnel complexities however desirable that would be. Yet, the basic rudiments of personnel issues and concepts do require the attention of EAP persons at all levels of endeavor. For instance, clients do get involved with EEO and affirmative action. The EAP assessor/counselor needs to be acquainted with these offices and endeavors within the government agency or corporation. Also, he will see persons on workmen's compensation and who may be in some phase of rehabilitation. Just what does this involve and what is the process? The same would follow for ERISA, or COBRA, or OSHA. Just what is a policy of commitment to fair treatment? And, what is the company's process of action where sexual harassment is alleged?

Undoubtedly, a professional with an EAP relationship with a company will have much to do with the department of human resources. It is the hope of the authors that a brief sketch of important personnel concepts and definitions will be of assistance.

Demographics

The Demographics (mix) of the workforce in most organizations is multifaceted. Factors that need to be considered when evaluating new programs are age, sex, ethnic background, current income level, and socioeconomic background. When these factors are complied and graphically displayed, then informed decisions can be made as to the method of program implementation.

Performance Appraisal Systems

Performance appraisal systems, although known by many names, are all intended to accomplish one goal. That is, to inform employees of their performance as it relates to the objectives of the organization. These appraisals may be as informal as a periodic conversational exchange between supervisor and subordinate relating to achievements and/or deficiencies or as complex as the completion of a multifactor rating form, a lengthy feedback session, and an ultimate performance rating. Many companies base salary adjustments on this rating, others use it strictly as a communication tool. No matter what technique is used, the purpose of performance review is to guide the employee toward becoming a more effective and productive member of the organization.

Note: This chapter is reprinted from *Employee Assistance Programs: A Basic Text* (1988) with permission of the author, the book's editors (Dickman, Emener, & Hutchison, Jr.), and the publisher (Charles C Thomas, Publisher, Ltd.).

EEO and Affirmative Action

Companies employing 15 or more employees and/or doing business with federal, state, or local government agencies are required to comply with federal guidelines for hiring, promoting, and discharging employees. These guidelines take into consideration race, sex, age, religion, handicap, and veteran status.

Major employers must develop and adhere to an affirmative action plan, which provides, among other things, goals, and timetables for attaining parity between the work force and the community.

Most business organizations have recognized this as being a civic responsibility and companies that elect to disregard affirmative action are subject to loss of contracts and costly litigation.

Workers Compensation/Rehabilitation

All states through their Labor Departments administer an insurance program designed to protect workers that are injured on the job, or while carrying work-related duties. The extent of such coverage is specifically prescribed in the statutes of the state and each state is different in terms of payment for lost wages, fee schedules for doctors and hospitals, and dollar values for permanent disability ratings. This insurance is provided to the employees at no charge. The company, unless self-insured, pays a premium to the state, based on past claims experience and the "level of risk" for that particular job. Workers whose injury precludes their returning to the same or a similar job are often times sent to rehabilitative training to provide new skills with which to earn a living. The cost of this training in most states is covered by the workers compensation insurance program.

ERISA/COBRA

The Employee Retirement Income Security Act (ERISA) is the federal agency that regulates pension funds, profit sharing plans, and other contributory and noncontributory company sponsored savings plans.

This agency was formed in 1974 to prevent risky or sometimes even unscrupulous investments of the employees' pension fund money.

ERISA requires that detailed explanations on the status of these various plans be provided periodically to all participants. Once a plan is approved as ERISA qualified, no changes can be made without first obtaining additional approval.

COBRA

The Consolidated Omnibus Reconciliation Act of 1986 was formed during the Reagan administration in an effort to reduce the cost of social services. This act requires that employers that provide health insurance to their employees offer this insurance to resigning employees for an additional 18 months and 36 months for employees who are discharged.

The employee must, however, bear the entire cost of the insurance, not just the contributory amount, plus a two percent administrative charge payable to the company.

OSHA

The Occupational Safety & Health Act of 1970 is a federal act intended to formulate and enforce standards that provide for a safe working environment for employees in private industry.

Annual reports are provided to this agency providing the statistical information on the number of accidents, the degree of seriousness and the number of lost time days due to employee accidents. OSHA publishes standards and codes, which must be complied with, and periodic inspections of worksites are conducted by this company.

Failure to comply with OSHA regulations can result in monetary fines or the closing of the worksite.

Supervision

The key individual in the attainment of the organization's goals is the first-line or front-line supervisor. This person in the link connects organizational management with employees that actually do the job. It should go without saying that the success of any new program or policy rests solely on the support of these supervisors.

Union and Nonunion Operations

The private sector work force is either represented by a labor union or operated on a nonunion basis.

This section is not intended to discuss the pros and cons of either, but, only to demonstrate how each functions.

Union Shop

The employees in this situation are covered by a collective bargaining agreement, generally referred to as a contract. This contract generally spells out wages, type of work to be accomplished, hours to be worked, and grievance procedures.

The employees are represented by a labor union and officials of that union negotiate with company management on behalf of the rank and file employees for increased wages and improved working conditions. Employees covered by this contract typically pay monthly dues that are used to fund the administration of the union.

One important aspect of the collective bargaining agreement, is the grievance procedure. Although this process varies with each contract, the intent is basically the same. The grievance procedure provides a step by step process that is used to settle employee complaints. The complaints vary but the most common relate to work being performed by an individual in an unauthorized classification or by a nonunion employee and disagreement with disciplinary measures.

Generally, a union shop steward will represent the employee to management and typically, grievances are heard at the first line supervisors level, then to general foremen and last at the plant or location managers level.

If efforts to resolve the grievances are unsuccessful, the final decision can be made by a federal arbitrator. These individuals are appointed on the basis of their labor relations experience and their decisions in grievances are final and binding.

Nonunion Shop

If it is the objective of the company to maintain a union free organization, then the management must operate in a similar manner to that of a union organization. Supervisor here again is key in communicating the organization philosophy. Supervisors must maintain an equitable and fair application of the company's rules and regulations.

The two main issues that are generally associated with a union organizing campaign are job security and consistent treatment of employees. In order to deal with these issues, it is necessary to establish a process for appeal. This allows employees who feel that they were mistreated to discuss the issue with management. Another tool that is used in a nonunion environment is the periodic performance appraisal. This is the means by which an employee learns how management feels about the kind of job that he does.

Generally, the supervisor evaluates the performance over the past period, reinforcing the positive achievements and coaches the employee on methods to improve weaknesses. Often a plan is established for future performance by setting measurable objectives.

The use of the performance appraisal can sometimes help to avoid disciplinary action by pointing out potential trouble areas. However, if it is necessary to take disciplinary action, this should be done in an objective, professional and well planned manner. Rules should be clearly stated so that they are easily understandable. The most important aspect of disciplinary action is that it is applied the same for all employees.

Employee Benefits

Employee benefits are generally thought of as nonmonetary compensation, as the value does not show up on the paycheck. There are however, costs associated with these benefits and management takes these costs into consideration when developing or adjusting the compensation package. The range of benefits varies according to the organization.

Generally included in the "Fringe benefit" package are:
1. Medical insurance coverage sometimes including dental and vision coverage. This benefit can be given free to the employees or a payroll

deducted premium can be charged.

2. Vacation, usually the amount of time is based upon years of service with the company.

3. Holidays, these are days that are paid but usually not worked by the employee.

Other benefits that are available in some organizations are: tuition reimbursement, free meals, free uniforms, stock purchase plan, pension, and profit-sharing plans.

Training and Career Development

Basic orientation and "on-the-job" training is usually a division of the Personnel department. Depending on the complexities of the organization, these training programs can be very structured or casual in nature.

Successful training programs equip individuals to perform specific functions. Results of such a program can be measured and modification made if the objectives are not met.

More sophisticated programs are developed to assist the employee in achieving his/her goals in the organizations. It should be noted that an honest evaluation be made and stated to individuals who have unrealistic ambitions. This approach, though sometimes uncomfortable, will help to avoid frustration and long term disgruntled employees.

Safety and Security

Although these two topics appear dissimilar at first glance, they are not so far apart in their interaction. Safety is a must for any organization. Depending on the type of the organization, the need for safety can vary. An active program with good participation at all levels can make a big difference on any company profit margin, not to mention how one views the company. On the other hand, you can give security the same connotation. A strong safety and security program can maintain employees at a level of fitness that is conducive to the goals of the organization. Screening is accomplished at all stages of employment by utilizing both safety and security techniques.

Health and Wellness

An out-clinic probably coins this concept, "Be Your Best." To be at your best, one must be fit both mentally and physically. This can be accomplished through nutrition and exercise programs.

These programs have demonstrated savings in insurance costs, lost workdays due to illness and better productivity. (Also see Chapters 3 and 5 on Wellness.)

CONCLUSION

EAP professionals have constant contact with departments of Human Resources. Indeed most "in-house" (see Chapters 7 & 10) programs are organized within these departments. And while a major thrust of this goal is EAP "separateness," close cooperation with Human Resources is absolutely a necessity.

COMMENT/UPDATE

Human Resources and the EAP: A Human Resources Practitioner's Perspective

MARK W. EVANS

The chapter previously written by Fred Dickman entitled, "Human Resources: Basic Definitions and Concepts for the Employee Assistance Programs Professional" captured the essence on how the Human Resources function had evolved and how those significant changes impacted the role of the EAP in organizations. The notions Dr. Dickman discussed concerning the interface between the Human Resources function and the various facets of its role are as true today as ever. Since that writing, a number of cultural and legal changes have occurred which have created significant challenges for the Human Resources and EAP professionals alike. As we explore these in this "update," it will become apparent that while the world of Human Resources and EAP professionals has become increasingly more complex in recent years, the opportunities to have a significant and positive affect on the organizations they serve has never been greater.

The Decline of Unionism

Companies continue to deal with union issues, although in some industry sectors unionism among employees has in fact declined, leaving employees in the position of having to trust the company to fill the role they once entrusted to their union leadership. The company was portrayed as the "adversary" and was not to be trusted. How, then, is the employee going to be heard when a real-life problem enters his or her life? Can the company be trusted to handle their concern with compassion, respect, and dignity? This dilemma offers a real opportunity for the forward-thinking organization to provide professional EAP assistance to help build and maintain trust through confidentiality and respect for the individual.

Workers Compensation/Rehabilitation

The injured worker is supported by most companies with Workers Compensation insurance and in many cases, company-sponsored health insurance and disability income protection benefits in some form. While the employee usually has some measure of financial protection for these events, there can be a strong sense of a loss of self-worth the longer a person is unable to contribute due to their injuries. How does an injured employee "get back into the habit" of working, rather 'than being nonproductive? It may have taken weeks or months to "get out of the habit" of coming to work

every day. In some cases, the relationship between the company and its employee can be strained depending on the nature and reasons for the injury. The EAP can be effectively used to help recovering employees prepare for their return to work with confidence and healthy anticipation rather than with fear and apprehension.

The Americans With Disabilities Act of 1990

This law was enacted to attempt to prevent people from feeling the effects of discrimination due to their disability status. Employers with 25 or more employees must comply with the law by adopting nondiscriminatory hiring practices and providing a "reasonable accommodation" to a person with a disabling condition so they can perform the "essential functions" of the job they are hired to perform.

In this act, there are strict definitions of what constitutes a "disability" and what practices and recordkeeping procedures must be implemented to comply with the ADA. For example, employers may not ask questions which are designed to ferret out or determine the extent of a real or perceived disability during the hiring process. Only after the offer of employment is made can a company use such means as a fitness-for-duty physical exam to determine suitability for employment in the position the employee has just been offered. Once evidence of a disabling condition is learned, whether by self-disclosure by the employee or through other means initiated by the company, the company is bound to explore the notion of what "reasonable accommodation" might be appropriate under the circumstances.

A job offer may not be rescinded until the evidence shows that it is due to "business necessity" or if the disability poses a "severe threat to the health or safety of others." As with many employment laws, the burden of proof lies solely on the company if challenged. The penalties for noncompliance or discrimination can be severe, and employee plaintiffs are entitled to a jury trial. It will be many years before the law is well defined and will undoubtedly be the fertile ground for many lawsuits.

Employees with disabilities have legal protection, which enables them to become productive members of society without discrimination by the company who hires them. How does an employee who has a disabling condition deal with the reality that will confront him or her on the shop floor? Laws cannot legislate employee perceptions of those who are, or who appear to be different from themselves. Employees with physical, mental, or emotional conditions may be treated differently by many who do not have compassion or understanding for their plight. In these situations, the EAP counselor can intervene once the problem surfaces and help both the employee and the company understand the moral and legal implications of their behavior. The EAP can serve to assist the company by counseling employees affected by the presence of the disabled person in the workplace to promote some measure of understanding and tolerance.

The human resource department is responsible for ensuring compliance with the ADA and similar laws in most companies, and it does so through training and education to employees and management as to the law and their respective rights and responsibilities under it. The EAP counselor who is connected to the efforts made by HR to educate and inform employees, as well as the corporate culture they are surviving in will be better equipped to deal with ADA issues in the workplace when they surface.

Family and Medical Leave Act of 1993

This law has been said to be one of the most far-reaching and least-understood laws in employee relations by both employees and management. It is one of the most complex and difficult to administer and comply with for most companies. In some cases, companies are still learning how to fully comply with its mandates.

The goal of the Family and Medical Leave Act (FMLA) is basically simple—employees who experience certain life events and may need (or elect) some time away from work may request unpaid leave time. If the request meets FMLA criteria, the company must grant unpaid leave time and must preserve the employee's job, pay and benefit sta-

tus until the leave period ends and the employee has returned to work. An employee may request up to 12 weeks of unpaid leave in a 12-month period according to the rules and policies set up by the company in compliance with FMLA.

In the past, a female employee who was pregnant and gave birth to a child was considered to be "temporarily disabled" and was granted time off (often with some pay) to give birth and recover from the rigors of childbirth in order to return ready to work. What if she was not ready emotionally to leave the new baby with others? What if there are no others ready and willing to care for the child? Asking for more time off was sometimes looked upon unfavorably by many companies. She either returned to work or faced the possibility of losing her job.

What about the male employee (father) who wants, or may need some time off to help care for the mother, baby or other family members? What about the employee who must take off work to take care of a seriously ill child? Or perhaps a seriously ill parent? Many companies took a dim view of granting an employee more than a few days off without running a risk of having his future employment in possible jeopardy. This is not to say that companies were not compassionate toward their employees. In the practical world of deadlines, production quotas and customer demands, a company is forced into making hard choices in order to accomplish their mission. Employees who are not at work when they could be are hindering the ability of the company to meet its obligations.

The Family and Medical Leave Act addresses all of these potential situations and gives direction as to how the company and employees must handle them when they arise. The rules are complete with detailed forms, procedures, etc., to hopefully prevent abuse or disparate treatment by either the employee or the company.

Human Resource professionals know that while the law can be seen as a restrictive one, the reality seems to be that very few employees actually take unfair advantage of the FMLA law. They see it as a "safety net" if something bad happens to them and they need to take some time off. They know they will not be "fired" indiscriminately based on their need to take care of family concerns or serious medical conditions. In most cases, an employee cannot financially afford to take 12 weeks of unpaid time away from work every year. It is also likely that the need to take this much time off from work may not present itself every year.

While it can be debated as to whether the law addresses all concerns of all parties in its application, FMLA gives the EAP counselor a powerful tool, which if used appropriately, can help preserve and balance an employee's home and work life. If and when the need arises, however, an astute EAP professional can intervene to help the employee solve such a problem and suggest the use of FMLA leave when appropriate.

Health and Wellness Programs

Many larger companies have adopted the notion that employees who have more healthy lifestyles will live longer, be more productive employees and cost their employers less in terms of absenteeism, utilization of benefits, and fewer debilitating injuries. They were among the first to implement "wellness" programs offering encouragement, and in some cases, direct incentives to achieve a more healthy state by making lifestyle changes. The literature is full of stories about companies who have reduced their costs and improved their performance through the use of such programs.

But how does a smaller company with limited resources get involved? Smaller companies can get the same positive effects and potential cost savings that are available to the larger entities, but the costs of implementation may outweigh the benefits in the near term. What can the EAP professional do to help?

Most HR practitioners know that employees with hypertension; those who may be overweight, those who do not get enough exercise; those who smoke; or those who may have substance abuse problems, put their companies at significant financial risk, not to mention the risks to their own personal health. If they believed that they could provide support through a cost-effective effort to create positive change, many would be interested and would work to convince their executive manage-

ment of the benefits of such a program and would seek their support to develop. This is where the EAP counselor could make a significant and long-lasting contribution to the future success of the enterprise.

An EAP counselor has access to an array of literature and educational materials concerning healthy lifestyles. In addition to dealing directly with employees who may have individual lifestyle concerns, a low-cost approach may be the sharing of such information with groups of employees at "wellness meetings" during or after work hours. Some companies offer such meetings during the normal lunch break.

Another tool that can be effectively used is the "health risk appraisal," an instrument which allows an employee to answer a series of lifestyle questions and have their "health risk" measured and plotted in light of their answers to the lifestyle questions. EAP professionals have access to such tools and knowing the culture of the organization can recommend various methods to communicate wellness information in an effective manner. While near-term results are hard to measure, there is no denying the long-term benefits in human terms from making positive changes in one's health and life.

Violence in the Workplace

While some may argue that the news media has made us somewhat immune to violence these days, the thought that we cannot feel safe where we live or work is foreign to many of us. Recent accounts of violence in the workplace have struck a fearful note with employees, HR professionals and managers at all levels alike. The thought of someone attempting to settle a dispute through violent means within the framework of the workplace can be unsettling at best, or downright scary at worst. What can we do to protect ourselves from such violence? How far do we responsibly go to protect employees from potential danger while remaining focused on our business objectives? Progressive companies have a resource in the EAP professional if they choose to take advantage of it.

What is the profile of the potentially violent person? Most HR practitioners, company managers, supervisors, and employees do not know. Even if they know what to look for, they may not know what to do if confronted with the situation. Many companies are responding by establishing policies to address these issues. A policy is only as effective as the manner in which it is carried out. People must be trained to know when and how to act in such situations. The EAP counselor can assist in helping company officials understand the profile of the potentially violent person and what may drive them to this level. The counselor may recommend other resources at his or her disposal to assist in this training effort for the company. The organization should take full advantage of any information it can give to its employees so they can effectively act to protect themselves and their fellow employees from potential harm due to such violent behavior.

CONCLUSION

Most Human Resource professionals understand that there are direct benefits to having a work force that has achieved a higher level of balance between their personal lives and their work lives. They understand that obvious work-related problems can be symptoms of other problems occurring outside the workplace, perhaps much more serious in nature. They also understand that these employees can be rehabilitated through proactive intervention by Employee Assistance Programs and the professionals who run them.

One of the important roles that the EAP counselor should assume should be that of "management trainer" in behavior-related issues. The EAP counselor must work in tandem with the HR practitioners in recognizing when an employee may be "out of balance" by the obvious (or perhaps not too obvious) behaviors displayed. They must work together to effectively use the current laws and other tools at their disposal to allow the employee to learn to bring their lives back into balance. Recognizing the legal, moral and ethical boundaries that must be maintained between HR and EAP professionals, the more they can work together to resolve such problems in the early stages, the more effective they can be. In the business world, one of the measures of success is effectiveness.

Chapter 17

HUMAN RESOURCE DEVELOPMENT IN EMPLOYEE ASSISTANCE PROGRAMMING: AN OVERVIEW

WILLIAM G. EMENER

Important and critical to the concept, **Human Resource Development**, is Prather's (1970) observation: "When I outgrow my names and facts and theories, or when reality leaves them behind, I become dead if I don't go on to new ways of seeing things." Commensurate with this philosophical observation, Stephens and Kneipp (1981) stated, "We can consciously manage only that which we can perceive. If our perception of the world is limited, our ability to conceptualize and choose among alternative courses of action will be even more limited" (p. 87). It is generally agreed that the world and people are constantly changing; interestingly, it has been observed that in the past decade the most observable form of change has been the spiraling rate of change. People, especially those working in employee assistance programs, must remain appreciative of the constantly changing nature of the world and commensurately the constantly changing nature of experience. People are constantly involved in refining their perceptions and the interpretations they give to their experiences (Hultman, 1979). For those individuals working in employee assistance programs, perception of what is possible and the ability to go beyond what was once considered expected, acceptable, and preferred, is directly related to one's capacity for intellectual, emotional, and functional growth. One of the major goals of employee assistance programs is to assist individuals (employees) in maximizing their ability to grow–to become what they are potentially capable of becoming. It would appear fitting to assume that a helper's capacity to help another person grow is related to the extent to which he or she is growing. If this is true, then it equally would make sense to assume that by systematically expanding our perception of the world and adding to our repertoire of knowledges, skills, and abilities (as a function of our lifestyles), our potential ability to meaningfully contribute to the lives of others and the programs in which we work will be realized. Basically, this represents the **a priori** rationale for the importance of having a "human resource development philosophy" meaningfully built into the infrastructure of employee assistance programming. Commensurately, this chapter will: (a) discuss the concepts of education, training and development; (b) concretize the importance of a human resource development component of employee assistance programming; and, (c) conclude with extensional and futuristic suggestions for the overall development of employee assistance programs with a focus on the continuing development of the personnel working in them.

Education, Training and Development

Tantamount to appreciating the ways in which a "human resource development philosophy" can be an integral part of the infrastructure of employee assistance programming, is the understanding of how this philosophy impacts the connotations

Note: This chapter is reprinted from *Employee Assistance Programs: A Basic Text* (1988) with permission of the author, the book's editors (Dickman, Emener, & Hutchison, Jr.), and the publisher (Charles C Thomas, Publisher, Ltd.).

and denotations of education, training, and development for employee assistance program personnel. For example, the phrases, "We need trained staff" and "Our staff needs inservice training" frequently implies the traditional conceptualization of training. "Training" literally means the act or process of directing or forming, typically by instruction, formal discipline, and/or drill. Implicit to the acts of formal discipline and drill is the implication that the recipient engages in a passive role and the provider engages in an active role. The "trainer" trains the "trainee." Human beings, however, tend to unfold and change gradually; moreover, their attitudes toward themselves and toward change play an integral role in their ultimate learning and potential change. People have even been known to resist training—for a number of understandable reasons. People tend to not like being treated like a "trainee." As one trainee stated to this author during an inservice training session, "I'm not a seal or a lion you know. Just because my boss made me come here and I am here, that doesn't mean that I will benefit from the program!" Obviously, this person's boss's attitude toward training and staff development had an important impact on this person's overall benefit (nonbenefit) from the program.

As developed by Nadler (1979), "human resource development" is a series of organized activities conducted within a specified period of time; importantly, it is designed to produce behavioral change. Two key ingredients, however, must exist; (a) the individual must feel that the intended activities and overall outcomes are for his or her benefit (along with the fact that the activities and outcomes are also intended to benefit the program and the program's clientele); and (b) the activities must be organized with predetermined specific processes and outcome goals. If there are no specific outcome goals of a human resource development program, or if there are no expected behavior changes, then it would appear reasonable to question the existence of the human resource development program in the first place. It is important to remember that when planning human resource development activities for employee assistance personnel, the releasing and maximizing of human potential is the ultimate

goal, and outcome goals should be thought of in terms of behavior change.

The following three primary forms of human resource development activities will be discussed in order to demonstrate the influence of the "human resource development philosophy" and also relate them to human resource development in areas relevant to employee assistance programs.

1. **Education** includes those learning activities designed to increase and enhance the individual's overall learning and human potential over time. For example, a preservice education program for employee assistance professionals should be designed to prepare students for a career in employee assistance programming not just a specific job in an employee assistance program. This career orientation is an important attribute of a human resource development program that is educational in nature. Whereas training will typically focus on the needs of the employer, the program, or the company, education focuses on the needs of the learner. Education is less concerned with maximizing compliance, uniformity, and sameness among personnel; education is concerned with individuality, diversity, and future ability to function autonomously. By focusing on more generalized knowledges, skills and abilities, education also prepares an individual to be able to cope, adapt, and adjust to a variety of situations, settings, and circumstances. A counselor working in an employee assistance program enrolled in a business management course at a university, is a good example of continuing education from a human resource development perspective. Such a course would appropriately involve theory (a general orientation); skill development aspects of the course for this individual would be future, career oriented (he or she is currently a counselor and could understandably be considering an upward mobility opportunity as a program manager or program director).

2. **Training** typically involves activities designed to assist an individual in improving a specific job task or set of job tasks. For example, a secretary-receptionist employed in an employee assistance program may attend an inservice training program on bookkeeping and filing. As this clearly indicates, such a program would be expect-

ed to enhance his or her bookkeeping and filing job tasks. Training also entails the connotative notion of minimizing individual differences among staff and enhancing uniformity. While the counselors working in an employee assistance program may work differently with their clients, which from a clinical perspective is very understandable, it would appear very important for the program's clerical staff to do their bookkeeping and filing in a very similar manner. Quite frequently, program maintenance and accountability functions such as these have to be uniform for overall program efficiency purposes. Nonetheless, attributes of training programs such as these should be explained to employees prior to their participating in training programs so that their individual feelings (e.g., such as feelings emanating from their need to be considered unique individuals) do not detract from nor minimize their overall benefits from the training program.

3. **Development** is typically directed toward the future and may include education and/or training. A key element of "development" is the possible element of risk on behalf of the organization, the company or the program. Basically, development activities are designed to move the organization and the employees toward the future, toward new directions and frontiers, and toward the development of possible new program developments and activities. The risk factor emanates from the realization that such future possibilities could entail change, and as most people have experienced, change can be very scary. Nonetheless, it is very wise for employee assistance programs to assure that "development" is an ongoing part of their programs of operation. Nadler (1979) poignantly described the importance of development to an organization:

> As individuals seek to grow on jobs, they need a legitimate and available mechanism for growth and development. If the organization does not provide it, they will either take their creativity and potential off the job or leave the job. (p. 96)

Consistent with the underpinnings of human resource development addressed at the beginning of this chapter, the assumption herein is that human beings not only appreciate and value growth and development as a person, but they will seek it out if it is not available in their environment.

CONCLUDING COMMENTS

An excellent article by This (1980) addressed eight critical issues facing managers in the 1980s. Three of them are very relevant to the importance of assuring that "development" is an integral aspect of the infrastructure and the overall working environment of an employee assistance program. **First,** all the numerous issues regarding the constantly changing worker values and motivation are critical to highly intensive work environments. Employee assistance programs tend to be highly intensive in nature, and it is not uncommon for the employees (clients) seeking assistance from an employee assistance program to be working in a high intensive work environment themselves. As the world changes around us, as people who seek our assistance are amid constant changes, it only seems fitting for us to experience change and development ourselves and continually seek out ways to help our employee assistance programs to be maximally responsive to such changes. **Second,** quality definition, quality assurance, and quality control have become increasingly important to human service programs in the past decade. And, there are many good reasons for this. Nonetheless, if the personnel of an employee assistance program perceive their organization from a "growth and development" perspective, there is a lesser likelihood that they will be resistant to change and more apt to be aware of growth and development needs and potentials on behalf of the organization. As one director of an employee assistance program once said to this author, "My only concern about the growth and development and improvement of our program, is being able to support all of the good ideas for improvement that I am constantly getting from my staff.

They seem to always be looking for ways to improve our organization!" (That is a good concern to have!) **Third**, it is not uncommon for employee assistance programs to have more work to do than they have the time and the staff to do it with. Increasing the resources available to the program is typically easier said than done. Thus, in a resource stabilization mode, program efficiency and effectiveness can really become strained. When the personnel of a program are vigilant of potential ways of growing and expanding, they also tend to be vigilant of ways of enhancing the efficiency and effectiveness of currently existing program components and resources. People in a growth and development-oriented environment, tempered with a genuine appreciation for reality, can be very creative in discerning ways of doing more and doing better with what they have (as well as thinking about what else they could be doing if increased resources were available).

As addressed by Knowles (1980), we are no longer thinking of staff development in the traditional ways of having someone other than the employee deciding what the employee needs, hiring a trainer to didactically tell the employee what he or she needs to know and learn, and then expecting the employee to passively participate and learn, grow, benefit from and enjoy the experience. Our tasks as administrators, managers, supervisors, and human resource development specialists in employee assistance programs, are: (a) to assure that our employees working in our programs experience an internalized desire to develop and grow to their fullest; (b) to help them feel good about themselves when they sense that there may be ways that they could improve themselves and be better than they are; and, (c) to make available to them opportunities for them to maximize their potentials. In his discussion regarding the growth and development of rehabilitation counselors, Emener (1986) stated:

> While professional trainers and professional educators are challenged to assess, plan, develop, implement, and evaluate their programs to maximize their potentials, the professional rehabilitation counselor is reminded that the one person who is ultimately responsible for the continuing education and development of the rehabilitation counselor is the individual rehabilitation counselor! (p. 222)

Thus, it is suggested that within our human resource development programs for our employee assistance program personnel, e.g., preservice, inservice, and continuing education, that this "human resource development philosophy" be part of the infrastructure and the bloodstream of our organizations so that our most precious commodity—our human resources, our personnel—are genuinely concerned about their own growth and development. Commensurately, our employee assistance programs will therefore grow and develop, and our programs will provide better, higher quality, and growing and developing services to those who come to us for assistance.

COMMENT/UPDATE

MICHAEL R. TELVEN

As the profession of Human Resources (HR) enters the twenty-first century, it finds itself to be a specialty in transition. This transition has been ongoing for the past decade and will continue into the next as HR wrestles with the questions of "Why HR exists?" and, "What value it contributes to the organization and what will be the role of HR in the future?" This is important to the EAP professional who most certainly will have frequent interactions with the HR department, especially for "in-house" programs, a department and function in flux.

Primarily, HR has been concerned with the administrative and employee relations functions of the organization. More and more, HR is being scrutinized by senior management and asked to add value by providing strategic partnership with the executive functions and to contribute meaningful change strategies to meet environmental demands. Simultaneously, HR is being asked to reengineer itself to create more efficient processes and to outsource customary functions to external providers such as benefits administration and recruiting.

As an alternative to its customary functions, HR is being asked to provide higher levels of contribution and more meaningful responses and capabilities that are multifunctional. Important issues for the EAP professional in relation to the HR function, include "How to partner with Human Resources by being familiar with their internal and external pressures?"

Within this context let's review the basic concepts of HR, current and evolving. These can be understood within three views: (1) administrative functions; (2) employee relations challenges; and (3) strategic implementation change events.

Administrative Functions

Traditionally, HR has had the responsibility for processing numerous and ever-growing personnel management functions within the organization. The EAP professional may find their clients are involved with some of these issues. An overview of some of those functions follows.

EEO and Affirmative Action

Generally, HR is authorized within the company to ensure the company is in compliance with Equal Employment Opportunity (EEO) regulations, hear employee complaints and conduct investigations. Companies with at least 15 employees or who have business contracts with any government agencies are required to comply with federal guidelines for employment practices.

Some of these regulations are the Title VII of the Civil Rights Act of 1964 (Title VII), which prohibits employment discrimination based on race, color, religion, sex, or national origin; the Equal Pay Act of 1963 (EPA), which protects men and women who perform substantially equal work in the same establishment from sex-based wage discrimination; the Age Discrimination in Employment Act of 1967 (ADEA), which protects

individuals who are 40 years of age or older; Title I and Title V of the Americans with Disabilities Act of 1990 (ADA), which prohibits employment discrimination against qualified individuals with disabilities in the private sector as well as in state and local governments; Sections 501 and 505 of the Rehabilitation Act of 1973, which prohibits discrimination against qualified individuals with disabilities who work in the federal government; and the Civil Rights Act of 1991, which, among other things, provides monetary damages in cases of intentional employment discrimination. The U.S. Equal Employment Opportunity Commission (EEOC) enforces all of these laws. EEOC also provides oversight and coordination of all federal equal employment opportunity regulations, practices, and policies.

Additionally, large employers with government contracts must develop affirmative action plans to ensure the work force reflects community diversity through action plans and timetables.

Workers Compensation

Workers Compensation statutes are insurance programs designed to protect workers that are injured on the job. Statutes differ in interpretation and application by individual states. The company pays for the cost of the insurance through a fee paid by the company to the state based on their "risk" history. Workers can also receive new skills training from the state through Workers Compensation if their injuries prevent them from working at their former job. Basically, Workers' Compensation laws are designed to ensure that employees who are injured or disabled on the job are provided with fixed monetary awards, eliminating the need for litigation. State Workers Compensation statutes establish this framework for most employment situations. Some laws also protect employers by limiting the amount an injured employee can recover from an employer in most accidents.

ERISA

The Employee Retirement Income Security Act (ERISA) was enacted to ensure that employees receive the pension and other benefits promised by their employers. Many provisions of ERISA and the IRC are intended to ensure that tax-favored pension plans do not favor the highest-paid employees over rank-and-file employees in the way benefits are provided. To achieve these ends, ERISA has a complex series of rules that cover pension, profit-sharing stock bonus, and most "welfare benefit plans," such as health and life insurance. ERISA supersedes almost all state laws that affect employee benefit plans and has thus created a single federal standard for employee benefits.

COBRA

The Consolidated Omnibus Budget Reconciliation Act of 1985 (COBRA) requires most employers with group health plans to offer employees the opportunity (at the cost of the entire monthly insurance premium and minor administrative charges) to continue temporarily their group health care coverage under their employer's plan if their coverage otherwise would cease due to termination, layoff, or other change in employment status.

OSHA

The Occupational Safety and Health Act of 1970 formed the agency called OSHA whose mission is to prevent work-related injuries, illnesses and deaths. Since the agency was created in 1971, occupational deaths have been cut in half and injuries have declined by 40 percent.

Employee Benefits

Benefits will differ by the company. Generally, most companies make medical insurance coverage available but the comprehensive nature of the coverage will differ by each company as will the monthly contribution required of each employee. Current programs employ highly creative methods of administration including programs called Health Maintenance Organizations, Preferred Provider Organizations, Point of Service and Managed Indemnity to try to control escalating

medical costs. Very few companies provide cost-free medical insurance in the current market for employee health care.

Likewise, most companies have moved away from company sponsored pension programs due to escalating costs and have installed and encouraged the usage of 401k-type plans. The 401k plan allows participants to contribute to their retirement fund and employers partially match those contributions. In return participants receive tax advantages, greater control over their funds and investment options.

Other benefits a company might offer include vacation time, holidays, tuition reimbursement, stock purchases, child care, award programs, wellness programs and EAP services.

Compensation

Human Resources administers compensation programs that include standards for salaries, external salary surveys, job value comparison systems, salary increases, promotion increases, bonuses, merit awards, pay for performance programs, stock options and other actions that impact directly on remuneration for contribution.

One of the major goals of the compensation program is to establish an attractive compensation package to attract the best qualified applicants. Another goal is to create programs that will motivate employees to exhibit greater performance for acceptable pay. Equally important is the goal to establish internal equity to maintain a sense of fairness based on competencies and contribution throughout the organization.

Employee Relations Challenges

Human Resources is being challenged by its clients to provide practices that will increase employee commitment and performance within the context of increasing demands, fewer resources, a changed employment contract from security to flexibility and flattened hierarchies that create fewer opportunities for promotions and advancements. The challenge for HR is to find creative ways to increase the meaning of the work, find joy in work processes, promote teamwork and establish opportunities for personal and professional growth within the organizational framework. The current challenge to Human Resources is a far cry from the traditional organizational framework of security, stability and corporate paternalism.

The traditional HR programs for employee relations challenges are the performance appraisal, disciplinary procedures, grievance procedures, disciplinary practices and motivation programs. The effectiveness of these programs depends on how the culture of the organization encourages an environment of control or support.

Performance Appraisals

Performance appraisal programs have become very sophisticated over years of research and practice. Yet in practice they still range from basic traits appraisals that evaluate an individual according to personal characteristics to highly sophisticated behavioral and competency tools. Overall, appraisal tools that measure the direct contribution of the performer without resorting to inferences will ultimately be more effective. Some of the best programs focus on the developmental aspect of the job for future performance as well as the communication aspect between leader and associate. It is also helpful to conduct performance feedback more frequently than simply annually, such as quarterly or semi-annually.

Most performance appraisal programs are still tied into budgetary processes because of their connection to salary increases and are delivered on an annual basis. On the negative side, performance appraisals systems can impact the feelings of fairness that drive morale due to concerns about accuracy, timeliness, judging others and separating individual contribution from group contribution.

Grievance Policies

One of the challenges for Human Resources is to surface issues before they become major problems and to assure employees that their concerns are heard. Most companies will establish a policy that ensures employees can bring their issues to their team leaders, or if not possible, to someone within the organization. The policy may include a step-by-step process whereby successive levels of supervision review the concerns and issue judgments. Other policies are less formal and include internal facilitators to ensure the issues are moved to resolution. Either way, the goal is to attain due process and a sense of fairness for the individuals involved.

Disciplinary Procedures

Human Resources is generally the guardian for the disciplinary practices within the organization to ensure fairness and due process among supervisors. From the days of high unionization we still have the three-step disciplinary process that is called progressive discipline and proceeds from a verbal warning of the infraction, to a written warning and to a final warning. Then the problem employee is terminated if sufficient improvements are not implemented. The problem with this procedure is that the process is more legalistic than behavioral, having been developed in union environments that were generally protective rather than improvement oriented. Behavioral programs such as "Positive Discipline" focus more on the worker as an adult who must choose to make their own improvements. They focus on confronting the individual with the specific problem, giving them time to think about if they want to make the adjustments and then having them develop a plan with needed resources to correct the problem. The individual is also given the opportunity to resign if they believe the environment is a bad fit for their interests and style.

Motivation Programs

Motivation programs are extremely diverse and range from doling out gifts and rewards to involving people in important programs and decisions. HR must assess the culture of their organization and determine appropriate performance improvement programs. They can be monetary or opportunity driven. In the end, appreciation and encouragement, a simple thank-you and positive reinforcement seem to work wonders.

The demand on Human Resources in the current business and international environment is to find ways to improve performance, competency and commitment in an era with increasing demands and competition, changing cultural expectations and decreasing opportunities.

Strategic Partners

While Human Resources has greater challenges to be more efficient in its process and program delivery and more responsive to employee challenges, the greatest pressure is coming from the expectation that HR will become a strategic partner with management to help implement the key strategies and change initiatives. The expectation is that HR will make valuable contributions to the success of the business enterprise. To this end senior managers are asking HR to reduce its own costs while providing a more comprehensive and multifaceted contribution to the core of the organizations business. Many of these initiatives are requiring HR to learn new competencies related to the everyday business drivers while still retaining their HR expertise.

Related to this need to translate strategy into action is the requirement to be a change expert. HR professionals are being required to learn all the different roles in the change process, from Catalyst to Facilitator to Champion or Sponsor, and how these roles interact throughout the multi-level change process.

EAP Professionals and HR Professionals

The EAP and Human Resources are professions that have many interests in common and are yet quite distinct. While needing to maintain a professional "separateness" from HR there are many entry points for cooperation and partnering between the HR Department and the EAP. Hopefully this chapter has given an understandable overview of some of the places where the EAP client will be involved with HR and also some of the possibilities where EAP and HR can partner.

ENDNOTES

For the best current work on the challenges faced by Human Resources in today's marketplace, consult David Ulrich, *Human Resources Champions, The Next Agenda for Adding Value and Delivering Results* (Boston, Harvard Business School Press, 1996).

For a description of the call for the reinvention of Human Resources, consult Jerry W. Gilley and Ann Maycunich, *Strategicaly Integrated HRD, Partnering to Maximize Organizational Performance* (Reading, Massachusetts, Addison-Wesley, 1998).

An excellent source on the internet for EEOC information is maintained by the Federal Government at www.eeoc.gov.

REFERENCES

Emener, W. G. (1986). *Rehabilitation counselor preparation and development: Selected critical issues.* Springfield, IL: Charles C Thomas, Publisher, Ltd.

Hultman, K. E. (1979). The path of least resistance. Austin, TX: Learning Concepts. Knowles, M.S. (1980). Malcolm Knowles on the challenge of the '80's. *Training and Development Journal, 34* (1), 42–44.

Nadler, L. (1979). *Developing human resources* (2nd Ed.). Austin, TX: Learning Concepts.

Prather, H. (1970). *Notes to myself.* Moab, UT: Real People Press.

Stephens, J. E., & Kneipp, S. (1981). Managing human resource development in rehabilitation. In W. G. Emener, R. L. Luck, & S. J. Smits (Eds.), *Rehabilitation administration and supervision.* Baltimore, MD: University Park Press.

This, L .E. (1980). Critical issues confronting managers in the '80's. *Training and Development Journal, 34* (1), 14–17.

Chapter 18

ALCOHOL AND DRUG ABUSE AWARENESS: IMPLICATIONS FOR INTAKE INTERVIEWING

HELEN FRYE DAHLHAUSER, FRED DICKMAN, WILLIAM G. EMENER and BONNIE YEGIDIS-LEWIS

American society's commitment to being responsive to the psychosocial health care needs of its citizens has been witnessed in the growth, expansion, and enrichment of counseling programs. Community-based counseling centers are typically designed to be responsive to persons with categorical difficulties, e.g., mental health, spouse abuse, marital and family problems, sexual dysfunction, and rape crisis, among others. Tantamount to the quality of service delivery at such centers has been a unique practitioner–the professional counselor. "The counseling practitioner is in a unique position to influence the behavior of others" (Galvin & Ivey, 1981, p. 536). Moreover, it must be remembered that this influence may be "for better or worse," for counseling and psychotherapy can help as well as harm (Hadley & Strupp, 1976). Helpful counseling is many times meaningfully influenced by the initial, intake interview.

Tyler (1969) stated that "the first interview is in many ways the hardest" (p. 40), and offered three major goals of the initial interview: ". . . the foundation for a relationship between counselor and client will have been laid down . . . to open up all of the psychological realities in the client's situation . . . to 'structure' the situation for the client" (pp. 53–55). Wolberg (1954) articulated several other goals including the gathering of pertinent information from the client to help establish the tentative dynamics and make a tentative diagnosis. Hollis and Woods (1981) identified four questions

that should be answered during the intake interview: (a) can the agency provide the help the client needs? (b) length of treatment required? (c) location of the problem? and (d) who is to be seen? It is the contention of the authors that most of the goals and objectives of initial interviews are the same goals for intake counseling. Intake counseling is a critical aspect of community-based counseling programs, requires specialized expertise, and is more effective if clients perceive the intake counselor to be an expert–viz, "the client's belief that the counselor possesses information and means of interpreting information, which allow the client to obtain valid conclusions about and to deal effectively with his problems" (Strong & Dixon, 1971, p. 562). The intake counselor's expertness is critical for numerous reasons. It is important for the accurate communication of empathic understanding and to influence the client's attitude toward counseling. Keefe (1976) believed empathy provides the impetus for change in clients. Altmann (1973) stated:

> The findings suggest that the dimension of accurate empathy plays a vital role in determining whether clients will continue or terminate counseling after the initial interview . . . empathy is almost exclusively related to terminating or continuing counseling after the first interview. (pp. 227–228)

Empathy training, initial interviewing, and intake counseling have been and are critical components

Note: This chapter is reprinted from *Counseling the Troubled Person in Industry* (1985) with permission of the author, the book's editors (Dickman, Emener, & Hutchison, Jr.), and the publisher (Charles C Thomas, Publisher, Ltd.).

of counselor preparation programs (Gilmore, 1973; Ivey & Authier, 1978).

Given the importance of intake counseling to community-based counseling programs and the importance of empathy and expertness in the intake counseling process, the purposes of this paper are to: (a) highlight the relevance of alcohol and drug abuse to community-based counseling; (b) describe a pilot observation which demonstrates the relevance of alcohol and drug abuse awareness to community-based intake counseling; and, (c) offer recommendations for pre-service and inservice counselor education and training, and suggested research and demonstration needs.

Relevance of Alcohol and Drug Abuse

Correlational findings among alcohol and other drug use and abuse and individual and family problems have been documented. Expressed individual and family problems, such as those that follow, are those typically encountered by intake counselors at community-based counseling centers.

Divorce

Studies summarized by Shuckit and Morrissey (1976) have indicated a significantly higher divorce rate among families experiencing alcohol problems than is true in the general population. (Divorce in American society has witnessed an escalating incidence rate over the past decade).

Family Violence

A positive relationship appears to exist between alcohol and other drug use and family violence. For example, in Emerson's (1979) survey of all cases of family violence handled by the Los Angeles police department over a period of five years, over half the cases were associated with alcohol or other drug use.

Spouse Abuse

While spouse abuse is not directly linked with alcohol abuse, drinking and other drug use and spouse abuse are associated. For example, in a survey of women who sought emergency aid in Ann Arbor, Michigan, over half of the abusive husbands were excessive drinkers and drinking was involved in 66 percent of the incidents (Congressional Record, 1978). Langley and Levy (1977) reviewed several studies of drunkenness and physical abuse and estimated that 40–95 percent of spouse abuse cases are directly linked to alcohol abuse. Other studies have indicated a significant relationship between spouse abuse and drinking by both spouses (Carder, 1978; Hindman, 1979).

Child Abuse

As in spouse abuse, excessive alcohol and other drug usage are associated with child abuse. A study attempting early detection of family pathology in a medical outpatient clinic found relationships between alcohol abuse and child abuse (Bekling, 1978). The same study found a relationship between child abuse and spouse abuse. A summary of studies by Kempe and Helfer (1972) estimated that as many as one-third of all cases of reported child abuse are alcohol related. Alcohol has also been related to child sexual abuse. Several studies (Epstein, Cameron, & Room, 1977; Julian & Mohr, 1980; National Center on Child Abuse and Neglect, 1981) have reported alcohol as a factor in incestuous families.

Sexual Dysfunction

Alcohol abuse and alcoholism has been definitely associated with lower testosterone level in males (DeLucca, 1981). This would corroborate clinical findings (Forrest, 1976) that alcoholics of both genders have an unusually high rate of sexual dysfunction.

Interpersonal Communications

In a study of both alcoholic and nonalcoholic couples, Ritchey (1979) found that drinking increased negative affective responses in both couples. The author concluded that ethanol introduction into couple interaction enhances the probability of negative emotional interaction. The increase in negative affect was highly significant for alcoholic couples and, while less significant, marked for nonalcoholic couples. (It may be that couples seeking counseling in communication skills would enhance these skills simply by not drinking, or by at least being aware of a pattern.)

Relevance to Community-Based Counseling Centers

The complex problems listed above are common complaints brought to community-based counseling centers. Since the relationship between typical individual, marital, and family problems and alcohol and other drugs is well-documented, it follows that the more "alcohol and drugs aware" intake counselors are, the better their understanding of client problems. For example, it is unusual that the problem family will mention drinking as a factor unless alcoholism has developed to an advanced stage. Alcoholism authorities recognize denial as a universal defense mechanism (DeLucca, 1981; Hirsch, 1967; Kissin & Begleiter, 1977). Yet drinking may be associated with the presented problem and in need of attention. If drinking or drug use is a pattern in spouse abuse, child abuse, sexual dysfunction, or other difficulties, problems may be somewhat minimized, or in some cases eliminated, with the cessation of drug intake or at least in the recognition of its involvement. As rehabilitation counselors continue to seek and obtain employment in settings involving work with clientele having alcohol and drug abuse difficulties (consult Dickman & Emener, 1982), it is critical for them to be professionally prepared to see alcohol and drug abuse as potentially being meaningfully related to clients' problems. In her article on intake and referral in an alcoholism setting, Petropoulos (1978) concluded that accurate assessment and referral are essential for successful rehabilitation of clients. Being aware of alcohol and drug abuse, is sine qua non to accurate empathy, perceived expertness, and overall effectiveness in the intake counseling process. The authors conducted a pilot observation to explore the criticalness of this "awareness" phenomenon.

A Pilot Observation

The purpose of this investigation was to explore the extent to which an intake counselor would/could identify the relatedness of alcohol and drug abuse to client problems. A comparison was made between intake counseling conducted by an intake counselor "untrained" in alcohol and drug abuse and an intake counselor "trained" in alcohol and drug abuse. All intakes were conducted at a community-based counseling center [the Family Service Agency, Clearwater, Florida.]

The "untrained" intake counselor (female) had a B.A. and several years experience as a volunteer in a rape crisis center. It was reported that: (a) almost all interviews were conducted by telephone; (b) the purpose was to determine the present emotional state of the caller and solicit information relevant to the presented problem(s); and (c) callers were questioned about their motivation for calling and their expectations of services. At the conclusion of each interview, she would determine whether to refer the client to another agency or assign the client to one of the counselors at the receiving agency. If she determined that the client was appropriate for the receiving agency, she needed to get certain specific information for the agency's records, such as: (a) names; (b) sex; (c) dates of birth and ages of each member of the household; (d) home address and phone number; (e) work phone number; (f) marital status; (g) by whom the client was referred; and (h) previous counseling. If appropriate, an appointment was made and the information was written up on an agency form and given to the counselor to whom the client had been assigned.

The "trained" intake counselor (female) had a B.A. and was completing a Master's degree in Rehabilitation Counseling. She had had one introductory course in the theoretical aspects of alcohol and drug abuse. Similarities between the "untrained" and "trained" intakes included: (a) most interviews were conducted by telephone; and (b) recorded necessary data remained the same. At the beginning of the telephone conversation, the "trained" intake counselor volunteered that all information was confidential and that it would be helpful in meeting the client's needs. She also checked specifically for the relationship of alcohol and drugs, legal or illegal, to the presented problem(s). This was frequently handled indirectly during the intake interview with questions such as: (a) "Has there been a change in lifestyle for you and/or any member of your household?" and (b) "How do you and members of your household handle stress?" When appropriate, she directly asked if drinking or the use of drugs accompanied certain behavior(s). For example, a man called for help because he hit his girlfriend on several occasions. When asked if he drank, he responded that he rarely did. When asked if he had been drinking in each instance when he hit her, he reported that he had. Another example of a drug-related problem was in the referral by the police of a six-year-old rape victim to the agency. When the intake counselor asked if drugs or alcohol had been involved, the response was that the offender was picked up in the front yard of the victim's home

unconscious from the intake of too much alcohol. In another example, a call was received from a woman who asked for help because she was having marital problems. When specifically asked how she and her husband coped with stress, she said her husband locked himself in a room and drank heavily till he was drunk enough to get to sleep.

Observed Data

When the "untrained" counselor's intakes for a six-month period were analyzed, out of 343 intakes, 21 (6.1%) of the problems were recorded as alcohol and/or drug related. The pilot observation conducted by the "trained" intake counselor over a two-month period of time, revealed that out of 138 intakes, 84 (60.8%) were reported as alcohol and/or drug related.

CONCLUSIONS, IMPLICATIONS, AND RECOMMENDATIONS

Individual, marital, and family problems appear to be associated with alcohol and other drug use and abuse. Unfortunately, intake counselors and therapists may not be aware of such associations or may give a low priority to the role of drugs and alcohol. This lack of awareness may cause counselors to focus on marginally relevant symptomatology rather than addressing primary aspects of presented problem(s). Community-based counseling centers are progressively utilizing intake counselors as part of the overall service delivery processing. It is critical that intake counselors accomplish the goals of initial contacts with clients (Altmann, 1973; Hollis & Woods, 1981; Strong & Dixon, 1971; Tyler, 1969; Wolberg, 1954). Thus, it is concluded that the documented association between alcohol and drug abuse and many of the problems for which clients typically come to community-based counseling centers, clearly illustrates the importance of intake counselors having high level alcohol and drug abuse awareness.

Implications such as these translate into numerous recommendations for the counseling profes-

sion–such as:

1. Preservice, inservice, and continuing education programs for counselors should include alcohol and drug abuse awareness content (e.g., to distinguish between alcohol and drug use and abuse, problem drinking and alcoholism, and how drinking and drug use patterns are associated and differentiated from abusing patterns); specific skill-building in intake counseling should sequentially be included as well;

2. Research and demonstration projects should be conducted to empirically test the findings and recommendations of the authors' pilot observation; and,

3. Where known associations between alcohol and/or drug abuse and individual, marital, and family problems exist, research and demonstration projects should be conducted to see if cessation of the associated alcohol and drug abuse reduces, minimizes, or remediates the client problems (e.g., spouse or child abuse, sexual dysfunction, interpersonal communications problems).

It is also suggested that the outcome findings of such research and demonstration investigations would have direct and indirect impact on accreditation, certification, and licensure issues.

American society's commitments to its troubled citizens connotes efficient, effective, and timely service delivery. And as was clearly delineated in the Fall, 1981 issue of the *Journal of Applied Rehabilitation Counseling* [*12* (3)], which featured a Special Section containing five solicited articles focusing on alternative job markets for rehabilitation counselors (pp. 145–149), rehabilitation counselors are championing this commitment on behalf of society in a variety of settings–including community-based counseling centers. The observations, suggestions, and recommendations herein, although interpolated and extrapolated in nature, call for specially prepared "alcohol and drug abuse aware" intake rehabilitation counselors–the proposed benefits to clients are too compelling to ignore.

REFERENCES

Altmann, H. A. (1973). Effects of empathy, warmth, and genuineness in the initial counseling interview. *Counselor Education and Supervision, 12* (3), 225–228.

Bekling, D. W. Comprehensive care clinic: Findings relative to domestic violence and alcohol abuse. Paper presented at National Council on Alcoholism Meeting, St. Louis, 1978.

Carder, J .H. Families in trouble. Paper presented at 24th International Institute on Prevention and Treatment of Alcoholism, Zurich, 1978.

Congressional Record. Hearings on domestic violence prevention and services act. *Congressional Record,* 1978.

DeLucca, J. R. *Alcohol and health.* Fourth Special Report to the U.S. Congress, Washington, D.C.: U.S. Department of Health and Human Services, January 1981.

Dickman, F., & Emener, W. G. (1982). Employee assistance programs: An emerging vista for rehabilitation counseling. *Journal of Applied Rehabilitation Counseling, 13* (3), 18–20, 24.

Emerson, C. D. (1979). Family violence: A study by the Los Angeles County Sheriffs Department. *Police Chief, 46* (6), 48–50.

Epstein, T., Cameron, T., & Room, R. Alcohol and family abuse. In Aarens, M., Cameron, T., Roizen, J., Roizen, R., Room, R., Schneberk, D., & Wingard, D. *Alcohol, Casualties and Crime.* Special report prepared for the National Institute on Alcohol Abuse and Alcoholism under Contract No. (ADM) 281–76–0027. Berkeley, Calif.: Social Research Group, University of California, 1977.

Forrest, G. G. (1976). The diagnosis and treatment of alcoholism. Springfield, IL: Charles C Thomas, Publisher, Ltd.

Galvin, M., & Ivey, A. E. (1981). Researching one's own interviewing style: Does your theory of choice match your actual practice? *Personnel and Guidance Journal, 59* (8), 536–539.

Gilmore, S. K. (1973). *The counselor-in-training.* New York: Meredith Corporation.

Hadley, S., & Strupp, H. (1976). Contemporary views of negative effects in psychotherapy. *Archives of General Psychiatry, 33,* 1291–1302.

Hindman, M. (1979). Family violence: An overview. *Alcohol Health Research World, 4* (1), 2–11.

Hirsch, J. (1967). *Opportunities and limitations in the treatment of alcoholics.* Springfield, IL: Charles C Thomas, Publisher, Ltd.

Hollis, F., & Woods, M. E. (1981). *Casework: A psychosocial therapy.* New York: Random House.

Ivey, A. E., & Authier, J. (1978). *Microcounseling: Innovations in interviewing, counseling, psychotherapy, and psychoeducation* (2nd ed.). Springfield, IL: Charles C Thomas, Publisher, Ltd.

Julian, V., & Mohr, C. Father-daughter incest–profile of the offender. Denver: National Study on Child Neglect and Abuse Reporting, 1980.

Keefe, T. (1976). Empathy: The critical skill. *Social Work, 21,* 10–14.

Kempe, H., & Helfer, R. E. (1972). *Helping the battered child and his family.* New York: Lippincott.

Kissin, J., & Begleiter, L. (1977). *The biology of alcoholism: Treatment and rehabilitation of the chronic alcoholic* (Vol. 5). New York: Plenum Press.

Langley, R., & Levy, R. (1977). *Wife-beating: The silent*

Acknowledgment: The authors express sincerest appreciation to the Family Service Agency, Clearwater, Florida, for the helpful cooperation and assistance received during the conduction of the pilot observation.

crisis. New York: Dutton.

National Center on Child Abuse and Neglect. *Study of the incidence and severity of child abuse and neglect.* 1981, in press.

Petropoulos, A. W. (1978). Intake and referral in an alcoholism agency. *Social Casework, 59,* 21–26.

Ritchey, D. Marital interaction of alcoholic couples: Changes in affective communication during experimental drinking. Doctoral dissertation, University of Pittsburgh, 1979. (University Microfilms No. 7924738).

Shuckit, M. A., & Morrissey, E. R. (1976). Alcoholism in women: Some clinical and social perspectives with an emphasis on possible subtypes. In Greenblatt, M., & Shuckit, M. A. (Eds.), *Alcoholism problems in women and children.* New York: Grune & Stratton.

Strong, S. R., & Dixon, D. N. (1971). Expertness, attractiveness, and influence in counseling. *Journal of Counseling Psychology, 18,* 562–570.

Tyler, L. E. (1969). *The work of the counselor.* New York: Appleton-Century-Crofts, Inc.

Wolberg, L. (1954). *The techniques of psychotherapy.* New York: Grune & Stratton.

Chapter 19

THE PREPARATION AND DEVELOPMENT OF EMPLOYEE ASSISTANCE PROGRAM PROFESSIONALS

WILLIAM G. EMENER

*An EAP education and development program's greatest strength
is vested in its diversity and tolerance of difference.*

The number of employee assistance programs (EAPs) throughout the United States, especially over the past three decades, has been escalating at a geometric rate (Dickman, Emener & Hutchison, 1985). Commensurately, increased attention and energy has been given to the staffing, professionalism, and personnel preparation issues relevant to the advancements and continued developments of employee assistance programs. Recently, for example, Maiden and Hardcastle (1986) stated:

> There are currently more than 8,000 EAPs in American work organizations, including 80 percent of the Fortune 500 companies. In light of this growth, the development of standards and professionalization of employee assistance programs is receiving increased attention. (p. 63)

Human service professionals increasingly have been seeking employment opportunities in the private sector human service arenas (consult Dickman & Emener, 1982; Emener, 1986; Lynch & Martin, 1982; and McMahon, Matkin, Growick, Mahaffey & Gianforte, 1983). More pointedly, recent surveys of graduates of rehabilitation counselor education programs (e.g., Janes & Emener, 1985) and social work education programs (e.g.,

Maiden & Hardcastle, 1986) have reported high percentages of rehabilitation counseling and social work graduates seeking and obtaining employment in employee assistance programs. From a clinical service delivery perspective, this makes sense in view of the fact that current EAPs are typically characterized by a helping/rehabilitative orientation operationalizing the philosophy that personal problems, whether caused by work-related or nonwork-related events or situations, do affect the individual as well as the organization and the environment in which the individual is working.

In addition to fostering a helping/rehabilitative orientation, professional preparation programs should also be sensitive to the importance of their "developmental" mission (as discussed in Chapter 28 of this text). In his recent book focusing on the professional preparation and development of the rehabilitation counselor, Emener (1986) articulated this career orientation attitude: "They (rehabilitation counselor education programs) should be committed not just to their students, in view of their students' jobs as rehabilitation counselors, but to their students, in view of their students' life-long careers in the field of rehabilitation" (p. 176). Thus, it would appear equally important for professional preparation programs whose graduates

Note: This chapter is reprinted from *Employee Assistance Programs: A Basic Text* (1988) with permission of the author, the book's editors (Dickman, Emener, & Hutchison, Jr.), and the publisher (Charles C Thomas, Publisher, Ltd.).

are seeking and obtaining employment in EAPs, to be cognizant of their role(s) in preparing students not just for specific jobs in EAP's but for careers in EAP service delivery which may include the eventual holding of numerous job positions in EAP's during their future professional lives.

Along with the continuing developments in preservice, inservice, and continuing education programs for EAP professionals, the recent past has witnessed increased attention to employee assistance program data, knowledge and information in textbooks, magazines, journals, and other assorted forms of information dissemination media. For example, Desmond (1982) recently stated:

> The Performance Resource Press in Troy, Michigan, has established itself as a leading resource center for training materials in the EAP field, including the EAP Digest. Other helpful journals and magazines are Alcoholism: The National Magazine, published by Alcom, Inc., and Alcohol Health and Research World, published by the National Institute on Alcohol Abuse and Alcoholism (NIAAA). (p. 30)

The professional publications of national associations of professionals in the fields of rehabilitation, social work, psychology, medicine, etc. have also witnessed an increasing number of refereed articles and reports addressing the aspects of employee assistance programming. The important aspect of this is that there is a growing body of knowledge in the EAP field, and that knowledge is in appropriate repositories of knowledge, and is available to professional education and programs for their use.

This chapter will: (a) discuss important and critical aspects of educational programming development relevant to employee assistance programs; (b) present and discuss important educational constructs and content areas; (c) review and discuss alternative learning modules, prerequisites and sequencing; (d) present important curricula areas of study; and (e) conclude with recommendations for the future of professional preparation programs for EAP professionals.

Important Aspects of Educational Programming for EAP Professionals

Professional literature is replete with textbooks, monographs, journal articles, and guides relevant to the important and critical aspects of professional education and development programming. The purpose of the following is not to repeat, duplicate, or review all of such existing material. Rather, the following is designed to address those attributes and aspects of professional preparation and development programming that are relevant and germane to EAP professionals.

Student-Trainee Issues

One of the numerous sets of critical issues related to students in a professional preparation program, is that involving student recruitment and selection. Program faculty constantly should be aware of the preferred attributes of the students who enter their programs. In turn, faculty should identify and activate as many recruitment possibilities available to them (e.g., personal visits and presentations to student groups in colleges and universities, to professional groups at meetings and conferences; the mailing out of recruitment information and materials to potential sources of students). Student selection is a very important function on behalf of the faculty. Typically, there are admissions standards and criteria, which supercede those of an individual program (e.g., for a graduate program, there usually are minimum grade point average and graduate record examination criteria). Standards such as these can be established by the program's home institution (e.g., college or university) or by the program's relevant national, professional accreditation body associated with the program's individual discipline (e.g., for a rehabilitation counseling program, this would be the Council for Rehabilitation Education; for social work, the Council on Social Work Education; for psychology, the American Psychological Association). In addition to admissions standards and criteria such as these, the faculty should also consider admissions criteria relevant to professional practice in an employee assistance program. In this regard, some programs require all applicants to have a personal interview with members of the program's admissions committee. Quite frequently, a counselor, social worker, or administrator from an EAP can interview applicants and provide very helpful and useful information and feedback to the program faculty. This also is a very helpful recruitment measure in that applicants can readily see that the program values and works closely with professional practitioners from the field.

Another important aspect of a professional education program for EAP professionals is the extent to which the program operationalizes a "career orientation" toward and with its students. In view of the suggested "developmental philosophy" of an EAP professional education program (as discussed in Chapter 28 of this book), students, prospective and current, should be cognizant of the importance of their developing themselves for a career–not just a job. Fittingly, recruitment materials and presentations, EAP orientation workshops and courses, and the overall attitude of the program's faculty and staff should reflect this orientation. In such activities, moreover, applicants and students should be encouraged to engage in reality testing with regard to their intended career in employee assistance programs. For example, it can be very exciting for an applicant or a student to see that beginning salaries in EAP's are in the $20,000 range and that EAP directors can earn up to $100,000 per year, plus expenses. The glamour and glisten of envisioning a plush office, a new company car, nice clothes, and a private secretary can be very appealing. Nonetheless, as Desmond (1985) pointed out, there are other realities too:

> The aspiring EAP counselor also will encounter other aspects of EAP work, which will be different from what would be found in more traditional rehabilitation settings. The counselor in an EAP may be required to travel extensively. An EAP in a headquarters setting may provide services to distant branches or plants of the organization. Personnel from the home office may set up EAPs at satellites, and either deliver services directly to workers in those settings or train personnel in those sites to deliver services. In the latter case, the satellite EAP

> staff must be trained, monitored, and supervised. Counselors also will encounter the expectation in industry that referred employees should "get better soon." Thus, it is likely that an EAP counselor will be expected to "produce" the desired improvement more quickly than would a counselor in a public or private, nonprofit agency. For the most part, EAP jobs are not 9 to 5 jobs. Counselors may be confronted with a crisis and be expected to produce results quickly. In serious situations, attention may be needed nearly around the clock. Lastly, EAP personnel are expected to have good writing skills. Reports must be well-written since copies may go to medical directors, plant managers, and other administrators. (p. 29)

Indeed, there are numerous intrinsic and extrinsic rewards for working in EAP programs. The importance of assuring that applicants and students are realistically aware of what professional EAP work activities and job tasks entail, however, should be a basic element of the infrastructure of a professional education and development program.

Students should also be encouraged to explore the details of their professional career orientation. It is important for a professional to understand the multiplicity of professional identities and appreciate the potential role ambiguity and role strain that such multiplicities can present. For example, an individual's professional self-concept is frequently related to the ways in which he or she responds to questions such as: "Am I a professional rehabilitation counselor (social worker, psychologist, etc.) who happens to be working in an employee assistance program?" or, "Am I a professional EAP counselor who happened to be educated and trained in a rehabilitation counselor (social work, psychology, etc.) education program?" An individual's response to questions such as this, moreover, will have a meaningful impact on what professional associations he or she will join, what journals he or she will subscribe to and read, and what professional conferences and workshops he or she will most likely attend.

Educational Program Issues

There are numerous educational program

issues which are critical and important to an EAP professional education and development program–too many to address in one part of one chapter of one book. Nonetheless, the experience of the author suggests that the following issues deserve special consideration. In his discussion of key constructs and contents of rehabilitation counselor education, Emener (1986) suggested what he considered to be the two pivotal questions confronting professional program educators:

1. What contents and constructs should be included in a rehabilitation counselor education program? and,
2. How should such contents and constructs be determined? (p. 115).

Typically, an EAP education and development program's response to questions such as these will be a function of the basic discipline of the college, department, or program in which it is housed. For example, if the program is housed in a college of education OR a college of arts and sciences, OR if the program is housed in a department of rehabilitation degree requirements and departmental, disciplinary professional accreditation standards will dictate certain requirements of the program.

This reality, however, is not a negative or "bad" condition. Predicated on the assumption that professional disciplines deserve educational program "departmental" or sanctioned "program" status within a college or university (in this configuration they also enjoy the safeguards provided by respective accreditation bodies), then "employee assistance programs" are considered employment settings in which a variety of professionals work and not professional disciplines unto themselves. Fittingly, employee assistance education and development programs are typically options, specializations, or tracks within rehabilitation counseling, social work, guidance and counseling, and psychology (to name a few) degree programs. When faculty develop an "EAP specialty" (track, option, etc.) within their department's or program's degree, the first activity is to identify the special knowledges, skills and expertise necessary for successful employment as a professional in an employee assistance program. Sources of such

information are available in the literature. For example, using the critical competency areas identified by Sink and Porter (1978), Hastings (1984) developed a questionnaire with 60 skill statements relevant to the professional work tasks in an employee assistance program. The nine competency areas were: (a) locating persons in need of services; (b) determining eligibility; (c) using diverse community resources; (d) assisting clients with the development of a rehabilitation plan; (e) insuring community services; (f) determining diagnostic procedures needed; (g) interpreting data to clients; (h) developing and maintaining a counseling relationship; and (i) using appropriate techniques to effect job placement and job retention of clients. For determining the extent to which persons working in EAP's thought rehabilitation counselor skills were applicable to the EAP field, Hastings (1984) sent her questionnaires to 50 companies thought to have EAPs. Respondents were asked to indicate (a) whether each of the individual skills listed was important in terms of the respondent's job in the EAP in his or her company, and (b) whether each of the individual skills listed was important in terms of the field of EAPs. Among her results, Hastings (1984) reported:

> The competency areas on which these respondents agreed for both relevancy levels were: locating persons in need of services; determining eligibility; using diverse community resources; insuring continuity of services; and, developing and maintaining a counseling relationship. Specific skill statements [which had high response frequencies] in relevancy to the EAP field included: can identify varied strategies for effective referral of clients to specialists; utilizes efficient case management and recording techniques; can use a systematic problem solving approach in counseling with clients; can demonstrate empathy, genuineness, warmth, concreteness, and respect across a variety of clients; is able to set mutually agreeable goals with clients; and, demonstrates an understanding of the ethical considerations of confidentiality. (p. 30)

Thus, as demonstrated by this illustration, the first step is to identify outcome expectations of the EAP education and development program.

It is also important to identify available resources within the immediate, on-grounds proximity of the program, faculty, and students (e.g., on campus) that are critical to a successful EAP education and development program. Such resources would include:

1. Adequate library holdings–textbooks, professional journals, films, audio and videotapes, and microfiche (among others). Basically, the program has to have an up-to-date knowledge base to draw from.
2. Counseling and learning laboratories–a counseling lab with two-way mirrors and accommodations for individual and group sessions (appropriate audio and video equipment can be very helpful for research and instructional purposes), learning laboratories with computer facilities and media equipment. The learning environment is very important to an EAP education and development program.
3. Cognate educational programs within the institution (e.g., departments of psychology, social work, rehabilitation counseling, guidance and counseling, schools of business and schools of continuing education) can provide opportunities for students to choose elective coursework, for faculty to consult and request presentations, and for the program to have an overall base of expertise not readily available within it.

Essentially, it is most desirable for an EAP education and development program to be located in an environment that will support, enhance, and challenge it.

The surrounding community is another important environment to an EAP education and development program. For example, in a surrounding community which has local industries and businesses which have flourishing and successful EAPs, there would tend to be numerous opportunities for the program to: (a) have a large selection of EAP professionals from whom guest lecturers, guest presenters, and adjunct faculty could be recruited and used in the presentation of coursework; (b) opportunities for field site visits, practica and internships for students to have real, in-the-field learning experiences could be formally developed; and (c) settings and populations for basic and applied research on behalf of faculty and students would be available. When there are EAPs in the surrounding community, it also is advisable for the faculty to ask nearby, practicing EAP professionals to help the EAP education and development program with its organizational and operational activities by serving on the program's Advisory Committee, Curriculum Committee, Admissions Committee, and other assorted task force groups charged with the design, implementation, and evaluation of the program. Likewise, it is not uncommon for nearby, community EAPs to ask faculty and students to assist them in designing, conducting, and evaluating their own inhouse staff development and continuing education programs. Arrangements like this allows for the sharing of information, educational and training materials, and equipment.

It has generally been accepted that the most important resource to an education and development program is its faculty. Organizationally, it has been suggested that no program will exceed the effectiveness of its leadership (Emener, Luck & Smits, 1981). Fittingly, while it is advisable to have collective wisdom involved in the planning, designing and conducting of an EAP education and development program (i.e., through the use of advisory, admissions and curriculum committees), it is very helpful if one member of the faculty who is committed to professional employee assistance programming be "in charge" of the program. Basically, it is recommended that the program have a program Director or Coordinator. It is also important for the remaining faculty to be appreciative of employee assistance programming and to be committed to the program's missions and objectives. Students typically take courses with a variety of faculty, and the overall faculty members' collective and individual attitudes toward EAPs represent a very critical influential force in the students' development as professionals.

As discussed earlier, some EAP education and development programs are separate programs within colleges and universities and others (most) are programs housed within one department or program having a traditional, professional disciplinary base (e.g., rehabilitation counseling, social work, etc.). Nonetheless, it is recommended that the EAP education and development program operationalize a multidisciplinary approach. For example, it is important for the program's organizational structure to include professionals (viz, faculty) from a variety of cognate departments and disciplines (e.g., psychology, business, etc.). Students should be encouraged to take elective coursework in other departments, with faculty from other disciplinary backgrounds. Here again, the value of the "development philosophy" can be appreciated; disciplinary incestuousness should be guarded against at all times. As comforting as it can be for everyone to tend to see things in similar ways, in the students' overall, long-term "development" it is very valuable for them to be exposed to a variety of approaches, understandings, and styles.

Curriculum Issues and Content

Employee assistance program educators and human resource development specialists, assuredly are aware that circa 1987 there are numerous colleges, universities, and continuing education programs that have established curriculum and coursework for employee assistance professionals. It can be very tempting to go to a library or contact a university or continuing education program and simply implement their "canned" curriculum. It is strongly suggested, however, that in the long run this is a very poor approach. People typically have great difficulty investing themselves and their energies into "someone else's" program. From an organizational development point of view, it is very helpful for the leadership and faculty of an EAP education and development program to review and study what others have done ("there is no need to reinvent the wheel"). At the same time, however, it is equally very important for the program's leadership and faculty to "build their own program." For example, a good place to start is for the faculty to work together to develop their responses (answers) to the two questions suggested by Emener (1986): (1) What contents and constructs should be included in the program? and (2) How should such contents and constructs be determined? When the leadership and faculty of a

program work together and develop their program, for their students, and for their community, the probabilities of their investing themselves into their program will be enhanced tremendously. When the program is then implemented, the faculty will invest themselves into the programs more because they want to, not just because it is their job.

Curriculum Planning and Development Issues

In the process of planning and developing an EAP education and development program, there are numerous important issues to be considered. Identifying and operationalizing appropriate learning approaches, discerning appropriate learning module areas, and then developing specific coursework are three important areas of consideration.

Learning Approaches. Two sets of differential approaches to the students' learning outcomes are deserving of the faculty's attention and consideration. First, there are alternative "models" of education to consider. For example, there is the Arts and Science Model, and there is the Professional School Model. Emener and McFarlane (1985) discussed the uniqueness of these two models:

> Among other constructs, the arts and sciences approach encourages coursework in the traditional, basic disciplines (e.g., sociology, psychology, humanities). The professional school approach . . . encourages coursework in applied, within-the-specific-professional-discipline area (e.g., social work, rehabilitation counseling), and also emphasizes supervised clinical practice (practica and internship). The arts and sciences model is more basic and generic in nature; the professional school model is more focused and applied in nature and has a strong "practice" component. (p. 8)

It is important for the faculty to discuss the pros and cons of these two models and their relevance to the overall program and curriculum and the individual courses. In most EAP education and development programs, combinations of both models can be found. Second, coursework can be presented in (a) a formal, in class, didactic format (e.g., the instructor lectures and the students listen, ask questions and take notes) or in (b) an experiential, in-the-field, learn-by-doing format (e.g., in a practicum setting under supervision, the student learns about counseling by doing counseling). Here too, in most EAP education and development programs, combinations of both approaches can be found. Overall, in terms of these differential learning models and approaches, possibly the most important reason for the faculty to attend to them is so that the faculty know what they are doing and why they are doing what they are doing.

Learning Module Areas. As already underscored earlier in this chapter, the first step in developing an educational and development program is to identify the necessary knowledges, skills, and expertise that the program's students will need after they complete the program and practice their profession. For example, the faculty at East Texas State University developed the first interdisciplinary counseling and human resource management program emphasis at the doctoral level, and the first step of their five-step program development tasks was:

1. Close examination was made of the roles and duties of human resource training and development (HRD/T&D) professionals in business and industry. Studies such as the Pinto and Walker (1978) ASTD research were extremely helpful. (Smith, Piercy & Lutz, 1982, p. 108)

Likewise, rehabilitation counselor education program development efforts will consult rehabilitation counselor competencies such as the 12 competency areas developed by Emener and Rasch (1984); social work education development efforts will consult social worker competency areas such as the six major areas identified by Maiden and Hardcastle (1986); and, employee assistance program personnel development efforts should consult studies such as Hastings' (1985) in which at least 10 different types of competencies were identified as important and needed by EAP professionals. Interested professionals are encouraged to consult other sources of needed and important

EAP professionals' competencies and their relationship to curriculum development; an excellent place to begin such an investigation would be to consult the July/August, 1986 issue of *EAP Digest* and the October and November, 1985 issues of **The ALMACAN** (the national publication of the Association of Labor/Management Administrators and Consultants on Alcoholism [ALMACA]). It is interesting to note that ALMACA has developed and recommended coursework for the professional development of EAP professionals, and in doing so ALMACA identified three learning module areas within which recommended courses are listed: (a) Understanding the Worksite: Work Organization as EAP Client; (b) Employee as EAP Client; and (c) EAP Courses.

After studying published EAP professionals' competency studies (e.g., ALMACA's, and Hastings, 1985) and recommended curricula and coursework (e.g., ALMACA's), and after tempering such information with his own experiences as a human service practitioner, educator, and educational program developer and administrator, the author of this chapter identified four learning module areas in which EAP education and development coursework and course content are recommended. The following lists these four modular areas and discusses: (a) the nature of the coursework and the fundamental elements considered critical to the courses in each area; and (b) possible sources of courses that may be available in a college or university that could be used (as they already exist, or adapted or modified) by an EAP education and development program.

1. **Module 1–Work, Employment, and Industry.**

Nature/Elements: psychology/sociology of occupations; basics of vocational guidance and career development; industrial and organizational psychology; industrial relations; structures and processes of work and work settings; the role(s) of work in society; the business side of industry.

Sources: courses with content such as these could be found in departments of guidance and counseling, psychology (viz, industrial/organizational psychology), sociology, rehabilitation counseling, vocational education, and assorted departments in business colleges.

2. **Module 2–Human Conditions: Employees and Clients.**

Nature/Elements: psychology of personality; abnormal psychology; addictions and chemical dependency; interpersonal problems and mental health; occupational stress; human relations; psychosocial aspects of disability; human development.

Sources: courses with content such as these could be found in departments of psychology, rehabilitation counseling, allied health, nursing, social work, educational psychology, home and family life, gerontology, and assorted departments in colleges of education, allied health, and social and behavioral sciences.

3. **Module 3–Employee Assistance Program Service Delivery.**

Nature/Elements: principles and procedures of training; assessment and evaluation of techniques; counseling skills and techniques; case management; EAP consultation and development; community analysis and intervention; industrial consultation; organizational development; vocational guidance; group counseling; the entrepreneurial side of human services; the business side of EAP service delivery.

Sources: courses with content and skill development such as these could be found in departments of human resource development, counseling, social work, occupational and vocational guidance, industrial and organizational psychology, and assorted departments in business colleges.

4. **Module 4–Organization, Administration, and Management.**

Nature/Elements: human resource management in business and industry; principles of human resource behavior, innovation and change; policy analysis and development; administration and supervision; principles of management and marketing.

Sources: courses with content and skill development such as these could be found in departments of administration, management, organization and industrial psychology, public administration, counseling, social work, and assorted allied health programs.

The actual recommending of specific courses that should be included in an EAP education and development program was considered to be outside the scope of this chapter. For example, the coursework suggestions within the above four learning module areas are far from inclusive! Moreover, there are numerous and very important curriculum contents that transcend these four modular areas and specific courses–for example, research, ethics, and legal issues. Furthermore, as discussed earlier, it is more important for the faculty and instructors in an EAP education and development program to work with each other and their respective advisory groups and committees and develop their own curriculum and their own courses for their own program. Decisions such as these, as well as decisions regarding whether a program should teach its own courses or explore the possible use of existing appropriate courses in other departments within the program's college or university, represent important decisions that should be made at the local level by the people who ultimately will be responsible for the implementation of the program.

Curriculum Implementation Issues

Once the leadership and faculty have identified the program's curriculum, the courses and the necessary policies and procedures (e.g., standards for admission), the program is then ready to be implemented. (This could be a good time for faculty to visit an already existing EAP education and development program, or to "work out some of the minor bugs and details.") At the outset and during the implementation stage, especially, other decisions have to be made.

For example:

• Who will be teaching what classes? What attributes, knowledges, skills, and abilities should the instructors for the specific courses have?

• Should there be any maximum class enrollment sizes established for any specific courses? Should there be any specific prerequisites for the individual courses? Should the courses that students take be sequenced in any special way?

• When and in what ways should students take their supervised field work? How should fieldwork sites (for practica and internships) be identified, approved, and utilized?

- What exit requirements should be considered, e.g., should students have to pass a comprehensive examination? What kind of certificate, diploma, degree conferment should the students receive?

Questions such as these are very important to the overall veracity and integrity of an employee assistance program education and development program. It also should be appreciated that questions like these should never be finitely answered–questions like these deserve constant address by the program's leadership and faculty. The price of movement toward excellence is constant vigilance and questioning.

Recommendations for the Future of Education and Development Programs for EAP Professionals

In their forecasting of the future of employee assistance programs, Dickman and Phillips (1985) discussed future increased attention to stress and the expanding developments of "wellness" programs. Commensurately, they forecasted increases in the needs for targeted services and specialty program emphases such as: communication skills training, assertiveness training, parenting, retire-

ment preparation, sexuality and changing sex roles, loss and death, victim assistance, and daycare (pp. 263–264). Furthermore, Dickman and Phillips (1985) envisioned future EAPs focusing not only on remediation and restoration, but, in concert with the increased "wellness" movement, focusing on prevention as well.

In the development, design, and implementation of an education and development program for EAP professionals, it is obviously critical for the program to prepare students "for what it is really like out there." Nonetheless, as discussed at the beginning of this chapter, the world is amid rapid, geometrically escalating change. Fittingly, the program must be ready to change itself: (a) to meet current changing demands; (b) to prepare professionals for the EAPs of the future; and (c) to prepare EAP professionals who will not only be a part of change in the future but who will play vital and proactive roles in the changes that will occur in the future. Obviously it would be very important for education and development programs for EAP professionals to build appropriate learning knowledges (content) and skills development components into their programs today so that when their students graduate they will be ready for tomorrow–"tomorrow when the world will be different than it is today"!

REFERENCES

Desmond, R. E. (1985). Careers in employee assistance programs. *Journal of Applied Rehabilitation Counseling, 16* (2), 26–30.

Dickman, F., & Emener, W. G. (1982). Employee assistance programs: Basic concepts, attributes and an evaluation. *Personnel Administrator, 27* (8), 56–62.

Dickman, F., & Phillips, E. A. (1985). Employee assistance programs: Future perspectives. In J. F. Dickman, W. G. Emener, & W. S. Hutchison (Eds.), *Counseling the Troubled Person in Industry: A Guide to the Organization, Implementation and Evaluation of Employee Assistance Programs* (pp. 262–267). Spring-

field, IL: Charles C Thomas, Publisher.

Emener, W. G. (Ed.) (1986). *Rehabilitation counselor preparation and development: Selected critical issues.* Springfield, IL: Charles C Thomas, Publisher, Ltd.

Emener, W. G., Luck, R. S., & Smits, S. J. (Eds.) (1981). *Rehabilitation administration and supervision.* Baltimore: University Park Press.

Emener, W. G., & McFarlane, F. R. (1985). A futuristic model of rehabilitation education. *Journal of Applied Rehabilitation Counseling, 16* (4), 5–9.

Emener, W. G., & Rasch, J. D. (1984). Actual and preferred instructional areas in rehabilitation education.

Note: For her technical suggestions and critical reading of earlier drafts of this chapter, sincerest appreciation is extended to Margaret A. Darrow, a master's degree candidate in the Department of Rehabilitation Counseling, University of South Florida, Tampa, Florida.

Rehabilitation Counseling Bulletin, 27 (5), 269–280.

Hastings, M. A. (1984). Employee assistance programs: A place for rehabilitation counselors? *Journal of Applied Rehabilitation Counseling, 15* (4), 29–30, 56.

Janes, M. W., & Emener, W. G. (1985). Rehabilitation counselor education graduates' perceptions of their employment and career satisfaction. *Rehabilitation Counseling Bulletin, 29* (3), 182–189.

Lynch, R. K., & Martin, T. (1982). Rehabilitation counseling in the private sector: A training needs survey. *Journal of Rehabilitation, 48* (3), 51–53, 73.

Maiden, R. P., & Hardcastle, D. A. (1986). Social work education: Professionalizing EAPs. *EAP Digest,* November/December, 63–66.

McMahon, B., Matkin, R., Growick, B., Mahaffey, D., & Gianforte, G. (1983). Recent trends in private sector rehabilitation. *Rehabilitation Counseling Bulletin, 27* (1), 32–47.

Sink, J. M., & Porter, T. L. (1978). Convergence and divergence in rehabilitation counseling and vocational evaluation. *Journal of Applied Rehabilitation Counseling, 9* (1), 5–20.

Smith, R. L., Piercy, F. P., & Lutz, P. (1982). Training counselors for human resource development positions in business and industry. *Counselor Education and Supervision, 22* (2), 107–112.

Part VI

SPECIAL ISSUES

Chapter 20

PROFESSIONAL, ETHICAL, AND PROGRAM DEVELOPMENTS IN EMPLOYEE ASSISTANCE PROGRAMS

WILLIAM G. EMENER and WILLIAM S. HUTCHISON, JR.

Pivotal to any human service program or delivery system is its perceived credibility. In the case of employee assistance programs (EAPs), especially with the increased penchant for accountability and the burgeoning managed care models of the 1990s, companies and industries, as well as the public at large, are demanding assurance, culpability and accountability, all of which are cornerstones of credibility. In many ways and for numerous reasons, enhanced professionalism, adherence to ethical standards and the development of program standards on behalf of EAPs, have significantly contributed to their perceived credibility within the business and industry, and the public at large. The purposes of this chapter are three-fold: (1) to discuss the *importance of professionalism* in EAPs; (2) to illustrate the EAP movement's commitment to *adherence to ethical standards* on behalf of EAP practitioners; and (3) to illustrate how the EAP movement is striving for adherence to *professional program standards* on behalf of EAPs.

Professionalism

In the delivery of human services, there are three critical attributes of professionalism: (a) *licensure*, (b) *certification*, and (c) *accreditation*. Basically, when professional practitioners are licensed or certified, recipients of their services enjoy an embellished and reliable sense of trust that the licensed or certified practitioners possess the knowledge, skills, and attributes necessary for quality service delivery. In effect, licensure and certification connotes that "a credible group of

professionals who know what they are looking for and know what they are doing is verifying that people can trust that this licensed or certified practitioner is good at what he or she is doing." Moreover, when programs are accredited, individuals receiving services from or through the auspices of the program enjoy an embellished and reliable sense of trust that the programs are designed, organized and operated in compliance with standards that have proven to be efficient and effective. In effect, accreditation connotes that "people can trust that an accredited program will do what it professes to do."

Professional Service Delivery and Ethical Standards

Most, if not all, EAPs exclusively utilize certified and licensed professionals (e.g., Certified Rehabilitation Counselors, Licensed Clinical Social Workers). Certification typically is awarded by a national certification body (e.g., the Commission on Rehabilitation Counselor Certification), which attests to the certificand's specialized credentials, knowledge, skills, and areas of expertise. Licensure typically is awarded by a state licensing board (e.g., through the auspices of a state Department of Professional Regulation), which not only attests to the licensee's specialized credentials, knowledge, skills, and areas of expertise but also allows the individual to practice independently and autonomously.

The EAP movement also has witnessed the inclusion of a certification process specifically for EAP professionals: the *Certified Employee Assistance*

Professional (CEAP). As announced in the Fall, 1995 CEAP Update, the Employee Assistance Certification Commission (EACC) upgraded its CEAP examination eligibility requirements:

CEAP EXAM ELIGIBILITY
REQUIREMENTS CHANGE FOR 1997

Beginning in 1997, there will be new eligibility requirements to sit for the CEAP examination– Two options are provided to qualify for the exam, based on whether the candidate has a related graduate degree:

- **Graduate degree** in related discipline (area approved by EACC) or equivalent outside the U.S.; and
- **2000 hours** within 2 to 7 years of supervised work experience in an EAP setting. Supervision must be EACC-approved; and
- **15 PDHs** completed prior to taking the exam. PDH process to be phased in at 5 PDHs per year beginning in 1997 (i.e., 5 PDHs for those taking the exam in 1997, 10 in 1998, 15 in 1999 and thereafter).
- professional credential in psychology, social work, rehabilitation or a related field of study based upon the standards of professional practice in effect within the given country

OR

- **3000 hours** within 2 to 7 years of supervised work experience in an EAP setting. Supervision must be EACC-approved; and
- **60 PDHs** completed prior to taking the exam. The PDH process will be phased in at 20 PDHs per year beginning in 1997 (i.e. 20 for those taking the exam in 1997, 40 in 1998, 60 in 1999 and thereafter).

The EACC is continuing to define the terms of the supervision process, the PDH process and accepted degrees. Further details will be provided as these definitions and processes are determined. (p. 1)

Current and future EAP professionals are encouraged to read the *CEAP Updates* and stay in touch with the EACC to remain abreast of changes in CEAP requirements as well as the dates and locations of CEAP examination sites.

Most EAP professionals belong to the professional association, the Employee Assistance Program Association (EAPA). Among EAPA's numerous professional development activities, it has strongly encouraged and enforced its members' adherence to its professional codes of ethics. This is very important because one of the marks of a professional is that he or she adheres to a code of ethics (Emener & Cottone, 1989). "The Oath of Hippocrates provided an early philosophical source for contemporary codes of ethics in the helping professions" (Davis & Yasak, 1996, p. 11). The Hippocratic principles that guide human service professionals' relations with their patients and clients include:

a. *autonomy*–respect for the consumer's right to free choice;
b. *nonmaleficence*–the injunction to do no harm to others;
c. *beneficence*–the duty to help others and do good;
d. *justice*–the obligation to attempt to achieve equality of resource distribution; and
e. *fidelity*–the duty to honor obligations (Beauchamp & Childress, 1983; Emener & Cottone, 1989).

An example of encouraged and facilitated adherence to ethical standards on behalf of EAP professionals is observed in the following formal document which was approved by EAPA's Board of Directors on April 10, 1988:

EAPA CODE OF ETHICS
REVISED

This document was drafted in final form on December 4, 1987 and approved by EAPA's Board of Directors on April 10, 1988.

Preamble

The EAPA Code of Ethics serves as a code of professional conduct for EAPA members. In cooperation with labor and management, EAPA members' primary objective is to provide the most effective employee assistance services to individuals and their families suffering from emotional, behavioral, alcohol and drug-related problems. The following principles are in accord with this goal and serve as guidelines for duly constituted national and local ethics committees in their efforts to educate EAPA members regarding ethical professional conduct. Members of EAPA affirm their endorsement of the Code of Ethics and acknowledge commitment to uphold its principles by signing the membership application and subsequent renewals.

Professional Responsibility

EAPA members help protect labor, management and the community against unethical practices by an individual or organization engaged in employee assistance programs, direct treatment, or consultation activities. When an EAPA member knows of an apparent ethical violation by another EAPA member, it becomes his/her ethical responsibility to attempt to resolve the matter by bringing that alleged unethical behavior to the other member's attention. If a resolution of ethical matters between members is not achieved, further informal consultation with colleagues and/or the local chapter's ethics committee is recommended, prior to any formalized national Ethics Committee review of a member's complaint.

Procedures for Review of Member Conduct

Per Article III–Section XI of Bylaws

Members of EAPA shall comply with its Bylaws and with its Code of Ethics. *Any member* who shall be found in violation thereof shall be subject to the action of the EAPA Board of Directors.

a. To be considered, a complaint against a member from any source shall be submitted in writing to the National President. The National President shall designate an appropriate investigating committee. If in the judgment of the appropriate committee the complaint warrants a hearing, the committee will prepare a formal charge and request that a hearing be scheduled. The charge shall state clearly the section or sections under which the violation is charged, as well as the alleged conduct of the member constituting the violation.

b. A copy of the formal charge shall be delivered to the member either in person or by registered or certified mail, and the member shall be given not less than thirty (30) days' notice by registered or certified mail of the time and place of the hearing on the charge. A closed hearing shall be conducted by the member's Regional Representative and the Chairperson of either the National Bylaws or Ethics Committee as appropriate. The member is entitled to be present at such a hearing and any continuation thereof, and may present oral or written evidence. The member may be represented in the closed proceedings by any voting member of EAPA in good standing. A written summary of the proceedings shall be made. Technical rules of evidence shall not apply.

c. When the hearings have concluded, the Committee Chairperson and the Regional Representative shall in executive session determine if a violation has occurred and prepare a written confidential report for the Bylaws or Ethics Committee with their findings. The Bylaws or Ethics Committee upon receipt of the report shall within thirty (30) days prepare a recommended action to dismiss the complaint, to refer the individual for a professional assessment and treatment if appropriate, to request a letter of resignation, to censure, suspend or expel the member, or any combination of these actions.

d. The Board shall no later than its next scheduled meeting act upon the report and the recommendations of the Bylaws or Ethics Committee. The member shall be informed promptly by registered or certified mail of the action of the Board.

e. The findings of fact of the Regional Representative and Committee Chairperson shall be conclusive. However, the member may appeal to the Board of Directors concerning the interpretation of the facts or the proposed penalty. The member may request permission to appear before the Board and, if such permission is granted, the member may be accompanied by a voting member of EAPA if so desired, to present arguments. The Board shall have the right to impose reasonable time limitation upon such a presentation. The Board's final decision shall be conveyed promptly by registered or certified mail to the member.

Confidentiality

EAPA members treat client information as confidential. Members inform clients fully about their rights regarding the scope and limitations of confidential communications elicited during the assessment, referral, and treatment process. They do not disclose information without client consent except where failure to disclose would likely result in imminent threat of serious bodily harm to the client or others.

Professional Competency

EAPA members who are Employee Assistance Program (EAP) providers are expected to possess knowledge of work organizations, human resources management, EAP policy and administration, and EAP direct services. All members are expected to have knowledge of chemical dependency, addictions and emotional disorders, and acknowledge the necessity of continuing experience, education and training to maintain and enhance proficiency. While membership in EAPA may not be used to suggest professional competency, attaining the status of a Certified Employee Assistance Professional (CEAP) does attest to meeting the requisite standard of knowledge for

competency in EAP practice.

Consumer Protection

EAPA members do not discriminate because of a client's race, religion, national origin, physical handicap, gender or sexual preference. They conduct research that respects and safeguards the welfare of research participants. EAPA members make full disclosure of the functions and purposes of the Employee Assistance Program as well as of any affiliation with a proposed therapist or treatment program, do not give or receive financial consideration for referring clients to particular therapists or treatment programs; do not engage in sexual conduct with clients; and do not act in any manner which compromises a professional relationship.

Assessment and Referral

Members are to make assessment and referral decisions only within their area of specific competency and to seek consultation or supervision when clinically indicated. To avoid appearances of conflicts of interest, it is recommended that members who do the initial assessment refer clients to individuals or entities not affiliated with the referring EAP or original referral source. Should a treatment decision be made to refer to the initial evaluator or an affiliated program, that disposition is to be done only if the client and contracting organization is informed of any financial interest in such a referral and it can be demonstrated that the referral is in the client's best interest.

Public Responsibility and Professional Relations

EAPA members agree that practitioners, both nondegreed recovering persons, as well as other professionals, form a partnership in providing employee assistance services.

As such, members: are responsible for educating and fostering the professional development of trainees; are encouraged to promote EAPA to the public and to provide public statements based on objective information; and are expected to work cooperatively within their professional communities. Cooperation within a professional community precludes denigrating other professionals to promote one's own interests, as well as fraudulent or grossly misleading advertising practices, and requires that one's professional qualifications be presented to the public in an accurate and truthful manner.

EAPA members are encouraged to assist another member to seek treatment if that member's professional functioning becomes impaired through the use of alcohol, drugs, and/or mental illness.

f. Any member who resigns, fails to maintain his membership during the pendency of these procedures or is expelled, shall be eligible to reapply for membership *only* upon conditions, if any, specified by the Board.

g. For the convenience of EAPA, the National President may agree to accept the member's resignation as an alternative to these procedures. (pp. 2–5)

Thus, it is clear that the EAP movement, especially over the past few years, has strongly encouraged and worked hard to ensure continuing professionalism in EAP service delivery.

EAP "Program Standards"

EAPs currently are not accredited. Nonetheless, it remains critical for EAPs to be designed, organized and operated in accordance with currently accepted EAP program standards. The following are the "Program Standards" which provide the spirit, intention and guidance for efficient and effective EAPs and EAP service delivery.

INTRODUCTION

Purpose

The purpose of these Employee Assistance Program (EAP) Standards are to:

- Define the EAP field as a profession
- Describe the scope of EAP services
- Educate the community regarding EAP services
- Suggest applications for program standards, guidelines and definitions
- Serve the needs of the EAPA membership

History and Background

The Standards for Employee Alcoholism and/or Assistance Programs were originally drafted in 1981 by a joint committee representing these national groups:

- The Association of Labor/Management Administrators and Consultants on Alcoholism (ALMACA)

- The National Council on Alcoholism (NCA)
- Occupational Program Consultants Association (OPCA)
- The National Institute on Alcohol Abuse and Alcoholism (NIAAA)
- The American Federation of labor and Congress of Industrial Organizations (AFL-CIO)

At that time, there were approximately 8,000 programs and 2,800 EAP professionals who belonged to EAPA. By 1990, the number of EAPs had increased substantially to an estimated 20,000, and EAPA membership had grown to more than 6,000 professionals.

In 1988, EAPA recognized the need for more detailed standards reflecting advancements in the EAP field. The EAP Association appointed a Program Standards Committee to develop revised Program Standards. The Committee developed a two-part document.

Part One sets forth specific Program Standards each of which is accompanied by a statement of

---

Note: Part Two of this document, *The Consumer's Guide*, is not included in this chapter. Interested readers, however, can obtain a copy of the *Guide* directly from the Employee Assistance Program Association.

Intent. These Program Standards identify the core ingredients of employee assistance programs and professional standards for carrying them out. The Program Standards are organized into six general areas:

- Design
- Implementation
- Management and Administration
- Direct Services
- Linkages
- Evaluation

Part Two, The Consumer Guide, consists of recommendations for applying these Program Standards in the EAP field. The recommendations provide organizations and EAP providers with practical guidelines for the development, implementation, maintenance, and evaluation of an employee assistance program in accordance with professional program standards.

It is hoped that the availability of this two-part document will encourage and assist management and union leaders in establishing EAPs in accordance with EAPA's Program Standards.

EAPA thanks the National Institute on Drug Abuse for the use of its documents relating to employee assistance programs within federal agencies.

I. DEFINITION

Standard

An employee assistance program (EAP) is a worksite-based program designed to assist in the identification and resolution of productivity problems associated with employees impaired by personal concerns including, but not limited to: health, marital, family, financial, alcohol, drug, legal, emotional, stress, or other personal concerns which may adversely affect employee job performance.

The specific core activities of EAPs include (1) expert consultation and training to appropriate persons in the identification and resolution of job-performance issues related to the aforementioned employee personal concerns, and (2) confidential, appropriate and timely problem-assessment services; referrals for appropriate diagnosis, treatment and assistance; the formation of linkages between workplace and community resources that provide such services; and follow-up services for employees who use those services.

(NOTE: This definition was approved by the EAPA Board of Directors in 1988 and has been written into a number of state statutes.)

II. SIGNIFICANCE AND USE

The objectives of an employee assistance program are these:

- To serve the organization, its employees, and their families by providing a comprehensive system from which employees can obtain assistance addressing personal problems which may affect their work performance;
- To serve as a resource for management and labor when they intervene with employees whose personal problems affect their job performance;
- To effectively, efficiently, and professionally provide assessment, referral, and follow-up services for mental health, alcohol, and other drug related problems in the workforce.

This document identifies a coordinated set of policies, procedures, services, and consultation activities designed to ensure that EAPs effectively meet these objectives. Adherence to professional standards and policies will ensure a viable program, which earns the respect and support of employers and employees. Effective programs are comprehensive enough in scope to respond to a wide range of employee problems, whether they are brought to the attention of the EAP by the employee, labor, or management.

Smaller organizations often provide EAP services by participating in a community consortium. Regardless of the exact structure of the EAP, ethical considerations are present in every aspect of the design, implementation, delivery and evaluation of the program.

III. PROGRAM DESIGN

A. Advisory Committee

Standard

There shall be an advisory function at a high level within the organization involving representatives of all segments of the work force.

Intent

Program acceptance and utilization is directly related to the degree of support from top management and involvement by employees, supervisors, management, and unions. One technique for maximizing the potential for a highly effective program is to form, at the earliest opportunity, an Advisory Committee representing all the various labor and management groups. To ensure that the EAP is supported by and located at the highest possible organizational level, committee membership should include top management and union/employee association officials as well as representatives from the following groups: medical, personnel/human resources, benefits, safety and occupational health, finance, legal, training and development, and EAP operations. This Committee can formulate a policy statement as well as specific strategies and procedures for implementing an EAP and criteria for evaluating its performance.

B. Needs Assessment

Standard

Program design shall be based on an assessment of organizational and employee needs as they relate to EAP utilization. The background information and organizational data to be factored into program design will include at least:

- an organizational profile
- an employee needs assessment
- surveys of supervisors and union representatives
- a review of service delivery models

Intent

Program planning and development should always include an assessment of the needs of the employee population and the organization for which they work. This assessment will help the advisory committee determine the most appropriate methods of providing EAP services.

C. Service Delivery Systems

Standard

Employee assistance program services shall be provided through a comprehensive, formal delivery system.

Intent

Employee assistance professionals and/or an advisory committee shall develop service delivery methods consistent with organizational and employee needs. Professional guidance is available through EAPA National, local chapters, or professional EAP consultants. There are a number of service delivery models, including:

- Internal programs through which services are delivered by EAP professionals employed by

the organization;
- External programs (known as "service centers") through which services are delivered by EAP professionals under contract with the organization;
- Combined programs through which services are delivered by a core group of EAP profes-

sionals employed by the organization and contracts with external EAP vendors for certain services;
- Consortia of smaller organizations that jointly contract with an independent EAP vendor to provide services.

IV. IMPLEMENTATION

A. Policy Statement

Standard

The policy statement defines the EAP's relationship to the organization as well as describes the EAP as a confidential resource for the organization and its employees. Additionally, it shall state the scope of the program's services as well as the program's limitations. The policy statement shall include at least the following concepts:

- The organization providing EAP services to its employees recognizes that a mentally and physically healthy employee is an organizational asset and that the availability of appropriate EAP services is beneficial to both labor and management
- Alcohol and other drug abuse, emotional, marital, family and other related problems affect job performance, employee health and quality of life. Such problems are treatable and are the legitimate concern of employers. Employees who experience these problems may be unable to function efficiently, effectively, and safely on the job.
- Employees who need EAP services can voluntarily seek assistance, or they can be referred through constructive intervention. Job security will not be jeopardized as a consequence of seeking EAP services, except where mandated by law. However, employees who use an EAP are expected to adhere to the job performance requirements of the employing organization
- All EAP records will be kept strictly confidential and will not be noted in any official record or in the employee's personnel file. Information

from the EAP may be released only with the written permission of the employee, or in response to the organizational EAP policy or from a court or other legal order (e.g., a subpoena).

Intent

Program implementation will be preceded by the development of a policy statement clearly communicating the organization's rationale for instituting an EAP. The policy statement should not be confused with operating procedures or with any contractual agreements with an external EAP provider. Because operating procedures may need to be adjusted in response to emerging needs, they should not be incorporated into a policy document that is difficult to modify.

B. Implementation Plan

Standard

An implementation plan shall outline the actions needed to establish a fully functioning EAP and set forth a timeline for their completion. The program implementation plan shall establish the EAP as a distinct service within the organization.

The implementation plan shall cover the following:

1. Policies, procedures, and objectives

2. Logistics of service delivery, including:
   - location
   - staffing ratio

3. An operations plan, including:
   * program promotion and employee communications, orientation, and education
   * training of supervisors and union representatives
   * review of health/mental health benefits coverage and possible benefits redesign
   * identification of community resources
   * strategies for program integration

4. A management plan, including:
   * budget projections
   * record-keeping
   * reporting procedures
   * quality assurance
   * liability coverage

5. An evaluation system, including:
   * measurable objectives
   * appropriateness
   * efficiency
   * progress
   * outcomes

Intent

An implementation plan should articulate the responsibilities of the organization and the EAP professionals. It should include realistic objectives and criteria for ongoing evaluation and, if necessary, program modification. Successful implementation encourages "ownership" by all sectors of the workforce. Special provisions may be needed for program implementation in worksites geographically distant from organization headquarters.

V. MANAGEMENT AND ADMINISTRATION

A. Policies and Procedures

Standard

To achieve consistent and effective delivery of services, standardized policies and procedures for program administration and operation shall be developed in response to program objectives and organizational needs.

Intent

The intent of this standard is to develop clearly defined administrative policies and procedures to insure a smoothly functioning and effective EAP. Standardized systems for program management and administration, combined with clear cut definitions of the program's scope, help delineate the program activities and guide the amount of resources dedicated to them. A clearly defined program may be better received and more frequently used. Standardized procedures are easier to monitor and adapt to changing needs, and may protect program staff from becoming overextended.

B. Staffing Levels

Standard

An adequate number of EAP professionals shall be available to achieve the stated goals and objectives of the program. Organizations that choose to contract for EAP services shall have at least one liaison person with formal responsibility for coordinating the delivery of services and monitoring contract performance.

Intent

EAP staffing patterns, and the number of professionals, vary according to the type of program and the scope of services provided. Whether the EAP is internal or delivered by external contractors, the number and qualifications of EAP professionals should match program needs.

C. Staff Qualifications

Standard

Each EAP shall retain professionals qualified to perform their duties. Measures of qualifications should include evidence of specialized understanding of alcohol and other drug problems and certification in employee assistance programming (CEAP). EAP professionals shall adhere to all government regulations regarding their scope of practice.

Intent

Staff competence is critical to program success. Depending upon the type of services provided, various levels of experience, education, certification, credentialing and licensure may be required.

Individual EAP professionals are responsible for recognizing the limitations of their competence and making certain that all work is performed within those limitations. Those individuals who are called upon to provide services for which they are not fully trained and experienced should be supervised by a person who is qualified in those areas. Consultation and referral can also supplement practitioner capability.

D. Community Networks

Standard

The EAP shall identify, foster, create, utilize, and evaluate community resources, which provide the best quality care at the most reasonable cost.

Intent

Delivery of quality services responsive to the individual needs of employees requires that the EAP develop and maintain an effective community network of local treatment resources, health organizations, and self-help groups. This activity is required on an ongoing basis.

E. Confidentiality

Standard

The EAP professional shall prepare and implement a confidentiality policy consistent with all professional standards and ethics, and adhere to all other regulations that may apply to information in the possession of the EAP. Disclosures specified by government guidelines and EAP policy will be communicated to users of EAP services. The limits of the confidentiality policy shall be disclosed in writing to those who use the EAP.

Intent

Program success and credibility may hinge, to a large extent, on employee confidence that the EAP respects individual privacy and adheres to confidentiality requirements and procedures.

F. Liability

Standard

All EAP professionals shall have adequate professional and other appropriate liability coverage.

Intent

The EAP needs to have resources to answer legal challenges to its delivery of services. The organizations should demonstrate financial responsibility to ensure continuation of the program during and following any litigation.

G. Ethics

Standard

EAP professionals shall adhere to the codes of ethics espoused by their professional organizations and by appropriate licensing and certifying bodies. Any actual or perceived conflict of interest among EAP professionals and service providers shall be avoided. Conflict of interest statements shall be filed when appropriate.

Intent

The intent is to ensure professional behavior and provide consumer protection. EAP professionals are responsible for the consequences of their actions.

A potential conflict may arise when an EAP provides ancillary services beyond the core EAP services. This should be clearly addressed in the contract and/or internal philosophy of the EAP.

VI. DIRECT SERVICES

NOTE: EAPs deliver comprehensive, quality services to three target groups: employees and covered family members, supervisory and union personnel, and the organization as a whole.

A. Crisis Intervention

Standard

The EAP shall offer responsive intervention services for employees, covered family members, or the organization in acute crisis situations.

Intent

The EAP must be prepared to respond to emergencies and urgent situations in a timely fashion, consistent with organizational policies. Timely intervention may prevent or lessen long-term dysfunction.

B. Assessment and Referral

Standard

EAP professionals, or an assessment service under contract to the organization, shall (1) conduct an assessment to identify employee or family member problems, (2) develop a plan of action, and (3) recommend or refer the individual(s) to an appropriate resource for problem resolution.

Intent

The intent is to match the identified problems with the appropriate care. Accurate assessment and appropriate referral should result in improved job performance and employee well-being. In the course of assessment and referral, EAP professionals may offer short-term problem resolution services so as to assure timely and effective help for the individual.

C. Short-Term Problem Resolution

Standard

EAP professionals shall determine when it may be appropriate to provide short term problem resolution services, and when to make a referral to community resources. Long-term, ongoing treatment is not part of the EAP model.

Intent

In accordance with program policy, there are occasions when it may be more efficient and effective for the EAP professional to provide short-term problem resolution services than to refer to an outside resource. At no time will the EAP professional operate outside his/her scope of expertise and licensure or accept financial reimbursement other than that allowed by EAP design or contractual arrangement.

D. Progress Monitoring

Standard

The EAP shall review and monitor the progress of referrals. This shall include assisting in reintegration to the worksite if the employee is taken off the job for treatment.

Intent

The EAP is in a unique position to monitor and review the progress of referrals; ensure quality assurance; provide ongoing support to the treatment professional, the supervisor and the employee; and assist the employee with reintegration into the worksite if the employee is taken off the job for treatment. Progress monitoring and the reintegration process will vary depending on the individual employee's needs.

E. Follow-Up

Standard

The EAP shall provide follow-up services to employees, covered family members, supervisory and union personnel, and the organization to monitor and support progress in the resolution of personal problems and improvement of job performance.

Intent

The availability of follow-up services can enhance EAP credibility and ensure timely problem resolution. By providing ongoing follow-up services, the EAP demonstrates a commitment to the well-being of individuals and organizations.

F. Training

Standard

The EAP shall provide training for supervisory, management, and union personnel to give them an understanding of EAP objectives, procedures for referring employees experiencing job performance problems to the program, and the impact of the program on the organization.
The following subjects shall be covered:

1. Understanding EAP
   * impact of employee well-being on job performance
   * management of employees with problems

2. Consultation
   * recognition of an employee's need for assistance
   * methods of referral to the EAP

3. Program operation
   * relationship of EAP to personnel actions
   * confidentiality
   * reintegration
   * relationship to federally mandated drug testing and training

The EAP shall ask those who attend the training to provide written feedback after taking the course.

Intent

The intent of regularly scheduled training sessions is to encourage early recognition, intervention, and appropriate referral to the EAP.

G. Supervisor/Union Consultation

Standard

EAP professionals shall provide individual consultation to supervisors and union representatives regarding the management and referral to the EAP of employees with job performance and other behavioral/medical problems.

Intent

The purpose of such consultation is to ensure that EAP professionals provide technical support and policy-based advice to supervisors charged with monitoring job performance and taking appropriate action in dealing with problem employees.

H. Organization Consultation

Standard

EAPs shall be both proactive and responsive when organizational developments and events impact employee well-being and fall within the EAP professional's areas of expertise.

Intent

The intent is to ensure that the EAP functions as an integral part of the organization. EAP professionals can offer a valuable perspective as part of the organizational team confronting external and internal developments and changes.

I. Program Promotion

Standard

EAPs shall ensure the availability and use of promotional materials and activities, which encourage the use of the program by supervisors, union representatives, peers, employees, and covered family members.

Intent

The EAP should be highly visible and presented in a positive light to encourage members of the organization to fully utilize the program services. Program promotion should be ongoing and should be directed to all levels of the organization.

J. Education

Standard

Information about the EAP and its services shall be part of new employee orientation and ongoing employee education.

Intent

Employee education is an essential EAP function and should emphasize primary prevention and self-care. Regularly offered presentations should include information designed to develop or increase employee awareness of factors that affect their personal well-being and impact on job performance.

VII. LINKAGES

A. Internal Organizational Activities

Standard

The EAP shall be positioned at an organizational level where it can be most effective with linkage to the executive office. The EAP should establish working relationships with a variety of internal departments and committees, including:

- Human Resources/Personnel
- Benefits
- Safety
- Equal Employment Opportunity
- Medical
- Security
- Risk Management
- Legal
- Training
- Organizational Development
- Employee Relations
- Union

Intent

The EAP operates at its optimal level when it is fully integrated with internal organizational activities. Close involvement and collaboration improves EAP visibility and increases its ability to have an impact. Linkages within the organization should maximize program effectiveness and decrease potential liabilities. Adaptations may be necessary in response to changes in organizational dynamics.

B. External Community Organizations and Resources

Standard

The EAP shall develop and maintain relationships with the external health care delivery system and other community resources which provide EAP-relevant services.

Intent

The EAP operates at its optimal level when it is fully acquainted and maintains working relationships with the referral and support resources available in the community.

C. Professional Organizations

Standard

EAP professionals shall maintain and upgrade their knowledge through such activities as belong to one or more organizations specifically designed for EAP professionals, such as the Employee Assistance Professionals Association (EAPA), attending training and/or continuing education programs, and maintaining regular, ongoing contact with other employee assistance program professionals.

Intent

The intent is to enhance the knowledge and skills of EAP professionals and ensure that they are aware of new developments and technologies in EAP service delivery.

VIII. EVALUATION

Standard

An EAP shall evaluate the appropriateness, effectiveness, and efficiency of its internal operations. Measurable objectives shall be stated for both process and outcome evaluation.

Intent

Meaningful evaluation of an EAP depends upon having measurable program objectives and data collection mechanisms. These should be developed early in the program planning process.

In addition to guiding the implementation and operations of the EAP, measurable objectives allow the organization to judge the program's progress and usefulness and to identify the need for program modifications. The procedures for achieving each objective should be reviewed periodically to assure that the objectives are obtainable.

Data that measure program effectiveness should be gathered routinely and analyzed to evaluate progress toward achieving each objective. Components for which data could be collected for program evaluation may include:

* Design effectiveness
* Implementation
* Management and administration
* Completeness of the program
* Direct services
* Linkages

A review of the daily operation of the program does not necessarily measure its total impact on the organization and the effectiveness with which it reassesses the needs of the organization.

As can readily be seen, these Standards are rather specific and rigorous, and clearly are designed to maximize an EAP's potentials for efficient and effective EAP service delivery to its identified primary consumer group.

CONCLUDING COMMENT

It is predicted that EAPs will continue to be a viable, integral and significant humanistic component of business and industry in the decades ahead. EAPs' continued positive impact is assured because of (1) the continuing, developing professionalism on behalf of EAP practitioners and (2) the continuing developments in EAPs' program and operational standards. As EAPs proceed in these ways, everyone will win—unions, management, and especially labor.

REFERENCES

Beauchamp, T. L., & Childress, J. F. (1983). *Principles of biomedical ethics.* Oxford: Oxford University Press.

Davis, A., & Yasak, D. (1996). Supporting a colleague in ethical conflict: Resolving problems of common sense. *Journal of Applied Rehabilitation Counseling, 27* (3), 11–16.

Emener, W. G., & Cottone, R. R. (1989). Professionalization, deprofessionalization, and reprofessionalization of rehabilitation counseling according to criteria of professions. *Journal of Counseling and Development, 67,* 576–581.

Chapter 21

LEGAL ISSUES CRITICAL TO
EMPLOYEE ASSISTANCE PROGRAMS

RANDY K. OTTO and JOHN PETRILA

Regardless of the setting in which services are delivered, the work of health care professionals is governed by relevant law, ethics, and practice standards. In this chapter we discuss in general terms the legal and ethical issues that are most likely to impact health care professionals working in Employee Assistance Programs (EAPs). Because laws, unlike practice standards and ethics, vary from jurisdiction to jurisdiction, a detailed discussion of the law most relevant to EAP practice in all states cannot be provided. We emphasize here the necessity that the reader be knowledgeable about the law in the particular jurisdiction in which he or she practices. We begin with a brief discussion of the issue of the role of the EAP professional, which is a critical determinant regarding legal and ethical issues that such professionals are likely to encounter. We then discuss a number of contemporary issues that may confront EAP professionals, including informed consent, confidentiality, drug testing, malpractice, and licensing complaints. The chapter concludes with a brief discussion of emerging issues regarding drug testing, genetic testing, and the Americans with Disabilities Act. Given space limitations, the discussion of each is necessarily brief. However, the discussion should alert the EAP professional to the general legal and ethical parameters of each of these issues. Those interested in exploring these issues in more detail are referred to the references; those with specific legal or ethical questions arising from practice are referred to an attorney who specializes in these issues or the applicable licensure board.

Role Definition

The importance of establishing and making clear the EAP professional's role with respect to the employee and employer cannot be overestimated. This is because the role that the professional has with respect to his interactions with the employee and employer determines the legal and ethical duties owed to all parties. If EAP professionals fail to understand their roles and responsibilities vis-à-vis the employee and employer, they may find it difficult to discharge their ethical and legal duties. This may also result in confusion in communications between the EAP professional and other parties. It is important to identify and communicate one's role early in the process, as it will set the stage for subsequent interactions with the employee and employer. Problems and complications are most likely to be encountered when the EAP professional is not clear about his or her role, or takes on multiple roles with the parties.

The EAP Professional as the Employee's Therapist

In the majority of cases the EAP professional will provide therapeutic services to the employee, as a work related benefit.[1] In such cases, the EAP professional acts as the employee's therapist. Any and all legal and ethical duties that attach to traditional therapist-client relationships apply in such cases, since the primary purpose of the EAP-based relationship is to bring about an improvement in the employee's emotional, behavioral, or physical health and adjustment, which may ultimately affect work adjustment and productivity. As discussed in more detail below, the legal and/or ethical precepts of informed consent, confidentiality, and privilege all apply when the EAP professional enters into a therapeutic relationship with the employee, though there may be confusion regarding the issue of confidentiality in particular in some situations. That the services are an employee benefit, are authorized by the employer, are required by the employer as a condition of continued employment, or are paid for by the employer do not affect the duties the EAP professional owes to the employee-client, to whom the EAP's professional owes allegiance.

The EAP Professional as Consultant-Evaluator to the Employer

In some cases the EAP professional does not act as the employee's therapist, but rather, acts as a consultant to the company. In such circumstances the EAP professional is typically called on to assess the employee's behavioral, emotional, and/or physical functioning and describe how such might affect the employee's work ability. In such cases interactions with the employee occur for the express purpose of providing the employer with information about the employee and the employee's condition that is relevant to his or her continued employment. When functioning in this capacity, EAP professionals may evaluate employees with respect to workers compensation, short or long-term disability, or fitness for duty (see Oher, 1999 for an overview and discussion). In such cases the EAP professional and the employee do not establish a therapist-client relationship and many of the ethical and/or legal duties owed to therapy clients (e.g., confidentiality, privilege) do not apply, or are more limited in their application. In such circumstances the employer, not the employee, should be considered the client since the evaluation is conducted at the request of the employer and with the understanding that any information gained during the consultative evaluation will be provided to the employer to assist its decision making regarding the employee. When acting in such a capacity, it is important to make

clear to the employee the nontherapeutic nature of the relationship and how this relationship differs from a more traditional and common therapeutic relationship. This is true particularly because many people simply assume that all contacts with health care professionals are for therapeutic purposes, with confidentiality and privilege applying.

Multiple Roles, Mixed Roles, and Confused Roles

EAP professionals are most likely to encounter difficulties when they assume both a therapist role with an employee and a consultant-evaluator role with the employer (either at the same time or sequentially), or they are not clear about their role with the employer and employee (Greenberg & Shuman, 1997).[2] Difficulties will ensue in either case as the different roles impose different duties and allegiances on the EAP professional, and the employer and employee may have conflicting expectations of the EAP professional.

Some EAP professionals may work in settings in which they are called on by employers both to provide treatment services to employees and evaluate employees for the purpose of assisting with the employer's decision making about them in the context of fitness for duty, worker's compensation, and/or disability. Serving in each capacity with different employees is not problematic in and of itself. Providing that the EAP professional adopts only one role (i.e., as a therapist or consultant-evaluator) with an employee and makes clear his or her role, no difficulties are likely to occur. However, it will be important for EAP professionals who engage in both activities with an employer to make sure that the employer and all employees are aware of their role in each case. The role distinctions that require the EAP professional to act in various ways in different cases may not be so clear to the employer, who may interpret such behavior as simple inconsistency or an unwillingness to be helpful in some cases. In addition, it will also be important for the EAP professional to assure that he or she is acting consistently with applicable ethical guidelines regarding multiple roles.

Informed Consent

Informed consent is both an ethical and legal precept that is rooted in the principle of autonomy, and ensures that individuals make informed decisions about evaluation and treatment (Appelbaum, Lidz & Meisel, 1987; Melton, Petrila, Poythress & Slobogin, 1997). For consent to be informed it must be knowledgeable, competent, and voluntary. Prior to initiating any assessment or treatment, the EAP professional must ensure that the individual understands the nature and purpose of the proposed intervention including likely benefits and risks. The EAP professional, therefore, must provide the employee with information about the proposed evaluation or treatment, any relevant alternatives, and potential benefits, risks, and outcomes associated with each alternative. A decision to undergo evaluation or treatment must also occur voluntarily and without coercion. Thus, the decision to participate in evaluation or treatment must be made freely by the employee. For purposes of informed consent, assuming that the employer has a good faith justification and basis, it is unlikely that requiring participation in an evaluation or treatment as a condition of employment will be interpreted as negating the voluntariness requirement. Finally, the employee's decision about participating in a proposed evaluation or treatment must be competent. That is, the employee must have the ability to consider various options, and weigh and balance information relevant to the various decisions (see Grisso & Appelbaum, 1999 for a more detailed discussion). This requires the EAP professional to consider the employee's decision-making capacity and ability to understand relevant information that is provided to him or her. Evaluations or treatment should not be conducted with persons whose capacity to deliberate about possible choices is significantly impaired. In the last few years, considerable research has emerged regarding capacity to consent, particularly but not exclusively regarding the relationship between mental illnesses and capacity (see, for example, Grisso & Appelbaum, 1998; Berg, Appelbaum, Lidz & Parker, 2001; Stiles, Poythress, Hall, Falkenbach & Williams, 2001).

Privacy, Confidentiality and Privilege

The value Americans place on privacy is reflected in the law regulating provision of health care as all states have laws ensuring the privacy of these records in some manner. In almost all states, however, privacy of health care records is addressed in legislation focused on services providers, institutions, and specific conditions (e.g., HIV and other communicable diseases, mental disorders). This patchwork of legislation is often piecemeal and unorganized, and sometimes inconsistent internally. Indeed, as of 1999 only two states had comprehensive laws detailing the privacy of such records (Pritts, Goldman, Hudson, Berenson & Hadley, 1999). In addition, state laws are often inconsistent with each other and with federal law (Petrila, 2000). Discussed below are issues of privacy that are related to provision of services by EAP professionals, including the Health Insurance Accountability and Portability Act (HIPAA) which was enacted by Congress in an effort to create minimum national standards for the protection of health care information.

Confidentiality

Confidentiality is best conceptualized as the health care professional's ethical and legal obligation to keep client communications private and confidential. The law regulating the practice of, and ethical principles relevant to, all health care professions requires that communications made in the context of a therapeutic relationship remain confidential, with some exceptions. Thus, EAP professionals who are involved in a treatment relationship with an employee are obligated to keep information relayed to them by the employee confidential with some exceptions, which are discussed below (see, e.g., *Vardiman v. Ford Motor Company*, 1997; *Rogers v. CHM2 HILL*, 1998). In contrast, EAP professionals who are evaluating the employee at the request of the employer in the context of worker's compensation, disability, or fitness for duty have no obligation to keep information gained during the course of the evaluation confidential, at least insofar as they can provide the information to the employer. The EAP professional, of course, remains obligated to respect the employee's privacy and disclose the information to no one other than the employer. In addition, the EAP professional must disclose to the employee limitations on confidentiality, whether the relationship is therapeutic or consultative to the employer.

Health care professionals are subject to both state and federal laws regarding confidentiality. EAP professionals are obligated to comply with confidentiality laws in the state in which they practice which, as noted above, may vary with respect to defining confidentiality and its limitations. Additionally, EAP professionals in all jurisdictions are obligated to comply with federal law regarding confidentiality of health care records.

STATE LAW REGARDING CONFIDENTIALITY OF RECORDS. Confidentiality, the duty to protect it, and the law's recognition of it are not absolute. Ethics or the law may provide for instances in which the general guarantee of confidentiality may or must be breached. The most obvious limitation to confidentiality is when it is expressly waived by the client, who directs the professional to provide the confidential information to a third party. Strictly speaking, provision of confidential information to a third party in such circumstances should not be considered a "breach" of confidentiality since it is done at the direction and with the permission of the client.

All states require health care professionals to breach confidentiality in order to report suspected abuse, neglect or abandonment of a child (Gostin, 1995; Kalichman, 1999). Some states have expanded this limitation to confidentiality and the associated reporting requirement to other populations that are considered vulnerable including disabled adults and elderly persons (see, e.g., Florida Statutes 415.102 and 39.201).

Jurisdictions vary with respect to whether they require health care professionals to breach confidentiality in cases where they suspect that their client/patient poses a risk of harm to third parties. Some states require health care professionals to breach confidentiality to protect third parties (e.g., California, see *Tarasoff v. Regents of the University of California*, 1976), while other states allow but do not require mental health professionals to breach confidentiality in such circumstances (e.g., Florida, see Petrila & Otto, in press). Thus, EAP professionals who are providing therapeutic services to employees must remain aware of the status of the "duty to protect" in their jurisdiction, including whether specific action (e.g., warning or notifying the intended victim) or more general action (e.g., taking steps to protect the intended victim other than warning) are required or permitted.

FEDERAL LAW REGARDING CONFIDENTIALITY OF RECORDS. In 1996, the United States Congress mandated the establishment of standards for privacy of health care records via enactment of the Health Insurance Accountability and Portability Act (45 Code of Federal Regulations Sections 160 and 164; HIPAA). The act establishes a national standard for protecting the privacy of health care information; however, it is worth noting that state laws that are *more protective* of privacy than HIPAA still control the law of the particular state. In other words, HIPAA sets a minimum standard but states are free to set more stringent standards for protecting the privacy of health care information.

HIPAA requires health care professionals to inform patients about their privacy rights, adopt clear procedures to ensure privacy of health care records, train employees so that they are aware of and can carry out privacy procedures, designate an employee who is responsible for ensuring privacy of records, and secure patient health care records so that privacy is ensured. HIPAA does *not* prohibit disclosure of information to another health care professional for treatment purposes, when authorized by the client, or when authorized or required by other laws. Although the HIPAA privacy rule became effective in April 2001, compliance was not mandatory for most health care providers covered by the rule until April 2003. While some have criticized the privacy provisions of HIPAA, it is considered by many to be an important piece of legislation devoted to ensuring the privacy of patient records (Scott, 2000).

Predating HIPAA are federal regulations regulating the confidentiality of persons who received treatment for substance abuse in "federally assisted" alcohol and drug abuse programs (42 Code of Federal Regulations Sections 2.1–2.67). These regulations, which apply to health care professionals in all states and federal jurisdictions, identify the nature and limitations of the confidentiality of the health care records of persons receiving alcohol and drug abuse treatment. More specifically, this federal code directs that such treatment records that could identify an individual as receiving alcohol and/or drug abuse treatment are confidential and can be released only in very limited circumstances, including with the written consent of the patient or, without the patient's consent, to medical personnel in the context of a medical emergency, for purposes of research and program evaluation (providing the patient's identity cannot be discerned), in response to a valid court order after the court has followed certain steps required by the regulations, or in order to comply with child abuse reporting requirements. This code also requires the treatment provider to provide to patients a summary of their confidentiality rights.

Privilege

Privilege refers to the law's recognition of confidentiality in legal proceedings in which the protected material otherwise would be subject to disclosure. Although privileged communications are protected from being revealed in the course of legal proceedings, nonprivileged communications have no legal protection in such proceedings. In many states, communications made to certain health care professionals are privileged (Shuman, 2000; Shuman & Wiener, 1982). Some privileges are specific (e.g., physician-patient privilege) while others are more general (e.g., psychotherapist-patient privilege). For example, in their survey of privacy law, Pitts et al. (1999) reported that 37 states provided for some kind of psychotherapist-patient privilege, 33 provided for some type of physician patient privilege, 14 provided for a social worker-patient privilege, and 8 provided for a victim/sexual assault counselor-patient privilege.

Even in those states in which privilege is granted, however, it is not absolute. For example, exceptions to the privilege in some jurisdictions include when the client waives privilege, raises his or mental state as an issue in a legal proceeding, initiates a licensing complaint or litigation against

the treating professional, or is the subject of a commitment proceeding. Thus, it is important that EAP professionals be familiar with the law of privilege in their jurisdictions.

In *Jaffe v. Redmond* (1996), the United States Supreme Court ruled that Federal Rule of Evidence 501 allowed federal courts to recognize a psychotherapist-patient privilege protecting confidential communication between a patient and psychotherapist. Of particular interest is that this case involved provision of clinical services by a licensed social worker via an EAP (Beyer, 2000). However, the Supreme Court, in recognizing a federal privilege, did not hold specifically that the privilege applied to EAPs–rather the Court ruled that psychotherapists enjoyed the privilege. The Supreme Court left the exact nature of the privilege, including exceptions, to be decided by courts over time (Svetanics, 1997; Klein, 1998; see Nielsen, 1997, Poulin, 1998; Nelken, 2000 and Aronson, 2001 for reviews of federal case law interpreting and applying the Supreme Court's decision in *Jaffe*, including discussion of what kind of communications the privilege applies and exceptions to the privilege).

Some post-Jaffe case law provides unique insight into how the courts may come to interpret the psychotherapist-patient privilege in the context of EAPs. In *Oleszko v. State Compensation Insurance Fund* (2001) the Ninth Circuit Court of Appeals extended the psychotherapist patient privilege enunciated in *Jaffe* to unlicensed EAP counselors. In *Greet v. Zagrocki* (1996) a federal district court allowed the psychotherapist-patient privilege to extend to records from a police department's EAP in which the service providers were peer counselors with no professional training.

Privacy, Confidentiality, Privilege, and Informed Consent

As the above discussion regarding informed consent might suggest, it is important that the EAP professional inform the employee about the nature, extent, and limitations of confidentiality and privilege as part of the informed consent process, and prior to establishing any kind of a professional relationship with the employee. Moreover, federal regulations require health care professionals to apprise clients of their privacy and confidentiality rights (see discussion of HIPAA and 42 Code of Federal Regulations 2.1–2.67 above). Of course, the nature of this disclosure will vary as a function of the jurisdiction in which the EAP professional practices, specific ethical principles applicable to the EAP professional, and the nature of the EAP professional-employee contact (i.e., whether the EAP professional is serving in a therapeutic or consultative-evaluative capacity).

Liability and Professional Sanctions

EAP professionals who fail to perform at the appropriate standards of care can be sanctioned in one of three ways: via a finding of malpractice in civil court, via discipline imposed by the relevant professional board which supervises the discipline which the licensed EAP professional practices, and via discipline resulting from any proceedings conducted by any professional organization of which the professional is a member.

Malpractice

Malpractice actions are tort or personal injury claims in which the plaintiff (the party bringing suit) claims that a health care professional caused harm by an action or omission that deviates from the prevailing standard of care within the particular profession (Petrila & Otto, in press). Plaintiffs may seek compensation for the losses allegedly suffered as a result of the professional's malpractice. Employee Assistance Program professionals who are health care professionals owe a duty to their clients that they would owe in any other context, depending on their specific discipline, as well as the nature and extent of the relationship. It should be noted at the outset that there are very few reported liability cases involving EAP professionals, reflecting the fact that most malpractice litigation involving mental health and health care professionals has arisen from other practice settings.

In *Reich v. Price and Southern Bell Telephone and Telegraph* (1993) the Court of Appeals of North Carolina affirmed a trial court's granting of summary judgment (in other words, a verdict was granted by the court without full trial) for the defendant, Michael Price, who administered the EAP operated by the plaintiff's employer, but who was not a licensed health care professional. The plaintiff alleged that, during the course of seeking consultation with Price and gaining a referral to a psychiatrist, she consumed drugs and alcohol, and had sexual relations with him. The appellate court affirmed the trial court's granting of summary judgment to the defendant on the grounds that the plaintiff's nonspecific claim of "professional malpractice" was vague and failed to establish the nature of the defendant's profession.

Employee Assistance Program professionals also may be involved in malpractice suits either as defendants or through providing consultation and testimony as expert witnesses for the plaintiff or defendant. As an expert witness, the EAP professional may testify about one or more of the following issues: (1) the appropriate standard of care in a particular case; (2) whether the defendant health care professional breached or met the professional standard of care; (3) the nature and extent, if any, of injuries suffered by the plaintiff; and (4) the relationship between the defendant professional's actions and the plaintiff's injuries, and the prospective treatment that may be necessary to treat the plaintiff's injuries.

In general, psychiatrists and nonmedical mental health professionals are sued for malpractice less frequently than physicians more generally (Simon, 2001). A review of state and federal appellate case law reveals little litigation involving EAP professionals specifically although, as noted above, EAP professionals will be held to the standard of care appropriate for their specific discipline or profession. However, because of professional concerns regarding malpractice, it is useful for the reader to understand the elements of a malpractice claim.

ELEMENTS OF A MALPRACTICE CLAIM. A plaintiff, in bringing a malpractice action, must show that: (1) the professional owed a duty of care to the plaintiff as a result of a professional relationship; (2) the professional breached the duty of care by failing to act consistently with prevailing professional norms; (3) the plaintiff suffered some kind of damages as a result of the professional's failure to act appropriately; and (4) the professional's actions were the proximate cause of the injuries suffered by the plaintiff.

The plaintiff must prove by a preponderance of evidence that the professional breached the prevailing standard of care and that the breach was the proximate cause of the damages claimed. The prevailing professional standard of care for a given health care professional is that level of care, skill, and treatment that, in light of relevant circumstances, is recognized as acceptable and appropriate by reasonably prudent health care professionals like the defendant. The existence of an injury, in and of itself, cannot create an inference or presumption of negligence against the health care professional.

EXPERT TESTIMONY. Although malpractice testimony addressing some of the elements of the malpractice action is typically offered, and is usually required, expert testimony need not be offered in cases in which common sense or ordinary judgment suggest the breach of a standard of care.

Licensing Complaints

Clients as well as others may file complaints alleging substandard practice with the state board that regulates the EAP professional's discipline (e.g., psychology, medicine, social work, and nursing). Although the nature, composition, and operation of professional boards vary from jurisdiction to jurisdiction, they have in common the responsibility of protecting the public from the substandard practice of professionals.

Although they are sometimes filed in tandem, complaints filed with licensing boards differ from malpractice actions in some important ways. The licensing complaint process is designed so that complaints can be filed easily and without legal assistance or representation. In contrast, almost all malpractice actions involve legal representation of the plaintiff. In contrast to malpractice actions, the complainant need not prove that harm occurred in a licensing complaint, but only need prove that the professional failed to meet the applicable stan-

dard of care or violated standards established in the licensing statutes in some other manner. Whereas a judge or jury decides whether a professional's conduct meets the elements of the claim in a malpractice action, the decision maker in the case of a licensing complaint is the relevant professional board, although the board's decision can be appealed to the courts. The professional board can impose a range of sanctions when it determines that a licensed professional has failed to meet the necessary standard of care. Sanctions may include letters of advisement or reprimand, imposition of fines, requiring remedial training or education, restriction of practice, and revocation of licensure in the most serious cases.

Discipline by Professional Organizations

Finally, professional organizations in which an EAP professional may enjoy membership may provide for discipline of members who fail to meet the standards or ethical principles promulgated by the organization. The complaint and review process can vary significantly among organizations, and the sanctions that can be imposed will be limited (e.g., public reprimand or letter of advisement, revocation of membership). These proceedings, however, may be relevant to and have an impact in licensing or malpractice actions.

Emerging Issues: Testing and the Americans with Disabilities Act

An EAP professional may be involved at least peripherally with workplace testing issues, specifically drug testing. An increasing number of states permit drug testing within the workplace and with a handful of exceptions dealing with random drug tests conducted, courts have been generally favorable toward drug testing (Wefing, 2000). In states that have adopted legislation authorizing such testing, a number of conditions may be established. For example, legislation enacted in Alaska (and based on that of other states, for example, Utah and Arizona) requires an employer to establish and distribute a written policy that: outlines the use of testing at least 30 days before its initiation; describes the employees who may be subject to testing; identifies when testing might be required; identifies the substances for which testing will be conducted; describes the types of testing to be used; describes the consequences of refusing to participate in testing; describes adverse personnel actions that might be taken based on testing results; identifies the employee's right to test results; identifies the employee's right to explain, confidentially, a positive test result; and describes the employer's policy regarding confidentiality (Zarou, 1999). In exchange for following the statutory guidelines, the employer receives broad protection from litigation resulting from the testing or actions taken as a result. Employees purportedly benefit from the increased emphasis on privacy established by such statutes, as well as from increased safety and health in the workplace associated with a drug-free workplace.

Another area of testing that has drawn increased attention is that of genetic testing. In contrast to drug testing, which has received a generally favorable public response, genetic testing often has been viewed with suspicion and distrust. At the same time, employer use of genetic information has increased in recent years; one recent summary noted that employers have used employee screening for genetic predisposition to disease and for a wide variety of health risks, including those related to smoking, reproductive hazards, HIV, drug use, and biological traits (Draper, 1999). While such testing raises serious issues, including scientific, ethical, and legal, the desire to use genetic information in making decisions in the workplace is likely to grow rather than diminish (Draper, 1999).

The EAP professional may have exposure to the issue of testing in a number of ways. First, the professional might suggest testing for drug use in some circumstances in which it appears warranted; second, an EAP professional might be called upon to provide treatment as a result of a drug test. Therefore, it is incumbent upon the EAP professional to be aware of the state of the law in his or her jurisdiction regarding the use of drug testing in the workplace. In such circumstances, it is also important for the EAP professional to understand and to communicate to the employee whether he or she is acting in a therapeutic role vis-à-vis the

employee or in a consultative role to the employer. The issues associated with the use of genetic information may lie somewhere in the future for many individuals working as EAP professionals, but those issues are emerging rapidly and so some knowledge regarding them will become increasingly important.

Finally, most EAP professionals are by now no doubt familiar with the Americans with Disabilities Act (ADA). The ADA, which became effective in 1992, prohibits discrimination on the basis of "disability" in a variety of areas, including employment. The ADA also requires that employers attempt to provide a "reasonable accommodation" to an employee with a disability, in order to enable the employee to work in circumstances when he or she might otherwise be unable to do so.

The EAP professional may become involved with ADA issues in a variety of ways. For example, he or she might be called upon by an employer to determine whether an employee has a disability within the meaning of the statute; to provide treatment to an employee with a disability; or to advise the employer on what might be a reasonable accommodation in a particular case.

The most important development in recent years regarding the ADA has been a trend in the United States Supreme Court to narrow application of the statute. The Court has done so principally though not exclusively by narrowing the definition of "disability." For example, in a recent case (*Toyota Motor Manufacturing v. Williams*, 2002) the Court ruled that in determining whether a particular impairment (in this case, carpal tunnel syndrome) was a disability, the legal decision maker was to look *not* at the effect of the impairment on the person's ability to work, but rather on its effect on activities of daily living, for example personal hygiene, household chores, and similar activities. This decision, combined with other recent Court cases, has the practical consequence of making it more difficult for employees to prove that they have a disability in a particular case (Petrila, 2002). It is important that the EAP professional recognize this trend and the general contours of the ADA in providing treatment or assessments that may be affected by the statute.

Summary

As this brief review suggests, the key threshold issue for an EAP professional to consider is the role he or she is playing in a particular case. If the role is that of treating professional, then the primary obligation is to the employee and the fiduciary duties of treating health care professionals govern. If the role is that of consultant to the employer, a very different set of rules may apply, particularly regarding the confidentiality of information obtained from the employee. In either case, it is important to notify the employee at the outset regarding what role the EAP professional is playing, and the implications of that role.

The particular profession of the EAP professional also plays a role, primarily because the professional's conduct will also be governed by the licensure rules of his or her profession. While malpractice litigation against EAPs or those who work under their auspice is rare, actions by the applicable licensure board may have an impact.

We have covered only some of the legal and ethical issues facing EAP professionals but in our judgment those presented here are at the core of practice. If the EAP professional practices according to prevailing professional standards, uses common sense, and is sensitive to potential role conflicts, the possibility of adverse legal action is comparatively remote. At the same time, it is important to understand at least the outline of the legal and ethical principles that govern practice, and the material presented in the references should prove valuable to those who wish to pursue specific topics in more detail.

ENDNOTES

1. For purposes of this discussion, those cases in which the EAP professional simply provides a referral to a third party for treatment should be considered as applying here since the purpose of the EAP professional-employee contact was to facilitate treatment.
2. We acknowledge that we have not exhausted the roles that EAP professionals may adopt in their interactions with employers and employees (e.g., EAP professionals may sometimes serve as educators) but we believe that the roles we have elucidated and discussed are the common roles and are most likely to prove problematic with respect to duties owed.

REFERENCES

Aaronson, R. H. (2001). The mental health provider privilege in the wake of *Jaffe v. Redmond*. *Oklahoma Law Review, 54,* 591–621.

Appelbaum, P., Lidz, C., & Meisel, A. (1987). *Informed consent: legal theory and clinical practice.* New York: Oxford Press.

Berg, J. W., Appelbaum, P., Lidz, C. W., & Parker, L. S. (2001). *Informed consent: Legal theory and clinical practice* (second edition). New York: Oxford Press.

Beyer, K. (2000). First person: *Jaffe v. Redmond* therapist speaks. *The American Psychoanalyst, 34* (3), 1–4.

Draper, E. (1999). The screening of America: The social and legal framework of employers' use of genetic information. *Berkeley Journal of Employment & Labor Law, 20,* 286–324.

Florida Statutes, 14 Fla. Stat. Ann. S. 415.102(1)(West 2002).

Florida Statutes, 14 Fla. Stat. Ann. S. 39.201(1) (West 2002).

Gostin, L. (1995). Health information privacy. *Cornell Law Review, 80,* 451–528.

Greenberg, S. A., & Shuman, D. W. (1997). Irreconcilable role conflict between therapeutic and forensic roles. *Professional Psychology: Research and Practice, 28,* 50–57.

Greet v. Zagrocki (1996 U.S. Dist LEXIS 18635, U.S. District Court for the Eastern District of PA).

Grisso, T., & Appelbaum, P. S. (1998). *Assessing competence to consent to treatment: A guide for physicians and other health professionals.* New York: Oxford.

Jaffe v. Redmond, 518 US 1, 116 S. Ct. 1923, (1996).

Kalichman, S. (1999). *Mandated reporting of suspected child abuse: Ethics, law and policy* (2nd edition). Washington, DC: American Psychological Association.

Klein, J. S. (1998). Note: "I'm your therapist, you can tell me anything": The Supreme Court confirms the psychotherapist-patient privilege in *Jaffe v. Redmond*. *Depaul Law Review, 47,* 701–726.

Melton, G. B., Petrila, J., Poythress, N., & Slobogin, C. (1997). *Psychological evaluations for the courts: A handbook for mental health professionals and lawyers.* New York: Guilford.

Nelken, M. L. (2000). The limits of privilege: The developing score of federal psychotherapist-patient privilege law. *Review of Litigation, 20,* 1–27.

Nielsen, W. J. (1997). Note: Privileged communications–The psychotherapist-patient privilege as adopted in the federal courts includes not only communications to licensed psychiatrists and psychologist, but also all communications to licensed social workers in the course of psychotherapy–*Jaffe v. Redmond. Seton Hall Law review, 27,* 1123–1141.

Oher, J. M. (Ed.) (1999). *The employee assistance handbook.* New York: Wiley.

Oleszko v. State Compensation Insurance Fund, 243 F.3d 1154 (9th Cir. 2001).

Petrila, J. (2000). Legal and ethical issues in protecting the privacy of behavioral healthcare information. In Gates, J. & Arons, B. (2000). *Privacy and confidentiality in mental health care.* Baltimore. Brookes.

Petrila, J. (2002). The U.S. Supreme Court narrows the definition of disability under the Americans with Disabilities Act. *Psychiatric Services, 53,* 797–798, 801.

Petrila, J., & Otto, R. K. (In press). *Law and mental health professionals: Florida* (2nd edition). Washington, DC: American Psychological Association.

Pitts, J., Goldman, J., Hudson, Z., Berenson, A., & Hadley, E. (1999). *The state of health privacy: An uneven terrain. A comprehensive survey of state health privacy statutes.* Washington, DC: Health Privacy Project, Institute for Health Care Research and Policy, Georgetown University. Available at www.healthprivacy.org/resources.

Poulin, A. B. (1998). The psychotherapist-patient privilege after *Jaffe v. Redmond:* Where do we go from here? *Washington University Law Quarterly, 76,* 1341–1382.

Reich v. Price and Southern Bell Telephone and Telegraph Company, 429 S.E.2d 372 (1993, NC App).

Rogers v. CH2M Hill, 18 F.Supp.2d 1328 (1998, Middle District of Alabama, Northern Division).

Scott, C. (2000). Is too much privacy bad for your health? An introduction to the law, ethics, and HIPAA rule on medical privacy. *Georgia State University Law Review, 17,* 481–505.

Shuman, D. (2000). *Psychiatric and psychological evidence* (2nd edition). Minneapolis, MN: West Group.

Shuman, D., & Weiner, B. (1982). The privilege study: An empirical examination of the psychotherapist-patient privilege. *North Carolina Law Review, 60,* 893–915.

Simon, R. I. (2001). *Concise guide to psychiatry and law for clinicians.* Washington, DC: American Psychiatric Press.

Stiles, P., Poythress, N., Hall, A., Falkenbach, D., & Williams, R. (2001). Improving understanding of research consent disclosures among persons with mental illness. *Psychiatric Services, 52,* 780–785.

Svetanics, M. L. (1997). Note: Beyond "reason and experience": The Supreme Court adopts a broad psychotherapist-patient privilege in *Jaffe v. Redmond. St. Louis University Law Journal, 41,* 719–739.

Tarasoff v. Regents of the University of California, 529 P.2d 533 (vacated) 551 P.2d 334 (1976).

Toyota Motor Manufacturing, Kentucky v. Williams, 122 S. Ct. 681 (2002).

Vardiman v. Ford Motor Company, 981 F.Supp. 1279 (1997, Eastern District of Missouri).

Wefing, J. (2000). Employer drug testing: Disparate judicial and legislative responses. *Albany Law Review, 63,* 799–832.

Zarou, M. (1999). The good, the bad, and the ugly: Drug testing by employers in Alaska. *Alaska Law Review, 16,* 297–327.

Chapter 22

DRUG AND ALCOHOL TESTING: CURRENT EMPLOYEE ASSISTANCE PROGRAMS DILEMMAS

ALISSE C. CAMAZINE

Recently, employers have become more aware of the impact which substance abuse has on the workplace. Increased accidents, absenteeism, workers' compensation claims, and other similar circumstances have made employers aware that substance abuse problems may exist in their workplace. Numerous companies have, as a result, taken steps to attack this growing problem. Many Fortune 500 and smaller companies alike have chosen to institute drug screening programs in an attempt to curtail substance abuse problems. Removing employees with substance abuse problems from the workplace reduces the risk of injury to co-employees and provides a safe workplace.

Basic Guidelines for a Drug Policy

If your company is planning to institute a drug screening policy, the policy must meet the objectives of the company and at the same time meet certain legal requirements. Additionally, the policy should be developed in conjunction with union representatives, personnel managers, management, security and legal advisors in order to avoid any intercompany conflicts regarding the procedures of the policy.

The policy should be clearly written, clearly communicated to employees, and uniformly enforced. Each employee should receive a copy of the policy. Company manuals and bulletin boards should be updated and include the policy. Any policy statement regarding drug screening should

address the following issues:

1. The company should demonstrate the need for a drug screening policy by making employees aware of the substance abuse problems in the workplace. The employees should also be advised about the company's concern for the health and safety of its employees, as well as the safety, productivity and security problems associated with substance abuse.

2. The company must provide clear, explicit notification of the policy to all employees. This policy should advise the employees of the company rules regarding the use of illegal drugs, alcohol and prescription drugs, both on and off the company property. The employees should be advised that they will be subject to drug testing under certain circumstances, and those circumstances should be set forth in the policy. The policy should also define the consequences for refusal to take a test.

3. Disciplinary action which will be taken as a result of a violation of the policy should be set forth. An employee should be aware that he may be removed from his job pending a drug screen, or that he may be discharged or terminated.

4. The policy should clearly state which employees are subject to the test and under what circumstances.

5. Notification to employees of positive test results must be provided. Employees should be given an opportunity to contest the results before dis-

Note: This chapter is reprinted from *Employee Assistance Programs: A Basic Text* (1988) with permission of the author, the book's editors (Dickman, Emener, & Hutchison, Jr.), and the publisher (Charles C Thomas, Publisher, Ltd.).

ciplinary action is taken. A hearing should always be permitted before terminations. Hearing procedures should be specifically set forth in the policy.

6. The company should advise the employees that it is the intent of the company to help troubled employees in overcoming drug, alcohol, and other problems, which are or may affect job performance. In order to accomplish this goal, the policy should provide for referrals to the company EAP following a positive drug or alcohol screen. Employees should also be encouraged to seek assistance at the EAP on a voluntary basis before more severe problems develop.

7. If the policy is going to be effective and at the same time avoid civil liability, safeguards for protecting employee confidentiality must be established. Results of the tests must be kept confidential and disclosed to only limited people. These policies should include to whom the information will be released and what will happen to the information after released. No results should be disclosed until a second test has confirmed the positive results.

Who Should Be Tested?

The company must determine from the outset, which groups of employees will be subject to testing. The potential legal problems involved in testing the different groups of employees have assisted companies in making their decisions about whom to test.

Many companies have chosen to limit testing to preemployment screens only. The companies hope that this will discourage drug users from joining the workplace. At the same time, there are few legal problems associated with preemployment drug and alcohol testing.

Employers have the right to require employees to be free from the use of drugs as a condition of employment, especially since those individuals who are abusing alcohol and drugs may cause danger to co-workers.

All applicants should be tested, rather than testing applicants randomly and prospective applicants should be advised that they will be tested for drugs as part of the preemployment process. Employers should obtain a consent from each applicant that acknowledges that there will be testing and that the applicant is providing his/her consent.

Some companies have chosen to perform testing on those employees whose actions create a reasonable suspicion of drug use, as a result of being involved in an accident or being unable to work. In order to have such testing "for cause" there must be suspicion based on specific facts that the employee is under the influence of alcohol or drugs. Such reasonable cause includes, but is not limited to deteriorating work performance, excessive tardiness, absenteeism, an accident on the job, or suspect behavior. Documentation must be maintained to substantiate why an employer or supervisor believed circumstances justifying "for cause" testing existed.

Based on recent cases, it is clear that "for cause" testing has met constitutional challenges. In *McKechnie v. Dargan* (E.D.N.Y., April 28, 1986, No. C. V. 84–4339), the testing of a police officer was upheld when the department has reasonable grounds to suspect that the officer was intoxicated or under the influence of alcohol. In this case, the officer's gun was used by a friend in a crime. Additionally, there had been deteriorated work performance over an extended period of time. Similarly, firefighters who exhibit signs of intoxication and smell from alcohol create a reasonable basis to require testing. *Korlick v. Lowery*, 26 N.Y. 2d 723 (1970). Refusal to take a drug test, if based on reasonable cause, can result in dismissal. *King v. McMickens*, 501 N.Y.S. 2d 679 (1st Cir. 1986).

In *Division 241 Amalgamated Transit Union v. Suscy*, 538 F. 2d 1264 (7th Cir. 1976) the bus operators' union filed a complaint attacking the constitutionality of a rule enacted by the Chicago Transit Authority. The rule provided that employees who were suspected of being under the influence of alcohol or drugs while on duty may be required to take a blood and urinalysis test. The United States Court of Appeals held that the state had a paramount interest in protecting the public by insuring that bus drivers were fit for duty. The court balanced the drivers' rights to privacy against the public's interest in safety. The court further said that before there could be testing, employees had to be involved in an accident or suspected of being under the influence. As a result, the court found that there could be testing under the rules as enacted by the Chicago Transit Authority.

In *Fraternal Order of Police, Newark Lodge No. 12 v. City of Newark* (N.J. Sup. Ct. Essex Co., Mar. 20, 1986), the court upheld a police department's order requiring all members of the narcotics bureau to submit to mandatory screening. The court required that the department take some steps to assure the accurateness of the tests and to insure the privacy of the officers. Similarly, in *Seeling v. McMickens* (N.Y.L.J. August 7, 1986), a state court upheld urine testing for correction officers who were required to drive prison vans because of the safety-sensitive nature of the job.

Many companies have taken the drug screening one step further and have instituted drug tests which are performed randomly and unannounced. These companies have justified these screens based on the inherent danger to the employees from working with other employees who have substance abuse problems and who are working in safety-sensitive positions. There have been many recent conflicting cases regarding the legality of such random tests. For example, in *Shoemaker v. Handel,* 608 F.Supp. 1151 (D.C.N.J. 1985), the court held that New Jersey had a legitimate interest in testing jockeys for drugs and alcohol in order to reduce the possibility of accident and death while racing. The basis of this decision was that horseracing is a closely regulated industry, which has traditionally been subject to close supervision and regulation. Additionally, there were substantial safeguards to protect confidentiality. Results were considered confidential and access to positive results was limited to Commissioners of the New Jersey Racing Commission and the Executive Director or his designee, unless there is a contested matter. The Racing Commission also stated that no information would be shared with any state agency regarding criminal prosecution.

In Marietta, Georgia, employees of the Marietta Board of Lights and Water were asked to submit to random drug tests. This occurred after the manager began receiving reports of drug usage by board employees. The company thought that the drug use may have been responsible for what they believed to be a large number of injuries to employees. Because of the extremely hazardous nature of the work performed by the employees, the manager felt that such drug usage constituted a threat to the safety of the employees and the public. After the random drug tests were completed, each of the employees tested showed positive for marijuana. The testing was challenged, but the court held that the tests were administered as part of the government's legitimate inquiry into the use of drugs by employees engaged in hazardous work. The court found, therefore, that the tests were not unreasonable. *Allen v. City of Marietta,* 601 F Supp. 482 (N.D. Ga. 1985).

In the case of *Jones v. McKenzie,* 638 F. Supp. 1500, (D.C. 1986) the court held that subjecting a school bus attendant to testing without probable cause violated the attendant's Fourth Amendment rights. In this case, there was no evidence that the individual in question ever used drugs or was under the influence of drugs either on or off the premises. Additionally, the employer did not confirm the positive test result with a second confirmation test. However, the court stated that its ruling might be different for school bus drivers or mechanics who are directly responsible for the operation and maintenance of buses and that those employees might reasonably be subjected to urine tests without suspicion.

Many other recent cases have held that public employees, even in safety-sensitive positions, may **not** be subject to urine tests unless there is reasonable suspicion that the employee is using drugs and/or alcohol. In *Capua v. City of Plainfield,* 1 IER Cases 625 (9/18/86), firefighters employed by the City of Plainfield were ordered to submit to a surprise urine test. In this case, there was no notice, no collective bargaining with the union, immediate termination for positive test results, surveillance during urine collection, no reasonable cause or suspicion, and no confidentiality safeguards. As a result, the court found such testing to be unconstitutional.

In *Caurso v. Ward* (N.Y. Sup. Ct. July 2, 1986, No. 12632/86) the court invalidated a New York City Police Department rule requiring random drug testing. The Department argued that the police were serving in safety-sensitive positions. The court held, however, that there must be reasonable suspicion before an officer can be required to take a urine test. Courts have recently issued similar decisions relating to other police departments and firefighters. See also *Turner v. Fraternal Order of Police,* 500A.2d 1005 (D.C. 1985).

It is clear from the recent court decisions regarding random drug tests that these cases will be decided on a case-by-case basis. It is difficult to predict what the United States Supreme Court will finally decide on this issue. Until there is more guidance from the courts, testing should be limited to preemployment screening and "for cause" testing, rather than .utilizing random screening. This approach to testing should limit liability and lawsuits.

Off-Duty Use of Drugs

Many employers would like to take disciplinary action if an employee is involved with drugs off duty or if an employee is involved in other off duty criminal conduct. Generally, the case law indicates that what an employee does on his or her time, outside of work, is not subject to workplace discipline. However, if the conduct of the employee could affect the business reputation of the company, render the employee unable to work or affect morale, then discipline is permissible.

In *Trailways Southeastern Lines, Inc.,* 81 Lab. Arb (BNA) 712 (Gibson, Arb. 1983) an employee pled guilty to breaking and entering with the intention of murdering his ex-wife. The driver was put on probation for the criminal offense. As part of the probation, the driver had to attend an alcoholic rehabilitation program, as well as attending Alcoholics Anonymous. Additionally, he was ordered not to consume any alcoholic beverages. A news article appeared in a local paper reporting the plea and identifying the employee as a Trailways bus driver. Other newspaper articles identified the individual as a Trailways bus driver and included details of the charges, including the fact that the driver had been carrying a gun. The arbitrator held that the publicity of the case and of the defendant as an employee of the company jus-

tified discharge. See also *City of Wilkes Barre,* 74 Lab. Arb. (BNA) 33 (Dunn 1980).

Similarly, in *Martin-Marietta Aerospace,* 81 L.A. 695 (1983), an arbitrator upheld the termination of an employee who had been convicted of selling cocaine off company premises. The arbitrator felt that the employer had a legitimate concern that the employee might attempt to sell drugs to other employees at the workplace.

In a contrary decision, an arbitrator found that an employer had no right to force an employee to submit to a drug test when a marijuana cigarette was observed in the employee's car after work hours. The employee in this case was on company property when drugs were found in his possession although his presence on the property was not related to his employment. *Texas Utilities Generating Co.,* 82 Lab. Arb. (BNA) 6 (1983). This case may indicate that an employee's drug use does not extend to off-duty use of drugs, unless the employer can show that the employee was unable to work as a result of the drug use, that the employer's reputation was harmed, or that the employee poses a risk to co-workers.

Constitutional Issues

The state and federal constitutions do not generally apply to the actions of private employers because the requisite "state action" is not present. Therefore, most of the challenges to drug testing have been brought by those individuals employed in the public sector. Challenges to testing in the private sector will generally be based on different grounds than those in the public sector. If, however, private companies are subject to a high degree of governmental regulation, the companies should be aware of the possibility that they may be subject to constitutional limitations. The following addresses the most frequent bases for constitutional challenges.

Right to Privacy

The first legal challenge raised by those opposing drug screening is an allegation of a violation on one's right to privacy. Although this right is not specifically enumerated in our constitution, the courts have found that specific guarantees exist in the Bill of Rights, the right of privacy being one of them.

In *Treasury Employees v. Von Raab,* 1 IER cases 945, (Nov. 14, 1986), an injunction was filed in Federal Court seeking to block the United States Custom Service from further urine collection as part of a drug testing program. The program required that the service workers who seek promotion into certain positions submit to drug screening, as a condition of employment for placement into these positions. A collector was physically present in the bathroom during the urination process. The representative placed dye in the urinal and then stepped back behind a partition. The court found that the testing "detracts from the dignity of each customs worker covered under the plan and invades the right of privacy such workers have under the United States Constitution."

Excreting bodily wastes is a very personal bodily function normally done in private; it is accompanied by a legitimate expectation of privacy, in both the process and the product. The Customs directive unconstitutionally interferes with the privacy rights of the Customs workers." It is important to note in this case that there was no evidence of drug problems among the work force, nor was there any reasonable cause to suspect that the employees were using or selling drugs at the worksite. See also *McDonell v. Hunter,* 612 F.Supp. 1122 (D.C.Iowa 1985), below.

Unreasonable Search and Seizure

The next constitutional challenge raised is that the testing violates the Fourth Amendment right to be free from unreasonable searches and seizures. It must be remembered that the Fourth Amendment protects individuals from governmental searches and seizures. In determining whether an individual has a reasonable expectation of privacy and whether the governmental instructions are reasonable, the courts will balance the need to seize against the invasion.

In *McDonell v. Hunter,* three correctional institution employees challenged the constitutionality of an Iowa Department of Corrections policy, which subjected the employees to searches of their vehicles and persons, including urinalysis and blood tests. The court found that the testing was an unreasonable search because there was no reasonable suspicion, based on specific objective facts that the employee was under the influence of alcohol or controlled substances.

Similarly, a court prohibited a local school board from performing drug testing of teachers considered for tenure because there was no reasonable suspicion of drug usage. *Patchoque-Medford Congress of Teachers v. Board of Education,* Case No. C85–8759 (N.Y. Sup. Ct. Suffolk City 1985).

The constitutionality of a police department order was tested in *Turner v. Fraternal Order of Police,* 500 A. 2d 1005 (D.C. App. 1985). The department order provided that upon suspicion of drug abuse a Department Official may order any member of the force to submit to urinalysis testing. The Court held that the department may compel officers to submit to the testing based on suspected drug abuse. The court considered whether, under the circumstances, an officer has a legitimate expectation of privacy and whether the department's order is unnecessarily intrusive. The court further stated that the department had a paramount interest in protecting the public. Based on the type of work in which officers engage, and the need to be alert to carry out such duties, the court believed that the use of controlled substances by police officers was a situation that created serious consequences to the public. Because the order required that there be suspected drug abuse, the court held that the intrusion was not unreasonable.

Due Process Rights

Opponents of drug testing argue that such testing violates an individual's due process rights. Such claims allege that the drug tests are inaccurate and insufficiently related to work performance. These allegations also relate to whether or not there is proper notice of the circumstances under which testing will be performed, and whether the employee had a right to contest the results. Due process requires that no adverse action be taken without a second confirmation test.

Many drug screening policies have been found to be unconstitutional based on Due Process challenges. These challenges have been brought based on the fact that the test results do not and cannot indicate impaired job performance. Many courts, however, have accepted the notion that any detectable use of drugs may impair job performance, especially in safety-sensitive positions. See *Turner v. Fraternal Order of Police,* above. In *Brotherhood of Locomotive Engineers v. Burlington Northern,* 117 LRRM 2739 (D.C. Montana 1984) the court granted the union's request for an injunction against the employer's new policy of using drug tests to detect possession of controlled substances by its employees because the employer failed to bargain with the union. In a union-represented workplace, it is necessary to discuss drug screens and searches with the union representatives before an employer can unilaterally make changes in the workplace rules.

Courts have also found that drug testing violates due process rights because the drug testing plan was far from an infallible system and was fraught with dangers of false positives. See *Treasury Employees v. Von Raab,* above. There can also be a violation of due process rights if the employee is not provided with an opportunity for a hearing before discharge. See *Jones v. McKenzie,* above.

These cases emphasize the importance of the proper development of a drug testing program. Many legal problems can be avoided by consulting with legal counsel and following constitutional safeguards to protect an employee's basic rights.

The Arbitrator's Views

Arbitrators will look unfavorably upon those companies who perform testing and do not provide the rehabilitative services of an Employee Assistance Program. For example, in *Alleghany Lundlum Steel Corp,* 84 Lab. Arb. 476 (1985), an arbitrator held that where misconduct is alcohol-related and the company has an EAP, the employee must be allowed to seek assistance. This was true even though neither the company nor the union had any knowledge of the employee's problem before the discharge. The arbitrator felt that the grievant had not been provided with an oppor-

tunity to seek assistance from the EAP because the dissemination of information regarding the EAP was inadequate.

Arbitrators may also consider the consistency of the treatment of employees. In *Indianapolis Rubber Co.,* 79 Lab. Arb. (BNA) 529 (1983) the arbitrator found that the employer had previously reinstated terminated employees who successfully completed a rehabilitation program. The arbitrator, therefore, believed that the company improperly discriminated against another employee by refusing to reinstate him when he completed the same program.

The arbitration decisions indicate that the arbitrators will consider whether progressive discipline was used, the length of employment, work history, the type of job involved, and whether there is danger to the public or others because of an employee's conduct. Notice requirements must be met for an arbitration decision to be upheld and the company must bargain with the union regarding the drug testing. In *Gem City Chemical Inc.,* 86 L.A. 1023 (1986) an employee refused to submit to a urine test during a physical examination. The arbitrator held that the employee had been improperly discharged because the request was not based on reasonable cause. Additionally, the testing was not discussed or incorporated into the union's collective bargaining agreement. The employer also did not provide notice of the test.

Arbitrators will expect that reputable laboratories, with accurate results be chosen to perform the tests. Disciplinary action should only be based on the second confirmation test. In *Washington Metropolitan Area Transit Authority,* 82 L.A. 151 (Bernhardt, 1983), an arbitrator upheld the discharge of a bus driver who was tested for drugs following an accident. The specimens were confirmed and positive results obtained both times. In a Federal Court of Appeals case, the court overturned the discipline of air traffic controllers who tested positive for drugs because the samples were not maintained for independent verification. *Banks v. Federal Aviation Administration,* 687 F.2d 92 (5th Cir. 1982).

It is clear that the arbitrators will scrutinize drug testing procedures. Employers should be aware of the principles considered by the arbitrators.

Arbitrators will favor use of an EAP prior to discharge, but will generally not have much sympathy for an employee who fails to recover or follow a "last chance" agreement. Arbitrators will require uniformity in discipline and will consider whether progressive discipline was utilized. Constitutional safeguards must be maintained if a discharge is going to be upheld.

EAP Involvement in Testing

The EAP should not be required to do the testing itself because this creates a conflict for the EAP whose primary purpose is rehabilitation, not discipline. An EAP should be involved in setting up a "last chance" agreement, which addresses and includes a plan for treatment, and requirements for continued employment. Employees should be advised that the use of the EAP represents a "last chance" and not a guarantee that the employment will be maintained. Further, the use of the EAP will not provide protection against discipline. Failure to improve deteriorated work performance or continued drug use following treatment may result in termination.

The plan should be in writing and should be signed by the employee. Those persons who will receive the follow-up information regarding whether or not there is improvement and/or recovery should be listed in the plan so that there will be no question regarding breach of confidentiality if information is disclosed.

The plan should be specific and should be clearly written so that there can be no subsequent disputes regarding what is and is not expected of the employee.

CONCLUSION

In summary, it is clear that there are many conflicting decisions regarding the legality of drug and alcohol testing. It is hopeful that in the near future, the United States Supreme Court will provide guidance on this subject. Until that time, if a company is going to institute a drug screening policy, certain constitutional safeguards must be followed. Without these safeguards, it is unlikely that the validity of the program will be upheld.

If preemployment testing is going to be performed, all applicants must be notified in advance. Testing on the basis of reasonable suspicion has, so far, met legal challenges, if the testing is performed in accordance with constitutional safeguards. In comparison, the validity of random testing is questionable at this time, even in safety sensitive positions. The lack of uniformity in the recent decisions indicates that the courts may invalidate these programs in the future. Further clarifying decisions are necessary in order to provide the answer to whether random testing will be allowed in the future.

UPDATE/COMMENT

JUDITH K. SCHEMM

At the federal level, large scale drug testing began in 1986 with President Reagan's "drug-free workplace" (Executive Order No12564, 1986). State and local governments followed suit and by 1996 81 percent of private corporations reported drug testing employees (American Management Association, 1998).

The term "drug-free workplace place" still evokes concern, intimidation and skepticism among some employee assistance professionals. Many see it as the opposite of good EAP practice. Some equate the phrase with drug testing, which is considered punitive, whereas an EAP is regarded as rehabilitative. This need not be the case, as more and more companies are giving employees who test positive a second chance. During this process the EAP professional can provide the employer a treatment plan to help with unresolved problems, establish treatment goals and give a time frame for the employee to reach goals. This affords the employer with a reasonable expectation that if goals are not met the employer can still follow another course of action, e.g., temporary discharge or termination.

Washington is among the many states that offer incentives for employers to implement a drug-free workplace program. Washington is the only state program that requires that each employee be offered a second chance if tested positive and that the process be monitored by the EAP. The drug-free workplace program in Washington conducted a survey of the EAP/drug-free workplace programs and these important objectives were reported.

1. Employee rehabilitation is not a benefit granted by a tolerant employer, but a good business decision. A reversal of the "War on Drugs" mentality where the drug using employee was seen as a problem, employee rehabilitation is seen as a choice. Either chose to comply with EAP recommendations or choose to leave the company (in Washington approximately 40 percent choose to leave). Those who choose to stay help themselves and their employer. This in turn is good for morale and improved employee/employer relations.

2. The EAP is an essential strategy in an effective drug free workplace program. Without the EAP, a drug-free workplace program can be only partially successful. Drug testing alone is not enough. Direction is needed to assist the worker in becoming a contributing employee. EAP intervention assures the employee that he/she may continue to work and privately address their drug/alcohol problems.

3. EAPs and drug testing are complementary strategies in an effective drug-free workplace program. Proponents of drug testing argue that it helps to identify employees who have substance abuse problems. Once identified, the business plays an active role facilitating the person's referral to EAP for treatment and reintegration back into the work force. In 1996, President Reagan's call for a "drug-free work-

place" included a mandatory referral of person's with a positive drug test to federal employee assistance programs.

Pre-employment testing continues to be the most valuable element in creating a drug-free workplace. Random testing, though problematic, continues to be the most powerful deterrent to drug use for current employees (Govert, 2001).

However, drug testing and privacy continue to be dilemmas for EAPs. A question remains as to limits on the on employer's incursion, into workers personal conduct. Claims of invasion of privacy have been leveled against an employer's prerogative in establishing workplace standards. Drug testing is a controversial issue in public sector employment. A compromise between employer need for a drug-free workplace and employee privacy must be considered. One of the first legal challenges raised by those against drug screening was the possible violation of one's right to privacy, guaranteed by the Bill of Rights. However, drug screening continues to be seen as a viable option at pre-employment and at random intervals once employed. Most cases that have been tried regarding privacy and drug testing have been settled in favor of maintaining a drug-free workplace unless the individual has proven unreasonable search and seizure and there was no reasonable suspicion. In *Skinner v. Railway Labor Executives' Association* (1989), the Court adopted a less stringent standard for privacy while at work. It found that the intrusions on privacy are acceptable in order to prevent injuries caused by impaired railway workers. In weighing the interest of both parties, the Court looked favorably on the potential deterrent value of drug testing (Brunet, 2002).

Ten years ago the Americans with Disabilities Act (ADA) created some of the most sweeping reforms ever issued by the U.S. government. The ADA was written to guarantee that people with disabilities would not be discriminated against in the workplace. This included employees addicted to drugs. Although ADA does not protect those who are current drug users or those who work under the influence of drugs, ADA rules do apply to long-term employees who claim addiction. If an employee is addicted to drugs, the employer is obligated to send the employee to treatment if the company has an EAP. After completion of treatment the worker must be offered his/her job back or an equivalent position. Employers only have to offer treatment once; if the employee does not stay sober the employer may be able to terminate the employee (Watts, 2001).

In *Skinner vs. Railway Labor Executives* and in similar cases in accordance appears to be developing among the federal courts about what makes a government mandated drug test reasonable. The courts have ruled the following: (1) drug testing that target a narrow set of workers whose drug use imposes a threat to fellow workers, the public, or the agency are considered constitutional; and (2) random testing of all workers within a specific job if used as a deterrent to future drug use will also be seen as constitutional (Brunet, 2001).

Based on these findings, drug and alcohol testing will continue to be part of today's work force. Drug testing and EAPs both have a function that the other cannot perform. Each should recognize the value and constraints of both approaches. Drug testing will not always identify workers with problems. EAPs continue to use other identifiers to discover troubled employees such as changes in behavior, presentation, chronic absenteeism, etc. EAP professionals are progressively more accommodating to drug testing, as they will continue to offer rehabilitative support needed by both employer and employee.

REFERENCES

American Management Association. (1998). *1998 AMA survey on workplace testing and monitoring.* New York.

Brunet, J. R. (2002) Employee drug testing as social control. *Review of PublicPersonnel Administration, 22* (3) 193–215.

Govert, H. (2001)) Drug-free workplace programs *CEAP, EAPA Exchange, 31* (1), 8–9.

Watts, C. (2001). Ten years after: Working with the ADA. *EAP Digest, 21* (4) 34–36.

Chapter 23

CRITICAL INCIDENT STRESS:
PRINCIPLES, PRACTICES, AND PROTOCOLS

MICHAEL G. RANK and J. ERIC GENTRY

Extreme emotional and psychological reactions to distressful situations and events are a natural part of the human experience. It is highly unlikely that one can live a lifetime and not experience a potentially traumatic event or situation. These extreme emotional and psychological reactions are unique to the individual and often do not follow a logical or predictable course. Most individuals who have experienced a traumatic event or situation are able to put the event into a philosophical perspective, make sense of the event, and return to living their life with minimal difficulty. However, some individuals struggle with returning to normative living and are at risk for developing posttraumatic stress disorder (PTSD), other anxiety disorders, personality disorders, or depression, just to name a few of the possible maladaptive outcomes. It is impossible to accurately predict by the nature of an event whether any given individual will develop PTSD (Rank, 1997). According to the American Psychiatric Association (2000), studies have found that eight percent of the adult population in the United States has developed PTSD and between one-third to one-half of at-risk individuals (survivors of rape, military combat, politically motivated internment and genocide, etc.) have developed the disorder.

The APA (2000) states that PTSD cannot be diagnosed unless symptoms persist after four weeks have elapsed from the traumatic event. This gives mental health professionals a window of less than 30 days to assist at-risk individuals to resolve their traumatic stress symptoms and to prevent posttraumatic stress disorders. If intense symptoms persist after two days following a traumatic event or situation, an individual may be at risk for developing acute stress disorder (ASD). The diagnostic criteria for ASD are almost identical to those for PTSD (APA, 2000). Diagnostically, ASD evolves into PTSD if symptoms persist past four weeks. It is critical therefore that the mental health professional intervenes in a sensitive, timely, and effective manner.

The term *Critical Incident* (CI) is the actual event that has the potential to bring about a crisis response; it is sometimes confused with the human response (the critical incident response) to the event (Mitchell & Everly, 2001). The terms *critical incident stress* (CIS), *critical incident stress debriefing* (CISD), and *critical incident stress management* (CISM) were initially employed by Mitchell (1983), Everly & Mitchell (1999), and Mitchell & Everly (2001). CIS originally described the emotional and psychological reactions of first responders (fire, rescue, disaster, law enforcement) to traumatic events or situations. CISD originally was the professional intervention to assist those personnel to mitigate their distress resulting from the traumatic event or situation. CISD is a group crisis intervention technique designed to alleviate the acute symptoms of distress resulting from a traumatic event or situation (Everly & Boyle, 2001). CISD is not group therapy. CISM has evolved into a 10-component comprehensive, integrated crisis intervention system of which CISD is a part (Everly & Mitchell, 1999; Mitchell & Everly, 2001).

CIS has since expanded to apply to anyone who has experienced a traumatic event or situation (Spitzer, 2002) and the CISD protocol has been adapted for various survivor populations. Additionally, CISD's have also been labeled as *Psychological Debriefing* (Bisson, McFarlane, & Rose, 2000; Raphael & Wilson, 2000).

The focus of this chapter is on preventing the development of ASD, PTSD, and other associated maladaptive resolutions to normative life following the experience of a traumatic event. This chapter will present the principles of critical incident stress (CIS), the practices associated with resolving CIS, and protocols intended to mitigate CIS.

Literature Review

Much of the literature about CIS, critical incident stress debriefings (CISD), and critical incident stress management (CISM) is intended for the mitigation of maladaptive stress reactions in first responders, police, firefighters, and other emergency service personnel. The International Critical Incident Stress Foundation (ICISF) specifically tailors their protocol to these populations (ICISF, 2002). The authors of this chapter expand the concept of CIS and the CIS intervention to survivors of any type of traumatic event or situation in a community and/or workplace context.

Critical incident stress is a unique type of personal condition that occurs when an individual experiences or witnesses an event that is unusual, extraordinary, or violent (Rank, 1997). The immediate human reaction to these unusual events is called a critical incident response (CIR) (Family Enterprises Inc., 1993). This response involves a vacillation between numbness and hyperarousal, blocking out feelings and recollections of the event, and a myriad of physiological symptoms. An individual's response to a stressor is highly unique, depending upon one's interpretation of the event, coping style, and support system (Rank, 1997). Responses to traumatic stress vary among individuals, communities, cultures, and nations.

The professional intervention employed to individuals or communities who have experienced a traumatic event is generally referred to as a Critical Incident Stress Debriefing (CISD) or Psychological Debriefing (PD). There are many debriefing models (ARC, 1991; Everly & Mitchell,

1997; FEMA, 2002; ICISF, 2002; Mitchell, 1983; Mitchell & Everly, 1996; Rank, 1997; Young, Ford, Ruzek, Friedman, & Gusman, 1998). All debriefing protocols reference and build upon the Mitchell model (1983), however some protocols add and delete components based upon the perceived needs of specific populations.

Research into the effectiveness of CISD reveals mixed results (Bisson, Jenkins, Alexander, & Bannister, 1997; Deahl, Gillham, Thomas, Searle, & Srinivason, 1994; Dyregrov, 1989 & 1998; Rapheal, 1986; Rapheal & Wilson, 2000; Shalev, 1994). Many of these authors and researchers chronicle the success of the intervention. However, some of these researchers question the effectiveness of a CISD, view the intervention as potentially damaging, and believe participants may be at risk for developing additional symptoms as the circumstances of the event are recalled, articulated, and expressed. According to Rose, Bisson, & Wesseley (2002), there is no current evidence that psychological debriefing is a useful treatment for the prevention of posttraumatic stress disorder after traumatic incidents.

It is the opinion of the authors of this chapter, based upon years of experience as critical incident stress debriefers, that the intervention, if done correctly, is the single most effective tool that can be employed to immediately address ASD, prevent the development of PTSD, and assist the survivor in rapidly returning to pre-morbid functioning. Participation in a CISD does not guarantee that participants will not subsequently develop stress-related disorders, however articulating one's perceptions and experiences about a traumatic event in a group setting, under a trained professionals guidance, has the potential to significantly reduce traumatic symptoms that lead to the development of ASD and PTSD (Everly & Mitchell, 1997; Mitchell, 1983; Mitchell & Everly, 1996; Rank, 1997; Young, Ford, Ruzek, Friedman, & Gusman, 1998). The Federal Emergency Management Agency (FEMA) and the American Red Cross employ the use of critical incident stress debriefings (FEMA, 2002; ARC, 1991 & 2002). Additionally, there are local, regional, and statewide teams trained to perform critical incident stress debriefings especially for emergency service personnel. Although there are many local programs functioning at various levels, there is no organized national intervention network for community and workplace critical incident response.

Post-event use of health care services and the effectiveness of critical incident stress debriefing sessions and other coping interventions were examined by Smith, Christiansen, Vincent and Hann (1998). Their research explored how experiencing a traumatic event in the workplace affects employee physical health. Critical incident stress debriefing interventions were rated as helpful by 78 percent of employees who attended.

Based upon an evaluation of existing empirical studies about PD and CISD, Bisson, McFarlane and Rose (2000) state that overall the intervention is well received by participants. They conclude that PD and CISD are useful interventions to facilitate the screening of at-risk individuals, to disseminate information and education, provide referrals for follow up, and to boost morale. In a meta-analysis of empirical studies evaluating the effectiveness of CISD's, Everly and Boyle (2001) note that CISD was never intended to be employed as a "one shot" intervention, however single session protocols were used out of necessity and time constraints. In the five studies evaluated by Everly & Boyle (2001), they conclude the following:

> The results of the aggregated participant studies assessing the CISD intervention are compelling, indeed. A large effect size was revealed attesting to the power of the CISD to mitigate symptoms of psychological distress. This beneficial effect was revealed despite the wide variety of subject groups, the wide range of traumatic events, and the diversity of outcome measures. (p.121)

Principles, Practices, and Protocols

This section is dedicated to helping employee assistance professionals understand and develop the skills necessary to provide prompt and effective intervention services for civilian and workplace survivors of critical incidents. The authors of this chapter are the co-directors of the International Traumatology Institute (ITI), a multination-

al program dedicated to training professionals and paraprofessionals to effectively serve survivors of trauma. The ITI began offering its training curriculum in 1997 and since that time the Institute has trained thousands of individuals to become effective responders and clinicians working with both critical incident and posttraumatic stress. The ITI's Field Traumatology curriculum integrates current research in the area of traumatic and critical incident stress, discussed previously in this chapter, as well as the practice experience and wisdom gained from work with survivors from natural disasters and human-induced catastrophes, including the bombing of the Murrah Building in 1995 and the terrorist attacks upon the United States on September 11, 2001. From our work with synthesizing current research, and through the process of sitting with survivors as they relate their horrifying narratives of loss, pain, and devastation, we offer the principles, practices and protocols detailed below to help employee assistance professionals to better serve the survivors of overwhelming experiences.

It is important that the reader not attempt to substitute the written material of this chapter for training and experience in the area of critical incident stress intervention. It is our experience that while this material may seem simple and commonsensical when read in the comfort of one's own home or office, when working with recently traumatized individuals, families, and communities in the context of the incident, with all the anxieties present, this work becomes increasingly complex and difficult. There is no substitute for thorough training and ongoing supervised experience towards building mastery with critical incident stress intervention.

Principles and Practices

NON-ANXIOUS PRESENCE. It is important for someone who has experienced a traumatic event to re-establish a sense of safety and stability as soon as possible following the event. The experience of trauma and the subsequent development of posttraumatic stress symptoms often involve the person's loss of a subjective sense of safety and control. We need to do whatever we can, in our initial interventions, to assist the survivor in re-establishing this safety and control. This goal of safety and stabilization may be said to underlie all critical incident stress interventions.

We have found that the most important and crucial ingredient to be effective in helping survivors of traumatic experiences regain this sense of safety and stability, and to minimize future symptoms, is the ability of the *helper* to develop and maintain a nonanxious presence through all phases of the work with survivors. This nonanxious presence is the cornerstone of all our training at the ITI and our work in supervising intervention teams. From a nonanxious presence the responder is able to continue to utilize all his/her training and cognitive faculties, offering the survivor a menu of services and interventions in a titrated manner that is responsive to the needs of the survivor. As a responder becomes increasingly anxious, we have witnessed good clinicians begin to offer services and interventions in a less coherent and sometimes more desperate, intense, and even coercive fashion. If the responder allows him/herself to become anxious beyond his/her ability to self-regulate (one's ability to maintain minimal anxiety levels), then the work may be perceived as threatening and the responder will then become increasingly compelled to *do something* to or for the survivor in order to manage his or her own anxiety. From this anxious stance, the responder is functioning with diminished cognitive and motor capacity (Sapolsky, 1998; van der Kolk, 1998; Scaer, 2001). It is from this anxious state of caregiving, in our opinion, that survivors can be either over or underserved by the caregiver with the potential for causing harm growing as anxiety increases. Bowen (Kerr & Bowen, 1998), in his seminal text on working with anxiety in families, identified the most important factor in helping families to reduce their anxiety and regain stable optimal functioning, was the ability of the clinician to retain a nonanxious presence in the context of the family's anxiety. We believe the same is true when working with trauma survivors–the better the responder is able to self-regulate and lessen his/her anxiety, the more effective will be the interventions. Additionally, and equally important, we are convinced that the responder who

maintains a nonanxious presence is much less susceptible to the deleterious effects (e.g., compassion fatigue, secondary traumatic stress, burnout) of helping trauma survivors (Gentry, 2002).

A true nonanxious presence is much different than the ability to affect an outward sense of calm, something that many of us have been taught to do effectively through our training. A true nonanxious presence involves the ability to elicit the dominance of the parasympathetic nervous system over the sympathic nervous system (Sapolsky, 1998) or, said more simply, the ability to engage the relaxation response and keep muscles loose even when perceiving threat and danger. If the caregiver is able to maintain relaxed abdominal and pelvic floor muscles (soft pelvic floor) while working with the trauma survivor, a nonanxious presence, and full utilization of one's cognitive and motor capacities, is maintained. We believe this capacity to be the hallmark of mature caregiving and, through our trauma intervention training at ITI, has become the requisite and foundational skill upon which all other intervention principles and skills are built with our students.

PEOPLE SKILLS. With a nonanxious presence developed and maintained, we have found that another important skill for the trauma responder to develop is the ability to be warm, open, and engaging with survivors of recent traumatic events. This is an area in which critical incident skills differ greatly from clinical skills. Often in clinical contexts we await the client to take initiatives in soliciting and continuing treatment–the client is seeking our professional help to address and resolve some discomfort and/or acquire desired states. In this context the clinician and her/his services are desired and usually purchased by the client with the clinician in a position of dominance in the power hierarchy between the two. In critical incident response, the responsibility for contacting, engaging, and intervening with the survivor rests solely with the responder, which is now a reverse of this power relationship. Often survivors are understandably less than enthusiastic about meeting and talking with a stranger during or immediately following a critical incident. These initial contacts, which require a warm and engaging presence, are areas in which we have seen many seasoned clinicians struggle as they work to develop these different sets of skills. It is not uncommon to initiate contact with survivors who have difficulty or resist communicating their thoughts and feelings about the incident, or who may even be openly antagonistic or hostile toward the responder. It is important that the responder be prepared for a myriad of response possibilities from the survivor and able to maintain a warm, inviting, and engaging, not solicitous, presence throughout the trajectory of contact with the survivor.

THE SCHWOOP: COGNITIVE-AFFECTIVE-COGNITIVE. Jeffrey Mitchell (1983), in his hallmark and seminal article on critical incident stress, mapped the critical incident intervention process and to which all subsequent critical incident work with survivors has, seemingly, adhered. This process has been identified as the "Mitchell Model," the "Mitchell Dip," and the "CISD Model" (Mitchell, 1983, Everly & Mitchell, 1995, Rank, 1997) and is used to describe the process through which the survivor is facilitated in debriefing a critical incident. This process seems to be a natural one that survivors undergo as their narratives of the traumatic event(s) unfold(s) and this natural process should be supported by the responder. This process of beginning and ending with cognitive and objective information, with the survivor enjoying a sense of distance and safety from the event, added to the middle phases of the intervention providing an opportunity for the survivor to explore and express more subjective thoughts and feelings associated with the trauma has become the blueprint for all critical incident intervention strategies. All critical incident interventions should begin with assessment of safety that is kept in the "thinking" and "present" realm. As the intervention progresses and as the survivor develops rapport with the responder, there will be a movement into remembering and feeling the traumatic event–the "affective" and "past" realms. As these interventions reach closure, the survivor should be answering questions about the future and feeling in control of the present.

These interventions may occur individually, one-on-one, in a clinician's office or on-site immediately following the critical incident (once the sur-

vivor has achieved safety and stabilization). They may occur in a group immediately following the critical incident or several days, weeks, months, even years following the event at the site of the incident, in a clinician's office, or at some neutral location.

One of our faculty at the International Traumatology Institute, who has worked extensively with thousands of survivors through scores of critical incidents including the Murrah Building bombing and several months of effective service delivery in New York City following the events of September 11, 2001 (Figley, Figley, & Norman, 2002), has named this cognitive-affective-cognitive process "The Schwoop" (personal communication with J. Norman, 1/19/99; Gentry, 2002). We have found that the ability of a critical incident responder to "make sense" of the symptoms and processes that a survivor experiences in language that is easily accessible and understood, to be very helpful in mitigating the negative effects of the traumatic event for the survivor. Explaining the natural process that the survivor often experiences following a trauma of moving from the cognitive here-and-now perspective to the affective there-and-then as simply, *"you're just in the schwoop,"* and helping them navigate successfully through this "schwoop" back to a cognitive and objective control has been invaluable with the numbers of survivors with whom we have worked. Using the language of the "schwoop" to help normalize the experiences of the survivor, as well as helping them to map and navigate their way through the jungle of images, sensations, and feelings associated with the trauma is just one of the valuable uses of employing this concept. Additionally, if the responder works enough critical incident situations, she/he will find some pattern responses among the survivors. One interesting behavior in which survivors engage is the unconscious and involuntary fixation of their eyes while they are reviewing visual material often associated with the recent event. We have called this "schwooping." While the survivor is accessing the visual material they most often are also experiencing uncomfortable feelings associated with the event(s). Cataloging the frequency, duration, and intensity of these "schwoops" exhibited by a survivor can assist the interventionist with the triage assessment. A survivor who is experiencing intense affect and visual intrusions ("schwoops") will likely need acute mental health assistance in the form of individual and/or group debriefing toward preventing future PTSD symptoms.

Another useful adaptation of the "schwoop" is when an individual is fixated in the affective and visual intrusions of a recent trauma an intervention specialist may use the construct of the "schwoop" to (a) point this out to the survivor (e.g., "what are you looking at right now?") and (b) to assist the survivor in moving out of the overwhelming affect and back into cognitive control. By explaining the "head-gut-head" processing of the "schwoop," the interventionist helps the survivor to both normalize and predict his or her experiences after a critical event. With this understanding the survivor is empowered to begin developing effective strategies for self-rescue and self-regulation that rapidly moves him/her out of the "schwoop" and into the effective functioning of recovery.

EXPRESSION OF AFFECT. Another important principle in working with survivors of recent traumatic events is the ability of the responder to tolerate many levels of expression, or lack of expression, of affect. Research has failed to conclusively demonstrate whether or not catharsis and emotional ventilation is useful and necessary toward mitigation of and recovery from posttraumatic symptoms results (Bisson, Jenkins, Alexander, & Bannister, 1997; Deahl, Gillham, Thomas, Searle, & Srinivason, 1994; Dyregrov, 1989 & 1998; Rapheal, 1986; Rapheal & Wilson, 2000; Shalev, 1994). In our work with survivors, we have employed the maxim "work with what presents." We have witnessed harm caused by interventionists who have failed on both ends of the continuum around this issue. We have seen responders, uncomfortable with the expression of high levels of intense affect, attempt to cull and silence the expression of these feelings when a nonanxious "bearing witness" of these feelings was prescribed. Other times we have witnessed well-meaning responders, with the belief that affect must be expressed before resolution can occur, attempt to trigger and coerce the expression of pain, anger,

terror, or grief to the point that the survivor is retraumatized by the intervention itself. This is not good critical incident stress intervention. With participants in our trainings, we suggest that they relinquish their beliefs, theories, and biases about what "should" happen and work with what "is" happening during the contact with the survivor. We suggest to the responder that she/he is unable to control the outcomes of the intervention and, most times, does not know what, exactly, is needed for particular individuals to resolve and recover from traumatic events. In the matter of the survivor expressing or not expressing affect during interactions and interventions, we urge the responder to develop tolerance and mastery with the many variable presentations with which the survivor may present. With this in mind, it is important that the responder remain flexible and able to respond to the needs of the individual survivor in the specific context. In this chapter we offer some generic components that are common to most critical incident intervention protocols and contexts. The specific needs of the unique, individual survivor are met consistently only by well-trained and experienced critical incident responders—there is no substitute for either of these important ingredients.

NORMALIZE RESPONSES/SYMPTOMS. A mantra heard often by anyone who has received training in critical incident stress management from the International Critical Incident Stress Foundation (ICISF) or who has worked on critical incident stress management teams is: *"You are a normal person having a normal response to an abnormal event."* This phrase captures the essence of critical incident stress intervention in that it helps the survivor begin to understand that the symptoms they are experiencing are resulting from the traumatic event and are not indications of any weakness or pathology on their part. We have seen many a frightened and overwrought survivor brighten measurably when informed that most people who experience a traumatic event recover fully with minimal intervention or treatment. A brief explanation of how brain mechanics and memory systems function relative to posttraumatic stress symptoms can be helpful (Sapolsky, 1998). An additional explanation that posttraumatic symptoms are attempts by our body's natural healing mechanisms to make sense of, resolve, and recover from the event are also helpful. If the responder is able to indicate that the procedures being used in the intervention are not "therapy," or "treatment," but instead designed to facilitate and accelerate these natural healing and resolution processes, the survivors' resistance to participation in critical incident intervention activities may be relaxed.

SOCIALIZE FOR POSSIBLE SYMPTOMS. A handout of possible symptoms (i.e., nightmares, increased or diminished appetite, difficulty sleeping, irritability, difficulty concentrating, etc.) that the survivor may begin to experience over time can be helpful in preparing them for a possible protracted recovery from the traumatic event. This handout and any explanation of these symptoms should be accompanied by contact and referral information for mental health professionals who specialize in treating traumatic stress. These handouts and discussions during critical incident interventions with survivors should also include an inventory of good self-care skills that can minimize symptoms' intensity, frequency and duration (i.e., physical exercise, good eating habits, enjoyable recreation activities, time spent with loved ones, spiritual/religious practices, etc).

CONNECT WITH SUPPORT. The final area of important principles and practice with survivors of recent traumatic events is connecting them with indigenous and ongoing support systems. Support during and after critical incidents has been identified as a critical component of rapid and thorough recovery from the effects of the traumatic event (Mitchell & Everly, 2001). Helping the survivor to identify and contact family members, friends, clergy, co-workers or other individuals and groups that can provide this necessary support should not be overlooked or minimized by the critical incident responder.

TEAM WORK. It has become a well-established modus operandi that critical intervention work is done in teams, or at least pairs. We strongly caution the reader to never attempt critical intervention work alone. There are several reasons in utilizing a team approach. First, the work is difficult and complex and quite often even the most seasoned veteran will need assistance with some phase of the work. Second, the workload and bearing of the traumatic material should be distributed between team members so that no one responder is becoming overwhelmed. Related to that function, having team members to "watch our backs" in terms of ongoing objective assessment of the beginning to experience possible compassion fatigue symptoms and can serve as an early warning and/or debriefing source for the responder. Third, utilizing a team means that there are a much more of an ability to be varied and creative in service delivery. Finally, post-incident debriefing assists with minimizing risk for compassion fatigue as well as an opportunity for updating and evolving serve plans and protocols.

Protocols

In this section, we will provide a brief introduction to the most common critical incident protocols utilized by critical incident stress management teams and individual responders to mitigate the effects of traumatic events upon the survivors of these events. While these protocols and interventions can have a powerfully therapeutic effect for the survivors who participate in them, they are not therapy or treatment. They are simply interventions designed to lessen the impact of the event and facilitate rapid recovery. None of these interventions, with the possible exception of the Individual Defusing Protocol, should be attempted without in-depth training and supervised experience. A list of resources for training in critical incident intervention is provided at the end of this chapter.

INDIVIDUAL DEFUSING. This highly skilled intervention is probably the most important activity when working with civilian survivors of a critical incident. The Individual Defusing Protocol is the process of helping these survivors through the employment of a brief conversation. The most important factor of this important brief intervention is making contact with the survivor and establishing a warm relationship. From this connection with the survivor, the interventionist can begin a process of assessment, triage, service planning, and assistance. Much of the effectiveness of future interventions with the survivor and mitigation of posttraumatic symptoms can be said to be contingent upon the quality and thoroughness of this primary activity. This defusing process has been euphemistically described as "sly-chology" by veteran field traumatologists to denote the series of interventions and assessments that are employed by the responder in a manner that is unobtrusive and conversational with the survivor.

The Six Step Guide for Defusing (Young et al., 1998) has been developed by the National Center for Posttraumatic Stress Disorder Education and Clinical Laboratory, building upon previous work by longtime disaster expert Dianne Meyers (1987). This defusing protocol has been adopted for fieldwork and has become an integral part of the International Traumatology Institute's Field Traumatology training. The Six Step Guide for Defusing is described below:

1. **Make Contact.** The defusing begins with a warm, inviting introduction and informal socializing. The defuser should be careful to introduce her/himself by first name, with a handshake, and without making reference to professional status or credentials unless asked (i.e., *Hi, my name is _____ and I'm helping out here today. What's your name?*). This contact may involve offering the survivor some thing to drink or eat and should focus upon nonthreatening, unobtrusive material until the beginnings of rapport have been developed. A detailed account of the recent events should not be solicited from the survivor.

2. **Make Assessment.** Any medical emergencies, physical pain, or somatic discomfort reported by the survivor should be reported immediately to an emergency medical professional (EMS). Ideally, EMS will have already provided triage and services to those survivors in need so that the critical incident stress responder. There are times, however, when a survivor's medical condition has been missed and it is important that the responder remain vigilant in assessing any physical difficulties (e.g., shortness of breath, dizziness, chest pain, irregular heart beat, profuse sweating) that may appear to be the normal sequelae following a traumatic experience but still need EMS attention and

clearance. When the responder is certain that the survivor is medically stable, an assessment of the survivor's level of functioning should follow. Is the survivor able to attend to the responder? Is she/he able to manage and contain intense affect associated with the event? Is she/he oriented to time, place, person or unable to focus on anything but the recent event? Open-ended questions such as, *"How can we help you while you are waiting?"* is an excellent tool for both gathering information about how the responder can be helpful as well as assessing the survivor's ability to organize thoughts and speech. If the survivor is unable to attend to the responder's questions and/or has difficulty managing him/herself, then a referral to acute mental health services may be the likely and appropriate next step for this survivor. During the course of this conversation the responder should notice any abnormalities in the survivor's speech, affect, movements or behaviors in order to connect this survivor with appropriate services following the defusing.

3. **Gather Facts.** By asking the survivor questions about the facts associated with the recent trauma, the responder provides a gradated and objectified approach to discussing the traumatic event. This will allow the responder to continue with the assessment while also gaining important risk information from the survivor, such as exposure to life-threatening situations, death, loss, or other traumatic stimuli that may be associated with possible future posttraumatic stress symptoms. Discussing the facts of the experience seems to be easier for survivors than the more threatening and personal areas of thoughts and feeling associated with the event.

Helpful Questions

- "Where were you when it first happened?"
- "What did you do first . . . what did you do next . . . ?
- "Where is your family?" (Young et al., 1998, p. 41)

4. **Inquire About Thoughts.** The responder can use the answers culled during the above phase to develop questions about the survivors'

thoughts during the experience. By moving from the facts of to thoughts during and about the event, the responder is helping the survivor to gently move from discussing the objective to narrating and integrating the personal aspects of the traumatic event.

Helpful Questions

* "What were your first thoughts when this event began?"
* "What thoughts ran through your mind during the event?"
* "What thoughts do you think will stay with you after this event?"
5. **Inquire About Feelings.** If the survivor has been able to navigate successfully through the "Thought Phase" above, then the responder may want to elicit some of the affective reactions the survivor had during and since the event. Young et al. (1998) offer the following warning regarding this step of the defusing:

Remember, defusing is a brief intervention and it precludes in depth exploration and ongoing support. Consequently you must use care in regard to any questions about feelings. It is important to avoid heightening a survivor's sense of vulnerability to the degree that it causes overwhelming anxiety. Obviously, under such time constraints, assessing capacity to manage anxiety is difficult, so it is best to proceed conservatively, i.e., continually monitor the survivor's reactions during the course of talking about their feelings and reassess the need to refocus the survivor's attention on the present and action-oriented steps to solve problems. If the survivor is able to tolerate talking about feelings, look for opportunities to validate common emotional reactions and concerns. "De-pathologize" survivor's reactions, that is, inform them about the normal reactions to an "abnormal" event to provide reassurance. (pp. 41–42)

6. **Support, Reassure, Provide Information.** While this is identified as the final step, these activities should permeate all phases of all critical incident interventions. The responder provides support to the survivor by maintaining a warm and nonanxious presence that serves as a bridge for the survivor to reconnect with other people and services that will be helpful in mitigating and resolving the effects of the traumatic event. The responder should take great care to be certain that the survivor is reconnected with a support system as soon after the event as possible. The survivor should be provided with important information about food, shelter, transportation, and other details necessary to begin re-stabilization. In the cases where a survivor needs specific information about the event (i.e., a missing loved one, extent of damage, etc.), the responder will want to assist or accompany the survivor acquiring this information through appropriate public information officers. At the conclusion of the defusing, the responder, at a minimum, should provide the survivor with a one-page informational handout that provides information about common stress reactions and symptoms, what to do to minimize the effects of traumatic stress, contact numbers for indigenous health and mental health practitioners, and, if possible, the schedule and availability of additional services (e.g., debriefings, family groups, massage, etc.) associated with the event.

DEMOBILIZATION (Mitchell & Everly, 2001). The Demobilization was designed as a quick informational and rest session for emergency service personnel (police, fire, EMS) after they have been released from service after a major critical incident that has affected over 100 personnel. This procedure is easily adapted to a workplace environment when there has been an incident that has affected the staff members. This is a short intervention lasting only 30 minutes during which the employee assistance professional provides a brief (10–15 minute) informational presentation followed by a rest period of 20–60 minutes during which food is provided. This rest period provides an opportunity for co-workers to socialize with each other, gain support, and for the employee assistance professionals to begin the Individual Defusing Protocol (see above) with staff who appear distraught. The goals of the Demobilization include: (1) assess the well-being of staff following an incident; (2) mitigate the impact of the event; (3) provide stress management information to personnel; (4) provide an opportunity for rest and food before returning to routine duties; (5) assess need for debriefing and other services. Handouts and other information on critical incident stress, such as referral information to employee assistance, should be made available to participants.

CRISIS MANAGEMENT BRIEFING (Mitchell & Everly, 2001). This is an intervention technique for a very large group, agency, company, or corporation. It is designed for use with groups of 300 or more and may be utilized with civilians immediately following a traumatic event, employees after a work-related crisis, and other critical incidents involving large numbers of people. It can be applied to critical incidents that involve terrorism, mass disasters, community violence, school crises, workplace crises, and military incidents. A Crisis Management Briefing typically lasts from 45–75 minutes. The goals of a Crisis Management Briefing are: (1) to provide information; (2) to control rumors and speculation; (3) stabilize chaos; (4) provide coping resources; (5) identify and facilitate follow-up care; (6) increase group cohesion and morale; (7) assess further needs of the group; and (8) restore adaptive functions of personnel. It is a four-step process that involves assembling the participants, providing facts regarding the crisis, discussing and normalizing common behavioral/psychological reactions to similar crises, and discussing personal and organizational stress management as well as directing the attendees toward further resources. The Crisis Management Briefing often falls within the job description of the employee assistance professional within a company or corporation.

GROUP DEFUSING (Mitchell & Everly, 2001). The Group Defusing is a shortened version of the Critical Incident Stress Debriefing (CISD–discussed below) and is utilized as a stop-gap measure to provide immediate assistance (0–8 hours) to groups following a critical incident and in lieu of a CISD. While this intervention has been previously targeted towards small groups of emergency service professionals, it is easily adapted to the workplace environment by employee assistance professionals. Group Defusings should be offered to small homogenous groups within the organiza-

tion (i.e., marketing departments, management, etc.) with the possibility of doing several Group Debriefings for the same incident. The goals of the Group Defusing are: (1) to mitigate the impact of the event; (2) accelerate the recovery process; (3) assess the need for additional services; and (4) reduction of posttraumatic stress symptoms. To conduct a Groups Defusing the employee assistance professional should: (1) establish a non-threatening neutral environment; (2) allow rapid ventilation of the stressful experience; (3) equalize the information across hierarchical lines; (4) restore cognitive processing of the event; (5) provide information on effective coping with stressful experiences; (6) affirm personnel and their resiliency capacity; (7) establish support and service linkages; and (8) develop future expectancies.

CRITICAL INCIDENT STRESS DEBRIEFING– CISD (Mitchell, 1983; Mitchell & Everly, 2001). The Critical Incident Stress Debriefing is the centerpiece and mainstay of all critical incident interventions. The CISD was originally developed by the United States Armed Forces to mitigate the effects of military accidents and maneuvers, as well as combat experiences (Mitchell & Everly, 2001). In 1983, Jeffrey Mitchell, founder and President of the International Critical Incident Stress Foundation, augmented this model to utilize with emergency service personnel. Since that time, the CISD has been utilized by a wide variety of groups in a vast array of contexts all over the world. The research, as reviewed previously in this chapter, generally lauds CISD as an effective intervention in mitigating the stress effects of traumatic events upon survivors. CISD, however, continues to remain embroiled in a bitter controversy regarding the empirical validation of its effectiveness. We can point to hundreds, if not thousands, of emergency service personnel and civilians who have participated in CISD's that could offer testimony as to the procedure's effectiveness; but conclusive empirical evidence to its efficacy and effectiveness is still forthcoming. As previously discussed, the CISD should not be utilized as a stand-alone procedure for critical incident intervention, but only as part of a comprehensive critical incident stress management program that includes all the principles, practices, and protocols discussed in this chapter. Mitchell & Everly (2001) define CISD as:

> The CISD and defusing process may be defined as group meetings or discussions about a traumatic event or series of traumatic events. The CISD and defusing processes are solidly based in crisis intervention theory. The CISD and defusing processes are designed to mitigate the psychological impact of a traumatic event, prevent the subsequent development of posttraumatic syndrome, and serve as an early identification mechanism for individuals who will require mental health follow-up subsequent to a traumatic event. (p. 89)

A CISD generally occurs 12 to 72 hours following a critical incident and is usually 90 minutes to three hours in duration. It utilizes the following mechanisms of actions to achieve these goals: (1) provides an opportunity for early intervention; (2) opportunity for catharsis; (3) opportunity to verbalize traumatic experiences; (4) provides structure to chaos of trauma; (5) provides group support; (6) provides peer support; (7) provides information for coping with stressful experiences; and (8) provides opportunity and vehicle for follow-up services (Mitchell & Everly, 2001).

The CISD occurs in the following stages:

Stage 1. Introduction Phase. In this stage the critical incident team members are introduced, the CISD process is explained, expectations are set, and the important ground rules are established.

Stage 2. Fact Phase. In this phase, the participants introduce themselves, describe their role during the incident, and identify the facts surrounding their first experiences with the incident.

Stage 3. Thought Phase. In the Thought Phase participants are asked to identify the cognitive experiences associated with the traumatic event. A question often utilized to elicit responses during this phase is "What thoughts did you have during and after this event that continue to stay with you?" The end of the thought phase heralds the transition from cognitive to affective processing of the event.

Stage 4. Reaction Phase. The Reaction Phase is where the participants are invited to share their emotional reactions during and since the event. It

is during this phase that most of the affective processing occurs. Very little, if any, interaction and intervention is required from the team during this phase. The team and participants should honor the sharing with eye contact and silent "bearing witness." A helpful question to elicit reactions in this phase is: "What was the worst part of the event for you?" or "What image from this event stays with you even now? This may be followed with "And how does remembering that experience affect you now?"

Stage 5. Symptom Phase. In this phase the team leader elicits from the participants the ways in which the critical incident has negatively affected them. A brief synopsis of potential stress symptoms may be helpful if participants are having difficulty identifying any changes in their functioning resulting from the event. The Symptom Phase marks the transition from affective back towards cognitive processing of the event.

Stage 6. Teaching Phase. In this phase the team leader often provides informational handouts on possible stress symptoms and coping techniques as well as helping participants "make sense" of and normalize the symptoms identified in the previous phase.

Stage 7. Re-Entry Phase. This phase is used to clarify any ambiguities, prepare for termination, facilitate closure, and prepare the participant for re-entry into normal daily functioning. It also provides an opportunity to arrange for follow-up and/or additional services, if necessary.

It is recommended at the conclusion of a CISD to provide an opportunity for food, refreshment, and socialization among the team and participants. This socialization period is an excellent opportunity for employee assistance professionals to provide referral information and ongoing support, if requested.

INDIVIDUAL DEBRIEFING. There will be many contexts where the CISD is either insufficient or inappropriate for an individual. In these circumstances, the employee assistance professional will need to employ the use of an Individual Debriefing Protocol. The most commonly utilized individual debriefing protocol is the adaptation of the CISD to the individual. This is done simply by following all the steps and phases of the CISD with a single survivor. Additionally, there are also many reports of CISD's adaptation to use with traumatized families.

An individual debriefing may occur on-site, in the employee assistance professional's office, or another neutral location. Individual debriefings should only occur after a thorough Individual Defusing, with all the requisite assessment, triage, and stabilization completed.

Eye Movement Desensitization and Reprocessing, or EMDR, (Shapiro, 1995) offers a protocol for resolving traumatic stress symptoms associated with recent events as does Traumatic Incident Reduction, or TIR (French & Harris, 1999). In the case of the above two protocols, it should be mentioned that these require specialized training, certification, and licensure prior to their utilization. With the recent escalation of frequency and magnitude of critical incidents around the world coupled with a growing interest in this area for professional training and academic study, we believe that many other protocols for individual and group debriefing and defusing will emerge in the near future.

COMPASSION FATIGUE. No text on critical incident intervention would be complete without discussing the potential dangers of this work. It has been conclusively demonstrated that working with survivors of traumatic experiences can produce deleterious effects for the caregivers (Deutch, 1984; Figley, 1995; McCann & Pearlman, 1990; Follette et al 1994; Schauben & Frazier, 1995; Cerney, 1995; Salston, 2000; Gentry, 2002). Secondary traumatic stress, vicarious traumatization, burnout, and compassion fatigue are all labels utilized to describe these effects that seem to mirror in the responder or clinician the symptoms of the survivor. No responder should ever work with survivors of traumatic experiences without a comprehensive self-care plan that is designed to minimize the deleterious effects of helping while maximizing resiliency. Some of the ingredients of this plan should include:

• Regular exercise;
• Good nutrition;
• Anxiety management strategies;
• Support persons and groups;
• Debrief-the-debriefer groups and individuals to dilute secondary traumatic stress;
• Recreational activities that provide the helping professional with recreation, joy, and a sense of aliveness;
• Ongoing professional supervision;
• Identification of and relationship with a mental health professional who specializes in traumatic stress for use if symptoms should develop;
• Ongoing professional development training, especially in the area of critical incident intervention and treatment of traumatic stress.

Critical Incident Training Resources

International Critical Incident Stress Foundation
10176 Baltimore National Pike, Unit 201
Ellicott City, MD 21042
(410) 750-9600
www.icisf.org

International Traumatology Institute
University of South Florida
4202 E. Fowler Ave. MHH116
Tampa, FL 33620
(813) 974-1191
www.outreach.usf.edu/trauma

The National Center for Posttraumatic Stress Disorder
VA Palo Alto Health Care System
Menlo Park, CA 94025
Executive Division
VA Medical & Regional Office Center
White River Junction, VT 05009
www.ncptsd.org

REFERENCES

American Red Cross (1991). Disaster Services Regulations and Procedures. *Disaster Mental Health Services.* (ARC 3050M) American National Red Cross.

American Red Cross (2002).
   http://www.redcross.org/sys/search/advsearch.asp

American Psychiatric Association (2000). *Diagnostic and statistic manual of mental disorders.* Fourth edition. Text revision. Washington, DC: APA.

Bisson, J., Jenkins, P., Alexander, J., & Bannister, C. (1997). A randomized controlled trail of psychological debriefing for victims of acute burn trauma. *British Journal of Psychiatry, 171,* 78–81.

Bisson, J. I., McFarlane, A. C., & Rose, S. (2000). Psychological Debriefing. In E. B. Foa, T. M. Keane, & Friedman, M. J. (Eds.). *Effective Treatments for PTSD.* New York: The Guilford Press. pp. 39–59.

Cerney, M. S. (1995). Treating the "heroic treaters." In C. R. Figley (Ed.). *Compassion fatigue: Coping with secondary traumatic stress disorder in those who treat the traumatized* (pp. 131–148). New York: Brunner/ Mazel.

Deahl, M., Gilliam, A., Thomas, J., Searle, M., & Srinivisan, M. (1994). Psychological sequelae following the Gulf War: Factors associated with subsequent morbidity and the effectiveness of psychological debriefing. *British Journal of Psychiatry, 165,* 60–65.

Deutsch, C. J. (1984). Self-reported sources of stress among psychotherapists. *Professional Psychology: Research & Practice, 15,* 833–845.

Dyregrov, A. (1989). Caring for helpers in disaster situations. Psychological debriefing. *Disaster Management, 2,* 25–30.

Dyregrov, A. (1998). Psychological debriefing–an effective method? *Traumatology, 4* (2).

Everly, G. S., & Boyle, S. H. (2001). Critical Incident Stress Debriefing (CISD): A Meta Analysis. In J. T. Mitchell & G. S. Everly, *The basic critical incident stress management course: Basic group crisis intervention* (3rd Edition). Ellicott City, MD: International Critical Incident Stress Foundation, Inc. pp. 119–123.

Everly, G. S., & Mitchell, J. T. (1995). *Critical incident stress debriefing (CISD): An operations manual for the prevention of traumatic stress among emergency services workers and disaster personnel.* 2nd Edition, Revised. Ellicott City, MD: Chevron Publishing Company.

Everly, G. S., & Mitchell, J. T. (1997). *Critical incident stress management (CISM): A new era and standard of care in crisis intervention.* Ellicott City, MD: Chevron Publishing Corporation.

Everly, G. S., & Mitchell, J. T. (1999). *Critical incident stress management (CISM): A new era and standard of care in crisis intervention* (2nd edition). Ellicott City, MD: Chevron Publishing Corporation.

Family Enterprises Incorporated (1993). Posttraumatic intervention institute. *Training manual.* Milwaukee, Wisconsin: Author.

Federal Emergency Management Association (FEMA) (2002). http://femaweb4.fema.gov/cgi-shl/web_eval uate.exe

Figley, C. R. (1995). *Compassion fatigue: Coping with secondary traumatic stress disorder in those who treat the traumatized.* New York: Bruner/Mazel.

Figley, C. R., Figley, K. R., & Norman, J. (2002) Tuesday morning September 11, 2001: The Green Cross Projects' role as a case study in community-based traumatology services. *Journal of Trauma Practice, 1,* 3 (4).

French, G., & Harris, C. (1999). *Traumatic incident reduction (TIR).* Boca Raton, Florida: CRC Press.

Folette, V. M., Polusny, M. M., & Milbeck, K. (1994). Mental health and law enforcement professionals: Trauma history, psychological symptoms, and impact of providing services to sexual abuse survivors. *Professional Psychology: Research and Practice, 25* (3), 275–282.

Gentry, J. E. (2002) Compassion fatigue: A crucible of transformation. *Journal of Trauma Practice, 1,* 3 (4).

International Critical Incident Stress Foundation (ICISF) (2002). http://www.redcross.org/sys/search/ advsearch.asp

Kerr, M. E., & Bowen, M. (1988). *Family evaluation.* New York: W.W. Norton & Company.

McCann, I. L., & Pearlman, L. A. (1990). Vicarious traumatization: A framework for understanding the psychological effects of working with victims. *Journal of Traumatic Stress, 3,* (1), 131–149.

Meyers, D. (1987). *Prevention and control of stress among emergency workers: A pamphlet for team managers.* DHHS Publication No. (ADM) 90–1496.

Mitchell, J. (1983, January). When disaster strikes: The critical incident stress debriefing process. *Journal of Emergency Medical Services,* pp. 36–39.

Mitchell, J. T., & Everly, G. S. (1996). *Critical incident stress debriefing: An operations manual.* Ellicott City, MD: Chevron Publishing Corporation.

Mitchell, J. T., & Everly, G. S. (2001). *The basic critical incident stress Management course: Basic group crisis intervention* (3rd Edition). Ellicott City, MD: International Critical Incident Stress Foundation, Inc.

Rank, M. (1997). Critical incident stress debriefing. In W. Hutchinson & W. Emener (Eds). *Employee assistance programs: A basic text.* Second Edition. Springfield, IL: Charles C. Thomas, Publisher, Ltd. p. 315–329.

Raphael, B. (1986). *When disaster strikes: A handbook for caring professions.* London: Hutchinson.

Raphael, B., & Wilson, J. (Eds.). (2000). Psychological debriefing: Theory, practice, and evidence. Cambridge: Cambridge University Press.

Rose S., Bisson J., & Wessely S. (2002). Psychological debriefing for preventing posttraumatic stress disorder (PTSD) (Cochrane Review). In: The Cochrane Library, Issue 3 2002. (http://www.update-software.com/abstracts/ab000560.htm)

Salston, M. D. (2000). *Compassion fatigue: Implications for mental health professionals and trainees.* A defended dissertation at Florida State University.

Sapolsky, R. M. (1998). *Why zebras don't get ulcers: An updated guide to stress, stress-related diseases, and coping.* New York: W.H. Freeman and Company.

Scaer, R. C. (2001). *The body bears the burden: Trauma, dissociation, and disease.* New York: The Haworth Medical Press.

Schauben, L. J., & Frazier, P. A., (1995). Vicarious trauma: the effects on female counselors of working with sexual violence survivors. *Psychology of Women Quarterly, 19,* 49–64.

Shalev, A. Y. (1994). Debriefing following traumatic exposure. In R. Ursano, B. McCaughey, & C. Fullerston (Eds.) *Individual and community responses to trauma and disaster: The structure of human chaos.* Chap. 9, pp. 201–219. Cambridge University Press.

Shapiro, F. (1995). *Eye movement desensitization and reprocessing: Basic principles, protocols, and procedures.* New York: Guilford Press.

Smith, D., Christiansen, E., Vincent, R., & Hann, N. (1998). Post event health and the effectiveness of critical incident stress debriefing. *Biostatistics and Epidemiology,* University of Oklahoma College of Public Health, University of Oklahoma Press.

Spitzer, W. J. (2002). Critical incident stress management. In R. R. Roberts & G. J. Greene, (Eds.) (2002). *Social workers' desk reference.* Oxford: Oxford University Press, pp. 447–451.

van der Kolk, B. (1996). The black hole of trauma. In B.A. van der Kolk, & A. C. McFarlane, (Eds) *Traumatic stress: The effects of overwhelming experience on mind, body, and society.* New York: The Guilford Press. 3–23.

Young, B. H., Ford, J. D., Ruzek, J. I., Friedman, M. J., Gusman, T. D. (1998). *Disaster mental health services: A guidebook for clinicians and administrators.* National Center for Posttraumatic Stress Disorder. (www.ncptsd.org)

Chapter 24

CYBERSPACE: THE NEW FRONTIER FOR EMPLOYEE ASSISTANCE PROGRAMS

MICHAEL A. RICHARD

Management in most organizations has embraced computer technology as a means of improving worker productivity and efficiency. It is seen as a way for employees to accomplish more in less time and with less effort. The computer and related information technologies (IT) such as the Internet, have provided employees and employers tools to organize and decimate information in ways never before possible. Furthermore, business sees many of their fiscal and competitive gains as being directly related to giving employees Internet capability. This technology has for many, if not most, successful companies become as essential as the telephone and the copy machine.

The gains for business, however, have had a down side. Cyberspace has quietly surfaced as a playground for many workers, who quietly send personal e-mail, buy CDs, download music, read sport news, etc, all while "on the clock." In addition to these seemingly "innocent" diversions, employees also send hate mail, harass co-workers, and frequent porn sites while at work. Employee Assistance Program (EAP) professionals are being asked to "help" those employees who have been identified as abusing or misusing the technology as it interferes with their ability to do their job, creates potential legal problems and in its most innocuous form, devours employee's time and capabilities to be productive. Before a discussion of the particular problems encountered with Internet use can be addressed, cyberspace as it relates to IT must be understood (Hines, 1994).

Information technology (IT) consists predominantly of computing, telecommunications and networking. IT also encompasses expert systems, imaging, automation, robotics, sensing technologies, and mechatronics (microprocessors embedded in products, systems, and devices). These interrelated expertise are increasingly allowing employees to be located out of the "office," in the home, on the road, etc. Work is no longer confined to the eight-to-five day and in fact IT now requires more flexible work schedules and environments. Information technology is still evolving and continues to reshape how work is done, be it on farms, factories, and hospitals, counseling offices or classrooms. It has been predicted that by 2010, IT will produce numerous changes, such as creating a more challenging and autonomous work environment, but it has and will continue to lead to increased depersonalization and boredom at work (Hines, 1994). Cyberspace offers disenfranchised or bored employees many nonwork-related options to occupy their time and avenues to vent their hostility. In addition, many of these options are inappropriate, crossing over the lines of acceptable behavior and into the realm of social deviance (Bellm, 1998; Greenfield & Davis, 2002).

On the positive side, the Internet offers employees a unique opportunity to affiliate socially and exchange information with professional peers whom they may never have met and who are half the globe away. These online contacts can enhance an employee's ability to do their job as new and prudent information can be accessed. However, the Internet can also provide employees near instantaneous access to inappropriate work-related diversions, such as pornography and gambling (Greengard, 2000). Furthermore, the seemingly harmless behavior of information seeking or "surfing" is a growing concern. "Surfing" the net may appear harmless, but employers are discovering that workers are often "online" gathering information when they should be doing something else, they are concerned that this has become a form of loafing, such as reading the newspaper while at work (Sunoo, 1996).

Gackenbach (1998) indicated that Internet users can be categorized as two types of people: those seeking information, and those providing information. To comprehend and intervene with any particular problem, it is important one have an appreciation of the basic reason the person is online (i.e., primarily to give or receive information). Within the context of these two core categories of Internet use, any number of work-related activities could take place, these include:

- Using private chat rooms available between two people with similar interests to explore solutions to a work-related issue.
- Private e-mail exchanges between two individuals to solicit information, public relations, etc.
- The ability of "user" groups to ask an "expert" a question by accessing her/his e-mail address.
- The ability to make announcements, post marketing information, etc.
- The ability of news networks to informally "poll" a captive audience and post results in a near immediate manner.
- The posting by corporations, business, nonprofit organizations, etc. mission, procedural, etc. statements.
- The ability to provide links to specific areas in the corporation.
- The ability to contact numerous and dispersed employees at once who are working on a project.
- Creation of discussion groups to facilitate problem solving.

All these functions are aspects of Internet use that enhance and improve a workers ability to do their jobs. Nonetheless, extreme misuse beyond the above has been the reason for EAP referrals. These instances of extreme "problems" with cyberspace use, is the primary concern of this chapter.

To begin it should be noted that problems associated with Internet use are not always extreme. Generally speaking the use of the Internet has contributed in minimally harmful ways to any number of employees. Innocuous ways in which most persons have misused the Internet include:

- Sending personal e-mail
- Accessing information for personal use such as concert information and sports scores
- Making appointments
- Paying bills
- Buying personal items such as CD's, books, etc.

Also, many employees have experienced some low level but manageable harm in regard to Internet use. Ways that these persons have been negatively impacted are as follows:

- Creation of an unfounded hope for a solution
- Acceptance of inaccurate information, just because it is posted
- Wasting time and getting behind on work
- Creation of unwarranted guilt, fear or anger
- Delaying a decision, by the continually seeking of information
- Alienation, or withdrawal from the organization through the use of various means of Internet diversions when bored.

These issues impact many persons who use the Internet, but most are able to reach some resolution to these situations on their own, or with minimal guidance. These common misuses have been presented to help the reader identify the normal negative experiences, from the problem behaviors. The fact that a company needs uniform criteria to differentiate between acceptable and unacceptable Internet behavior is a necessary factor for any counselor to consider. This company policy is imperative so that EAP providers can differentiate between the two; extreme misuses must be identifiable. This is necessary as many persons will be referred, some inappropriately, and the EAP professional must be able to identify those in most need. Therefore, the impact on the individual and the frequency of use that is considered unacceptable will be explored. In order to understand these issues, however, one must begin with an exploration of the cyberspace environment (Griffiths, 1995).

Online Environments

Face to Face (FtF) communication is dynamic and transactional; the direction and flow of conversation goes back and forth between participants. Each person exchanges the position of sender and receiver of information during the process. The Internet is also a transactional communication process and the flow of information is similar to being FtF; however, the conditions of attending to the process are different (Barnes, 2001 p. 9, 1998).

Online communication operates on the basis of "I am what I tell you," compared to FtF encounters where all of the senses are utilized. This occurs primarily because online users are able to project to others what they have had the opportunity to edit. Furthermore, the user, if he/she so desires, is able to hide location and identity. These abilities can allow some users to act and respond in a more uninhibited manner. This uninhibiting "online" effect can lead persons to escape the confines of the dominant social structures. Constraints are lifted due to the blurring of distance, class, gender, age and race when online. The obscurity of online interactions may be positive enabling communications between two persons where gender issues and stereotypes will not be a concern, unless parties decide to disclose such information. Some suggest that online communications enable people to have the opportunity to explore, present, and play with many aspects of personal expression, and this can and often is perceived by the user as a liberating experience (Wood, 1995 p. 62). Further, it permits people to communicate with others from around the world enabling them to develop relationships with persons from other cultures and backgrounds (Barnes, 2001 p. 9).

On the other hand, the downside of online communities is that they provide the individual environments where they can present a fragmented projection of self. The leeway afforded is that a person can become fixed and inflexible, and evade any social inner action where compromise and cooperation is required. In a time when team work and group enterprises are expected, online communication can and does contribute to failures in workplace collaboration. For instance, the inability of communicating parties to see body language and judge voice intonation presents challenges to users, challenges of which they are often unaware (Barnes, 2001 p. 9).

Those persons who are able to successfully navigate the Internet have been thought of as being resilient. Reliance has been described as the ability to change to suit the situation, and to devise new ways to meet the circumstances we have encountered while maintaining unity between all aspects of one's persona. It is the ability to have multiple moods, to change opinions, and have our beliefs evolve and thus allowing for the development and growth of the individual as well as the expansion of culture (Reid, 1998).

The previously described singularity of the online personality can be one of the greatest threats to individual growth and well being, as a person and as a worker (Reid, 1998). The Internet, as do substances offer the less resilient individual the opportunity, time and space in which they can escape from the confines of "social" necessity. However, as with drugs, sex, or power, it is an imagined haven (Reid, 1998).

Online Personality Issues

AGGRESSION. The disinhibiting effect of being anonymous, as well as the physical safety, a person's experience in the virtual environment often encourages inappropriate behaviors such as aggressive or abusive behaviors. The manifestation of aggressive behavior on the Internet has been called "flaming," a form of intense communication characterized by the uninhibited expression of anger or hostility toward another person or groups of persons. The aggressive or abusive user perceives a safety from the usual social sanctions, which occur, in (FtF) encounters. This is possible not just because of distance but even moderately skilled users can protect themselves by masking identity as well as location. A disturbing example reported by Reid (1998) describes a situation were an abusive user entered a chat room design to provide support for victims of rape. The intruder was able to send degrading and graphic descriptions of rape to all users in the chat room. The result, even for those least impacted, was that they had to discontinue use of the chat room, those more severely impacted reported their posttraumatic stress symptoms were exacerbated, compounding their existing trauma.

In business arenas, incidents of self-described innocent "flaming" in the form of responding to a sports-talk show host can lead to time away from work. However, in its extreme and problematic instances it can lead to public relations problems and often civil and monetary consequences. For example, Chevron and Microsoft were required in settlements to pay $2.2 million each in law suits because of "sexist" e-mails that were considered by the courts to create a "hostile" work environment. Many persons who at some point have been victimized by a user who has masked age, gender etc. report feeling a loss of trust, that everything online is a lie, and that no one online tells the truth about who they really are (Reid, 1998).

MULTIPLE ASPECTS OF SELF. The ability to obscure or even recreate oneself online allows a person to explore, as never before, dimensions of their "private" selves. For some users this can be a feeling and liberating experience, for others it can create a sense of support for the most deviant of behaviors. For example, chat rooms exist for persons who may want information about conditions such as disease or dysfunction. This information is easily and anonymously available to persons who might never seek it in face-to-face situations. However, chat rooms also exist for persons wanting to explore how to make a bomb, or rape a child and other perverse behaviors. The ability of a person to explore and express such deviant aspects of personality is only enhanced by the ability to mask ones identity when on the Internet (Johnson, 1998). This can cause some individuals to destabilize as they can loose their anchor in reality, and as they are able to find support in a venue where they can express deviant thoughts (Reid, 1998).

FRAGMENTATION. Related to the ability to freely express multiple aspects of ones self is the potential for fragmentation of the personality. Aspects of the personality necessary to continue and enhance relationships are qualities such as compromise, openness to change, and empathy. The online user has the ability to be inflexible,

opinionated to the extreme, and unsympathetic and express this by "flaming." Further, if a user so chooses online communications can be limited to only interactions with others who think as they think. This creates a situation were the normal qualities of compromise, openness and empathy are not necessary. This ability on one hand to express a rigid or deviant idea coupled with the ability to limit or curtail conflicting opinions enables a person to expand and explore hostility, anger or deviance beyond the limits they encounter in "real world" communications. This ability to express without censure can then diminish the modifying effects of social interaction. The persons will just remove themselves from FtF communications and become increasingly enmeshed in the cultures of cyberspace. This creates the potential to allow for the more deviant aspects of personality to be fragmented, isolated, and supported and to become somewhat immune from the effects of social modifiers (Johnson, 1998).

SOCIAL ISOLATION. A problem related to the combination of Internet use and the restructured work environment is isolation. As more and more people are able to work from home, the office culture is changing. For some persons this serves to intensify the processes of anonymously exploring multiple aspects of self and fragmentation. It can result in a decrease in human contact in the form of face-to-face communications. The combination of a visual computer screen and the transactional nature of e-mail can create a situation that enables a person to transform the void of cyberspace into a falsely perceived place for intimate human interaction (Barnes, 2001 p. 8).

Internet Addiction

When one considers the phenomena described above, it is apparent that social pathologies can and do find outlets and support in cyberspace. Further, accessing these outlets may lead to obsessive and seemingly out of control behavior. Also, even if the Internet use is appropriate as to material, the extreme use may impact one's ability to function in other aspects of their lives. This had led many social scientists to describe a phenomenon of Internet addiction (Ajayi, 1995; Griffiths, 1998).

Companies, furthermore, are concerned with "addiction" to Internet use that is not necessarily "inappropriate." Problems have been reported related to the frequency of use. For persons working in offices it can result in marked reductions in productivity due to excessive "searching" or "surfing" for information. Further, for employees who work at home it may result in increased isolation and distance from co-workers and family (Armstrong, Phillips & Sailing, 2000; Griffiths, 1995).

The idea of addiction to technology has been operationally defined as non-chemical (behavioral) addictions that involve human machine interactions. They can be passive (e.g., television) or active (e.g., internet use). Moreover, they usually include inducing and reinforcing features, which can contribute to the promotion of addictive tendencies (Armstrong, Phillips, & Sailing, 2000; Griffiths, 1995).

To refresh the reader, the core components of addictions are salience, modification of mood, and alterations in tolerance, symptoms during withdrawal, interpersonal conflicts, and the tendency to relapse (Davis, 2001). The question that remains to be addressed in regard to Internet addiction is: if it happens just what are people addicted to?

The stereotypes of Internet addiction are that these persons are "hackers," who tend to be socially inept teenage males, with little or no social life and who are labeled by such names as "nerd" or "geek." It would be beneficial to look at what research has indicated about the Internet users when studying Internet addiction. The following are demographic information related to excessive Internet use:

- The "average addict" uses the Internet 38.5 hours per week
- 72% of these persons self identify as Internet addicts.
- 10.6% as dependent on the Internet.
- The average IT worker uses the Internet about 18 hours per week.
- 13% of workers reported their Internet use was excessive and interfered with their personal lives.

- The majority of users are male.
- Pathological users (those considered addicted were predominantly male (12.2%) rather than female (3.2%) (Griffiths, 1998).

The Internet has been described as the *Prozac*® of communication as frequent users appear to be more friendly and open on the Net than in FtF communications (Griffiths, 1995). The jury is still out regarding this issue as problematic since some suggest that excessive use is not addiction but a means to compensate for pre-existing deficiencies in a persons life, such as poor or inadequate relationships, few friends, physical appearance, disability, etc. (Armstrong, Phillips, & Sailing, 2000; Griffiths, 1998). Another argument that it is not an addiction is the perspective that this is but another manifestation of societal trend for people to spend more time with technology than with people. The trend to use technology as a source of entertainment or social interaction began with the radio, followed by the television, and the next step is the Internet. Proponents of this perspective believe this is inevitable behavior given the reality of our society that people are becoming more and more isolated from one another and the Internet has become a means for people to connect (Ajayi, 1995, Barnes, 2001 p. 262).

One last issue related to excessive Internet use and the working environment is that employees who work at home who do not have the contact with colleagues and supervisors can more easily hide excessive Internet use as well as other problem behaviors. Addiction to Internet, gambling, and/or substance abuse can go unnoticed when people work in isolation. This isolation allows many problems to go unrecognized by co-workers and supervisors (Caplan, 2002). A role in the future will be for EAP professionals to educate workers and supervisors how to better identify the Internet abuser so that appropriate referral for EAP intervention can be made.

Dr. Kimberly Young, executive director of the Center for Online Addiction believes Internet addiction does exist and does interfere substantially with people's lives. She believes that zero tolerance policies do not work for Internet addiction and that employees must acknowledge its existence and be prepared to implement appropriate strategies to deal with the problem. This can be done by a company having a realistic policy on what constitutes Internet abuse, an effective education policy for employees as to what Internet addiction is, fair and equitable penalties for abuse, and referral to EAPs so that employees can once again become productive employees, not discarded (Greengard, 2000).

CONCLUSION

The reality is that most persons who use the Internet at work abuse it at some level. This is as much a reality as making personal phone calls. However, in its extreme form Internet abuse causes losses in productivity, increased security costs, unnecessary loads on networks, data security issues, and the increased risk of civil and criminal liability. The appropriate distinction between use and misuses must be explored, defined and enforced by each workplace. Then those who are identified as misusing to an unacceptable extreme should receive EAP intervention to effectively deal with their problem.

In closing, EAP providers may want to look at cyberspace as an opportunity. The Internet is becoming a fast and convenient way to link workers with work/life and EAP services. An added benefit is that some people, say for example someone in need of a child care referral or help handling a work conflict, feel more at ease confiding in their computer than talking directly to a specialist.

Employee Assistance Programs are becoming a desirable and common benefit, offered by nearly 90 percent of large employers. At the same time, e-mail, the Internet and intranets have revolutionized the way Americans seek and exchange information. That raises the prospect of EAP professionals expanding on ways to efficiently deliver psychosocial support to millions more people who may need it but would not seek it in a face-to-face encounter. The risks are many, confidentiality will have to be maintained, and users will have to be reassured that the communications are secure and safe before they will use computer technology to receive assistance with their most personal problems.

REFERENCES

Ajayi, A. (1995). Terminal addiction. *Internet and Communication Today,* May, p. 36.

Armstrong, L., Phillips, J. G., & Sailing, L. L. (2000) Potential determinants of heavier Internet usage. *International Journal of Human-Computer Studies, 53* (14), 537–550.

Bellm, M. (1998). Cutting down on Internet abuse at work. *Control Engineering, 45* (12), 62.

Caplan, S. E. (2002). Problematic Internet use and psychosocial well-being: development of a theory-based cognitive-behavioral measurement instrument. *Computers in Human Behavior, 18* (5), 553–575.

Greenfield, D. N., & Davis, R. A. (2002). Lost in cyberspace: The web at work. *Cyberpsychology Behavior, 5* (4), 347–353.

Greengard, S. (2000). The high cost of cyberslacking. *Workforce, 79* (12), 22–24.

Griffiths, M. (1998). Internet addiction: Does it really exist? In Gackenbach, J. (Ed)., *Psychology and the Internet: Intrapersonal, Interpersonal, and transpersonal implications.* San Diego, CA: Academic Press.

Griffiths, M. D. (1995) Technological addictions. *Clinical Psychology Forum, 76,* 14–19.

Hines, A. (1994). Jobs and infotech: Work in the information society. *The Futurist, 28* (Jan./Feb.), 9–13.

Johnson, A. (1998). Causes and implications of disinhibited behavior on the Internet. In Gackenbach, J. (Ed)., *Psychology and the Internet: Intrapersonal, Interpersonal, and transpersonal implications.* San Diego, CA: Academic Press.

King, S. A., & Moreggi, D. (1998). In Gackenbach, J. (Ed)., *Psychology and the Internet: Intrapersonal, Interpersonal, and transpersonal implications.* San Diego, CA: Academic Press.

Reid, E. (1998). The self and the Internet: Variations on the illusion of one self. In Gackenbach, J. (Ed).,

Psychology and the Internet: Intrapersonal, Interpersonal, and transpersonal implications. San Diego, CA: Academic Press.

Sunoo, B. P. (1996). This employee may be loafing. Can you tell? Should you care? *Personnel Journal, 75* (Dec.), 54–59.

Chapter 25

CULTURAL DIVERSITY ISSUES IN EMPLOYEE ASSISTANCE PROGRAMS

CHARLOTTE G. DIXON and TENNYSON J. WRIGHT

An ethnically diverse work force has emerged as a necessary and expected reality of the twenty-first century organization. Thomas (1991) stated: "Managing diversity is an idea whose time has come. More and more corporations and organizations of all kinds are awakening to the fact that a diverse work force is not a burden, but their greatest potential strength–when managed properly" (p. ix). Mayo (1999) identified several demographic and business trends that have combined to push diversity to the top of the business agenda. First, diversity is increasing worldwide. For example, *Canadian Social Trends* (cited in Mayo, 1999) reports that minorities are expected to make up 20 percent of all adults in Canada by 2016, which more than doubles the percent of adults in 1991. Additionally, 85 percent of the net addition to the U.S. work force by the end of the twenty-first century will be women and non-white men. More specifically, the Hudson Institute's Workforce 2020 (1997), indicate that ethnic minorities will constitute 32 percent of the labor force by the year 2020. Second, the consumer market has become increasingly diverse. Increased globalization has resulted in expanded markets to a wide variety of consumers. In order to pace with the competition and demand, smart companies have realized the need to improve their understanding of these emerging markets and are aggressively competing to attract and retain talented employees of diverse backgrounds. Third, the use of teams as building blocks of organizations is growing. Mayo (1999) indicated that increasingly business leaders believe that innovation, creative solutions and better decisions can be more easily reached by a diverse group of people. This assertion was supported in a recent survey by *Purchasing* magazine (cited in Mayo, 1999) that found that 57 percent of companies use multifunctional teams to make strategic decisions.

One of the primary strengths of an ethnically diverse work force is the different perspectives it brings to an organization. By facilitating an exchange of information among managers with dissimilar perspectives and a discussion of different viewpoints related to a task, a well-managed ethically diverse work force can have a positive impact on performance, morale, retention and achievement of the mission of the organization. However, retaining a diverse work force and building cooperation among it can present significant challenges. If managed properly, diversity can be the cornerstone of a globally competitive organization. But if mismanaged, diversity can be counterproductive and costly. In the past, human resource professionals have attempted to deal with these challenges on their own. Today, however, employee assistance programs (EAPs) offer a host of diversity-related services designed to address the challenges of meeting the needs of a diverse work force. "Organizational management has begun to realize that diversity issues, such as discrimination and cultural alienation, affect productivity" (Gale, 2002, p. 66). Consequently, the effective management of work force diversity has become a primary issue for EAPs. Overall, an ethnically diverse work force is a good human resource and business practice that benefits everyone.

A review of the literature reflects that management practices, supervisory relationships and diversity training programs are among the principle areas that must be considered and if necessary, created by organizations attempting to effectively manage an ethically diverse work force. The remainder of this chapter will address these three critical areas and the ways in which EAPs can assist in the effective management of a diverse work force.

Management Practices

According to Thomas (1991), diversity became an issue when three powerfully significant trends reached their own critical points at about the same time in the 1990s. He identified them as: "(1) The global market in which American corporations must now do business became intensely competitive.; (2) The makeup of the U.S. work force began changing dramatically, becoming more diverse.; and (3) Individuals began to increasingly celebrate their differences and became less amenable to compromising what makes them unique" (pp. 3–4). This has led to corporations and organizations seeking better ways of managing its human resources from a diversity perspective.

Thomas (1991) defined "managing diversity" as: ". . . a comprehensive managerial process for developing an environment that works for all employees" (p. 10). According to Soni (2000), managing diversity is predicted to be one of the most significant organizational issues of the coming decades. This will be the result of the projected changes in organizational demographics combined with employers' concerns about motivating and obtaining satisfactory levels of performance of a diverse group of employees. The projected changes have created an urgency to understand and recognize the value of diversity in virtually all organizations. However, whether the goal of effectively managing work force diversity is achieved depends largely on an organization's diversity climate (Cox 1993). Accordingly, managing diversity will require initiatives that are culturally and ethnically relevant, organizationally sound, and mission focused. These initiatives must be designed to: (1) increase sensitivity to cultural differences; (2) develop the ability to recognize,

accept, and value diversity; (3) minimize patterns of inequality experienced by women and ethnic minorities; (4) improve cross-cultural interactions and interpersonal relationships among different gender and ethnic groups; and (5) modify organizational culture and leadership practices (Carrell & Mann 1995; Cox 1993; Loden & Rosener 1991; Thomas 1991).

One of the critical tasks for managers is to help individual employees, including senior managers and middle managers, define themselves beyond organizational or divisional lines toward a team identity. Though important, individuality ranks second to the overall mission and goals of the organization. An effective manager must be able to cultivate a team identity that values and integrates the goals of the organization along with the demographic characteristics of its members. When necessary, managers must be able to redirect attention and resources away from the individual or diversity issues towards the mission and goals of the organization, while concurrently recognizing and rewarding individual efforts toward accomplishing team goals. These two tasks are not mutually exclusive and will require a delicate balancing act by a skillful manager. These tasks are critical to creating and maintaining an effective human resource management team.

Once a team identity has been established, consensus building toward achieving a common task or goal must occur. Managers should start by developing a common vision or mission to be achieved then unite all team members around shared values thereby fostering a sense of group identity. Managers must be able to help each member of the team view himself or herself as a whole unit striving for a common mission or goal. In other words, effective consensus building that demonstrates and engenders passionate commitment to the mission or goal must take place. Diversity within the unit should be viewed as a means to an end and should be valued for its significance to achieving the desired outcome.

Equally important, managers must be required to engage in leadership practices that maximizes the knowledge and social expertise inherent in an ethnically diverse work force. For example, the practice of matching tasks to people is a simple but necessary management tool. Several career counseling theories (e.g., Trait-Factor, Holland, Super) long have supported the value of matching people to tasks that are consistent with their interest, aptitude skills and abilities. Utilizing these theories will assist managers in making sound decisions relevant to the assignment of tasks and duties within the team. When one considers that one of the most common problem for managers is assigning employee roles that match their own stereotype rather than the individuals' skills and abilities (Mayo, 1999), the importance of matching becomes very apparent. In order to avoid engaging in such potentially problematic behaviors, managers will need to be aware of their own stereotypes and avoid allowing them to negatively impact their decision making. In order to avoid this potential problem, managers will need to effectively assess individual employee interests, aptitudes, skills and abilities, as well as establish a personal relationship with each, to avoid stereotypical decision-making. "EAPs offer a wide range of services, including training and consultation with managers and supervisors" (Zarkin, Bray & Karuntzos, (2001, p. 351) and can therefore assist managers to establish and implement the management practices outlined above.

Supervisory Relationships

The supervisory relationship is at the heart of effective diversity management and often transcends formal policies and programs. Dixon-Kheir (2001) reported and discussed the results of a recent survey of 500 employees between the ages of 21 and 30, 75 percent of whom were Black, Latino/Hispanic, Asian/Pacific Islander or Native American. When asked to identify key requirements for remaining in and having a long career with an organization, the overwhelming response was a quality supervisory relationship. The supervisory relationship was viewed as the primary factor that would have the greatest impact on their success within their organization. Respondents identified the following attributes of a quality supervisory relationship: (1) effective introductions to the organization; (2) recognition and support for career aspirations and contributions; (3)

facilitation of acceptance and inclusion in the organization and in professional groups and informal networks; (4) advancing their ideas and proposals to benefit the organization; and (5) supporting them in difficult situations and going to bat on their behalf in battles they cannot win on their own (Dixon-Kheir, 2001).

Quality reporting relations or communication was identified as a second essential requirement for remaining and having a long career with their organizations. Results of the survey of 200 managers identified as having established and sustained quality reporting relationships with employees from diverse backgrounds indicated that they: (1) set mutual expectations; (2) provided frequent feedback; (3) avoided generalities or stereotypes in communicating; (4) shared personal experiences and cultural knowledge of the organization; (5) acted as an advocate and provided visibility/exposure for employees; (6) were accessible and encouraged straight talk about the bad news as well as the good news; (7) knew and appreciated the employee's work; (8) coached and developed knowledge and skills; and (9) recognized and rewarded superior performance (Dixon-Kheir, 2001).

It is important to note that 80 percent of the managers reported that the quality of communication was more important than its frequency. It is not uncommon for supervisors to limit communications to work-related issues.

In the case of cross-ethnic, cross-cultural interactions, work-related matters may be identified as the only common denominator. Supervisors must make every attempt to bridge this gap and take the time to cultivate personal relationships with ethnically diverse subordinates. Relationship building between supervisors and subordinates will require the sharing of values and personal interests, goals and aspirations by both parties. A measure of the genuineness of the supervisors' actions may be assessed by the amount of time spent with subordinates during work and nonwork-related functions. Supervisors can encourage nonwork-related group activities, for example, having breakfast or lunch together, sponsor a unit picnic or Christmas parties where employees are encouraged to bring their families and share food, games, or other cultural/ethnically specific activity.

In addition to the above, Dixon-Kheir (2001) offer the following suggestions for creating quality relationships: (1) learn more about the employee; (2) learn how likely your employees are to leave; (3) set mutual expectations about the supervisory relationship; (4) schedule regular career and/or personal development meetings; (5) give regular feedback; (6) encourage dialogue about diversity; and (7) look for opportunities to support relationship building. Employees stay with organizations when they feel valued, are recognized for their contributions, are able to develop their knowledge and skills, and are compensated fairly for their work contributions.

Diversity Training

Diversity training programs are typically aimed at: (1) increasing participants' awareness of their own personal attitudes, beliefs, and values; (2) imparting culture specific knowledge about various ethnic groups; and (3) developing skills to enhance cross-ethnic, cross-cultural interactions (Atkins, Morten & Sue, 1997). Unfortunately, many participants of diversity training programs report negative learning experiences associated with such training and thus these programs have received less than stellar reviews (Beekie, 1997; Karp & Sammour, 2000). In many instances, diversity training programs have failed to achieve their intended outcomes. However, because diversity training is such an integral component of any effective diversity management initiative, it is important to examine problems typically associated with diversity training and to identify considerations for designing a quality diversity training program.

Common Problems with Diversity Training

There are several common problems associated with diversity training. First, diversity training is often met with extreme resistance. Because of negative personal experiences with diversity training or knowledge of others' negative experiences, participants who are *required* to attend diversity train-

ing tend to do so with a defensive, closed posture coupled with resistance, skepticism, and cynicism. Breaking down the barriers posed by attitudes of this nature must be addressed immediately by the trainer but can be very time-consuming. Karp and Sammour (2001) asserts that most diversity programs are value driven and emphasize how things "should be." These authors suggest that resistance stems from uninvited outside efforts by diversity trainers to tell the participants that they should change their attitudes, values and beliefs and they further suggest that such resistance serves to protect the integrity of the participant. Quality diversity training does not attempt to change one's attitudes, values or beliefs but rather attempt to bring about an awareness of how such attitudes, values and beliefs impact one's behavior and decision making. Unfortunately, pejorative preconceived ideas about the goal or purpose of diversity training prevents many employees from approaching training with an open mind and thus limits their ability to comprehend this simple yet fundamental distinction. Consequently, it is essential that this distinction be made clear from the beginning and re-emphasized throughout the training session.

Secondly, limited time is a common problem associated with diversity training. In addition to handling resistance, one of the principle goals of diversity training is increased self awareness of one's attitudes, values and beliefs relevant to other cultures and ethnic groups. True self-awareness is a process that occurs over time through deep reflection and introspection. At best, a one-day or two-day diversity training session may only begin to foster a willingness to consider the importance of expending such energy for the purpose of enhanced relationships with ethnically diverse co-workers. For those employees who approach diversity training with a flexible attitude and a willingness to learn, a one-day or two-day training session may only began to delve into the complicated issues surrounding self awareness.

Third, diversity training is often viewed as a necessary learning activity primarily for white males, or the majority culture. This view falsely assumes that persons of ethnic backgrounds lack attitudes, beliefs and values which could negatively impact their willingness or ability to establish productive working relationships with other ethnic group members and fails to recognize the heterogeneity within different ethnic groups. It is important that diversity training programs be able to address both within group differences and between group differences and emphasize the need for all employees to examine how personal attitudes, values, and beliefs impact their behavior and decision making when working with persons from different ethnic backgrounds.

Fourth, though diversity training is often viewed as being predominately necessary for white males, by in large, voluntary attendees are typically females and non-white males. In other words, when given a choice, most white males choose not to attend diversity training. Several explanations for this occurrence have been offered: (1) a lack of sensitivity on the part of diversity trainers toward white males; (2) a climate that promotes feelings of guilt and defensiveness; (3) personal attacks by diversity trainers against white ancestors; and (4) the perception that trainers have negatively judged one's value systems and are insisting that a change must occur (Atkinson, 2001).

Designing a Quality Diversity Training Program

Diversity training activities are typically conducted under the direction of human resource personnel or via EAPs. As such, it is important that both human resource and EAP personnel recognize the importance of due diligence in the planning, designing and implementation of diversity training activities throughout the organization. Without critical attention to factors such as selection and style of trainers, content of training materials, approaches to conflict, etc., diversity training activities will likely fail and the credibility of the organization's EAP will be sorely compromised.

If one of the objectives of diversity training is to enhance ethnic/culture specific knowledge, then knowledge specific to all populations, including minorities, females, and whites, must be valued and appreciated. Diversity training must include ways that men and women, or people of different races, reflect differences in values, attitudes,

behavior styles, ways of thinking, and cultural background (Thomas, 1991).

Diversity training usually concentrates on one of several of these general objectives:
- "Fostering awareness and acceptance of individual differences.
- Fostering greater understanding of the nature and dynamics of individual differences.
- Helping participants understand their own feelings and attitudes about people who are 'different.'
- Exploring how differences might be tapped as assets in the workplace.
- Enhancing work relations between people who are different" (Thomas, 1991, p. 25).

White American culture must be included in diversity training as well. White participants, male and female, are rarely prepared to answer the question "what does it mean to be white in America?" Few have ever considered or viewed themselves as part of a racial or ethnic group with a cultural experience uniquely their own. Consequently, notions of white privilege or group identity tend to be foreign concepts. Many ethnic group members view whites as white first and other characteristics secondary (e.g., white male, white female, white boss, white supervisor, etc.). This perception holds a deeper meaning for the ethnic group member and tends to be a novel idea to most white participants of diversity training. In other words, many ethnic group members believe that white Americans do indeed have a culture that have contributed to their place in society and in the workplace. It is this perception that needs to be thoroughly explored by diversity trainers. Few, if any work environments exist where white Americans are not employed. Consequently, not only is it essential for whites to possess and understand cultural specific knowledge about ethnic group members, but it is equally important for ethnic group members to possess and understand white American culture. And perhaps most importantly, for each to understand the perceptions that other ethnic groups' possess about cultures other than their own. A quality diversity training program will explore such issues and in so doing, increase the involvement and participation of white participants. Including and exploring discussions of white culture also tends to lessen resistance and is essential to demonstrating the value of learning about all ethnic groups.

It is important that diversity training not focus on the behaviors and sufferings of any particular ethnic group but rather that it should address to the anxiety and fears of employees that create barriers to positive acceptance and appreciation of all ethnic groups. Diversity trainers should strive to avoid narrow discussions of race and culture and seek to uncover the true source of discomfort and anxiety as well as to focus attention on characteristics common to all members of the group.

Achieving the goals of diversity training will not be easy. However, the need for sustained training and processing of these complex issues is imperative. Diversity training initiative will be integral to the success of the organization and therefore, the strategic plan should pay particular attention to diversity training issues. For example, Karp and Sammour (2001) identified the following six questions managers should entertain when planning diversity training programs: (1) Who should conduct the training?; (2) Who should get the training?; (3) Does the training address attitudes or behaviors?; (4) What's being said versus how it's being said?; (5) Does the training provoke feelings of guilt or empathy?; and (6) Does the training focus on victims or survivors of discriminatory practices? Clearly, sufficient time, attention and research should be devoted to designing a quality diversity training program; one which effectively addresses the selection of trainers, implementation, monitoring and evaluation of the training program. Serious consideration should be given to the identification of desired diversity training outcomes. Seeking employee input regarding the desired outcomes will bode the organization well in securing employee buy-in. Additionally, training evaluations can be valuable tools for improving the quality of the programs offered.

Organizations that are serious about maximizing their diverse work force should consider extended diversity training programs similar to those offered by many universities and corporations. These programs recognize the barriers inherent in diversity training and address them over longer periods of time, usually eight to 16 weeks. Most university-based diversity training classes incorporate books, videos, newspaper articles, personal reflections along with lectures and class activities in order to provide a richer, more in-depth learning experience. This approach also allows participants and instructors time to get to know each other, build a trusting relationship and foster a safe environment in which to explore such complex issues. Additionally, those who train/teach under such conditions are likely to possess a deeper, more complex understanding of the issues and in many instances, are more experienced trainers. Human resource personnel, university diversity officers and/or managers who are in charge of designing diversity training programs are encouraged to look to external, university-based trainers and to support training options for those employees seeking a deeper learning experience.

CONCLUSION

Globalization has made our world much smaller and far more inclusive. Organizations are diverse as are marketplaces and consumers. Clearly, when diversity fails the organization fails. Subsequently, the commitment toward diversity must be demonstrated from the top down and implemented throughout the organization (Griffin, 1994). Because it has been found that diverse groups of employees bring new input to their organizations by generating productive dialogue and contributing diverse perspectives that positively impact service and delivery, promoting an ethnically diverse work force should be viewed as a means to cultivate management creativity and competitive advantage in the marketplace. Subsequently, the most successful organizations of the twenty-first century will find ways to not only benefit from the experience, talents, and expertise of ethnically diverse employees, but also will strive to promote and maintain an organizational climate that respects, values and supports them.

Effective utilization of EAPs can positively impact an organization's ability to meet the demands of an ethnically diverse work force. However, it is important to note the results of a process evaluation conducted by Zarkin, Bray and Karuntzos (2001), which revealed several deficiencies that would impact the effective delivery of EAP services to ethnic minority employees. For example, they found that EAP staff members lacked awareness of cultural diversity issues that affected their ability to effectively counsel and refer diverse populations. Secondly, they found that (e.g., problem identification checklists failed to include "family" issues; confrontational approaches were not culturally sensitive) workplace training programs did not include information generally relevant to women and minorities. These findings exemplify the need for diversity training sensitivity across the entire work force, including human resource and EAP personnel.

REFERENCES

Atkinson, W. (2001). Bringing diversity to white men. *HR Magazine, 46* (9), 76–83.

Beekie, R. (1997). Diversity training's big lie. *Training, 24,* 122.

Dixon-Kheir, C. (2001). Supervisors are key to keeping young talent. *HR Magazine, 46* (1), 139–142.

Evans, R. (2001). A cultural gap. *Hospitals & Health Networks, 75* (9), 72.

Gale, S. F. (2002). Companies find EAPS can foster diversity. *Workforce, 81* (2), 66–69.

Gardenwartz, L., & Rowe, A. (2001). Cross-cultural awareness. *HR Magazine, 46* (3) 139–142.

Griffin, C. E. (1994). Improving rehabilitation service utilization among ethnic/racial groups: Rehabilitation administrator's role. *Journal of Rehabilitation Administration, 18* (1), 37–45.

Hayes, V. (1999). Beyond employment equity: The business case for diversity. *Ivey Business Review, 64* (1), 44–50.

Hilderbrand, K. (1996). Use leadership training to increase diversity. *HR Magazine, 42,* 53–54.

Judy, R. W., & Amico, C. D. (1997). *Workforce 2020: Work and workers in the 21st Century.* Indianapolis, IN: Hudson Institute.

Karp, H. B., & Sammour, H. Y. (2000). Workforce diversity: Choices in diversity training programs and dealing with resistance to diversity. *College Student Journal, 34* (3), 451–458.

Mayo, M. (1999). Capitalizing on a diverse workforce. *Ivey Business Journal, 64* (1), 20–26.

Merrick, N. (2001). Minority interest. *People Management, 7* (22), 52–53.

Ramsey, R. D. (2001). Supervising immigrant workers. *Supervision, 62* (11), 13–15.

Raphael, T. (2001). Savvy companies build bonds with Hispanic employees. *Workforce, 80* (9), 19.

Russell, J. (2002). Multiculturalism grows up. *Hispanic Business, 24* (4), 58.

Soni, V. (2000). A twenty-first century reception for diversity in the public sector: A case study. *Public Administration Review, 60* (5), 395–408.

Thomas, C. (2001). Challenges to diversity. *Pharmaceutical Executive, 21* (7), 10–14.

Thomas, R. R., Jr. (1991). *Beyond race and gender.* New York: American Management Association.

Zarkin, G. A., Bray, J. W., & Karuntzos, G. T. (2001). The effect of an enhanced employee assistance program (EAP) intervention on EAP utilization. *Journal of Studies on Alcohol, 62* (3), 351–358.

Chapter 26

CHANGES IN THE WORK FORCE AND CHANGES IN THE WORKPLACE CRITICAL TO EMPLOYEE ASSISTANCE PROGRAMS

MICHAEL A. RICHARD and JUDITH K. SCHEMM

The empires of the future are the empires of the mind.

Winston Churchill, at Harvard University, September 6, 1943

Winston Churchill's statement appears to have prophesized the current generation. This is due in large part to the far-reaching effects of information technology (IT). In the wake of IT, the foundations of the American workplace are being altered. Cities, once the centers of economic activity, such as Detroit and Pittsburgh, have yielded power and prestige to new centers, such as the Silicon Valley and the "Carolina Triangle." More than geographic, a basic transformation in what business produces has occurred. Industry once made cars, textiles and steel; today's businesses generates fodder for the "mind" information, services, and computer support technologies (Burris, 1998; Druker, 2000).

The ideal workers once were employed by a company, knew the their job, did them well, were loyal, and depended on their jobs until retirement. They performed tasks, an integral part of producing a product that could be seen, had dimension and physical substance. Today, IT workers have been described as self-employed, outsourced, retrained, and self-sufficient. These workers processes information, transport ideas/information, take orders, sort, label, categorize, and are able to prioritize work according to value. The work done by the workers of today represents an alteration from what was asked of industrial era workers (Rothman, 2000). Consequently, workers

of this millennium grapple with ever-evolving demands of a new work order, which produce a unique set of problems.

Workers today are being forced to re-evaluate basic values related to work, community and family. When you include the social and political changes which occurred in less than a generation, such as the changes in family, increased violence in the workplace, events in Oklahoma City and of September 11, 2002, the need to help workers adjust to a new world becomes evident (Gale, 2002; Galea, Resnnick, Ahern, Gold, Bucuvalas, Kilpatrick, Stuber, Vlahov & 2002). This chapter explores sources of worker problems as they relate to changes in the way work is done, which challenges basic values, beliefs and security. A sampling of specific IT problems related to cyberspace space, are discussed in another chapter of this book.

The source of change in work can be described as occurring on three levels: (1) the macro level, defined as "global"; (2) micro changes, or those related to community, work, family; and (3) individual level.

Macro Level Changes

Forces of the world have become more interdependent as a result of IT. Global networks, known as "the global economy," have proliferated, and the effects are being felt worldwide in many economic, political, and social contexts. Proponents of the "New Work Order" see fundamental changes in each of these areas as necessary to continue the globalization process, which is at the heart of modern business practices (Reich, 1999).

Globalization has been described as a hybrid, created when IT business demands and goals of developing countries encountered the IT business demands and goals of the developed nations. The need to incorporate the needs of both has provided the rationalization for a movement toward sociological singularity (Reich, 1999). The necessary conditions to accomplish globalization started with the development and implementation of the technological infrastructures of transportation and communication. This allowed for instantaneous communications and the ability to travel the globe in hours. The spread of the IT market has preceded unabated, and the pressure to maintain a "growth" orientation has persisted, coupled with pressure on governments to upgrade requisite IT skills of its citizens. Technology is seen as reigning supreme, being the fundamental element in a global culture (Logsdon & Wood, 2002; Rothman, 2000).

At the core of these changes are inconsistencies to nationalistic philosophies, which provided the moral foundations of the industrial era. Basic beliefs accepted by workers like "American products are superior", and the necessity to protect workers from "foreign" competitors are being challenged by the "global" world view (Carnoy, 2000; Reich, 1999). Logsdon and Wood (2002) describe this debate over a nationalistic versus global world views, as deliberated in business and economic communities. They suggest business leaders are increasingly optimistic about the future and value of global networks. Many see core values such as "American Pride" as inhibiting growth and expansion into global markets. Therefore, basic values are being reevaluated at the theoretical level.

In the global economy ideas and information are the commodity, time and space are no longer constraints. In fact, when time and space are imposed they serve only to inhibit economic expansion (Lipset & Ray, 1996).

This is the basis of the problem in the transformation of work, which is how to reframe the moral grounding and language for American citizenship. This grounding which once helped to define a world view, also was the foundation of American industrial era capitalism (Carnoy, 2000, pp 58–64; Lipset & Ray, 1996).

Expansions of global trade and investments have impacted many jobs especially those utilizing IT. Business leaders see globalization as desirable and necessary for economic growth (Kelly, 2000; Mohanty & Yadv, 1996). For example, the North American Free Trade Agreement (NAFTA) was enacted to the discomfort of organized labor during the Clinton administration, with the encouragement and overwhelming support of IT related business. Since its inception the United States government and business leaders have gone on to form and become principal members of the World Trade Organization (WTO). As the WTO's political and economic influence has grown, concepts which continue to impact American workers are being discussed by WTO members. Ideas such as implementing "flexible wages" to respond to changes in variations in supply and demand, are being discussed by the WTO and are given serious consideration. American business and national leaders at the "global" level already apply "flexible wages" in third world countries. Furthermore, many express the opinion it would be a desirable option in the United States. These changes in their infancy have already begun to impact the stability of US workers, such as values and beliefs (Logsdon & Wood, 2002; Reich, 1999).

Micro Level

As the world economy has evolved, so have concepts of work. Social scientists see this transformation as causing a postindustrial bureaucratic work organization characterized by decentralization, reductions in class structures, and greater economic polarization. IT and related enterprises demand that workers have more knowledge and technological skills in order to obtain jobs. Once employed, workers can anticipate a decrease in formal organizational structures to help in adjusting to new jobs, more autonomy, plus a substantial increase in personal responsibility (Kelly, 2000; Rothman, 2000).

This is not unexpected, as Salzman & Rosental (1994, p. 4) argued, in that workplaces are fashioned by the purpose and type of technology. Therefore, businesses dependent on computerized systems of manufacturing and/or information will differ considerably from work dependent on producing a consumable product. Computerized workplaces require workers to have more flexibility and greater skill variability, which create differing patterns of work organizations and demand structures.

CLASS STRUCTURE CHANGES. Socio/Economic changes related to the IT revolution have divided the work force into two groups, the "haves" and "have-nots." The "haves" people with up to date IT skills find great fiscal rewards. The "have-nots" those with no, few, or outdated technical skills, are consigned to the low end of the wage scale. This polarization most evident in IT related work is seen as acceptable, in part due to a false sense that those at the bottom of the technological worker heap, may eventually climb to the top (Murphey, 1999; Nord, 1999). There is a bright future for those fortunate enough to be appropriately skilled, educated, and technically proficient to qualify for good IT jobs. But for many it is a reality of retraining, layoffs, and difficult adjustments to new work demands, continued discrimination, and major disruptions in family life (Dariety, Guilkey, & Winfrey, 1996; McNerney, 1996; Kelly, 2000).

As the transition of work unfolds 55 percent or more of the total jobs are in the service/retail occupations whereas only 18 percent are in manufacturing (Occupational Outlook Handbook, 2002). The industrial companies share of the Gross Domestic Product (GDP), the broadest measure of goods and services produced in the United States, has fallen from 29 percent in 1950, to 18 percent. This has been accompanied by a remarkable growth in service and IT jobs resulting in an increased demand for qualified workers in each of these sectors (Berman, 2001; Thomson, 1999).

WORKPLACE DEMANDS ON WORKERS. The IT workplace demands that workers be more educat-

ed, better trained and willing to take greater career risks. IT employers expect workers to perform tasks involving sorting data, processing information, and the exchange information in multicorporate and multinational environments. Jobs often are more financially rewarding, but workers must be self-motivated and willing to accept increased responsibility often with less security (Clinton, 1997; Druker, 2000).

The increased risks can be illustrated by the numerous losses of jobs for persons employed by ENRON, WorldCom, and numerous dot.com companies, which have declared bankruptcy. Downsizing has also left many highly skilled employees unemployed, and disillusioned (Buhler, 2002; Druker, 2000). There is the risk of obsolescence as skills once considered critical can become outdated. A prime example, the frantic need for keypunch operators 30 years ago, which today is a job nonexistent.

Due to changes in the way service work is done, it has been catapulted up the socioeconomic ladder swallowing up many jobs previously described as "white-collar" such as attorneys, physicians, insurance salesman, accountants, bankers and others. Jobs in these professions and the "new IT professions," such as programmers, are foundations for career opportunities for workers in a broadened "service based economy." The other less valued occupations included in the "service" classification such as retail sales, housekeeping, lawn maintenance, food servers, etc., continue to maintain a subordinate image (Metters & Varges, 2000; Thomson, 1999).

IT, bureaucratic constraints are being relaxed to allow for creativity and work schedule flexibility. However, this has lead to increased pressure to perform, as accountability is now performance-based. These flexible schedules have resulted in family and self-identity issues which will be discussed later (Clinton 1997; Welty, 1997). Further, Hodson, (2001) reports worker autonomy, input into decision making, and salaries were dramatically different for IT engineers than their cohorts working in manufacturing.

ORGANIZATIONAL CHANGES. A dramatic change in work has been the emergence of less formal organizational bureaucracies. Industry typically has utilized clearly defined chains of responsibility and communication. IT firms more frequently rely on informal teams (Basin, 1996; Mankin, Cohen & Bikson, 1997).

Changes in work organization are most evident when high-tech work environments are compared to the traditional industrial environments. Industry typically was structured with specialized divisions of labor with many vertical shifts from high to low status jobs within the workplaces. The structure of information age work has fewer hierarchical levels and is exemplified by a "two-tier" polarized occupational arrangement (Carnoy, 2000; Hodson, 1988; Rocha & McCant, 1999; Rothman, 2000). This has resulted in delayering as many mid-level positions are reduced or eliminated with a subsequent skill and pays barrier separating the two tiers in most service and IT organizations. Polarization is exacerbated by the increased emphasis placed on education, external credentialing and recruitment from without the organization (Brauer, 1995). Even though this trend occurs most often in IT firms, delayering and outside recruitment are becoming more evident in low-tech organizations (Hodson, 2001; Murphey, 1999; Rocha & McCant, 1999).

As companies revamp their organizations, another trend is multifunctional activity, or teamwork, which utilizes the expertise of people from different departments and/or corporations. From the corporate perspective, these multidisciplinary teams result in improved output and the ability to better reward success and to identify sources of failure. Working in such performance-based environments puts added stress on team members, especially if the "team" fails (Lipset & Ray, 1996; Solomon & Marmer, 1999).

For industrial era workers, functional aspects of the job created stronger constituent relationships while the cross-functional personal contacts were minimal. This resulted in employees having a safety net of understanding colleagues when a corporate goal was not accomplished. The worker knew if he/she had done his/her job well that they would have the support of similar professionals. Today's employees often feel deserted, isolated and used as "rules," which once governed individual work have been replaced by new ones stress-

ing the importance of "group" outcomes (Chmiel, 1998). For example, a worker may be a marketing specialist but spend 75 percent of his/her time working on project teams with persons from other departments. Their office may be in the marketing department, but his/her ability to socialize and find support from those who think and act like a marketing professional has been greatly diminished. Consequently, a worker's professional identity is becoming weaker while demands for a multifunctional character increase (Challenger, 1999).

EAP professionals increasingly will face issues surrounding feelings of abandonment, loss of control, and loss of self-esteem. Advising a worker to just do their best to reap rewards may no longer be a realistic approach. The role of EAP professionals in such situations is seen as being able to teach employees to work more efficiently as a team member, teaching methods to maximize team effectiveness (Burns, 1999).

PROMOTION AND RETENTION. Recruitment has routinely been handled through traditional hiring practices and by human resource personnel, but some problems have been encountered (Murphey, 1999). To assist in understanding issues faced by employers, looking at the changing needs related to the hiring, retention and promotion issues of two different types of employers may be helpful. The service industry and the newly "automated" manufacturing environments will be examined to illustrate.

Screening for persons with strong "social" personalities and related skills needed in positions of high consumer contact is a growing concern for service industry employers. Traditional personality tests (Meyers Briggs, Self Directed Search, etc.) have proven useful in screening for competent persons (Adler, 2000). However, service firms are looking for more than competence. They want potential managers and supervisors to be persons who can quickly tell the difference between acceptable and unacceptable customer relations, and who are able to identify and prioritize work that creates new value. They are seeking applicants who are "going for the gold," rather than planning to occupy middle management positions (Metters & Varges, 2000). EAP professionals could serve a central role in this process, by aligning themselves with human recourses and perform in-depth interviews with qualified potential employees. This could help to more effectively identify persons who are willing to put forth the necessary effort to succeed in the service industry (Blair, 2002).

Further, as service employees prove themselves they become increasingly valuable to employers. Consequently, retention of "proven" employees has become a concern for service firms. The importance of retention has developed as training takes longer and is costlier. Moreover, customers more often report they are attracted to a service company because of the skilled personnel, rather than the lure of cheap prices or media advertising (Metters & Varges, 2000). Providing interventions to mediate the concerns of these valuable employees and help to keep them with the same company is seen by many employers as falling into the arena of the EAP professionals (Blair, 2002; Burns, 1999).

In manufacturing, which is becoming more automated, retention has also become an issue due to the rapid decline in the number and proportion of blue-collar workers needed (Berman, 2001). This decline has resulted in downsizing, layoffs, or expectations that workers upgrade existing outdated skills. To keep a job, employees often must agree to retraining to meet the technological demands of automation or to enter the "white collar" side of the company. This is an area traditional training professionals have not yet fully understood and have not handled well. If employees cannot or will not be retrained, it is often seen as easier to just replace them with new workers who have the required skills (Frazee, 1997; Rocha & McCant, 1999).

When retraining has been provided it often fails the "blue collar" workers. Especially those workers retrained for "white collar" positions. These workers often express difficulty adapting to the "corporate white collar culture" as they do not understand the subtle social cues involved in their new positions, and no training is provided to prepare them for "white collar culture." Further, workers who attempt to make this transition into the white-collar world indicate they were once able to ask for help when needed, but have found

out that "asking'" in the white-collar world is often considered the same as being "ignorant." Consequently, the struggle to adapt to a new working environment is for many a problematic situation (Lipset & Ray, 1996; Rocha & McCant, 1999).

A challenge for EAP providers in the next few years is to carve out new arenas of service provision. The role of screening, retention counseling, employee advocacy, social skills training, and supervisor sensitivity training are areas which must be and increasingly are being addressed by EAP providers (Blair, 2002; Burns, 1999; Lippman, 1998).

Individual Level Changes

Americans long have recognized work as, a series of discrete and interactive tasks requiring skill, dexterity and cooperation. Work took place in a shared space and time. An employee worked for a company during agreed-on predetermined hours and the process occurred in a consistent systematic "eight-to-five" day. Further, there were discrete parameters to work, as time "off the clock" was theirs. This expectation is vanishing for many of today's workers as the traditional eight-to-five "company man" is losing value (Kelly, 1999; Lipset & Ray, 1996).

Changes in the workplace and in society as discussed have contributed to a new cadre of problems and issues for today's workers and challenges to EAP professionals. The impact of the changed workplace on workers well being will be explored in five broad areas: (1) stress-related to the ever-evolving need for knowledge and education; (2) decreased opportunities and job security; (3) effects on family and individual roles in the family; (4) the differential impact of change on certain groups; and (5) other concerns.

EDUCATIONAL/SKILL REQUIREMENTS. The new technology as described requires entry level workers to know more in order to obtain entry level and well-paying jobs compared to the job market encountered a generation ago. Today's workers must bring many of the required skills to the job, as employers less frequently provide basic skills training (Burris, 1998; Chimel, 1998; Drucker, 2000).

For example, in 1962, a 24-year-old man returning from military service could realistically expect to be hired by any number of industrial firms and the company would train him in a skill (tire building, automobile assembly, etc.). Once proficient at the job, wages were respectable, stable, increased with seniority, and were secure given he stayed with the company.

The necessity that workers have requisite skills in technology began with the advent of the computer. Even though the use of computers is still in its early stages, workers skills have fallen behind employers needs. For instance, a 1994 Associated Press poll found that 36 percent of adults felt they lacked the knowledge necessary to keep up with technology, while others felt that they lacked the money (24%) or time (21%). Although, once the skills are obtained Americans workers generally feel positive about the new technology as it is seen as enhancing job performance (Lipset & Ray, 1996; Rocha & McCant, 1999).

EAP professionals can play a key role in providing support, goal-setting and esteem-building as workers grapple with the demand for greater skills and increased education. Many workers not prepared for the new work order may feel they have nothing to offer and are just "not good enough"(Blair, 2002).

JOB SECURITY AND ADVANCEMENT. If a person has the necessary skills and gets a "good" job, expectations for a secure future with one company are less likely. A new employee in 2002 can anticipate changing jobs more frequently, losing jobs due to downsizing or corporate failure, and that many of their skills will become obsolete due to the ever-changing technology. This is in large part due to the reality that many IT employers feel it is easier to replace workers whose skills become outdated (Clinton, 1997; Rothman, 2000). The EAP professional must be ready to deal with the issues faced by those workers who have and will experience challenges to their employment security (Burns, 1999; Lippman, 1999).

Promotion and advancement opportunities are eroding along with job mobility for many workers (Challenger, 1999; Frazee, 1997; Hodson, 2001). Requirement credentials (academic degrees, training, etc.) coupled with an increase in professional and managerial hiring from outside the organization has decreased the potential for "loyal workers" to receive in-house training or retraining, and/or promotion. This diminished prospect for promotion and mobility has frequently resulted in problems maintaining adequate worker motivation (Drucker, 2000; Rocha & McCant, 1999; Powers, 2000). Many employers are experimenting with processes such as quality control circles, worker participation experiments and EAP interventions at the group and individual levels to help offset the disillusionment resulting from decreased opportunities (Burns, 1999; Lippman, 1999).

Another issue that EAP professionals will face involves rejuvenating the enthusiasm of white-collar workers caught unprepared in corporate downsizing. Patterns associated with some of the layoffs in many companies are seen as having a long-term negative effect on employee motivation (London, 1996; Sheridan, 2000).

EFFECTS ON FAMILY. Families serve many purposes in our society such as, providing comfort, support and purpose in a person's life. In times of workplace transition, families are called on to ensure social cohesion. However, in times of fundamental cultural change, as currently experienced families are put under a great deal of stress adjusting to the changing demands of the new work order. Families historically provide the means of transmitting basic work values, skills and knowledge necessary to navigate the world of work to their children. Changes in the basic requirements of work and the way business views the world are impacting the family of today. For example, the traditional two-parent family is undergoing stress related to flex time and increased work demands placed on working parents. Furthermore, the makeup of families today takes on many different forms, such as single parent or dual employed families (Carnoy, 2000; Rosenberg, 2001)).

To better understand the dilemmas faced by today's workers consider the impact on families during the transition from an agrarian to an industrial-based economy. This was a time fraught with many social problems such as child labor abuse. However, to understand how this occurred is to look at how farming families passed on agricultural skills. These families typically required children at a very young age to learn the skills by accompanying parents into the fields. However, when this was attempted in factories, disastrous situations occurred including trauma related to some perceived loss in basic "family values." Eventually, the system of cooperative family work broke down in the industrial era and was replaced by what has come to be known as the nuclear family. The evolution from agrarian to nuclear family took many generations to develop passing through many stages of transition and adjustment. As a society, we will be faced with similar and evolving transition issues as work becomes more entrenched in information technology (Carnoy, 2000; Lipset & Ray, 1996; Spitze & Loscocco, 1999).

It is important to consider the impact of other social phenomena when we look at the family. Large numbers of women have rejected the burden of maintaining social norms and educating future generations. Smaller families enabled women to successfully enter the workplace and if desired reject the role of homemaker. Furthermore, in the last 30 years increasing numbers of women made the decision to "go it alone" as a single parent. Consequently, in today's workplace more and more single women are finding employment. For these women, the new work order is having a profound impact on their families. Working mothers in particular have felt the impact on their families. This often results from the changed demands in an IT economy resulting from "flexible" work schedules, modified work environments, and the expectation to excel in job productivity, performance, as well as a desire to be a good parent (Schroeder, 1999; Spitze & Loscocco, 1999).

DISCRIMINATION. The faces of American workers are also changing. Workers are more often women, less often white, and older. For example, as ethnic populations continue to grow it is anticipated they will make up the majority of the general population by 2050. Consequently, workplace changes will be more than technological but cultural. However, as minorities (African-Americans, Latinos, Asians, etc.), women, and persons who are older find jobs, discrimination persists.

Although these workers find employment, the jobs generally are those in the lower paying positions (Darity, Guilkey, & Winfrey, 1996; Staveteig & Wigton, 2001; Zarkin, Bray, & Karuntzos, 2001).

To better understand racism and sexism in the emerging workplaces, a major sociological/political factor compounding its effect should be addressed. Concurrent with the political and social movements of affirmative action occurring during the 1970s organizational restructuring also occurred. These changes resulted in the multitier organizational structure being replaced by a two-tier structure and also an increase in jobs in new areas, such as IT. The effect of company restructuring and increasing numbers of jobs helped to create a false atmosphere of social change. In hind site, the restructuring only hid the fact that the better opportunities available in the technologically-driven workplace employed primarily white men. This was due in large part to the reality that technological and educational opportunities had historically been more difficult for women and minorities to access. Therefore, in large numbers women and minorities were left without the requisite skills to enter the upper echelons of the new work order. Furthermore, the false perceptions of corporate responsiveness to mandated social change only served to thwart legal and social reforms targeted at the organizational level (Noyelle, 1987).

Polarization of the workplace which constricted the multitiered workplace, has served to amplified concerns of racism, sexism and ageism. Furthermore, the deemphasis on internal means of promotion more often has a negative impact on workers who are minorities or women (Gale, 2002; Thomas, 2001).

MINORITY WORKERS. Research efforts confirm the continued pervasiveness of racism in high-tech firms (Darity, Guilkey, & Winfrey, 1996; Thomas, 2001). The effects of racism and the ever-increasing diversity of the work force are discussed in more depth in a separate chapter of this text.

THE "AGEING" WORK FORCE. Today's labor market has also produced an intricate alteration in the generational/hierarchical dynamics of the workplace and related problems are being encountered. Managers, supervisors, etc. are younger while many workers seeking available jobs are older. This presents a formidable challenge to EAP professionals. As many issues are being faced by older workers: (1) the challenge of learning new ways of doing a job (i.e., working in multidisciplinary groups, etc.); (2) acquiring the new skills necessary to perform the job as currently required; (3) an increase in stress having to adjust to and accept intergenerational differences in communication, social behaviors, and work habits now pervading the workplace; and (4) understanding the realties of discrimination as it impacts older workers when dealing with younger, more powerful superiors (Douville, 2001; Taylor & Walker, 1998).

Another concern is skill obsolescence which results in many older workers not being offered training opportunities afforded many younger workers, due to supervisor stereotypes (Imel, 1996; Taylor & Walker, 1998). In a study of work force age demographics, Barth, McNaught, and Rizzi (1993) found 34 percent of managers surveyed report their companies spend little or no money training older employees, compared to 21 percent who report spending little or no money training workers under 35.

GENDER. As previously described, in the last 100 years of the industrial revolution families changed and many became single parent households, most often women. As the number of women in the work force approaches 50 percent, many are the primary providers for their families. The increase in the numbers of women rejecting the role of "homemaker" occurred just prior to the advent of high technology. This resulted in more educated women willing to work flexible schedules. Therefore, many women are and were willing to work under the new work "rules" and have been hired in great numbers in technical "support" positions (Jones, 2001).

Although more jobs have been available to women, ample documentation supports that gender stereotypes persist in the IT work place. These stereotypes view femininity as negating any high-level technical ability (Maume, 1999). The patterns of gender segregation at first glance appear to be changing when you see the increasing numbers of occupations providing support to comput-

er professionals. These jobs are much less gender segregated, (36 % women). However, the professional and managerial jobs remain predominately male (Maume, 1999). These support jobs offer women false hope for advancement and for many this has become the "glass ceiling "of the IT environment (Jones, 2001; Maume, 1999).

EAP counselors must be sensitive and skilled in dealing with issues of discrimination many women face and that they bring to sessions. However, issues of discrimination are not the only issues women employees encounter. Many women in the workplace are single, primary parents, and face multiple issues from outside the workplace that impact performance and job satisfaction. Consequently, issues of conflicting roles (family and employee) and abuse increasingly surface as primary presenting problems (Schroeder, 1999).

DOMESTIC VIOLENCE. Domestic violence is not confined to the home, it also invades the workplace. Often it is harassing telephone calls or stalking a woman in parking areas. Frequently, a former spouse or partner will attack a woman while she is working. This is a problem that cannot be ignored as the following FBI statistics emphasize:

- Abusive husbands and/or lovers harass 74 percent of employed battered women at work.
- Murder at work is the second leading cause of death on the job, but the No. 1 cause of occupational death for women. (Johnson & Indyik, 1999)

As more workers enter the work force who are not white males, the EAP professional must be skilled in working with persons who differ in ethnicity, culture, gender and lifestyle. In the future, the EAP professional can be assured they will be referred more diverse employees. Suffice it to say that EAP professionals must develop and become proficient in multicultural counseling techniques (Schroeder, 1999; Zarkin, Bray, & Karuntzos, 2001).

Other Issues

VIOLENCE IN THE WORKPLACE. The increasing incidence of violence, and incidents, such as September 11 has demonstrated the need for appropriate EAP interventions. Therefore, an entire chapter has been dedicated to crisis management in this text.

ELDER CARE. An average elderly person needs 18 years of some form of special care; 80 percent of that care is provided by family members (Administration on Aging, 2000), and many caregivers work. Caring for a dependent elderly family member, and successful job performance are at times competing demands for men, but more so for women. Women, have traditionally functioned in this role for aging parents. Yet unlike previous generations, today's women have more roles, and demands. Familial roles such as partners, homemakers, and mothers are more often coupled with roles of worker and as caregiving daughters to dependent parents. These women have often been described as being in the "sandwich generation," caught between caregiving for children and parents (Singleton, 2000).

CHILD CARE. A critical issue which often impacts productivity and which many workers, primarily women, struggle with is child care. Furthermore, as more families are dual career homes, concern for the care of dependent children often invades the workplace. It impacts job performance and time at work. When working with such workers it is important to remember the following:

- 75 percent of all mothers are employed
- 8.2 million preschool-age children have working mothers
- 18 million American children live in single-parent households (Michaels, 1997)

RETIREMENT PLANNING. Many aging Americans have grave concerns regarding their financial futures. Research suggests this is a valid concern as a substantial number of aging Americans are not adequately prepared financially to retire or leave the work force (Administration on Aging, 2000; Simon-Rusinowitz, 1999). There appears to be a variety of reasons for this lack of preparation, such as frequent changes in jobs, inconsistent contributions to retirement funds or a belief that Social Security would be adequate. Therefore, many workers will have inadequate funds available upon retirement (Rubin, White-Means, & Daniel, 2000; Thorson, 1999).

It should be noted this issue disproportionately impacts women and minority elderly populations due to insufficient employment histories (Silverstone, 1996). Minorities and women experience culture-specific constraints and barriers that affect career development (Marsella & Leong, 1995). Traditionally, they have been employed in lower paying, unskilled or semiskilled jobs and suffer from limited resources when compared to their white male counterparts. Consequently, many do and will rely on social security benefits as the sole resource when considering retirement (Darity, Builkey, Winfrey, 1996; Rappaport, 1998)

CONCLUSION

Advancements in technology are still evolving and offer for many a wide array of possibilities in their work lives. Many new and different issues can be anticipated as work continues to evolve. These are not known form our current vantage point. We have noted that the organization and approach to production has already undergone radical and fundamental changes. A new work order is developing, resulting in large part from the inherent intangibles of IT and a global economy. The business of business is now information, not tangible products. There is a marked change in demand skills and markets now have a global reach. The impact of technology has been and will continue to be evasive, it has affected fundamental aspects of life in some obvious and some subtle ways. These effects continue to alter the social fabric of our lives. We are just at the dawn of this new age and it will provide many disappointments and opportunities. It is not the worker who navigates these changes with excitement and skill who will challenge EAP professionals but those whose experience of change creates fear and anxiety.

POSTSCRIPT: In writing this chapter, we became overwhelmed at the extent of the changes which have occurred in the world of work in the last 20 years. It was a struggle organizing this chapter to capture all the factors, the magnitude of those factors and the interactive effect these changes have had on peoples' lives. We came to the conclusion this was not possible in the confines of one book chapter. Therefore, the reader is invited to explore the phenomena of change in the economy and work which has created an unstable workplace for many people. More importantly, we challenge the reader to understand that the

changes described also represent a fundamental alteration in how work and the world are seen. Indeed, EAP professionals must be prepared for the onslaught of problems related to these changes in work. To do an adequate job, it is imperative that she/he understands the extent of the transformation.

REFERENCES

Administration on Aging. (2000). AoA announces the availability of "a profile of older Americans, 2000." [On line]. Available http://www.aoa.dhhd.gov/.

Barth, M. C., McNaught, W., & Rizzi, P. H. (1993). Corporations and the aging workforce: In Mirvis, P. (Ed.) *Building the competitive workforce: Investing in human capital for corporate success.* American Association of Retired Persons.

Berman, J. M. (2001). Industry output and employment projections to 2010. *Labor Review, 124* (11), 39–56.

Blair, B. R. (2002) Consultative services: Providing added value to employers. *EAP Association: Exchange, 32* (2) 20–23.

Buhler, P. M. (2002). Survivors of organizational downsizing. *Supervision, 63* (1), 14–16.

Burns, J. (1999). For EAPs, corporations have become clients: rather than work strictly with employees, EAPs turn to organizational consulting. *Managed Healthcare, 9* (12) 46.

Burris, B. H. (1998) Computerization of the workplace. *Annual Review of Sociology, 24,* 141–57.

Carnoy, M. (2000). *Sustaining the new economy: Work, family and community in the information age.* New York: Russell Sage Foundation.

Challenger, J. (1999). There is no future for the workplace. *Public Management, 81* (2) , 20–23.

Chmiel, N. (1998). *Jobs technology and people.* New York: Routledge Publishers.

Clinton, A. (1997). Flexible labor: restructuring the American work force. *Monthly Labor Review, 120* (Aug.), 3–17.

Darity, W. A., Guilkey, D. K., & Winfrey, W. (1996). Explaining differences in economic performance among racial and ethnic groups in the USA: The data examined. *The American Journal of Economics and Sociology, 55,* 411–425.

Druker, P. F. (2000). The long view. *Training and Development, 54* (12), 27.

Frazee, V. (1997). Staffing services help workers upgrade

skills. *Workforce, 76* (Apr.), 21.

Galea S., Resnick H., Ahern J., Gold J., Bucuvalas M., Kilpatrick D., Stuber J., & Vlahov, D. (2002) Posttraumatic stress disorder in Manhattan, New York City, after the September 11th terrorist attacks. *Journal of Urban Health, 79* (3), 340–353.

Gale, S. F. (2002). Companies find EAPs can foster diversity. *Workforce, 81* (2), 66–69.

Johnson, P. R., & Indyik, J. (1999). Domestic abuse: The organizational benefits of assisting domestically abused employees. *Public Personnel Management, 28* (3), 365–374.

Jones, S. (2001). Silicon ceiling, glass ceiling for women in technology fields. *Crain's Chicago Business, 24* (46), 15–16.

Kelly, G. M. (2000) Employment and concepts of work in the new global economy. *International Labour Review, 139* (1), 5–32.

Lippman, H. (1999) This is not your father's EAP. *Business & Health, 17* (12), 42–49.

Lipset, S. M., & Ray, M. R., (1996) . Technology, work, and social change. *Journal of Labor Research, 17* (Fall), 613–626.

Logsdon, J. M., & Wood, D. J. Business citizenship: From domestic to global level of analysis. *Business Ethics Quarterly, 12* (2), 155–187.

London, M. (1996). Redeployment and continuous learning in the 21st century: Hard lessons and positive examples from the downsizing era. *Academy of Management Executive, 10* (Nov.), 67–79.

Marsella, A. J., & Leong, F. T. L. (1995). Cross-cultural issues in personality and career assessment. *Journal of Career Assessment, 3* (2), 202–218.

Metters, R., & Vargas, V. (2000). Organizing work in service firms. *Business Horizons, 43* (4), 23–32.

Michaels, B. (1997). Collaborating with a work-life consultant: Worker famiies. *HR Focus, 74* (Sept.), 7–8.

Murphey, D. D. (1999). An economic paradox? Displacement and polarization in a booming economy. *The Journal of Social, Political and Economic Studies, 24* (3), 349–371.

Nord, S. (1999). Sectoral productivity and the distribution of wages. *Industrial Relations.*

Powers, E. L. (2000). Employee loyalty in the new millennium. *Advanced Management Journal, 65* (3), 4–8.

Rappaport, A. M. (1998). Retirement security for women needs work. *National Underwriter* (Life and Health/Financial Services Edition), *102,* 39.

Reich, R. B. (1999). We are all third wayers now. American. *Prospect, 43* (Mar./Apr.), 46–51.

Rocha, C. J. (1999). Closing time: Workers' last call. *Forum for Applied Research and Public Policy, 14* (1), 65–68.

Rosenberg, L. F. (2001). Expanded services: More employers embracing EAPs. *Business Insurance, 35* (26), 10–16.

Rothman, H. K. (2000). What has work become? *Journal of Labor Research, 21* (3), 379–392.

Rubin, R. M., White-Means, S. I., & Daniel, L. M. (2000). Income distribution of older Americans. *Monthly Labor Review, 123* (11), 19–30.

Salzman, H., & Rosenthal, S. R. (1994). *Software by design.* New York: Oxford University Press.

Schroeder, S. (1999). JobWork/life: Managing the delicate balance. *Risk Management, 46* (8), 31–33.

Silverstone, B. (1996). Older people of tomorrow: A psychological profile. *The Gerontologist, 36* (1), 27–32.

Sheridan, J. H. (2000). Ready for the revolution? *Industry Week, 49* (2), 89–91

Simon-Rusinowitz, L. (1998). Future work and retirement needs: Policy experts and baby boomers express their views. (The baby boom at mid-life and beyond.) *American Society on Aging.* [On-line]. Available: http:iac.fcla.edu/.

Solomon, C. M. Stressed to the limit. *Workforce, 78* (9), 48.

Spitze, G., & Loscocco, K. (1999). Womens position in the household. *Quarterly Review of Economics and Finance, 39* (special issue) 647–661.

Staveteig, S., & Wigton, A. (2001). Racial and ethnic disparities: Key findings from the National Survey of American families.

Taylor, P., & Walker, A. (1998). Employers and older workers: Attitudes and employment. *Aging and Society, 18* (6), 641–658.

Thomson, A. (1999). Industry output and employment projections to 2008 employment outlook: 998–2008. *Monthly Labor Review, 122* (11), 33–50.

Thorson, J. A. (2000). *Aging in a changing society* (2nd edition). Philadelphia, PA: Brunner/Mazel, Inc.

Welty, G. (1997). For workers, high-tech can mean high anxiety. *Railway Age, 198* (Feb), 9.

Zarkin, G. A., Bray, J. W., & Karuntzos, G. T. (2001) The effect of an enhanced employee assistance program (EAP) intervention on EAP utilization. *Journal of Studies on Alcohol, 62* (3), 351–388.

Part VII

SELECTED SAMPLES

Chapter 27

IMPAIRED PROFESSIONALS: CURRENT CONCEPTS AND PROGRAM ELEMENTS

JOSEPH MOLEA

Here's the fellow who's been puzzling you.

(Alcoholics Anonymous, p. 23)

Any discussions of impaired professionals must include a review of the current brain-based understanding of addictive disorders. Today, most neuroscientists agree that the route of action, the final common pathway, if you will, of all mood-altering substances, including alcohol, is the mezzo limbic system of the brain.[1] The fact that not all individuals exposed to mood-altering substances become addicted points to an underlying neurochemical mechanism that predisposes certain individuals to addictive behavior. This assertion is supported by both the genetic research, the familial nature of addictive disorders, and the simple fact, known since the late 1930s, that the underlying problem of chemically dependant individuals is the dysphoric restlessness, irritability and discontent they experience prior to the relief found when ingesting a mood-altering substance.[2] This explains such seeming paradoxes as the progression of tolerance after abstinence and behavior states that lay between active use of the drug and recovery, such as the so-called "Dry Drunk" state and suicidality after abstinence is achieved.

When Bill Wilson, the author of the Alcoholics Anonymous text, described the "typical alcoholic" he selected adjectives that tended to the superlative. The typical alcoholic, he said, is a "fine fellow . . . perfectly sensible and well balanced . . . [with] special abilities, skills, and aptitudes . . . and a bright future," a list that could easily be used as the admission criteria for any professional school in

the nation.[3] The idea that professionals with graduate education and successful careers might fall around the median of the chemical dependency incidence curve, flies in the face of commonly held truisms about the disease of chemical dependence. Given an 18 percent lifetime incidence of chemical dependency (a conservative estimate), one wonders what people think these 43 million people are doing when they are not drinking or using drugs? This is a restatement of the Surgeon General's recent finding that 70 percent of all alcoholics are functional.[4] Estimates that about 3 percent of Americans will experience homelessness during their lifetime would seem to indicate that not all chemically addicted individuals are living under bridges.[5]

Premorbid vulnerabilities in chemically dependant individuals such as passivity and self-doubt, dependent personality configurations, and a pessimistic outlook match those found in many professionals. Overachieving, workaholic patterns also tend to predominate. Substance use, including tobacco, self-prescribing and self-treatment with prescription drugs (whether by writing illegal prescriptions, or by diverting medications from friends and family members), are all risk factors for chemical dependence in the professionals.[7] While debate still exists around G. Douglas Talbott's pioneering conceptualization of the special problems associated with addicted professionals, and, in specific, physicians, a careful review of the current state of the art will demonstrate the accuracy of his insight.[6] While much of this work was done in populations of health care professionals, in our experience the concept will generalize to all professionals, particularly licensed professionals. The hope is that this work will generalize further to all chemically dependent populations' given the high rate of success of such programs.

Behavioral Indicators

Detection of the professional with an alcohol or drug disorder is often delayed by the ability of the professional to protect his or her job performance at the expense of every other dimension of his or her life. The first realm to be affected by an addiction is family, followed by community, finance, spiritual and emotional health, physical health, and only then, job performance.[8] Still today, most providers view chemical dependency like passengers on the Titanic, viewing the surface problem and judging that disaster has been narrowly averted as the real devastation continues to churn away under the surface. Consequently, the great majority of dysfunction remains unidentified until late in the disease. By the time such an individual begins to ask for help, the disease is often well progressed and much has already been lost. Given the natural history of the disease, the Employee Assistance Program (EAP) professional must have a high index of suspicion for dependency and be willing to investigate suspicious behavior or refer the individual for a more formal evaluation even in circumstances that seem to have been adequately explained. The one salient fact, regardless of the plausibility of the alibi, will be the inappropriate or intemperate use of drugs or alcohol that has intruded into the workplace. Even the most flagrant abuser is loath to have this happen. The workplace is often the last bastion of sanity in the chaotic life of the addict.

A small amount of investigation will reveal a history of withdrawal from family activities, marital discord, extra-marital affairs associated with drug or alcohol use or occurring in places where drug and alcohol use is prominent. Embarrassing behavior at clubs or parties followed by DUI cita-

tion, legal problems, financial problems and other role discordant behavior will be evident. Changes in dress habits, personal hygiene, increasing medical complaints followed by medications seeking or self-prescribing, emotional crises, or unexplained illnesses will be noted. The work schedule of these individuals will often become disorganized allowing the individual to spend more time behind locked doors or will facilitate frequent absences from the office. The chemically dependant professional's work history will often include numerous job changes, frequent geographic relocations, unexplained time lapses between jobs, indefinite or vague letters of reference, and employment in one or more positions that are not appropriate to his or her qualifications. Finally, and most importantly for the vigilant EAP, decline in professional productivity will occur.[9] It is late-stage disease that leaves the professional poised for disaster. This is when the EAP will see him.

A Word about Disruptive Behavior in the Workplace

New onset disruptive behavior (however one defines it) is the herald sign of occult dependency. Recently, the Joint Commission on Hospital Accreditation (JCAHO) issued guidelines to hospital medical staffs outlining steps to be taken when the behavior of a physician falls outside accepted norms. Substance abuse or chemical dependence is identified in a large percentage of new-onset disruptive behavior.[10] As this scrutiny of here-to-for acceptable (if unpleasant) behavior becomes the norm, more individuals will begin to be evaluated for erratic behavior before the more classic signs of chemical dependency (alcohol on the breath, Monday morning absences) intrude into the workplace. This will place a greater responsibility on the EAP to identify soft signs of chemical addiction and will demand earlier referral to an addiction professional for formal evaluation and treatment. Interested parties are referred to the evolving literature of this controversial topic, an example of which can be found in an article by this author recently published by the American College of Physician Executives.[11]

Intervention

Anosognosia, a fancy name for denial, is an almost pathopneumonic sign of chemical dependency and communicates more effectively the neurologic character of the signs and symptoms of chemical dependency. Ignoring the obvious problem serves to absolve the addict of personal accountability through rationalization and justification of his or her using on the conscious level, but fills him or her with guilt, shame, and remorse on an unconscious level. Paradoxically, the individual blames his or her circumstances on others by projecting these uncomfortable emotions on those around him. Since the advent of drug-free workplace policy, this lack of ability to self-report a problem with chemical addiction compensated for in many industries by the use of random and for-cause urine drug screening. Most health care and legal professionals, as well as many other licensed individuals, do not adhere to such policies as Part 42 CFR of the Code of Federal Regulations opting for self-regulation. Without the benefit of urine drug screening in the workplace, most professionals find themselves the subject of an intervention of some sort, either by the family, the employer, a licensure agency, or a combination of the three, as a result of behavioral changes or indirect signs of chemical addiction.

Intervention is a procedure that occurs before referral for a chemical dependency evaluation. Intervention is necessary when an individual is either unaware of his or her addiction or when he or she is otherwise unable to recognize the seriousness of the disease. It is a specialized therapeutic technique that when properly administered may break through the dense denial of the professional and allow him or her to avoid the otherwise inevitable "bottom" of the alcoholic. If improperly conducted, however, it may lead to death.[12] This topic is too detailed to elaborate here, but interested parties are encouraged to review the guidelines elaborated by the Talbott et al. 1982 article on the subject.[13] The EAP may or may not be a participant in such an intervention, but should be aware of the circumstances that result in the client referral.

Assessment

Experienced interventionists, most state medical societies, and many state medical licensing boards recommend a comprehensive assessment in a specified treatment facility to determine the extent of the impaired physician's illness and treatment needs. The initial assessment has been found to be a very effective goal of intervention. This allows the intervention team to emphasize that they want the troubled professional to see an expert who will define the problem in an objective manner after which time, the nature of treatment, if any, will be recommended. The nature of the process–given the nature of denial and the licensure and legal implications of chemical dependency in professionals–is, by necessity, a forensic endeavor. In our institution, we have adapted the process of Forensic Distortional Analysis to identify deceptive responses with the utilization of standard objective mental health testing, multiple interviews in varying environments, and collateral contacts with individuals who have firsthand knowledge about the client's drug and alcohol use.[14] This information is then used to continue the intervention process by confronting the individual with their deceptive responses, to make a diagnosis, and to provide the employer with an objective opinion, if not of the individual's problems, of their veracity. These measures, when combined with biochemical studies, physical examination, and observation for delayed signs of withdrawal form a very effective device for identification of occult substance abuse and chemical dependency.

Treatment

The need for specialized treatment for chemically dependent health care professionals has been a major subject of discussion for some time. Controlled, large-scale evaluation studies have shown that abstinence-based treatment methods are indeed effective.[15] Treatment of the impaired professionals has many special features that combine the highest clinical standards and serve as a benchmark for the field of addiction medicine and the chemical dependence treatment field in general. Our experience indicates that most chemically dependent health care professionals benefit from a strong group setting both in the initial treatment process and in long-term aftercare. The addicted professional needs not only a peer-group setting of other patients with the same disease process, but also one combining fellow professionals. This helps to confront more effectively and empathetically the grandiosity, defensiveness, and denial that are typically seen in professionals.[16] The goal of treatment should be abstinence from alcohol and other psychoactive substance and recovery from associated medical and psychiatric disorders. Focusing as it does on the spiritual aspect of human perception and experience, recovery in general, and 12-step notions of recovery in particular, go beyond objective indicators to quality of life issues that may include issues of job satisfaction and a renewed focus on life outside of the workplace. The EAP should be prepared to discuss such issues with recovering professionals and support treatment recommendations that may include reduced or limited work week, change of job roles or status, or even career counseling and vocational rehabilitation.

Treatment centers that specialize in the care of impaired physicians generally offer levels of care that adhere to the American Society of Addiction Medicine Patient Placement Criteria.[17] This instrument is design to assist clinicians and third-party payers to standardize the placement of individuals in the appropriate level of care based on justifiable criteria. It is an interesting side note that most licensed professionals will code at a level III-5 (extended outpatient treatment while living in a therapeutic community) due to density of denial, access to drug of choice, treatment resistance, or having a work or home environment that is hostile to recovery.[18] Many of these individuals will suffer comorbid conditions that paradoxically help them succeed in some professional capacity (e.g., the flamboyant marketing executive with an undiagnosed bipolar disorder, the demanding, narcissistic neurosurgeon, or the antisocial—but successful—attorney). While some impaired physicians have attained true sobriety through intense and focused long-term participation in traditional outpatient treatment or even real engagement in Alcoholics Anonymous, or other recovery programs, the most consistently successful individuals engage in extended outpatient programs of 90 to 120 days while engaged in a therapeutic community. Given the risk to licensure and career and the tendency of boards and the like to adopt a "one strike and you're out" policy, the risk of relapse, even one that falls into the category of a "slip" demands an approach that contains such risk within the context of the treatment process.

The treatment team should be experienced in dealing with impaired professionals, and be knowledgeable about the legal and professional licensure issues that confront these individuals. We have found this so important that our team includes a full-time attorney to case manage legal issues for the large number of clients with legal issues and a liaison officer to deal directly with boards, monitors, and EAPs to assure that the treatment process addresses problems apparent to all the stakeholders involved thus reducing and, in most cases, eliminating re-entry problems. Listed below are the elements of a successful treatment experience that have been enumerated in the Textbook of Addiction Medicine of the American Society of Addiction Medicine in the Section dealing with drug and alcohol use in the workplace:[19]

1. *Understanding and Acceptance of the Disease Concept of Addiction.* Simply stated, this involves embracing the biopsychosocial nature of the disease of chemical dependency.

2. *Identification of Triggers.* This involves an understanding of the psychology of craving which involves the capacity of mood-altering substances to manifest conditioned responses in addicted individuals.

3. *Development of Nonchemical Coping Mechanisms.* This involves identification of stressful environments and activities and finding ways to avoid or alter the nature of such activities. Ironically, use of drugs and alcohol will rarely play a part in such activities, but will be reserved for the periods of relative boredom between such activities when the addict is attempting to deal with the anxiety of anticipation before the next stressful encounter.

4. *Changing Priorities to Achieve a Balanced Lifestyle.* Many professionals place their careers as the first priorities in their lives. Concepts such as

workaholism and perfectionism have grown out of the popular understanding of the successful professional. Such behaviors may become the trigger mentioned above. The impaired professionals must realize that recovery and growth come first and must include considerations of family and leisure concerns. Achieving a stable recovery involves the balance of these elements.

5. *Family Involvement in the Treatment Process.* Family involvement is critical to the diagnostic, treatment, and recovery process. Often a spouse may be at odds with the treatment process if the fear of job loss or career damage supercedes the concern for the addict. The family must be guided from a codependent-enabling stance to an acceptance of the disease concept for treatment to be successful.

6. *Involvement in Mutual Help Groups.* The merits of Twelve Step groups during and after treatment are well established. Recently, other programs have surfaced that shift the focus from a spiritual conception of the psychic change that occurs in recovery to a focused change of thought patterns. The success of such programs is not known.

7. *Peer-Oriented Therapy.* The overidentification that often occurs within professionals groups as a hedge against increasing distress and dwindling self-esteem can be used to enhance treatment by participation in group therapy with exclusively other professional. Such groups can be profession–specific (e.g., groups for doctors or attorneys) or, a combination. The important factor is that the groups are exclusive to professionals.

Aftercare/Monitoring

Because substance abuse is a chronic illness, treatment is but the beginning of the recovery process. Most treatment will involve structured aftercare (continuing care) programs that allow the patient to continue to work on issues identified in treatment after discharge. Most professionals see aftercare as an imposition curtailing as it does the ability to work late and "catch up" on work lost in treatment. Such hostile reactions are common in

early recovery, however, when aftercare is presented as a legal, licensing, or employment requirement, the degree of compliance, acceptance and gratitude usually improves. The planning of aftercare and monitoring should begin on the first day of treatment and involve the family and all other support systems of the recovering professional.[20]

Monitoring is an outgrowth of drug-free workplace policy and, in the licensed professions, is a modification of probationary requirements that demands access to body fluids, and observation of behavior as a assurance of the licensees ability to practice his or her profession with reasonable skill and safety. As such, these requirements seemed arbitrary, however. Studies have shown that those monitored for five years saw a drop of relapse rates to 20 percent, about that seen with other chronic illnesses.[21] In many states, physicians are expected to participate in their state medical society-sponsored physicians' health program. These programs have a dual function: to protect the public from the impaired physician and to help the impaired individual achieve recovery. Such groups have reported Recovery rates from 80–90 percent leading some to contend that physicians have better outcomes with the general population when long-term aftercare and monitoring are in place.[22] Such success argues for an expansion of such monitoring for other professionals.

Reentry

Reentry is a treatment issue that maybe addressed at any number of points within the treatment process. If strict monitoring is in place and evaluators have found a pattern of abuse rather than dependency, the client may be returned to the workplace during outpatient treatment or psychoeducation. Even in specialized, professional specific treatment with individuals residing in therapeutic communities, it is possible to return professionals to the workplace as an exercise to assess their ability to cope with workplace stress. There are also cases where individuals no longer meet the criteria for active treatment, but are still not ready to reenter the workplace in their former capacity. Good examples of this prin-

ciple include the anesthesiologist or nurse anes-
thetist in treatment for a narcotics addiction, or the
restaurateur who managed the operation from
behind the bar. Such individuals should be
reassessed at regular intervals to determine their
ability to return to the workplace. Most will undergo successful reentry within two years of adequate
treatment. Monitors and continuing care
providers should be prepared to aid in vocational
rehabilitation early to allow the individual to
avoid a mindset based on the notion of disability.[23]

Contracts signed with treatment centers,
employers, professional monitors, or even family
members have been effective in focusing the
recovering person on Twelve Step community
resources, personal spiritual development, and
family therapy. The possibility of relapse should
be recognized in such documents and outline an
approach to relapse that avoids assigning blame to
the individual and provides for action to be taken
should such a circumstance occur.

SUMMARY

Despite all of the advantages afforded professionals of early detection and specialized treatment promising better outcomes, it must be
remembered that chemical dependence is a chronically relapsing disease that can be controlled but
not cured. Current brain-based understanding of

the disease process may provide medicinal interventions or even genetic alteration as an ultimate
solution, but today, adequate control leading to a
productive, happy life is available for all that care
to avail themselves of it.

REFERENCES

1. Brick J., & Erickson C. K. (1998). *Drugs, the Brain, and Behavior: The pharmacology of abuse and depend-ence.* Haworth Press. pp. 180–181.
2. Alcoholics Anonymous, 3rd Edition, 1976, Alcoholics Anonymous World Services, Inc. pp. 21–22.
3. Alcoholics Anonymous, 3rd Edition, 1976, Alcoholics Anonymous World Services, Inc. pp. xxvi–xxvii
4. U.S. Department of Health and Human Services. Mental health: A report of the Surgeon General. Rockville, MD: *U.S. Department of Health and Human Services, Substance Abuse and Mental Health Services Administration,* Center for Mental Health Services, National Institutes of Health, National Institutes of Mental Health, 1999.
5. U.S. Conference of Mayors. "A Status Report on Hunger and Homelessness in America's Cities: 1998." U.S. Conference of Mayors, 1620 Eye St., NW, 4th Floor, Washington, DC, 20006–4005, 202/293-7330.
6. Talbott, G. D., & Benson, E. B. (1980). Impaired Physicians: The dilemmas of Identification. *Post-grad. Med., 68,* 56–64.
7. Vaillant, G. E., Soborale, N., & McArthur, C. (1992). Some psychological vulnerabilities of physi-cians. *The New England Journal of Medicine, 287,* 372–375.
8. Bissel, L., & Haberman, P. *Alcoholism in the profes-sions.* New York, NY: Oxford University Press, 1984, pp. 216–234.
9. Talbot G. D., Gallegos, K. V., & Angres, D. H. Impairment and recovery in physician and other health professionals, principals of addiction medi-cine, 2ed Editions, ASAM, 1998, p. 1271.
10. Molea, J. Managing disruptive physicians. *Healthcare Executive,* ACHE May/June 2001, pp. 68–69.
11. Molea, J. Dr. Jekyll./Dr. Hyde: Managing the dis-ruptive physician. *Click On-line Journal,* ACPE, March, 2001.
12. Talbot G. D., & Gallegos, K. (1990). Intervention with Health Professionals. *Addiction & Recovery, 10* (3), 13–16.
13. Talbott, G. D. (1982). The impaired physician and intervention: A key to recovery. *J. Fla. Med. Assoc., 69,* 793–797.
14. Molea, J. Detecting deception in evaluation and

assessment of substance abuse and dependency. Paper Presentation, *International Conference on Physicians Health,* American Medical Association, April, 1, 2000.

15. Vaillant G., & Clark W. et al. Prospective study of alcoholism treatment. *Am. J. of Med.* 1983, *75,* 455–463.

16. Talbott G., & Martin C. Treating impaired physicians: Fourteen keys to success. *Virginia Medical Journal,* 1986, *113,* 95–99.

17. Mee-Lee, Shulman, & Gartner. "Patient placement criteria for the treatment of psychoactive substance use disorders," 2ed Edition, 1996, American Society of Addiction Medicine.

18. Molea, J. Special modifiers to increase accuracy of the ASAM adult patient placement criteria for the for the treatment of psychoactive substance use disorders, 2ed Edition. Paper Presentation, *International Conference on Physicians Health,* American Medical Association, April, 1, 2000.

19. Talbot G. D., Gallegos, K. V., & Angres, D. H. Impairment and recovery in Physician and Other Health Professionals. *Principals of Addiction Medicine,* 2ed Edition, ASAM, 1998 pp. 1270–1271.

20. Gorski, T. (1986). *Staying sober: A guide for relapse prevention.* Independent Press.

21. George E. Vaillant, M.D. A long-term follow-up of male alcohol abuse. *Archives of General Psychiatry,* March 1996, pp. 243–249.

22. Reading, E. (1992). Nine-year experience with chemically dependent physicians: The New Jersey Experience. *Maryland Medical Journal, 41,* 325–329.

23. Harrington, R. et al. (1982). Treating Substance-use Disorders among Physicians. *Journal of the American Medical Association,* pp. 2253–2257.

Chapter 28

THE BAR AND THE BAR

RICHARD E. GENTRY

The primary concerns of state Bar Associations are protection of the public from impaired conduct and protection of the integrity of the court system. As officers of the court, judges, clerks, and other court and professional personnel must be able to rely upon the representations of attorneys. Attorneys handle funds without daily scrutiny and to a large extent, the future of many members of the public.

Although drug/alcohol addictions are medical problems affecting numerous individual members of the Bar, until quite recently, state Bar Associations viewed addiction only in its regulatory role. Therefore prevention, intervention, supervision, and aftercare were not within the scope of lawyers' regulation. In the past, attorneys who engaged in inappropriate conduct due to the addiction process, have been suspended or disbarred, and no measures were taken to reach the source of the conduct.

Attorneys and Bar Associations have always been leery of looking too deeply into their fellow attorneys' private lives. Merely "accusing" someone of being addicted could result in slander actions.

However, most state Bar Associations insure their members' escrowed funds. This self-interest has led to prevention efforts, which try to avert actions requiring draconian punishments. In the State of Washington the Bar's prevention measures are supervised by the self-insurance fund. The prevention measures may include education, a hot line, referral network, or actual intervention.

The education efforts routinely include information about addiction as a disease, symptoms and the state Bar's attitude. This information is published in state Bar journals, newspapers and local Bar publications. The state Bar's attitude about addiction seriously affects the willingness of its members to admit addiction prior to violating one of the rules. If the Bar is supportive, the result will be a better attitude about reporting impaired attorneys prior to disaster, or as is rarely the case, self-reporting.

In the 1970s the only mechanism for reporting impaired conduct was after noticeable misconduct occurred. Showing up drunk in court was not always reported, as sometimes it affected no one adversely; missed court dates were rescheduled. A simple denial was taken at face value. Once the disease had begun its active deterioration phase, local Bar committees simply waited for disaster to strike, then they stepped in to prevent further abuse of the public.

With the advent of the 1980s, programs such as California's "Other Bar," Florida's "Impaired Attorneys' Program," and others were instituted. These programs go into the area of referral prior to misconduct. Basically, the systems call for confidential peer referral, followed by an investigation by the appropriate persons. With the well-justified assumption that lawyers are litigious, these are nonprofit corporations separate from the Bar itself.

One state has all attorneys arrested for driving while intoxicated referred directly by the police agency. The arrest process is generally a good time

Note: This chapter is reprinted from *Employee Assistance Programs: A Basic Text* (1988) with permission of the author, the book's editors (Dickman, Emener, & Hutchison, Jr.), and the publisher (Charles C Thomas, Publisher, Ltd.).

for intervention, as denial is significantly lowered. In all other states outside of discipline, referral is a casual process in which the impaired attorney will be fortunate if referred by friends or other compatriots prior to discipline.

Intervention on nondisciplined attorneys takes great skill and patience. Attorneys are trained in avoidance, debate, cross-examination, and verbal self-defense. In my experience it is the brave intervenor who comes out of the intervention understanding why he impugned the integrity of this attorney. Preparation must be exhaustive, facts presented (under the Johnson model) must be nonarguable, and the intervention site chosen to minimize avoidance techniques.

The Florida Bar utilizes one full-time intervenor and should expand in 1987–88 to include several part-time assistants. The response from Bar members has been appropriate and helpful, although there is a long way to go before acceptance is total. Currently the Bar's intervenor confronts the member and refers for assessment by the appropriate agency. The member then enters into a private contract with the Impaired Attorney Program, which states what the member will do to prevent further drug/alcohol abuse.

Normally an addicted attorney will have come to the attention of the regulatory process prior to intervention. Impairment does not constitute a defense for lawyer misconduct, although "voluntary" assessment and treatment will mitigate punishment. The Florida Supreme Court has recognized that a lawyer has a better chance at recovery, and any restitution to clients (unearned fees, missing funds, etc.) be paid by the attorneys on probation rather than while suspended or disbarred.

It is important that an individual attorney take responsibility for his actions while addicted and that he/she will be given a chance to make other victims of his/her disease whole. Any other course of conduct would breach the duty of the Bar to protect the public.

Most state Bar Associations are currently developing programs for detection and treatment of drug-impaired attorneys within the framework of peer reporting. A better approach would be through a statewide "Employee Assistance Program" which would direct education and prevention efforts to the home environment where the effects are noticeable prior to on the job.

Attorneys develop a thick skin and often do not identify clients' problems with their own. A family is in a better position to see developing problems, and if they could solve the problem without adversely affecting the breadwinner, they should be given the chance.

There are currently no programs to reach the families of attorneys for earlier detection. By the time the referral process has begun, the family denial is a necessary adjunct to family survival and the walls are effectively erected.

Chapter 29

PROFESSIONAL SPORTS AND EMPLOYEE ASSISTANCE PROGRAMS

FRED DICKMAN and BEN HAYES

This chapter is designed to show how an Employee Assistance Program can be effective throughout the system of a Professional Sports organization. The example used is the minor league system of a professional baseball club. The program has been in operation about four years.

The baseball organization used as a model has teams of various levels located in seven different locations and comprises approximately two hundred players, managers, coaches, and trainers.

The chapter's intent is to explain how and why the EAP was begun, to trace the development over four years, to describe the kinds of issues brought to the EAP for assessment, counseling, and follow-up and to discuss its evolution or utilization rate.

History

Minor league organizations have not been constrained by labor/ management contract from performing drug testing on its personnel. Consequently, the organization discussed decided a little over four years ago that players under contract with the organization would be drug free. Tests were mandatory and given to all personnel universally. This was done during spring training when all personnel were together. Out of 200 persons tested, 12 (or 6%) were positive. Consistent with the club's policy, an evaluator was called to assess each of the 12 persons, so as to determine what treatment was needed if any. Out of these evaluations it became evident that problems other than drugs existed in most cases and, in those cases, general counseling was recommended. Testing was done several other times during that season and, where a positive was found, the same result was found. A few needed substance abuse counseling; most needed and wanted assistance for other problems; problems such as performance anxiety, general stress, family issues, life-style stress, etc.

At the next spring training, in a general all-day session and small seminars, more was done than drug testing, and alcohol and other drug education. Topics such as handling pressure, performance anxiety, and family relationships were offered with an enthusiastic response. Managers, coaches, and trainers were given special seminars on identifying the "troubled" player and players performing below their ability. During that season, a "hot line" was installed for persons to call collect to get help for a problem or a feeling. Management could and did call for the EAP counselor to come to that city to see a specific player. Spring training instruction as to lifestyle and psychological issues has gotten bigger and alcohol and other drug use has gotten less attention. At the last drug testing, only four were identified, and total positives continue to be less and less. Either the message has gotten across or use is down even among the (each year) new players. The average of 2–3 percent is far less than the general population. Spring training EAP sessions have gotten more elaborate with national speakers on topics of inter-

Note: This chapter is reprinted from *Employee Assistance Programs: A Basic Text* (1988) with permission of the author, the book's editors (Dickman, Emener, & Hutchison, Jr.), and the publisher (Charles C Thomas, Publisher, Ltd.).

est chosen by the players. The EAP counselor goes on three to four day trips to each city and his time is used confidentially by the players and managers, whom coaches and trainers refer freely.

Issues Brought to the EAP

The most frequent concerns brought to EAP counseling/assessment session were the following:

1. **Insomnia:** A surprising finding (but logical when thought about) was that a considerable number of players had trouble going to sleep. This was not due to going out and staying out for long hours after the game. The great majority of players try to go to sleep reasonably soon after the game, especially on the road, but tend to toss and turn. It is difficult to stop obsessing about the game whether mistakes were made or success enjoyed. An attempt was made to teach relaxation techniques and for those who came for a session (or sessions) with this problem a tape was made and sent to him with relaxation on one side and visualization (for either a hitter or a pitcher) on the other.

2. **Enhancing Performance:** Players came with a desire to utilize visualization to enhance concentration, focus, relaxation, and to "hold" the ball or "slow" the ball through mind control. Many athletes have the sense of being so grounded at times that everything seems in slow motion. Other times they have a sense of time acceleration and play seems actually faster than reality. Techniques of visualization often assist in more often capturing the former state.

3. **Family Problems:** Relationships: parents, wives, or girlfriends were a concern. Some were counseled and referred to family service centers if severe. These young people have relationships back home and when they are away, they worry. Then too, some are married and long road trips put a severe strain on the marriage. The lifestyle involving games every night, sometimes up to midnight, takes a special kind of tolerance and understanding to survive a marital or any other close relationship.

4. **Patience:** Many players, especially in the lower leagues, have trouble waiting for a chance to play. This entails learning patience, developing trust that they will be given a chance, dealing with resentment, keeping a positive attitude about themselves, and continuing to work hard in practice.

5. **Anxiety:** Believing in themselves, staying too much in the (immediate) past or future, feeling "light" or "not here" are problems of deeper, nonperceived anxiety. Practice in proper breathing, relaxation, and grounding appeared to help. However, when a self-image problem clearly created a marked discrepancy between ability and function, a referral to a psychologist for weekly sessions was in order.

6. **Lifestyle Problems:** There is a temptation to sleep until noon or beyond. Players don't have to report for pregame practice until 2:30 p.m. The game is over around 10:00 p.m. unless it's a double header. Then midnight or later is the average. Players who can get to sleep soon after the game and get up at least by midmorning usually feel less sluggish. Diet is another problem in this lifestyle. Past 11 or 12 p.m. only fast food places are open. Those who learn to keep fruit around and find some way to balance diets fare much better in the long run. Turning this around is not easy but worth it to the dedicated players.

7. **Substance Abuse Issues:** This part of the lifestyle requires special attention, more by management and the EAP philosophy (to assist players reach their potential), than the players themselves. While drug use is not to be permitted, and checks are made, drinking is an accepted part of the lifestyle. Hence, there is apt to be more denial and enabling than attentive caring confrontation and intervention. Some players are concerned and resist peer pressure. The majority do not. The effects of overuse, abuse, and alcohol's effect on the nervous system have to be addressed in workshops, management training, and in counseling sessions. It is especially an appropriate issue when the problem is underperforming or performance associated with undue anxiety.

Mini-Workshops

Opportunity is given on road trips to present thirty-minute workshops each day in the clubhouse. These elaborated on spring training workshop themes in addition to problems learned about during the formal and informal sessions.

Among the topics were:
1. "Performance Anxiety"
2. "Relaxation Training"
3. "Insomnia–Causes and Remedies"
4. "Diet"
5. "Thinking Positive–Rational Emotive Therapy"
6. "Being in the Now"
7. "Learn From, Rather than Ruminate Past Mistakes"
8. "Being Grounded–Breathing, Listening, to Your Body"
9. "Visualization–Making the ball bigger and slower for the hitters; the reverse for the pitchers"
10. "Sitting on the Bench and Still Being Involved"

Informal Counseling Sessions

During the three-to-four-day team visitation, the EAP counselor/assessor had an opportunity to just "be around" during practice and the game, in the dugout or bullpen during a game, and going for the late meal after the game with several players and/or managers. These periods provided the opportunity for helpful contacts and even short counseling encounters.

1986 Statistics

During spring training and the three to four day trips to various sites, the following statistics were accumulated for the 1986 season:
1. **Formal Interviews:** Twenty-one persons made formal appointments about various issues (discussed later in the report). These persons were seen in a clubhouse office; the contractor's motel room; over lunch, dinner or coffee/tea; or isolated locales on the practice field.
2. **Informal Contacts:**
   (a) Five to ten-minute sessions were possible behind the batting cage during practice, in the dugout just before a game, visiting the bullpen during a game, between practice and dressing for the game, running/jogging in the mornings from the on-the-road-motel, and sitting by the pool at the motel from 11:00 a.m. to 1:00 p.m. It is difficult to be accurate about the number of these contacts, but a conservative estimate is fifty.
   (n) After the game, suppers with managers, workers, and trainers were enjoyed at every visited locale. These were found to be extremely helpful in getting better acquainted with these gentlemen and a more in-depth perspective of the problems, both general and specific. As an aside, each person's grasp of the emotional aspect of the players was greatly admired.

Evaluation

The ultimate evaluation, of course, is how well a player does in relation to his ability. Some work is being done on this aspect of evaluation but the results will be long term. Some players who entered the program are already in the major leagues, but not enough evidence exists to infer the EAP program was a significant variable.

Another means of evaluation is utilization rate. So far, 90 persons have entered the EAP program for at least one session. This is nearly a 50 percent utilization rate taken at face value of 180 plus players. Adjusting this down for trades, new players from the draft, releases and trades to other organizations the utilization rate is approximately 30 percent. This type interest alone demonstrates the value of an EAP program for a minor league organization and maybe to all other sports organizations as well.

Chapter 30

GOVERNMENT AND THE UTILIZATION OF EMPLOYEE ASSISTANCE

JOHN L. DALY

The need for employee assistance programs (EAPs) and innovative mental health interventions in American government never have been more critical than it is today. Frequently, we read newspaper accounts and hear radio and television stories of public service gone awry. This is due partially to the stressful nature of work performed by public servants. For example, law enforcement personnel often encounter high stress and unpredictability in their work. Firefighters experience second thoughts about the handling of rescues, especially when loss of life results. Teachers and public health nurses increasingly are confronting violent encounters with those they are expected to serve. Social workers face threats of physical, mental and emotional burnout resulting from the heavy caseload demands they must manage. The recent incidents of domestic violence committed in the summer of 2002 by Special Operations soldiers stationed at Fort Bragg, North Carolina amplified the adverse impact that work in the public's service can have on one's family life due to immensely stressful work environments (Starr, 2002). In this instance, five murders occurred in a matter of weeks in military families stationed at Fort Bragg following the return of soldiers from combat duty in Afghanistan.

The pressures of work also can have detrimental impact on an employee's work commitment. Recently released research by Paul Light of the Brookings Institution reflects this concern. His research points out that an increasing number of federal employees are reporting that they are motivated primarily by a paycheck (even after September 11, 2001) more than they are by per-

forming work that benefits society. Today, 41 percent of federal respondents report pay as their most influential motivating factor. By comparison, 31 percent of the federal employees respondents queried during last year's survey (conducted in February-March 2001) indicated that their paychecks (as opposed to the work itself) were the most significant motivational factor (Miller, 2002).

Citizens often ask, "What is wrong with our government?" and "Why can't government (and its employees) perform more effectively like businesses do?" following highly adverse outcomes where public service personnel are involved. In part, answers to these questions are basic–stress induced environments (whether related to stressful jobs or family complications) ultimately result in diminished performance outcomes. Government employees, however, do not hold a monopoly on stressful work, but the nature of public service is fundamentally different from business.

Public servants operate in a context that is often more complex and stress-laden than in the private sector. Public servants at all levels and in all sectors work primarily in the public's interest. We expect more from our public servants, even though they do not always deliver results to our satisfaction. We also scrutinize public employees' actions and behaviors more closely, because they serve as the guardians of our tax dollars and have an obligation to act in the public's trust for their citizenry's best interest.

Two premises set the foundation for discussion regarding why employee assistance initiatives are so critical to government's success and its employees well being. The first premise–government differs from business—can result in an increased need for EAPs and requires greater vigilance on the part of human resources systems to remain attentive to a broad variety of employee-related problems. The second key premise—that performance outcomes often hinge on a healthy public work force—suggests that governments that discount the benefits of employee assistance programs often pay the price in other ways, including: higher employee turnover, lower work productivity, increased litigation, declining commitment to public service, and a loss of faith among the general public in the value of, and need for public service.

EAPs in the Context of Government

Three critical factors distinguish government operations from those in business. Functionally, organizations in both sectors (i.e., public and private) do the same things (i.e., plan, organization, staff, and control). Where the difference between business and government occurs is in the context that they operate in and the nature of the goals, objectives and missions they seek to accomplish. Many organizational behavioralists, including this author, believe that work in government settings is more challenging, and at times more frustrating, because of the context within which it operates. Three contextual distinctions, and their impact on EAP practices, are discussed below.

Distinction 1: Government's Increasing Role as Interdependent Service Provider

American government historically has existed to provide public goods and services to identified clients (e.g., citizens, other public agencies, qualified clientele). Traditionally, public organizations were granted sole authority and control over how, when, and by whom services would be provided. In return for being granted significant discretionary power over service delivery, public agencies were expected to act in the public's best interest, regardless of implementation costs or fiscal consequences on agency's resources.

Kettl notes that the domain of American public administration has radically changed in recent years. He stated that, "It is virtually impossible to identify any public program that a single government agency can manage on its own without relying on some partnership with other public agencies or private or nonprofit organization (1996)." Agency initiatives today require public managers to seek actively more insights and information from multiple stakeholders (often with conflicting goals and objectives) prior to public programs and policies implementation. Increasing shared power over agency actions typically slows the implementation process. This fosters the perception that government cannot make decisions in a timely fashion. It places public managers in highly stressful "no win" scenarios. They can act quickly, on partial information, thereby creating resentment from some stakeholders' interest excluded from the decision-making process. Or, they can act more deliberately, seeking broader input, thereby creating the general perception of being lethargic and incapable of action.

Private enterprise operates in a more "closed" decision-making structure. Businesses, through executive decision making, act quickly based on external feedback (e.g., a market analysis) to maximize their profit potential or market penetration. Likewise, consumers (often) have choices about whom to purchase goods or services from within the open marketplace. Individuals displeased with a vendor's product or service can choose to go elsewhere. Likewise, under most circumstances, businesses can decide to pull out of a market. Public agencies cannot easily dismiss their obligations to the public because of legal mandates. Whom can citizens turn to when their homes are on fire, other than their local fire department? Limitations of choice for citizens being served make it all the more critical that those public servants maintain the highest of caliber mental and physical well being. Because public agencies (realistically) cannot pull "out of the marketplace," government employees ethically must respond to their clients' demands even when resources are scarce. As noted, these workers also face increasing pressures to share power and control over how policies are shaped, implemented and distributed among a variety of clientele interests and needs. These circumstances result in higher stress levels for those acting in the public's interest.

Distinction 2: Constraints of the Civil Service Systems

Government also differs from business in its ability to terminate poorly performing employees. In business, especially in nonunion environments, individuals work on an "at will" basis. "At will" employment means that the employer can terminate employee "at will" (i.e., at any time) when business needs necessitate this action.

The "at will" concept provides employers the leverage needed to terminate redundant or unproductive employees. However, as McAfee and Champagne (1994) noted, "the legislatures and courts in several states have established what amount to exceptions to the at-will employment rule." Moreover, even with this at-will option available, many employers seek to retain high quality performers when they experience declining work performance due to personal problems. They do so because many organizations invest handsomely in their employees' training, which would be undesirable to lose. It is in the organization's best economic interest to try to "make whole" employees facing problems in order to regain higher performance levels. Rich literature exists indicating that employee assistance and employee wellness programs have demonstrable positive outcomes.

In many governments, at-will standards are not applicable. This is true especially for those individuals employed in middle to entry-level positions. Frequently, these public employees work under civil service system rules. Civil service provides greater due process rights to employees facing the prospect of termination. In these systems a public agency's effort to terminate is more difficult to obtain and more time-consuming than in comparable private sector situations. There must be a "just cause" for firing the individual as opposed to termination based on the "at-will" concept. Moreover, civil service policies frequently provide rehabilitative assistance (and a "second chance" for the employee) before termination proceedings can be carried out. Thus, public supervisors often must work with the civil service employee through his/her problem, more than do managers with "at-will" employees in the private sector. This pro-

vides both opportunity and challenge for the public manager and for the EAP service providers. It allows the organization to preserve its investment in its employee's knowledge, skill and ability and facilitates the retention of a talented employee once he is "whole" again.

Distinction 3: Public Scrutiny of Government Actions

Governments also operate in more accessible working environments. They frequently are required to respond to aggressive media and assertive public oversight. As an example, the state of Florida's "sunshine laws" mandate among the highest levels of public accessibility to governmental action and information. It is not uncommon for Florida media sources to report municipal policy changes under consideration before its work force is apprised of potential actions.

Public accessibility to government is a paramount element of American democracy. As a society, we demand public accountability to ensure that the public's interest is being served effectively. Broad public scrutiny benefits the community but can come at a cost for public employees. It imposes increased stressors on public employees resulting in increased needs for mental health interventions. Similar levels of public accessibility to information typically are not granted in private organizations. Corporate leaders can request that the media leave its facilities without comment to reporters' inquiries. Their stress resulting from media inquiries is lowered, because they have a high "zone of control" over information accessibility. Past research has documented a strong association between higher stress levels and declining mental and physical well being. It is also well known that stress increases for individuals when situational predictability declines and as workers lose control of their task environment. Both factors, loss of predictability and control, exist as a result of increased accessibility to government. In the case of upper-level officials (e.g., city managers and prominent elected officials), this situation also affects their families. These households must deal with the "fishbowl" effect (i.e., having their every movement under observation and scrutiny from their citizenry). Under these circumstances the need for EAP intervention, especially for family members of the public servant, can be significant.

Contextual Distinction and EAP Implementation

Human resource systems frequently serve as the interface between the problem employee needing aid and the employee assistance provider granting counseling and referral services. Specific federal laws mandate that an individual's medical history, including EAP counseling records, remain confidential. Negligent employers are liable legally for disclosing employee health records without prior authorization from the individual. Standard human resource procedures call for nondisclosure of this information until an employee release has been obtained. Nonetheless, once a release has been granted, employers should continue to distribute such information only on "a need to know" basis.

Substantial pressures exist for public organizations to disclose information to the public they serve. Public human resource systems, as retention sources for such confidential information, must take affirmative steps to secure "protected information" from general disclosure (including the media). To this end, confidential information customarily is secured in separate files outside the public's purview. Furthermore, operational personnel (especially immediate supervisors) must be informed about laws protecting the confidentiality of medical records. Employees must be informed that they will be held accountable (up to and including termination) for disclosing protected information about fellow employees without prior authorization to do so. Public agencies face constant pressure to provide information to media concerns, public and special interest groups, and other relevant public stakeholders. Maintaining high confidentiality standards, the government will be protecting the individual in need of assistance and itself, and will not be burdened with cost and time-consuming litigation for breaches of confidentiality.

Historical Evolution of EAP Programs in Government

The historical origins of employee assistance programs are founded in early alcoholism intervention strategies, which began to gain acceptance in the late 1930s. During this period, innovative industrial physicians at progressive corporations like DuPont, Eastman Kodak, and Consolidated Edison along with dedicated individuals principally affiliated with Alcoholics Anonymous (AA) began viewing problem drinking and alcoholism as a treatable mental health disease rather than as flaws of individual character. Prior to regarding alcoholism as a treatable disease, alcoholics customarily were institutionalized permanently in mental facilities. It is ironic that change occurred, not so much because of this horrific treatment approach, but as a result of needing to "work with the problem drinker" due to work shortages cause by World War II. Sustaining staffing levels ultimately led to new paradigmatic treatment approaches. This shift in attitude was also a blessing for American organizations following World War II, as millions of returning soldiers experienced readjustment problems discovered on the worksite in the form of increased employee drinking problems (Trice & Schonbrunn, 1981).

Changes in societal attitudes towards alcoholism were reflected also in the growing number of AA groups and members experienced between 1938 and 1944. Trice and Schonbrunn, in their research of early (1900–1955) job-based alcoholism programs report that only three AA groups and approximately 100 members existed in 1938. However, by 1944 the AA movement had grown to more than 300 groups serving more than 10,000 members (Trice & Schonbrunn, 1981).

The origins of the modern era EAPs commenced in the early 1960s when more comprehensive and holistic approaches to the counseling and treatment of employee (and employee dependents) problems began to appear. Dickman and Challenger (1988) indicate that in 1962, the Kemper Group expanded its program's thrust to "reach families of alcoholic workers and to persons with 'other living problems.'" These "broad brush" approaches expanded services to include "marriage and family problems, emotional problems, financial and legal problems, and other problems with drugs in addition to alcohol. This became the typical industrial counseling approach by the end of the 1970s, and during the 1980s the broad brush approached exploded (Dickman & Challenger, 1988)." The impetus for comprehensive government employee assistance approaches also grew as a result of the successes experienced in corporate EAPs and due to increasing legislation mandating mental health intervention.

Legislative Mandates and EAP Utilization in Government

Governmental adoption of occupational alcoholism programs was given a major boost in 1970 with the passage of the "Federal Comprehensive Alcohol Abuse and Alcoholism Treatment and Rehabilitation Act" (Challenger, 1988). This act obligated the federal Civil Service Commission (the forerunner to the Office of Personnel and Management (OPM)) to develop operating alcoholism intervention programs for federal employees. It also provided funding to all states for occupational alcoholism consultants to assist in the design and implementation of occupational alcoholism programs (Challenger, 1988). Over time, spin-off policies began appearing in state and local government. In addition, governments incorporated broadened program coverage, moving beyond occupational drug and alcoholism programs, towards more comprehensive mental health initiatives for its work forces.

As noted, growth in broad-brush governmental employee assistance programs was aided through new federal legislation. New federal acts significant to the expansion of governmental EAPS, include: (1) The Rehabilitation Act of 1973; (2) The Americans with Disabilities Act of 1990; and (3) The Drug-free Workplace Act of 1988.

The Rehabilitation Act of 1973 extensively influenced the early utilization of governmental EAPs. As part of its mandate, the Rehabilitation Act required that recipients (including state and local governments) of federal contracts and grants of more than $2,500 could not discriminate against individuals with physical or mental impairment. As an extension of this legislation, EAP services often were provided to those requiring rehabilitative assistance. One's disability status, as defined by this new law, existed when one or more of the individual's major life functions was limited (Thompson, 1990). Section 501 of this law (which pertains to federal employees) remains in force as the guiding disability and rehabilitation legislation for federal agencies.

The Rehabilitation Act also served as the forerunner for the Americans with Disabilities Act (ADA) of 1990. ADA now is the principal legislation protecting individuals' disability rights in state and local government and in the private sector. It applies to organizations employing 15 or more workers on a full-time basis. Both the Rehabilitation Act and ADA place obligations on organizations to make reasonable accommodations to assist employees experiencing problems that limit life's (including work-related) activities. Of note, however, is the fact that these laws do not protect current drug users or alcoholics from disciplinary action, including termination. In many instances, however, government as employer attempts to "make whole" individuals experiencing personal problems through counseling and referral, prior to proceeding with termination. This willingness to grant another chance through rehabilitative efforts occurs due to civil service protections granted to many government employees.

The Drug-Free Workplace Act of 1988 also has influenced positively the expansion of governmental EAP services. This act, passed as a part of the Anti-Drug Abuse Act of 1988, requires federal contractors and federal grant recipients receiving $100,000 or more [The Federal Acquisition Streamlining Act of 1994 (FASA) raised the threshold of contracts covered by the Drug-Free Workplace Act of 1988 from $25,000] to develop and implement a comprehensive substance abuse policy (U.S. Dept. of Labor website). Virtually all local governments and many other quasi-governmental bodies receiving funds (e.g., universities, nonprofit organizations) must follow the guidelines of this legislation as recipients of federal monies. Employers are expected to educate employees about their policy against drug use or possession. This legislation also recommends venues for assisting individuals requesting counseling and/or rehabilitative assistance.

Government Employee Assistance Programs Utilization

At any point in time more than 20 percent of America's work force falls into the category of "problem employee" (Myers, 1984). These problems include one or more of the following: alcoholism, drug dependency, mental and emotional disorders, compulsive gambling, marital discord, family problems, and legal issues. No matter what the specific problem is it is likely to result in declining individual work performance. In many instances, these types of problems influence the employee's behavior negatively, which eventually jeopardizes the organization's financial security through increased lawsuits and higher overall organizational litigation costs.

It makes prudent economic sense for governments to promote comprehensive health initiatives to aid their employees who are experiencing problems. Moreover, public organizations should encourage early self-referral as a means for improving the individual's potential for recovery. Installing a belief that the ultimate goal of the organization and its EAP is rehabilitative rather than punitive, facilitates the successful application of EAP services within ones work force. Cunningham reports encouraging news about self-referral trends among employees. She notes "there has been a dramatic shift in the proportion of 'involuntary' to voluntary clients in programs (Cunningham, 1994)." Furthermore, she notes, "in most EAPs the majority of employees seek help on their own without the intervention of their supervisors, and most are not exhibiting overt signs of declining work performance (Cunningham, 1994)." This indicates that the stigmas associated with EAP utilization among employees may have lessened over the past two decades as EAP programs have shifted from being labeled as "drug and alcohol" programs to ones focused on greater overall health of individual workers.

Counseling services generally are "purchased" rather than provided in-house. Privately contracted EAPs tend to be the norm in government today. A similar pattern exists in private enterprise where corporate-based, in-house EAPs still exist but are "a less standard format through which EAP services are offered (Cunningham, 1994)." A number of factors influence organizational preferences for "outside" EAP contractual providers.

First, governments are increasingly aware of, and concerned about, the potential for litigation as a result of improper disclosures of confidential EAP information. Selecting outside vendors to manage EAP services mitigates some of this litigation potential. In addition, selecting outside expertise to advise on the rehabilitative well being of the "problem employee" also may limit damages associated with future negligent retention lawsuits.

Government's desire to contain rising operational costs also explains its prevailing use of contractual EAP services. Smaller size municipalities often cannot afford in-house EAP services. Moreover, when they can, they still often choose contractual services because of lower per capita costs. In Hawaii state government, its EAP service provider charges a fee per employee range from $12.00 to $30.00 per employee annually. This rate is calculated according to the number of employees in the organization and the types of EAP services desired (Hawaii Health Assistance Services, 2002). Governments at all levels today face pressures to find venues to conserve their revenues and increase their organizational efficiency. Clearly, contracting services is highly desirable for many organizations that may not have the expertise on staff or the desire to expend resources through in-house service provisions. Minimizing liability, preserving limited fiscal resources for other needs, and obtaining high quality EAP expertise from outside sources are key driving forces for the "privatization" of EAP services in government.

In 1988, Robert Challenger noted the tendency for government employee assistance services to lag behind those provided in the private sector. He stated, "Unfortunately, there are still some states that have not fully recognized the benefits to be derived from such programs and lack the impetus and knowledge to install comprehensive programs for all their employees and family members" (Challenger, 1988). An analysis of all governmental units here is not feasible due to the sheer numbers. The 1997 Census of Government, for example, reports more than 87,500 units of government (Department of Commerce, 1999). However, the Appendix at the end of this chapter provides website locations for EAP programs in America's 50 state governments for the readers' review. These websites reveal interesting observations about state government EAPs. First, since Challenger observed in 1988, nearly all state governments today have actively functioning EAPs in place. This is encouraging as it indicates extensive growth in EAP utilization in state governments over the past decade. It should be noted, however, that these EAP websites vary considerably in terms of the quality and quantity of information available to interested parties.

The state website information in many cases, however, provides an initial understanding of the services available through state EAP providers. A number of these sites presents information indicating "comprehensive services" that are available to their employees. Further analysis of these sites indicates that many states have adapted services to reflect changing employee needs within their organizations. For example, intervention services due to instances of workplace violence and employee harassment have become common in many systems. In addition, programs providing assistance addressing quality of working life issues are offered now in many state systems. Program services to aid in planning for future employee needs–financial retirement planning, caring for parents/spouse/self in retirement, and living active lives in retirement–are examples of the changing scope of coverage provided by today's government EAP service.

Future Trends of Governmental Employee Assistance Programs

Government employee assistance initiatives will continue to evolve and adapt as the needs of society and organizations change in the coming decades. A number of factors are likely to affect the types of program offerings provided by government. One might anticipate that, with the aging of the work force, there will be increased calls for EAP services assisting "Baby Boomers" in transition from work to retirement.

Containment of rising health costs also will result in increased proactive emphasis by government on their employees' utilization of EAPs (and Employee Wellness) initiatives. For this to be effective, however, the cultures inherent in governments, as well as the citizenry's attitudes toward employee assistance programs, must change. Human resource systems can help here through proactive efforts (e.g., through effective marketing of programs) to encourage increased employee participation in EAP and wellness-related programs. Far too many public sector systems simply make this information available but do not progressively encourage employee service utilization. The offering of incentives for employee participation (e.g., "wellness" bonuses), especially in wellness-related programs, should be encouraged. Governments interested in pursuing this strategy, however, should anticipate and plan for resistance to the creation of programs and facilities specifically designed to enhance the physical health and wellness of the public employee. For example, a city that seeks to fund the building of its own employee wellness center is likely to face questions by citizens regarding why their tax dollars are to be used to support "country club" lifestyles of municipal workers. City leaders are likely to face bitter resentment and opposition to these initiatives even when it can be shown that the benefits of the program outweigh the costs for its implementation. In these instances, creative strategies should be considered, like that of building a new community recreation facility that offers public access while simultaneous offering employee-based wellness initiatives.

EAP emphasis on drug and alcohol assistance will remain a central focus of employee services. Their dominance, however, may lessen somewhat (especially for drug counseling) as declines in drug use continue in our society. This may be offset, however, by the need for increased alcohol counseling services. Over the past 15 years in Florida, for example, the level of "driving under the influence" has dropped from .15BAC (blood alcohol content) to .10BAC and now to .08BAC. It is even lower for those employed in positions (e.g., municipal transit drivers) required to meet Department of Transportation standards. Therefore, the reduced need for drug counseling services may be offset by the increased demand for alcohol abuse counseling as societal standards for alcohol abusive behavior are tightened.

These predictions in all likelihood will change as societal perception and attitude vary, as organizational leadership changes, and as new laws are enacted, modifying and mandating what existing EAP programs must accomplish. Regardless of the changes, one constant will remain—that is, government will continue to look to employee assistance programs as a means to enhance and sustain its work force's physical and mental well being in order to retain high levels of public productivity.

APPENDIX
STATE–HUMAN RESOURCE UNIT–EAP WEBSITE

Alabama–Department of Personnel–
http://www.riskmgt.state.al.us/empassis.html

Alaska–Dept. of Administration–
http://www.state.ak.us/local/akpages/ADMIN/drb/ghlb/98eapak.htm

Arizona–Human Resources & AZ Personnel Retirement–
http://www.hr.state.az.us/benefits/active-eap.html#top

Arkansas–Office of Personnel Management–
http://www.state.ar.us/dfa/odd/eap.html

California–Department of Personnel Administration–
www.dpa.ca.gov/benefits/other/eap/eapmain.shtm

Colorado–Division of Human Resources–
http://www.state.co.us/dhr/eap/eap.htm

Connecticut–Human Resources Services–
http://www.dmhas.state.ct.us/DSS/eap.htm

Delaware–State Personnel Office–
http://delawarepersonnel.com/benefits/eap.htm

Florida–Human Resource Management–
http://www.dep.state.fl.us/admin/depdirs/pdf/dep460.pdf

Georgia–Dept. of Human Resources–
http://www2.state.ga.us/departments/dhr/EAPcontact.pdf

Hawaii–Department of Human Resources Development–http://www.heas.org/about.html

Idaho–Idaho Department of Personnel–
http://www.isu.edu/humanr/ibhp.pdf

Illinois–Dept. of Employment Security & State Retirement Systems–
http://www.state.il.us/agency/dhs/eapbrochnp.html

Indiana–Department of Personnel–
http://www.in.gov/jobs/laborrelations/easy_pol.htm

Iowa–Iowa Department of Personnel
http://www.state.ia.us/government/idop/BenEAP.htm

Kansas–Division of Personnel Services
http://da.state.ks.us/ps/documents/bulletins/9701.htm

Kentucky–Personnel Cabinet–
http://kygovnet.state.ky.us/personnel/emphb/keap.htm

Louisiana–Dept. of State Civil Service & Office of Risk Mgmt.–
http://www.dhh.state.la.us/oada/employee_assist.htm

Maine–Bureau of Human Resources–
http://www.state.me.us/beh/
Note: Portions of the website, including the EAP section is *"under construction"* as of 8/24/2002)

Maryland–Office of Personnel Services and Benefits–
http://www.opsb.state.md.us/erd/eap.htm

Massachusetts–Human Resources Division–
http://www.state.ma.us/gic/eap.htm

Michigan–Department of Civil Service–
http://www.michigan.gov/ose/0,1607,7-143-6097_6273--,00.html

Minnesota–Department of Employee Relations–
http://www.doer.state.mn.us/eap/eap.htm

Mississippi–State Personnel Board–No state EAP or EAP website. Some agencies have "agency" EAPs.

Missouri–Division of Personnel–
http://www.mchcp.org/members/02se_eap_benefits.htm

Montana–State Personnel Division–
http://www.state.mt.us/doa/spd/css/benefits/eap.asp

Nebraska–Division of State Personnel–http://www.lincolnjobs.com/nepersonnel2.html

Nevada–Department of Personnel–
http://www.state.nv.us/personnel/eap.html

New Hampshire–Division of Personnel–
http://www.dhhs.state.nh.us/DHHS/EAP/
default.htm

New Jersey–Department of Personnel–
http://www.state.nj.us/personnel/annual98.pdf
(Annual Report on page 15)

New Mexico–Personnel Office–
http://www.state.nm.us/gsd/rmd/employee.htm

New York–Department of Civil Service–
http://www.ric.goer.state.ny.us/wbt/eap/default.htm

North Carolina–Office of State Personnel–
http://www.osp.state.nc.us/eap/seaphp.htm
(Note: Still *"under construction"* as of 8/25/2002)

North Dakota–Central Personnel Division–
http://www.state.nd.us/ndpers//eap.html

Ohio–Ohio Human Resources Division–
http://www.state.oh.us/das/dhr/eap.html

Oklahoma–Office of Personnel Management
http://www.doc.state.ok.us/humanresources/eap.htm

Oregon–Human Resource Services Division–
http://personnel.hr.state.or.us/Policy/POLICY4A.
htm

Pennsylvania–State Civil Service Commission–
http://www.drugfreepa.org/business_eap.htm

Rhode Island–Department of Administration–
http://www.lifewatch-eap.com/
(Contractual provider for the state)

South Carolina–Office of Human Resources–No state
EAP or EAP website. Many agencies contract with
private EAPs.

South Dakota–Bureau of Personnel–No state EAP
(Source: BoP e-mail correspondence of September
24,2002)

Tennessee–Department of Personnel–
http://www.state.tn.us/finance/ins/eap/eap.html

Texas–Human Resources Management–
http://www.hr.state.tx.us/advisory/eap.html

Utah–Department of Human Services–
http://www.hshr.state.ut.us/eap.htm

Vermont–Department of Personnel–
http://www.state.vt.us/pers/er/pm/pm193.htm

Virginia–Department of Personnel & Training–
http://www.dhrm.state.va.us/services/health/
empassist.htm

Washington–Department of Personnel–
http://hr.dop.wa.gov/eas/eashist.html

West Virginia–Division of Personnel–
http://www.state.wv.us/admin/personnel/classes/
erp/refbook.htm

Wisconsin–State of Wisconsin Dept. of Employment
Relations–
http://der.state.wi.us/static/eapdefault.htm

Wyoming–Human Resources Division–No website as
there is no state EAP.

REFERENCES

Challenger, B. R. (1988). Government. In F. Dickman, et al. *Employee assistance programs: A basic text.* Springfield, IL: Charles C. Thomas, Publisher, Ltd.

Cunningham, G. (1994). *Effective employee assistance programs: A guide for EAP counselors and managers.* Thousand Oaks, CA.: Sage Publications.

Dickman, F., & Challenger, B. R. (1988). "Employee assistance programs: A historical sketch," in F. Dickman, et al. *Employee assistance programs. A basic text.* Springfield, IL: Charles C. Thomas, Publisher, Ltd.

Hawaii Health Assistance Services (2002). Information downloaded from Internet site www.heas.org/about. html on August 31, 2002.

Kettl, D. F. (1996). "Governing at the millennium," in J. L. Perry, ed., *Handbook of public administration–Second Edition.* San Francisco: Jossey-Bass Publishers.

McAfee, R. B., & Champagne, P. J. (1994). *Effectively Managing Troublesome Employees.* Westport, CT: Quorum Books.

Miller, J. (2002). "Study: More feds work just for the money," *Government Computer News.* Article dated 06/05/02–Internet download from www.gcn.com/ vol1_no1/workforce/18889-1.html on August 13, 2002.

Myers, D. (1984). *Establishing and building employee assistance programs.* Westport, CT: Quorum Books.

Starr, B. (2002). "Fort Bragg killings raise alarm about stress," July 27, 2002 new release from CNN.com. Internet download from http://www.cnn.com/2002/US/07/26/army.wives/ on August 28, 2002.

Thompson, Jr., R. (1990). *Substance abuse and employee rehabilitation.* Washington, D.C.: The Bureau of National Affairs, Inc.

Trice, H. M., & Schonbrunn, M. (1981). "A history of job-based alcoholism programs: 1900–1955, *Journal of Drug Issues.*

U.S. Department of Commerce (1999). *1997 census of government* (Report GC97(1)-1, page XIII), Washington, D.C.: U.S. Department of Commerce. For additional information see http://www.census.gov/prod/gc97/gc971-1.pdf.

U.S. Department of Labor, The Drug-Free Workplace Act of 1988, download from http://www.dol.gov on August 28, 2002.

Chapter 31

THE CLERGY

FRED DICKMAN

Clergy present a unique problem and opportunity to the Employee Assistance Professional. This is particularly true regarding alcoholism. The problem is that clergy too often are forced to deny personal problems, especially problems of addiction. Consequently, the problems are apt to mushroom and be subjected to effective intervention much too far into the progression. The opportunity is that as a denomination is educated to the nature of personal problems in general, and addiction in particular, the clergy (both those who are recovering and those who are not) can, in turn, reach many more persons who are ill but in denial.

The purpose of this chapter is to focus on clergy and alcoholism. However as more churches embrace the EAP approach to early intervention, many more "EAP type problems," i.e., marriage and family, alcoholism, adult children of alcoholic parents, other drug addiction and general psychological issues will be identified and ameliorated at a much earlier time in each's progression.

The Clergy's Unique Problem

Not only is the clergy alcoholic person and his family subjected to the stigma of alcoholism, as is the general population, he has a deeper stigma as well. He is led to believe that were he to have enough faith he would not become alcoholic. Conversely, if he is an alcoholic, his faith must be either too weak or nonexistent. This "deeper" stigma is noticed anecdotally by the author as well as

implied by survey-type research (Moss, 1975). This phenomenon may well explain the often lack of interest in alcoholism among pastors and in the churches noticed by researchers (Banks, 1983). If it is true that clergy believe alcoholism (and mental illness as well) to be an indication of low or absence of a living faith, then the problem of reaching the alcoholic clergyman and his family is doubly difficult. Hence, the challenge and opportunity for the EAP professional who can penetrate the denial of church structures. Not only will the ill clergyman receive help sooner, but those whom he can reach early will be multiplied in that he is on the frontline of families approaching the church for help.

Paradoxical History

The double stigma felt by the clergy is all the more strange when viewed in the light of the history of Alcoholics Anonymous. Clergy and churches have been involved with AA since its beginnings in 1935 (Kurtz, 1979).

A prime example is the Reverend Doctor Samuel Shoemaker who was Bill Wilson's (Cofounder of AA) spiritual advisor in the early years of the latter's recovery (Kurtz, 1979). The Rev. Fr. Ernest Dowling is another example. With this shrewd Jesuit's early counsel, Bill and the early AA members kept Alcoholics Anonymous efficiently unattached from any form of organized religion.

In the early years churches of all faiths opened

Note: This chapter is reprinted from *Employee Assistance Programs: A Basic Text* (1988) with permission of the author, the book's editors (Dickman, Emener, & Hutchison, Jr.), and the publisher (Charles C Thomas, Publisher, Ltd.).

halls to AA groups for their "closed" and "open" meetings. To this day, only a cursory glance in any city will list well over half the meeting places as in the halls of churches.

A Growing Reversal

Increasingly mainline Protestant denominations and the Roman Catholic Church are breaking the double stigma; in that to have the disease of alcoholism is tantamount to having no faith.

The Episcopal Church under the leadership of Vernon Johnson of Johnson Institute and the Catholic Church with good experience with Guest House (a Catholic treatment center outside Detroit) have issued policy statements that alcoholism is a disease and not a sin. With this kind of growing atmosphere an EAP for each diocese, district or presbytry can make a significant contribution to the clergy, nuns, lay brothers, and the people to whom they are servants.

Church EAPs

As described above the climate may be appropriate for an Employee Assistance Program for the various church bodies for the following reasons:

1. **The Disease Concept.** A growing acceptance of the disease notion of alcoholism has filtered to many church leaders (Kellermann, 1958). Rather than viewing alcoholism as continuing sinfulness, there is a growing awareness that while faith is a necessary ingredient in alcoholism recovery (Roessler, 1982), the lack of faith does not cause alcoholism.

2. **History of Pastoral Concern.** Churches have long been involved in and sympathetic to the movement of Alcoholics Anonymous and alcoholism recovery in general. Early on (1932–1950), this support was spotty and evolved around pioneers such as Rev. Dr. Shoemaker and Fr. Dowling. As early as 1948 was the Hazelden experiment, and by 1952 the Lutherans sponsored a hospital-based treatment center in Chicago. More recently, churches sponsor treatment and training awareness throughout the community.

3. **Church Policy Statements.** As stated earlier the Episcopal Church and various Catholic Dioceses have issued policy statements adhering to the disease concept of alcoholism. These clearly offer treatment rather than discipline and punishment and are actively engaged in the rehabilitation of clergy alcoholics.

4. **Recovering Examples.** Each diocese, district and many congregations have found, as has industry, that recovering persons are productive and fruitful workers and stewards. On a national level, some of the most noted and successful teachers of alcoholic recovery are members of the clergy.

5. **Public Acceptance.** Eighteen years ago in the author's diocese he found it nearly impossible to return to an active parish ministry as a recent recovering alcoholic. Today that is changed. He has been offered many parishes in the past ten years and experiences no obvious rejection as he speaks to church groups about alcoholism. Many parishes, and other diocesan positions, are filled by recovering persons.

The EAP Approach

The clergy may be approached to get early assistance for alcoholism and other problems just as have persons in industry since the 1940s–through an EAP.

Once the bishop of the diocese, president of the conference, or district secretary is convinced, a healthy or EAP committee comprised of knowledgeable lay and clerical members may be established. This committee agrees upon a policy statement that alcoholism is a disease and that other incapacitating problems are "human" and not antithetical to faith. Then the committee speaks at conferences and in small groups to raise awareness to: (1) clergy can have problems, (2) to early (or late, for that matter) rehabilitate is highly likely with an EAP, and (3) it is to the best interest of all concerned to face and ameliorate the problem(s) rather than deny to the point of destructiveness.

On this atmosphere, intervention teams can be trained, adequate medical insurance provided, counseling/evaluation centers organized and treatment and follow-up plans initiated. The EAP coordinator, lay or clerical, is selected and the program can be launched. Not only does such a program work for those to whom it is intended, but the whole climate of the diocese/district is changed, so that lay people who have the disease of alcoholism and their families are more apt to seek help faster.

CONCLUSION

This chapter has attempted to demonstrate that clergy face a unique situation when they "catch" the disease of alcoholism. They too often blame themselves and are blamed for lack of faith or they would not have contracted the disease. It was pointed out that such an attitude is strange in view of the close and helpful history the churches have in the historical progression of the alcoholism recovery movement.

It was recommended that:

1. Various church organizations initiate EAPs to reach and rehabilitate clergy alcoholic persons, and
2. The time and spiritual atmosphere is ripe for such a movement.

Finally, clergy are well-trained and necessary persons to the community. When one clergyman and his family accepts his or her alcoholism, gets treatment and returns to the active pastorate everyone gains; the church, the clergyperson and his/her family and the parishioners, especially those who have problems themselves.

COMMENT/UPDATE

THOMAS P. SCHROEDER

When Bill Hutchison called to ask my help in updating this chapter regarding clergy and the need for and use of employee assistance programs, I had to wonder a bit, as I am certainly no expert in these matters and, certainly, my style of writing is less than scholarly. Although I am familiar with EAPs in general and have recently established an EAP for the staff at the Pastoral Center of Diocese of St. Petersburg, I haven't had a great deal of experience with how they work and, in particular, how they might benefit members of the clergy. On the other hand, I have had a good bit of experience over the past 20 years in working with a variety of clerical, religious and lay workers who are and have been involved in all sorts of ministry in the Roman Catholic Church and other denominations. First as chancellor in the Diocese of Saginaw and now as the Executive Director of the Department of Human Resources in St. Petersburg, I can speak from firsthand experience to the issues brought about by stress and its effects on the church "work force."

It is pretty elementary, but when I think of ministry in the church (regardless of denomination), I look at a very labor-intensive operation. We are about the business of providing ministry to parishioners and nonparishioners alike and this requires a large work force of both paid and unpaid staff. Providing ministry is not just reserved for the ordained or vowed religious but it is also a legitimate responsibility for the laity. Not only do we share in this sometimes awesome responsibility, we also share the many stresses that come with that ministry and this is why EAPs are such an important resource for all who work for the church.

Although a subject for another forum, it is important before we go much further, to consider a few of the complexities that are unique to the church as a workplace. These will have an impact on the applicability of EAPs in later discussions.

1. First, the work force in a parish is made up of both support staff and ministerial staff: Both are absolutely essential to the mission of the church and should not be in competition with one another (as is sometimes the case). This, along with all the attendant issues, creates a stress level that is often difficult to overcome.

2. Secondly, the work force in a parish is often made up of ordained clergy, vowed religious and members of the laity. With the latter, there are paid and unpaid (volunteer) staff. Though not always the case, all need to be considered "staff" and all need to be recognized as not only a part of the big picture but, also as making a valued contribution to that big picture . . . the ministry and mission of the parish. The differences in lifestyle, expectations, and lived experiences, often create confusion, resentment, and stress.

3. Somewhat linked to the above, the differences between Canon Law (the law of the Church) and Civil Law (the law of the land) also lend themselves to creating tension and stress within the work force. The "employment relationship" of clergy and religious is governed by Canon Law and the employment relationship of the laity is governed by literally hundreds of state and federal labor laws. These differences and lack of understanding of the differences can often bring about confusion, resentment, and stress.

4. Lastly, I would add that those who work in and for the church are often held to a higher standard than those who work in the secular world. Not that this isn't entirely appropriate, but the perceived standards are often unreasonable and, in some ways, unattainable. These so-called standards are imposed on church workers by themselves, by the church, by society in general, and their individual perceptions and interpretations of what "God wants." In management circles and in human resources, it is a commonly held tenet that workers should only serve one boss in order to maintain clarity in expectations, communications and accountability. In a sense, those working in the church environment have several bosses and this often creates a great deal of frustration, tension and stress. When looking at the stress of the workplace, we can each claim a certain amount of uniqueness and that our profession is stressful for certain characteristic reasons. On the other hand, there are certain stresses and stressors that are common between us and our calling makes no difference whatsoever. As employers

and as good stewards of the resources we have at hand (human resources), we need to sort through all those issues. We need to deal with those things that are unique, those things that are common and:

- Recognize the symptoms and their effect on the individual as well as the organization. (Symptoms are those things that may indicate the possible need for counseling and/or support of some other kind.)
- Identify the possible stressors that may be the root causes for the symptoms.
- Inventory all the various resources and means of dealing with the stressors and symptoms.
- Design a program, a comprehensive strategy, to reduce, relieve or manage stress in the best way possible for the individual and the organization.

On the next page is a chart that provides several examples of symptoms and stressors that are relatively common in the church as a workplace and that affect the various components of the work force: clergy, religious, and lay. The lists are in no way not all-inclusive and are provided as examples that I've come across in my work with the church over the past 20 years.

It wouldn't take much effort at all to identify more symptoms and stressors but that is not my main purpose here. I could also take a little more time and expand on each of those that I've identified and go into detail about why it is a particular problem or issue. What I do want to do though, is drive home the point that it would behoove us as employers to assess the overall need for a variety of mental and emotional health programs and try to provide for those needs . . . much the same as we do in dealing with physical health. It has been stated many times in many different places, but part of our mission, as "church" is to minister to the ministers.

Recommendation

My overall recommendation is for employers (whether they be in the secular world or in the church) to keep their finger on the pulse of what is happening and assess the various stresses that can and do affect their work force. This assessment can be accomplished through simple observation or

SYMPTOMS	STRESSORS
Addictive behaviors, e.g.	Approaching retirement
Alcohol abuse & dependence	Clergy shortage
Substance abuse & dependence	Depersonalization of workplace
Work addiction	Eldercare
Gambling	Heavy workload
Being reclusive & isolated	Image of church & ministry
Burnout	Inadequate job skills
Depression	Inadequate reward system
Excessive anxiety	Inappropriate Expectations
Extreme mood swings	Lack of accountability
Hostility	Lack of clear direction
Inappropriate angry behavior	Lack of support (friends or extended family)
Obsessive thinking	"Living over the store"
Over & under-eating	Loneliness & isolation
Over & under-exercise	Loss of meaning
Over & under-sleeping	Loss of spiritual center
Sexual acting out or repression	On-call nature of work & ministry
	Physical problems
	Power
	Role conflict
	Sexual abuse scandal
	Transition of another parish

through listening to individuals and/or groups. If the latter is used, care must be taken to listen carefully and with sincerity. Once these things are understood, then I recommend that a comprehensive and realistic strategy be designed to address all of the various issues at a number of different levels. There are a number of sources and resources for various types of assistance and support and it is helpful to provide a balanced mix of several, if not all, depending on the need. Although there may be others, the following is a list of resources that come to mind in looking at some of the needs I've identified within our church work force.

• *Education programs*

Quite often stress is the result of understanding possible stressors or, very simply, not having all of the skills necessary to do one's job or ministry. On the latter issue, I often recommend continuing education and skill development programs of one type or another. One that comes to mind right now, is the program in *Contemporary Administrative in a Church Setting* that we are offering for our pastors in the Diocese of St. Petersburg. This particular program recognizes that many pastors have not had the opportunity to build the skills necessary to be comfortable with the administrative side of their "job" as pastor. In addition to addressing professional skills, knowledge and abilities, other types of educational programs might address the more personal side of things. One might deal with retirement planning, which is often a source of stress for those who are uncertain about their future. Other topics might include understanding how your personality type might interact with others, classes in first aid and CPR, programs on substance abuse, overall wellness, family issues and how to deal with being part of the "sandwich generation," etc.

• *Family, Friends, Support Groups and Colleagues*

When people are feeling stressed, it is often

good to simply talk things through and occasionally vent a bit. Family, friends, colleagues, and a variety of support groups are often a good source for this type of help. One word of caution though is that one needs to be cautious and make sure that confidentiality will be respected and that the individuals can be trusted with what may be very sensitive and personal information. It's not always that malicious gossip will be the problem, but relatively harmless comments offered out of concern for an individual can be terribly damaging as well. Ideally, clergy support groups would have clear norms, including norms regarding confidentiality and accountability.

• *Prayer, Spiritual Directors and Retreats*

One's faith can be and is a tremendous source of strength and comfort when dealing with a variety of stress-related issues. Sometimes, depending upon the situation, a little more guidance or direction is necessary to get over a particular obstacle. In these situations, one's spiritual director can be a great resource. Also, taking time away from the daily routine and focusing on our relationship with God in a retreat setting can be helpful. Prayer is a wonderful source of strength and inner peace.

• *Employee Assistance Program*

Now, given the fact that this book is written about EAPs, this is the big one. It is an employee benefit that has been around for a while, but also one that is still relatively new within the church as an employer. As you may have read already, the history of EAPs is related to employers concerns over dealing with alcoholism and substance abuse.

Just for the sake of clarity, the EAP we established in the Pastoral Center is intended for the use of all who work here: clergy, religious, and lay. There was no distinction between state in life and the program works through a third-party vendor. We have contracted with Operation PAR for the coming year to provide five, prepaid counseling sessions for employees and/or members of their families. Although our health and medical insurance program has a mental health component, the EAP is seen as an opportunity to:

- resolve some issues early
- assess the seriousness of an issue prior to utilizing the insurance benefits
- determine what, if any, additional treatment or follow-up may be necessary

Participation in the program is self-elected and being that it is through a third party, respect for confidentiality is a very high priority. By it's nature, the program is also set up so that in some instances, the employer might recommend or require an employee to take advantage of the counseling. An obvious example might be a situation where someone is having a problem with alcohol or substance abuse.

The overall design of the program embraces the concept of total wellness. Although counseling is a major component of the EAP, education (as mentioned above) is also a very real concern and priority.

EAPs are typically thought of as "employee" benefits and clergy and religious aren't technically considered employees. My fear with our program is that members of the clergy may not be open to using it, because they don't view themselves as employees and that the counseling will not address their particular concerns as priests. Although I think we all suffer from many of the same stresses, I do acknowledge that we need to deal with these differences in some way. Rather than restructuring the program entirely, a clergy EAP for example, might simply be marketed differently and have a slightly different who are skilled in focus in its educational component. Further, it may be necessary to identify counselors or have an awareness of some of the issues unique to ministry and the church in order to be helpful to members of the clergy who wish to avail themselves of their services. Operation PAR, for example, had identified a number of "faith-based" counselors who may be able to respond to the needs of our priests, as well as our religious and lay employees.

In short, EAPs can be an important resource for those who work in the church because they are comprehensive (available to deal with a variety of concerns), confidential, self-elected, flexible, prepaid, etc.

• *Mental Health Counseling*

Where EAPs may leave off, more formal and involved counseling may be necessary depending on the seriousness or severity of the situation. If this is the case, the mental health component of many health and medical insurance programs may pick up the cost. In some ways, this type of counseling would be what I would consider to be outpatient counseling.

• *Treatment Centers*

Again, depending on the type of severity of the situation, more intense counseling and therapy may be necessary and an individual may need to be in a residential treatment facility. There are many of these facilities available around the country. Although a little dated (1995), the National Association of Church Personnel Administrators, headquartered in Cincinnati, Ohio has produced a Treatment Facility Resource Manual that may be of some help in designing a comprehensive program to deal with the more severe symptoms, stressors, and conditions.

The topic of EAPs and their application for those who work in the church is a matter that really cannot be dealt with adequately in just these few pages. My intention has been to briefly address the need for EAPs in the church setting, to look at a few of the symptoms, the stressors and a few of the possible resources for dealing with stress. Having done so, I hope that this will serve as a catalyst to encourage church employers (bishops, pastors, school principles, etc.) to look closely at their work force, and to assess the levels of stress in their respective workplaces. And, to take steps to design and implement a comprehensive program to assure a healthy and happy work force.

REFERENCES

Albers, R. H. (1982). The theological and psychological dynamics of transformation in the recovery from the disease of alcoholism. *Dissertation Abstracts International, 43* (4–A), 1198.

Banks, R. E. (1983). Attitudes and alcohol: The use of the semantic differential with different professional and drinking populations in east Tennessee. *Dissertation Abstracts International, 43* (9–A), 2896.

Desilets, R. (1968). Alcoholism and actual pastoral approaches. *Toxicomanies, 1* (1), 51–60.

Drummond, T. (1982). The alcoholic and the church: A pastoral response. *International Journal of Offender Therapy & Comparative Criminology, 26* (3), 275–280.

Fappiano, E. R. (1984). The alcoholic priest and Alcoholics Anonymous: A study of stigma and the management of spoiled identity. *Dissertation Abstracts International, 43* (4–A), 1211.

Fitzgerald, M. C., (1982). Correlates of alcoholism among Roman Catholic nuns: Psychological and attitudinal variables. *Dissertation Abstracts International, 43* (I–B), 246.

Kellermann, J. L. (1958). *Alcoholism: A guide for the clergy.* New York: National Council on Alcoholism.

Kurtz, E. (1979). *Not–God a history of alcoholics anonymous.* Center City, MN: Hazelden.

Mann, K. W., (1972). The mission of the church in a drugs culture. *Journal of Religion & Health, 11* (4), 329–348.

Merrigan, D. M. (1983). Pastoral gatekeeper participation in community alcohol abuse prevention. *Dissertation Abstracts International, 44* (6–A), 1700.

Moss, D. M. (1975). Parochial ministry, the Episcopal Church, and alcoholism. *Journal of Religion & Health, 14* (3), 192–197.

Roessler, S. J. (1982). *The role of spiritual values in the recovery of alcoholics.* Wesley Theological Seminary.

Sorensen, A. A. (1973). Need for power among alcoholic and nonalcoholic clergy. *Journal for the Scientific Study of Religion, 12* (1), 101–108.

Chapter 32

EMPLOYEE ASSISTANCE PROGRAMS FOR SCHOOL TEACHERS AND SCHOOL PERSONNEL

WILLIAM G. EMENER

There is a serious crisis in teaching in the United States. It jeopardizes this nation's ability to conduct its own public affairs through the workings of an informed electorate. It endangers the nation's capacity to compete effectively in a shrinking world where technological skill and inventiveness will determine leadership. (Feistritzer, 1983, p. 59)

Indeed, in the recent past there has been increased public attention to our schools in the United States. Observations and concerns such as Feistritzer's (1983) abound not only among professionals but among the general public as well. A variety of factors have contributed to the crisis in teaching, including population shifts, increased professional opportunities for women outside the teaching profession, and the declining caliber of those entering the teaching profession." (Raschke, Dedrick, Strathe & Hawkes, 1985). Within our schools and their environments, and within the working lives of educators and especially the working lives of teachers, there are identifiable attributes and characteristics, which meaningfully contribute to our present teaching crisis. Evidence of these "special" aspects of the teaching profession(s), provide compelling reasons for school systems to have employee assistance programs for their personnel—especially for their teachers. The remainder of this chapter will: (a) discuss some of the identified "problems" of school personnel (with a focus on teachers); (b) present convincing rationale for having employee assistance programs

in our school systems; (c) discuss important service delivery components of EAPs for school personnel; (d) address special concerns in need of attention in school system EAPs; (e) provide an example of a successful school system EAP; and (f) offer a concluding comment regarding the design, development, and implementation of an EAP in a school system.

Job-Related Problems of School Personnel (Teachers)

Over the past few years, our highly technological and complex society has added to people's pressures and stresses—especially on our educational systems and the professionals working in them. The president of a leading teachers' organization articulated these phenomena: "The dynamics of our society and increased public demands on education have produced adverse and stressful classroom and school conditions. These conditions have led to increased emotional and physical disabilities among teachers and other school personnel" (Moe, 1979, p. 36). Some attention recent-

Note: This chapter is reprinted from *Employee Assistance Programs: A Basic Text* (1988) with permission of the author, the book's editors (Dickman, Emener, & Hutchison, Jr.), and the publisher (Charles C Thomas, Publisher, Ltd.).

ly has been focused on the new, beginning teacher in terms of helping him or her to quickly develop and learn "basic survival skills" and hopefully avoid some of the deleterious effects articulated by Moe (1979). Boynton, DiGeronimo, and Gustafson (1985) stated: "Experienced and successful teachers appear to have an inexhaustible bag full of [necessary, personal survival] techniques, strategies, and methods going for them. Pity the first-year teacher. The new teacher comes to the profession with a nearly empty bag of experiences" (p. 101).

Recent studies have identified unique aspects of teaching that contribute to occupational difficulties and job-related problems. "Teacher isolation," for example, appears to have deleterious effects on classroom teachers. Goodlad (1983) reported that teachers are typically separated from one another in the schools and little is done to facilitate their coming together (e.g. to work on their curricula and instruction). Tye and Tye (1984) found that even though "sharing" is necessary and desired by teachers, most of them work alone in self-contained classrooms and have very little time to observe each other at work and to work together. Interestingly, Rothberg (1986) surveyed 196 teachers enrolled in graduate programs and in his findings he stated:

> Over 80 percent of each group (elementary, junior/middle, and senior high) felt, "Your classroom is a private world which no one besides you and your students enter." Senior high school teachers' perceptions were higher than others.
>
> In response to the question, "Do you feel your good work goes unnoticed?" over 85 percent of the elementary and middle/junior high school teachers said, "sometimes" or "frequently," while 85 percent of the senior high school teachers said, "frequently" or "always." (p. 320)

Feelings akin to "separation" have also been reported by teachers. Cox and Wood (1980), for example, found teachers to report feeling "alienated" within the school with little opportunity to be involved in decision-making. Unfortunately, emotive reactions to the classroom and the school environment such as these also contribute to the stress that teachers experience.

There is a dearth of systematic research on stress in teachers, especially elementary teachers (Pellegrew & Wolfe, 1982). Professional literature in this area appears to be limited to personal reports, anecdotal observations, and problem resolution techniques (Quick & Quick, 1979; Weiskopf, 1980; Werner, 1980). Even though daily stresses, student disruptions, verbal abuse from students, and less than preferable levels of administrative support have been associated with teacher stress (Chichon & Koff, 1978), there unfortunately remains very little systematic evidence that schools are attempting to rectify such conditions. It would appear reasonable to conclude, nonetheless, that some of these identified debilitative conditions are the types of conditions, which schools could address. For example, Raschke, Dedrick, Strathe and Hawkes (1985) studied 300 K–6 teachers from school districts of various sizes in the central Midwest and reported: "When asked to list three things they did not like about their job, 70 percent of the teachers cited excessive paperwork and nonteaching duties as two major concerns." (p. 562) The existence of these conditions, per se, is not necessarily the problem in and of itself; the prolonged existence of these conditions is what tends to contribute to the debilitating effects and the eventual "teacher burnout" discussed in professional literature.

Freudenberger and Richelson (1980) offered an understanding of burnout that would appear to be very relevant to teaching: ". . . state of fatigue or frustration brought about by devotion to a cause, a way of life, or a relationship that failed to produce the expected reward" (p. 26). In her review of literature, viz on burnout related to teachers, Weiskopf (1980) summarized six categories of stress which contribute to teacher burnout: program structure, work overload, amount of direct contact with children, staff/child ratio, lack of perceived success, and responsibility for others.

Thus, as revealed in this cursory review of available, related professional literature, while teachers experience the types of pressures and stresses that many people experience as a result of societal conditions (Gold, 1985), there are also special and unique conditions of teaching and working in our schools that add to the pressures and stresses experienced by teachers. It is also important to note that in our society over the recent past, there have been increases in alcohol and drug abuse, increases in marital and family problems (e.g., the rise in divorce rates), and increases in reported problems in daily living (Dickman, Emener & Hutchison, 1985). Furthermore, employees can have work-related problems (as discussed above), and all of these potential difficulties and problems on behalf of employees, e.g., teachers, have effects on their work performance (Dickman & Emener, 1982). The fact that teachers play an extremely important role in the development of our children, our future generations (Moe, 1979), we should feel energized to proactively attend to such matters.

Rationale for EAPs in Our Schools

As portrayed in current popular media (e.g., newspapers, television), professional publications (e.g., journals) and in reports from assorted national commissions (consult Griesmer & Butler, 1983), teaching is a beleaguered profession. In a nutshell, to a great extent "teaching" is not meeting important, human needs of our teachers. Kreis and Milstein (1985) recently stated:

There is a growing realization that our school boards and administrators who want teacher performance to improve will have to answer the age-old teacher question, "What's in it for me?" . . . Satisfying teachers' needs is complex, but is essential to improving the performance of our schools. (pp. 75 & 77)

As discussed in Chapter 28 of this book (i.e., the importance of "development"), if teachers are consumed with attending to their own needs, it will be difficult for them to attend to the needs of their students. And, it must be remembered that this involves large numbers of individuals. For example, the U.S. Department of Education's (1982) "Estimates of School Statistics: 1982–1983" revealed that over 1.1 million of the classroom teachers employed during the 1982–1983 academic year were elementary teachers–importantly,

they were responsible for the education of almost 24 million children. A propos of these data, Raschke et al. (1985) stated:

Administrators, school board members, and taxpayers need to play a more decisive and responsive role in reducing some of the sources of stress that lie beyond the immediate control of the elementary school teacher. When one considers the vital role elementary teachers play in nurturing the psychological, physical, and intellectual competencies of young children, it becomes patently clear that these teachers need more time to teach and plan innovative and enriched instructional programs. (p. 563)

Considering the numerous difficulties and problems that school teachers and other professional school personnel can have, considering the deleterious impact of such problems on the school experiences of school children, and considering the positive impact that an employee assistance program can have when made available to employees with the types of difficulties and problems teachers can have, it indeed would appear imperative for school systems to have employee assistance programs.

Service Needs Provided by EAPs in School Systems

Employee assistance programs in school systems should be able to provide a full compliment of services typically provided by EAPs (consult Dickman, Emener & Hutchison, 1985; and other chapters in this book). For example, services in the areas of personal, marital and family concerns, financial planning, substance abuse and addiction, among others, are usually considered "must" service areas. The following, nonetheless, is designed to illustrate some of the school-oriented service delivery areas that EAPs for school systems should consider. (Specific service needs should be determined via evaluation research surveys within the specific school system the EAP is going to serve.) Services provided by school system EAPs can be categorized into four groups: (a) direct services—those provided to employees on an individually need-determined basis; (b) indirect services–those provided to employees on an "available to everyone" participation basis; (c) professionally oriented–those focusing on work (e.g., teaching) oriented problems; and (d) personally oriented–those focusing on problems unique to the employee's personal life. (In most instances, there is much overlap among these areas of distinction.) The following, however, will illustrate some of the services among these four groupings.

I. Direct Service Delivery

A. Professionally-Oriented. Based upon positive feedback from recipients, Boynton et al. (1985) offer 45 helpful suggestions for first-year teachers to help them adjust to some of the realities of classroom teaching. Their 45 suggestions, in four categories (16 in "classroom management"; five in "classroom discipline"; nine in "instruction"; and 15 labeled "professional"), can be offered to a teacher whose difficulties and problems are related to his or her classroom experiences.

B. Personally-Oriented. Quite frequently, personnel will have a presenting personal problem that requires an individual service response. For example, Youngs (1985) analyzed questionnaires returned by 3,470 (69.4%) respondents from a population of U.S. superintendents and principals in a study of drug abuse. Among her findings, she reported that "nearly 60 percent of the respondents knew of others who used drugs while on the job in the listed classifications." (p. 41). Her study also identified specific suggestions designed to help school professionals with drug and drug-related problems.

II. System-Service Delivery

A. Professionally-Oriented. There are numerous activities that EAPs in school systems can initiate, or encourage the staff to initiate, that can help minimize feelings of alienation and help facilitate a sense of community and professionalism. For example, Rothberg (1986) suggested activities designed to reduce teacher isolation: "Anything to improve and increase social interaction with and

among staff would be meaningful . . . Attendance at professional meetings . . . Retreats at the beginning and/or at the end of the school year . . ." (p. 322)

B. Personally-Oriented. Examples of these kinds of activities were suggested by Gold (1985) in her descriptions of Stress Reduction Programs: "Inservice workshops, self-help groups, and stress clinics at teacher centers can help teachers make some necessary changes in their personal lives." (p. 211)

Employee assistance programs in school systems, as can be appreciated by these above illustrations, face the challenge of providing the "typical" array of EAP services provided by most EAPs and also providing and facilitating "school-system-specific" kinds of services that can be very helpful to personnel working in schools (especially teachers). Obviously, many of these service delivery components are more "wellness-oriented" (vis-à-vis remedial); nonetheless, their benefits have been documented and they certainly have demonstrated their worth.

Special Concerns of School System EAPs

As indicated in EAP literature (e.g., Dickman, Emener & Hutchison, 1985; and chapters in this book), there are numerous concerns and sensitivities of which an EAP must be aware if the program is to be successful. School system employees, management, and labor, each have their individual and unique concerns about the operations and activities of an employee assistance program. There are unique characteristics of the teaching profession and of school systems that deserve special consideration.

VERIFICATION. When a school system plans, develops and implements an EAP, there are usually some skeptics in the community, on the school board, in the administration and among the staff who have concerns about, and are against, the program. It is critical for all operations and procedures of the program to be carefully monitored and appropriately documented. Furthermore, a high quality program evaluation component should be built into the infrastructure of the EAP.

In these ways, the criticisms of the program's skeptics can be allayed, and the program's veracity and continuance can be assured.

CONFIDENTIALITY. Similar to numerous other professions in our society (e.g., professional athletics, law enforcement, clergy), there are public expectations regarding the lifestyles of teachers and school officials–on and off the job. School personnel tend to be very concerned about what others think about them, how they act, and what they do. Moreover, public opinion regarding teachers assuredly can influence their employment since they tend to be "in the public eye." This is especially true in small-town, rural areas. Thus, assuring the employees of the EAP's confidentiality is crucial.

MARKETING/TRUST. Establishing trust with an expectedly suspicious and fearful group should be a high priority in the EAP's marketing strategy. For example, it can be very helpful for EAP staff and school officials to attend faculty meetings and in "face to face" interactions explain the specific policies and procedures of the program. The bottom line is to convince the staff (especially the professional staff) that the program will respond to them and be helpful to them, and that they do not have to worry about being found out and/or punished because they come to the program for assistance.

Being sensitive and responsive to the uniqueness of the teaching profession, school system attributes and community attitudes, is critical to the effectiveness of an EAP in a school system. Sensitivity to these special considerations, such as the ones discussed above, should be an integral part of the EAP and the mindsets of all of the personnel associated with the EAP.

An Example of a Successful School System EAP

For the purpose of providing an illustration of the important considerations involved in the planning, development, and implementation of an employee assistance program for a school system, the following describes and discusses the Employee Assistance and Wellness Program of the Hernando County School System in Hernando County, Florida. Key aspects of the Program's activities and experiences are highlighted.

PLANNING, DEVELOPMENT AND IMPLEMENTATION. Following numerous discussions among members of the school board, school officials and selected members of the professional staff, a contractual agreement between the school system and an independent provider was developed and enacted. Basically, the school system's EAP is an "outhouse" program (vis-à-vis the "inhouse" type of program). The Program began on November 1, 1985. Early implementation activities included multiple marketing strategies. For example: brochures describing the Program and its features and benefits were included with employees' paychecks on a periodic basis; members of the EAP staff and representatives from the school system attended meetings with personnel groups (e.g., at teachers' meetings) in order to discuss the Program in a face-to-face manner; and supervisory training sessions were conducted to assure that supervisors knew how they were to "work with the Program." Program evaluation activities included contract compliance monitoring, formal, and informal observations of the Program's activities and their subsequent impacts and outcomes.

PROGRAM EVALUATION MEASURES. Formal evaluation of the Program and its developmental activities was contracted out to a program evaluation consultant. The Program's "Six Month Preliminary Report" (Hutchison, Jr., 1986) includes foci on the five major areas of the contractual agreement: (a) Referral and Assessment; (b) Program Evaluation; (c) Case Management; (d) Ongoing Treatment; and (e) Training and Consultation. Data from the "Report's" Fact Sheet reveal that: (a) the total number of persons covered by the Program was 1,629 (1,150 employees and 386 family members); (b) 89 sessions had been held with the 49 EAP cases; and (c) the Program's utilization rate during the first six months was .085 (49/1150 x 2). The Summary of the evaluation "Report" includes the following:

Findings support full contract compliance by HCEAP [the contractor]. The process evaluation indicates that the EAP service is being utilized at almost a 9% level by employees and their families.

The utilization rate is almost double the national average of 5% for similar programs and is a strong indicator of client satisfaction. In addition, direct service costs have run almost as projected for this time period.

The process evaluation provides additional support of client satisfaction with the EAP service as indicated by the fact that 100% of the clients responding to the survey [the Program's EAP Survey] felt they had been helped and would refer other persons to the program. In addition, clients feel they have been helped to decrease anxiety and depression as well as increase their work performance. The wellness program has served 65 employees and has been well-received. Participants indicate they were helped in a variety of areas including increased ability to relax, manage their time, and improve their work performance.

In conclusion, the EAP and Wellness program has been well-utilized by employees and their families. The services are helping them solve important life problems, which is improving both personal and work performance. The services are efficiently administered and program costs are well within budget projections. (Hutchison, Jr., 1986, p. 8)

Indeed, the Program's formal evaluation, thus far, is very complimentary to its efficiency and effectiveness.

The clinical staffs records from the employees' initial contacts to the EAP ("call ins"), indicate interesting data regarding the employees' initially, self-reported, presenting problem areas: (a) family relationships–40%; (b) marital–26%; (c) personal–23%; (d) legal–3%; (e) financial–2%; (f) substance abuse–1%; and (g) job stress–1%. The EAP's Wellness Program, nonetheless, provided cardiovascular screening tests and the tests revealed that between 2/3 to 3/4 of the employees who were tested indicated some above-normal levels of stress (Landers, 1987). While these observations are casual and not conclusive, they do underscore the importance of an EAP's providing a complete complement of services and the apparent cautiousness with which employees describe their concerns, difficulties, and problems to an employee assistance program at intake.

All indications are that this Program is doing very well, and there are no apparent reasons as to why it should not continue to be a meaningful component of the Hernando County School System.

CONCLUDING COMMENT

Our schools play an extremely important role in our society–especially in terms of tomorrow's society. Currently, there are numerous problems in our schools, and the working lives of our schools' most precious resources–**our teachers and administrators**, are experiencing difficulties and problems. To a large degree, one very unfortunate result of this is that the quality of education in our schools is not what it could, or should be. Employee assistance programs have demonstrated their abilities to positively impact on the efficiency and effectiveness of employees' work. Likewise, EAPs in school systems also have demonstrated such positive outcomes. There would not appear to be any "acceptable" reason as to why a school system would not have an employee assistance

program. And, with careful and professional planning, development and implementation, such as discussed in this chapter and as experienced in the Hernando County School System, employee assistance programs in our schools should do what they ultimately are designed to do–enhance the quality of education for our youth. Interestingly, when the author of this chapter was talking with officials from the Hernando County School System about the costs of their Employee Assistance Program, Landers (1987) poignantly stated: "It is not a question of whether or not we can afford our employee assistance program; in view of the outcome benefits to our school children, we cannot afford not to."

Acknowledgment: For his technical insights and suggestions, and his critical reading of an earlier version of this chapter, sincerest appreciation is extended to Dr. Roger R. Landers, Director of Health and Student Services, Hernando County Schools, Brooksville, Florida.

REFERENCES

Boynton, P., DiGeronimo, J. D., & Gustafson, G. (1985). A basic survival guide for new teachers. *The Clearing House, 59,* 101–103.

Chichon, D. J., & Koff, R. H. (1978, March). The Teaching Events Inventory. Paper presented at the annual meeting of the American Educational Research Association, Toronto.

Cox, H., & Wood, J. R. (1980). Organizational structure and professional alienation: The case of public school teachers. *Peabody Journal of Education, 58* (1).

Dickman, F., & Emener, W. G. (1982). Employee assistance programs: Basic concepts, attributes, and an evaluation. *Personnel Administrator, 27,* 8, 55–62.

Dickman, J. F., Emener, W. G., & Hutchison, W. S. (Eds.) (1985). *Counseling the troubled person in industry: A guide to the organization, implementation, and evaluation of employee assistance programs.* Springfield, IL: Charles C Thomas, Publisher, Ltd.

Feistritzer Associates. (1983). *The American teacher.* Washington, D.C. Author.

Freudenberger, H. S., & Richelson, G. (1980). *Burnout: The high cost of achievement.* Garden City, NY: Anchor Press.

Gold, Y. (1985). Burnout: causes and solutions. *The Clearing House, 58,* 210–212.

Goodlad, J. I. (1975). *The dynamics of educational change.* New York: McGraw-Hill.

Goodlad, J. I. (1983). A study of schooling: Some implications for school improvement. *Phi Delta Kappan, 64* (8), 555.

Griesmer, J. L., & Butler, C. (1983). *Education under study.* Chelmsford, MA: Northeast Regional Exchange, Inc.

Griffin, W. D. (1984). Teacher alienation and isolation. Unpublished Master's Report, University of Central Florida.

Hutchison, Jr., W. G. (1986). Six month preliminary report: District school board of Hernando County-Employee assistance & wellness program. Unpublished report. Department of Social Work, University of South Florida, Tampa, Florida.

Kreis, K., & Milstein, M. (1985). Satisfying teachers' needs: It's time to get out of the hierarchical needs satisfaction trap. *The Clearing House, 59,* 75–77.

Landers, R. R. (1987). Personal communication. Brooksville, Florida. (January 30, 1987).

Lortie, D. (1975). *Schoolteacher: A sociological study.* Chicago: University of Chicago Press.

Maslach, C. (1976). Burnout. *Human Behavior, 5* (9), 16–22.

Moe, D. (1979). Teacher burnout—A prescription. *Today's Education, 68* (4), 36.

Pagel, S., & Price, J. (1980). Strategies to alleviate teacher stress. *Pointer, 24,* 45–53.

Pellegrew, L. S., & Wolfe, G. E. (1982). Validating measures of teacher stress. *American Educational Research Journal 19,* 373–393.

Quick, J., & Quick, J. (1979). Reducing stress through preventive management. *Human Resources Management, 18,* 15–22.

Raschke, D. B., Dedrick, C. V., Strathe, M. I., & Hawkes, R. R. (1985). *The Elementary School Journal, 85* (4), 559–564.

Rothberg, R. A. (1986). Dealing with the problems of teacher isolation. *The Clearing House, 59,* 320–322.

Sparks, D. (1979). A teacher center tackles the issues. *Today's Education, 68* (4), 254.

U.S. Department of Education National Center for Education Statistics. (1982). Estimates of school statistics 1982–1983. *Digest of Educational Statistics,* Volume 34.

Weiskopf, P.E. (1980). Burnout among teachers of exceptional children. *Exceptional Children, 47* (1), 18–23.

Werner, A. (1980). The principal's role: Support for teachers in stress. *Pointer, 24,* 54–60.

Youngs, B. (1985). Drug abuse among superintendents and principals. *EAP Digest,* January/February, 41–46.

Chapter 33

CRIMINAL JUSTICE PRACTITIONERS

MAX L. BROMLEY and WILLIAM BLOUNT

This chapter focuses on the effects of job-related stress on practitioners within the criminal justice system, specifically police, correctional officers, and probation officers. It also includes a brief review of documented sources of stress in criminal justice agencies, and suggests the types of employee assistance program services and strategies that might be most useful to assist workers in the criminal justice system.

Approximately 1.8 million persons are employed at the federal, state, and local levels within the justice system (*Bureau of Justice Statistics Sourcebook,* 1995). Over the last 25 years, criminal justice administrators have come to realize that many of their personnel face personal problems beyond those experienced by individuals in the general population. Criminal justice employees have had to deal with substance abuse, marital problems, job burnout, and other stress-related issues on the job.

Numerous studies have been conducted that review stress within the context of criminal justice organizations. In the area of policing, for example, early stress-related research was conducted by Aldig and Brief (1975); Eisenberg (1975); Kroes et al. (1974); and Reiser (1974, 1976). Furthermore, Graupman (1983), Kroes (1985), Sewell (1981, 1983), and Spielberger et al. (1981) conducted investigations into stress issues within the police occupational world. A composite of work done by some of these researchers will be described later in this chapter.

More recently, according to McCafferty et al.

(1992), police officers are at risk to develop post-traumatic stress disorders during their careers either as a result of a single horrible experience or as the result of an accumulation of a series of stressors over the span of a career. Specialized officers such as homicide detectives may feel additional stressors given the pressures inherent in solving murders (Sewell, 1993).

With regard to probation officer occupational stress issues, for example, Smith (1982), Sigler and McGraw (1984), Sigler (1988), Whitehead (1985) and Whitehead and Lindquist (1985) focused primarily on the occupational characteristics of burnout and role conflict as experienced by probation officers. The populations studied included both federal and state level probation officers.

Stress experienced by correctional officers also has been the subject of empirical research. There is little question that working in a jail, prison or other correctional setting is both psychologically and emotionally demanding. In many ways, correctional employees are as confined as the inmates they supervise. Individual and organizational stress experienced by correctional officers has been studied by Cheek and Miller (1983), Flannery (1986), Horowitz and Baker (1987), Siegel (1986), Ganster and Schaubroeck (1991), Whisler (1994), and Simmons (1996).

Sources of Stress for the Criminal Justice Professional

As noted by Ayres (1990), Stratton (1978) found

Note: This chapter is reprinted from *Employee Assistance Programs: A Basic Text,* Second Edition (1997) with permission of the author, the book's editors (W.S. Hutchison, Jr. & W.G. Emener) and the publisher (Charles C Thomas, Publisher, Ltd.).

it useful to develop a composite of the sources of stress drawn from the works of a variety of researchers including Eisenberg (1975), Reiser (1976), and Roberts (1975). These categories are identified as follows:

1. External stressors (stressors from outside the law enforcement organization)
   a. Frustration with the United States judicial system
   b. Lack of consideration by the courts in scheduling police officers for court appearance
   c. The public's lack of support and negative attitudes towards law enforcement
   d. Negative or distorted media coverage of law enforcement
   e. Police officers' dislike of the decisions of administrative bodies affecting law enforcement functions
2. Internal stressors (stressors from within the police agency)
   a. Policies and procedures that are offensive to officer
   b. Poor or inadequate training and inadequate career development opportunities
   c. Lack of identity and recognition for good performance
   d. Poor economic benefits and working conditions
   e. Excessive paperwork
   f. Inconsistent discipline
   g. Perceived favoritism regarding promotions and assignments
3. Stressors in law enforcement work itself (stressors originating from within police work)
   a. Difficulties associated with shift work, especially rotating shifts
   b. Role conflicts between enforcing the law and serving the community
   c. Frequent exposure to life's miseries and brutalities
   d. Boredom, ultimately interrupted by the need for sudden alertness and mobilized energy
   e. Fear and dangers of the job
   f. Constant responsibility for protecting other people
   g. The fragmented nature of the job in which one person rarely follows a case to its conclusion

h. Work overload.
4. Stressors confronting the individual officer (stressors confronting the officer as an individual)
   a. Fears regarding job competence, individual success, and safety
   b. Necessity to conform
   c. Necessity to take a second job or to further education
   d. Altered status in the community due to attitude changes regarding a person because he or she is a police officer (pp. 4 & 5).

As mentioned earlier, considerable research also has examined the sources of stress for probation officers and correctional officials. Champion (1990) noted that stress among probation officers is derived from a number of sources including the following:

1. job dissatisfaction
2. role conflict
3. role ambiguity
4. client-officer interactions
5. excessive paperwork
6. performance pressures
7. low self-esteem and public image
8. job risk
9. liability

Holegate and Clegg (1991) described the correlation between high turnover among probation officers and job burnout. Problems identified by probation officers in their research included inadequate resources, relatively low pay and status, low mobility opportunity, role conflicts and role ambiguity.

Whisler (1994) found that major sources of stress for probation officers were not inherent in the job itself, but tended to generate from within the organization and its procedures. For example, inadequate salary, lack of promotion opportunities, job conflict, lack of participation in policy-making decisions, and inadequate support from the department, illustrated that the most significant stressors were administrative or internal to the organization. In a study examining the influence of job-related stress and job satisfaction on probation officers' intent to quit, Simmons (1996) also found that the major job stressors derived from the organization, and included inadequate salary, incompetent supervisors, and excessive paperwork. Job satisfaction, inversely related to job stress, was directly related to the intention to terminate.

Several authorities also have investigated causes of stress among correctional officers working in jails or prisons. According to Dahl (1981), for example, the two most significant stressors for correctional officers were found to be management ambiguity and inmate contact. Lombardo (1981) noted that poor communication between correctional officers and their administrators was one of the top three sources of stress in their work setting. Fear of inmates and feeling that they did not participate in decision-making also were noted by correctional officers in this study. In a study by Brodsky (1982), it was reported that correctional officers cited role conflict as a major stressor in their jobs. That is, society expects them to rehabilitate inmates when they were often unable to do so. Whitehead and Lindquist (1986) noted that administrative practices and poor communication led to stress and burnout among correctional officers. In another study by Lindquist and Whitehead (1986), correctional officers cited inconsistent instruction from supervisors as a major stressor in their jobs. Furthermore, younger officers seemed to experience job burnout at a higher rate when compared to older officers.

Finally, Whisler (1994) found that the comparison of probation officers' stressors with police officers' stressors indicated that while the most significant stressors for probation officers were internal to the organization, police officers emphasized job/task-related stressors such as fellow officers killed in the line of duty, killing someone in the line of duty, exposure to battered or dead children, physical attacks, etc. These dissimilarities appear to be the result of distinctly different job requirements for each group.

While the majority of research has been conducted on law enforcement officers and correctional officers, there are other groups associated with criminal justice agencies that experience similar kinds of stress such as ambulance and emergency service personnel. Firefighters, for example,

have been found to have similar sources of stress as police officers (Pendleton, Stotland, Spiers, & Kirsch, 1989). More closely related to the daily operations of law enforcement officers are telecommunicators, those individuals responsible for receiving emergency calls to the police and dispatching assistance. Whether they work within a police organization or within a 911 framework, Roberg, Hayhurst and Allen (1988) reported that dispatch personnel experience a significant amount of occupational stress similar to and often greater than that of sworn law enforcement personnel, and Decker, 1991, found a significant reduction in telecommunicator stress with an improvement in the work environment.

The Need for Employee Assistance Programs to Serve Criminal Justice Practitioners

Although the evolution has been slow in its development, a variety of employee assistant services are currently available for practitioners in the criminal justice field. Reese (1987) traced the growth of assistance programs in the law enforcement field back to the early 1950s. Many programs, such as those initiated in Boston, New York, and Chicago, were created to deal primarily with alcohol abuse problems.

In the 1970s, agencies such as the Los Angeles Sheriff's Office, the Chicago Police Department, and the San Francisco Police Department expanded their programs to include nonalcohol-related problems. In 1980, mental health professionals began providing personal and job-related counseling services to Federal Bureau of Investigation (FBI) personnel. Mental health professionals also were used to assist FBI managers with a variety of employee-related matters (Reese, 1987). By 1986, many of the largest police departments in the United States had formed "stress units" or other sections to provide help for officers having personal or occupational difficulties. In the early 1990s, the United States Customs Service provided stress management training for both its supervisory and nonsupervisory personnel throughout the country (Milofsky et al., 1994). According to Reaves and Smith (1995), the majority of law enforcement agencies with 100 or more officers now have written policies regarding providing counseling assistance services for their officers. Today, many law enforcement agencies formalized programs in place to provide critical incident stress debriefings (Mitchell, 1988; Mitchell & Bray, 1990).

Based on the research cited earlier in this chapter, probation officers and correctional officials also are in need of additional services in order to effectively deal with personal and occupational problems. While there may be some unique differences between problems experienced by police officers, correctional officials and probation officers, there are definite similarities among these criminal justice professionals. A few examples are offered to illustrate this point. Each of these professional groups are generally part of larger bureaucracies that tends to emphasize rather rigid rule-oriented approaches to policy matters. In addition, professionals in each of these groups are exposed to the suffering of others and often find themselves in personal danger. Frequently, the public views their occupational roles in different ways than those held by the criminal justice professionals themselves. Prolonged work hours and difficult shift work are commonplace in the criminal justice occupational milieu. Additionally, these criminal justice professionals may be subject to posttraumatic stress disorder based upon their exposure to a variety of situations.

Considerations When Developing Employee Assistance Services

At a minimum, three questions should be answered before a criminal justice agency decides to extend employee assistance program services to its personnel. The first asks what conditions or sources of stress affect the criminal justice practitioner? Second, how does a criminal justice agency take steps to reduce stress created by its own policies or practices? Finally, what will encourage the targeted practitioners to make use of the services?

There are a number of suggested management strategies for creating a healthy work environment designed to lead to a reduction in organizational stress. For example, Ayers (1990) suggested the following strategies be taken to help achieve this goal:

1. **An examination of the workplace.** In this part of the strategy, Ayers suggested that the organization examine itself, identifying internal stressors and developing plans for needed change. This would include a variety of techniques for obtaining anonymous information from agency personnel as well as suggestions as to how improvements can be made.

2. **Believing in the mission.** This strategy ensures that the department has clear direction that is well understood by all members of the department.

3. **Living the organization values.** In this strategy, management must change its approach from autocratic to one that emphasizes democratic principles and input from all of its personnel. This input helps to establish values upon which the organization will carry forth its mission.

4. **Encouraging upward communication.** This strategy requires a change from the rigid, military-like atmosphere found in many criminal justice agencies today. Effective communication must be two-way with open communication being allowed to flow from the bottom up and ideas being championed at any level within the organization.

5. **Pushing autonomy down.** This strategy implies that educated practitioners should be given more responsibility and discretionary power in performing their tasks. Decision-making will be forced to the lowest level of the organization.

6. **Ensuring fairness.** This strategy promotes fairness in all matters to include discipline, performance evaluations, and promotions.

7. **Caring about people.** This strategy ensures that all supervisory personnel must care about those employees that work for them. Emphasis here is on the critical role that first-line supervisors play in reducing stress by assuming the role of facilitators and coaches (p. 25).

Several similar strategies for reducing organizational stress for correctional personnel were suggested by Woodruff (1993). These steps are to be taken by department managers once organizational stressors have been identified by personnel working within the agency:

1. **Development of a mission statement, goals and objectives, and values for the organization.** Policies and procedures should then be consistent with the mission statement and values of the organization.
2. **Develop consistent written policies.** For policies to be effective, they must be done in writing and consistently applied by management and supervisory personnel.
3. **Foster participation in decision making at all levels.** Personnel working within the agency should be afforded the opportunity to participate in the development of policies and procedures that affect their work.
4. **Consistent policies, instructions and directives from top management to all levels.** This should serve to reduce role conflict and inconsistent instructions given to subordinates.
5. **Officer education and training prior to and on the job.** All personnel must be adequately trained in order to deal with the stressful situation that they will encounter on the job.
6. **Provide thorough management training programs.** Top level managers should be given training in the consistent application of policies and procedures. Additional training should be provided in all aspects of management and interpersonal communication.
7. **Ongoing training and education in stress awareness and management for all employees.** All individuals in the organization should be made aware of the devastating effects of stress and provided with strategies to help prevent or control their own stress.
8. **Fair and effective selection and performance evaluation procedures.** Promotions and performance evaluations should be conducted in a consistent, objective manner for all individuals.
9. **A comprehensive employee wellness program.** Training should be provided for all personnel in order to develop good health practices including information regarding proper exercise and nutrition (p. 74).

Stratton (1985) suggested that if an employee assistance program is developed within an agency, certain services are essential. Examples include counseling following a critical incident, e.g., if an employee is involved in a shooting incident or if an employee experiences the death of a family member. These services should be made available to agency personnel 24 hours a day. Other programs such as those that deal with substance abuse, financial problems, retirement planning and family concerns can also be of benefit. Stratton (1985) further noted that before establishing a full-scale EAP, administrators should review and establish policies regarding the following issues:

1. **Confidentiality and credibility.** The most successful programs are ones in which the persons providing assistance are seen as highly professional and that information provided to them will not be used by the administration against them.
2. **Voluntary versus involuntary.** While it is true that employees may be ordered to attend counseling, the most effective programs are those in which individuals themselves seek out counseling.
3. **Status of the EAP and its staff.** Individuals providing the service must be viewed as ethical and professional.
4. **Location and accessibility of the EAP.** Generally, the services should be provided at a location separate from the headquarters of the agency. Again, 24 hour services should be available for critical assistance.
5. **Additional programs.** Programs should be offered on a routine basis for purposes of health screening. Spouse orientation programs are also encouraged for those professionals working in the criminal justice field (p. 31).

Some authorities have suggested that many criminal justice practitioners may be hesitant to share personal or work-related problems with a mental health professional for a variety of reasons (Depue, 1979; Klein, 1989). Reasons include but are not limited to: if information is shared with a mental health professional, how will it be used by administrators; lack of faith in the mental health field, denial—criminal justice practitioners don't have problems, etc. In recognition of these issues, some agencies in the 1980s established peer counseling programs wherein fellow employees are trained and offer support and advice.

Klein (1989) described the various aspects of the peer counseling program established in California that was eventually certified by the Commission on Peace Officers Standards and Training:

Training Peer Counselors

1. The three-day course is team—taught by clinical psychologists and police officers.
2. Principles taught include establishing rapport, active listening, and taking action.
3. Peer counselors are also trained to recognize serious problems (i.e., delusions, suicidal tendencies) that require referral to a mental health professional (p. 2).

Areas in which the peer counselors have been used successfully include the following:

1. Stress
2. Posttraumatic stress
3. Relationship problems
4. Chemical dependency (p. 3).

CONCLUSION

In summary, the occupational world of the criminal justice professional is both emotionally and psychologically demanding. Sources of stress for practitioners include internal and external factors. Therefore, it would seem appropriate for criminal justice executives and assistance service providers to consider the development of comprehensive strategies to assist employees that include, at a minimum, the following components: (a) stress awareness and management training; (b) crisis intervention and postcritical incident services; (c) family counseling; and (d) substance abuse awareness. The International Association of Chiefs of Police has long recognized that police officers needed access to a variety of mental health services. In 1994, this group published a model policy for police agencies to meet these needs. This model policy includes both "peer counseling" and "mental health professional" components in recognition of the different level of services that might be needed for practitioners (IACP, 1995).

As noted earlier, there is substantial literature that indicates a major source of stress for many criminal justice employees related to management and supervisory policies and practices. Therefore, steps must be taken to develop organizational goals and values that recognize the needs of individuals and that seek to maximize their professional potential. Creative problem solving should take place within criminal justice agencies in order to facilitate and not hinder the efforts of criminal justice professionals. The programs and strategies suggested in this chapter are intended to promote thoughtful dialogue among those persons responsible for reducing stress in the criminal justice work environment, thereby enhancing employee productivity.

REFERENCES

Aldag, R., & Brief, A. (1978). Supervisory style and police stress. *Journal of Police Science and Administration, 6,* 362–367.

Ayres, R. N. (1990). *Preventing law enforcement stress: The organization's role.* Washington, DC: Bureau of Justice Assistance, U.S. Department of Justice.

Brodsky, C. (1982). Work stress in correctional institutions. *The Journal of Prison and Jail Health, 2,* 74–102.

406.

Bureau of Justice Statistics (1995). *Sourcebook of criminal hustice statistics–1994.* Washington, DC: U.S. Department of Justice.

Champion, D. J. (1990). *Probation and parole in the United States.* Columbus, OH: Merrill.

Cheek, F., & Miller, M. (1983). The experience of stress for correction officers: A double-bind theory of correctional stress. *Journal of Criminal Justice, 11,* 105–120.

Dahl, J. J. (1981). Occupational stress in corrections. In B. H. Olson & A. Dargis (eds.), *American Correctional Association Proceedings,* 207–222.

Decker, R. M., Jr. (1991). An Analysis of Telecommunicators Stress in Law Enforcement. Unpublished master's thesis, University of South Florida, Tampa, FL.

Depue, R. L. (1979). Turning inward: The police officer counselor. *FBI Law Enforcement Bulletin, 48* (2), 8–12, Washington, DC: U.S. Department of Justice.

Eisenberg, T. (1975). Job stress in the police officer: Identifying stress reduction. Techniques in W. H. Kroes and J. J. Hurrell (eds.), *Proceedings of Symposium,* pp. 26–34. Cincinnati: National Institute for Occupational Safety and Health (HEW Publication #76–187).

Flannery, R. B., Jr. (1986). Major life events and daily hassles in predicting health status: Preliminary inquiry. *Journal of Clinical Psychology, 42,* 458–487.

Ganster, D.C., & Schaubroeck, J. (1991). Work stress and employee health. *Journal of Management, 17,* 235–271.

Graupman, P. (1983). Permanent shifts as opposed to rotating shifts: An evaluation of sick time and use among police officers. *Journal of Police Science and Administration, 11,* 233–236.

Holgate, A., & Clegg, I. (1991). The path to probation officer burnout: New dogs, old tricks. *Journal of Criminal Justice, 19,* 325–327.

Horowitz, S. M., & Baker, W., Jr. (1987, Oct.) The relationship between lifestyle, distress, and absenteeism in male law enforcement officers. *Fitness and Business,* pp. 55–61.

Klein, R. (1989). Police peer counseling: Officer helping officers. *FBI Law Enforcement Bulletin, 58* (10): 1–4, Washington, DC: U.S. Department of Justice.

Kroes, W. H. (1985). *Societies victims–The police: An analysis of job stress in policing* (2nd ed.). Springfield, IL: Charles C Thomas, Publisher, Ltd.

Kroes, W. H., Margolis, B. L., & Hurrell, J. J., Jr. (1974). Job stress in policemen. *Journal of Police Science and Administration, 2,* 145–155.

Lindquist, C. A., & Whitehead, J. T. (1986). Burnout, job stress, and job satisfaction among southern correctional officers: Perceptions and causal factors. *Journal of Offender Counseling, Services, and Rehabilitation, 10* (4), 5–25.

Lombardo, L. X. (1981). Occupational stress in corrections officers: Sources, coping strategies, and implications. *Corrections at the Crossroads: Designing Policy,* 129–149.

McCafferty, R. L., McCafferty, E., & McCafferty, M.A. (1992). Stress and suicide in police officers: Paradigm of occupational stress. *Southern Medical Journal, 85,*

Milofsky, C., Ostrov, E., & Martin, M. (1994). A stress management strategy for US Customs Workers. *EAP Digest, 14* (6), 46–48;

Mitchell, J. T. (1988). The history, status, and future of critical incident stress debriefings. *Journal of Emergency Medical Services, 13,* 47–52.

Mitchell, J. T. & Bray, G. P. (1990). *Emergency services stress: Guidelines for preserving the health and careers of emergency services personnel.* Englewood Cliffs, NJ: Prentice Hall.

Pendleton, M., Stotland, E., Spiers, P., & Kirsch, E. (1989). Stress and strain among police, firefighters, and government workers: A comparative analysis. *Criminal Justice and Behavior, 16,* 196–210.

Reaves, B., & Smith, (1995). *Law enforcement management and administration statistics, 1993: Data from individual state and local agencies with 100 or more officers.* Washington, DC: U.S. Department of Justice.

Reese, J. T. (1987). *The history of police psychological services.* Washington, DC: U.S. Department of Justice.

Reiser, M. (1974). Some organizational stress on policemen. *Journal of Police Science and Administration, 2,* 156–159.

Reiser, M. (1975). Stress, distress, and adaptation. In Police Work in W. H. Kroes & J. Hurrel (eds.), *Job Stress and the Police Officer: Identifying Stress Reduction Techniques.* Proceedings of the Symposium, Cincinnati, OR, May 8–9, 1975, Washington, DC: U.S. Government Printing Office.

Roberg, R. R., Hayhurst, D. L., & Allen, H. A. (1988). Job burnout in law enforcement dispatchers: A comparative analysis. *Journal of Criminal Justice, 16,* 385–393.

Roberts, M. (1975). Job stress in law enforcement: A treatment and prevention program. In Kroes, W. H. & Hurrel, J. (eds.), *Job Stress and the Police Officer: Identifying Stress Reduction Techniques.* Proceedings of the Symposium, Cincinnati, OR, May 8–9, 1975, Washington, DC: U.S. Government Printing Office.

Sewell, J. (1981). Police stress. *FBI Law Enforcement Bulletin, 50* (4), pp. 7–11.

Sewell, J. (1983). The development of a critical life

events skill for law enforcement. *Journal of Police Science and Administration, 11,* 109–116.

Sewell, J. D. (1993). Traumatic stress of multiple murder investigations. *Journal of Traumatic Stress, 6,* 103–118.

Siegel, B. (1986). *Love, medicine, and miracles.* New York: Harper and Row.

Sigler, R. (1988). Role conflict for adult probation and parole officers: Fact or myth. *Journal of Criminal Justice, 16,* 121–129.

Sigler, R., & McGraw, B. (1984). Adult probation and parole officers: Influence of their weapons, rural perceptions, and role conflict. *Criminal Justice Review, 9,* 28–32.

Simmons, C. (1996). The effects of job satisfaction and stress on probation officers' inclination to quit. Unpublished master's thesis, University of South Florida, Tampa, FL.

Spielberger, C., Westberry, L., Grier, K., & Greenfield, G. (1981). *The police stress survey: Sources of stress in law enforcement.* Monograph Series 3, No. 6, Tampa: University of South Florida, Human Resources Institute.

Stratton, J. G. (1978). Police stress: An overview. *Police Chief, 45* (4), 58–62.

Stratton, J. G. (1985). Employee assistance programs: A profitable approach for employers and organizations. *Police Chief, 52* (12), 31–33.

Smith, J. (1982). Rekindling the flame. *Federal Probation, 46* (2): 63–66.

The International Association of Chiefs of Police (1995). Model Policy for Providing Mental Health Services.

Whitehead, J., & Lindquist, C. A. (1985). Job stress and burnout among probation/parole officers: Perceptions of causal factors. *International Journal of Offender Therapy and Comparative Criminology, 29,* 109–119.

Whitehead, J. T., & Lindquist, C. A. (1986). Correctional officer burnout: A path model. *Journal of Research in Crime and Delinquency, 23* (1), 23–42.

Whisler, P. M. (1994). A study of stress perception by selected state probation officers. Unpublished master's thesis, University of South Florida, Tampa, FL.

Woodruff, L. (1993). Occupational stress for correctional personnel–What the research indicates (Part 2), *American Jails, 8* (5), 71–76.

Part VIII

FUTURE DIRECTIONS

Chapter 34

EMPLOYEE ASSISTANCE PROGRAMS: FUTURE PERSPECTIVES

FRED DICKMAN and B. ROBERT CHALLENGER

The current trend in the broad field of health care is moving more and more in the direction of addressing the whole person (Hollman, 1981)–a "systems" approach to mental, emotional and physical wellness. Looking at a person as having many parts, functioning as a unit, it is not difficult to see how a problem in one area an have a significant bearing on one's functioning in other areas. An employee assistance program (EAP) sensitive to employee needs will do everything possible to adopt and promote this approach.

Awareness of this holistic concept by the EAP needs to be kept in front of the employees and their families. They need to be reminded continuously of the EAP's existence and philosophy. When an employee can see that the EAP is open to "any problem," that the employee or a member of the employee's family does not have to be in crises, employees will more readily avail themselves of the program's services.

Some of the general components of this holistic approach address:

Stress

Although change seems to be a common denominator for events perceived as stressful, literally anything may be termed stressful if a person is highly vulnerable and lacking a supportive environment. There is extensive research supportive of the relationship between stress and physical and psychological disorders (McGaffey, 1978).

An informed EAP which embraces the concept of "wellness" will include education on stress, its signs and symptoms, and prevention methods and alternate coping strategies.

This can be accomplished by raising employee awareness through lectures, films, seminars and workshops, and newsletters. Periodic monitoring of blood pressures and heart rates, availability of exercise equipment and exercise classes, nutritional and dietary information, and relaxation and meditation techniques all serve to prevent and reduce stress and promote physical wellness.

Physical Wellness

This is not discrete from stress, as noted, however, a few areas may be specifically addressed more appropriately under physical aspects of wellness. EAPs can make available to their employees general information on common prescription drugs and over-the-counter drugs, stressing interactions–especially with alcohol consumption and other drug use.

Seminars, information, and counseling should be available through a progressive EAP to assist employees with stopping smoking and overcoming eating disorders.

Education on the disease concept of alcoholism, the progression of addiction, and early signs of alcoholism and drug abuse is a most effective intervention tool. Alcoholism's effect on the family members and friends of an alcoholic per-

Note: This chapter is reprinted from *Employee Assistance Programs: A Basic Text* (1988) with permission of the author, the book's editors (Dickman, Emener, & Hutchison, Jr.), and the publisher (Charles C Thomas, Publisher, Ltd.).

son should not be overlooked.

Mental and Emotional Wellness

Education leads to new awareness, and awareness leads to opportunities for change. A supportive EAP offers programs, which promote mental and emotional wellness. These may include:

1. **Communication Skills Training.** Help workers with effective methods for interpersonal communications on and off the job.
2. **Assertiveness Training.** Assist employees in getting what they want, pleasantly and effectively.
3. **Parenting.** Helping parents become more effective and cope with difficult and potentially stressful problems involved in raising children.
4. **Retirement Preparation.** The current economic state is dictating a trend to more early retirements. Most workers can expect to live at least 20 years after retiring, and planning ahead can help this to be a productive, comfortable life stage.
5. **Sexuality and Changing Sex Roles.** Women make up over 40 percent of the national labor force (Solomon, 1983). A component designed to affect stereotypic attitudes and assumptions about women will increase EAPs' penetration. Research literature shows that supervisors with equalitarian attitudes toward women identified and referred more women to EAPs (Reichman, 1983).
6. **Loss and Death.** Support groups offering opportunities for sharing, and programs outlining coping strategies will help employees through difficult periods brought on by death of a loved one, divorce, and major geographical relocations.
7. **Victim Assistance.** EAPs can help immeasurably with personal, emotional, and financial wounds resulting from being criminally victimized. Often, these needs have not been attended to by the criminal justice system (Teems & Masi, 1983).
8. **Day Care.** Provisions for caring for young children of working parents would maximize the potential work force available to an employer.
9. **AIDS.** The disease of AIDS is already entering the ever-increasing list of problems that fit under the umbrellas of Employee Assistance Programs. Some counselors have the task and responsibility of assisting AIDS victims in developing coping mechanisms and initiated self-help and support groups. In addition, many work organizations are providing educational materials and workshops for their employees. Hopefully, the research and tests of our medical colleagues will eventually remove this fatal disease from our concerns.
10. **Gatekeeping and Brokering of Health Care Costs.** The ever rising costs of health care insurance premiums and treatment has led EAP providers into the total management of mental health, alcoholism and drug abuse benefits. The importance of short-term counseling and alternative treatment modalities is presently in the forefront in the containment of these rising costs. The successful EAP providers will need to be even more resourceful in the establishment of cost effective strategies and relationships with the therapeutic and medical community.
11. **Academic Curricula.** The provision of services industry is the fastest growing branch of our present economy. The EAP portion of that industry is enjoying success in that growth and has resulted in a growing demand upon institutions of higher education to begin to incorporate in their curricula courses aimed at specifically preparing future and present EAP personnel for the growing demand of professionals. The demand will continue for all EAP practitioners to participate in the academic arena to remain abreast and current in the expansion of the EAP field.
12. **Increased Professionalism.** As stated by Masi and Montgomery (1987) EAPs will increasingly demand licensure and other certification as the counseling role is added to that of assessment and referral. Companies who use EAPs as gatekeeper to health care costs containment will have to insure counseling with appropriate quality control.

13. **Various Legal Concerns.** Industry is facing a serious drug problem (Masi & Montgomery, 1987). One way to identify the abuser is through urine analysis. As seen in Chapter 31 this process raises serious problems–constitutional not the least of them. EAPs will be called upon to enter this debate if for no other reason than if they don't we will return to a dismissal policy rather than one of identification, intervention, and remediation.

14. **Displaced Worker Crisis.** Increasing automation and technology may create a new category of employee: the displaced worker. EAPs may (and probably should) be invaluable aids in needed retraining efforts. Testing, referral for retraining and placement can be necessary efforts in the total productivity of the nation.

Although most companies have yet to realize the benefits of a fully functioning EAP, in companies where data on program cost effectiveness is kept, the least return is $3 back for each one dollar spent. One company reported a $17 return on one dollar of EAP funding (Fetterolf, 1983).

Returns like this, coupled with knowledge of costs to industry incurred via on-the-job accidents, absenteeism, health and medical insurance costs, and lost production, the trend is becoming clear that business and industry cannot afford NOT to have some form of an employee assistance program.

There are alternatives for smaller businesses to have an EAP, which are covered elsewhere in this text. Smaller companies can form EAP consortiums, i.e., splitting the cost of a full-time EAP coordinator between two (or more) companies (McClellan, 1982; Quayle, 1983). Another alternative is contracting with local EAP professionals in the area. The more employees are touched by an employee assistance effort, the more effective and worthwhile the effort is–in terms of both human service and bottomline cost savings.

The trends discussed above have both decided advantages and, to these authors, an obvious danger. Some of the advantages and signs of growth are:
1. Industry and human services will be even more involved in a partnership in the future than previously. This means more people will have the opportunity for early intervention. More human service professionals will learn to relate and be effective in the workplace.
2. These trends mean that industry may be looking seriously at the notion that it not only hired people with problems, or potential problems, but it creates problems (McGaffey, 1978). Studies on industrial stress and its alleviation may teach us how some of this stress may be avoided or, at least, lessened at work.
3. As both government and industry decentralize, we as a society may take more responsibility for prevention and remediation of the kinds of human problems now involved with EAPs.

A Danger

Yet, as advantageous as these trends are, a clear danger exists. Simply put, it is that alcoholism may be lost in the shuffle as the occupational alcoholism program gives way to employee assistance programs; which, in turn, is supplanted by the employee enhancement program. There is already evidence to this effect.

Some time ago, the authors surveyed local companies in the Tampa Bay area as to their interest in learning about alcoholism in the workplace. Many were adamant that there was no alcoholism in their companies. Later, some of these same companies contracted with "new" EAP professionals who stressed employee enhancement, "playing down" alcoholism. Apparently, stress in the workplace is more acceptable than alcoholism. Recently, the authors asked some of the "new" EAP professionals about penetration rates in general and alcoholism in particular. Penetration rates were reported high, but alcoholism identification and rehabilitation rates were around 5 percent.

This is a frightening comparison with the 40 percent–60 percent rates of the occupational alcoholism programs of the 1940s through the 1960s and of the employee assistance programs of the 1970s. There is evidence that the trained interviewer does not find what he or she doesn't know about (Dahlhauser et al., 1983). If the new professionals contracting with industry do not know about alcoholism, they are not apt to see much of it–alcoholic people have been successfully deceiving these professionals for years.

This book ends, as the authors believe it should, where, in a way, it began. Alcoholism and its treatment conceived EAP strategy. Industry, in turn, was recognized as the best intervener for alcoholism treatment. This relationship may be lost unless industrial managers and employee enhancement program professionals maintain a high commitment to alcoholism rehabilitation, which clearly remains the major health problem in the community and in the workplace.

REFERENCES

Dahlhauser, H. F., Dickman, F., Emener, W. G., & Yegidis-Lewis, B. (1982). Alcohol and drug abuse awareness: Implications for intake interviewing. Manuscript submitted for publications.

Fetterolf, C. F. (1983). Acceptance remarks upon presentation of Ross Von Wiegand Award at the 12th Annual Meeting of ALMACA. *The ALMACAN, 13* (10), 1, 6–7.

Hollman, R. W. (1981). Beyond contemporary employee assistance programs. *Personnel Administrator,* (Sept.).

Masi, D., & Montgomery, P. (1987). Future directions for EAPs. *The ALMACAN, 17* (3), 20–21.

McGaffey, T. N. (1978). New horizons in organizational stress prevention approaches. *Personnel Administrator,* 26–32.

McClellan, K. An overview of occupational alcoholism issues for the 80's. *Journal of Drug Education, 12* (1), 1982.

Quayle, D. (1983). American productivity: The devastating effect of alcoholism and drug abuse. *American Psychologist, 38* (4), 454–458.

Reichman, W. (1983). Affecting attitudes and assumptions about women and alcohol problems. *Alcohol Health & Research World, 7* (3), 6–10.

Solomon, S. D. (1983). Women in the workplace: An overview of NIAAA's occupational demonstration project. *Alcohol Health & Research World, 7* (3), 3–5.

Teems, L., & Masi, D. (1983). Victims of crime as EAP clients. *The ALMACAN, 13* (10), 20–21.

Chapter 35

FUTURE PERSPECTIVES–1997

WILLIAM G. EMENER and WILLIAM S. HUTCHISON, JR.

By and large, the major theme of this book's 1988 futuristic perspectives chapter remains true for the 1990s. If companies continue to move ubiquitously toward a wellness model, alcohol rehabilitation indeed may be lost in the shuffle. (And that certainly would be a shame–there are thousands of good employees who could provide excellent work for companies if the companies' Employee Assistance Programs [EAPs] would genuinely embrace and operationalize an EAP model that would include a viable alcohol rehabilitation program component.) There is, nonetheless, an additional futuristic perspective for EAPs pertinent to what has been, and is, going on in the United States.

Over the first half of the 1990s, the United States has witnessed a suppressed economy. Wage and salary compression, shrinking employment opportunities, "downsizing" and "rightsizing" reconfigurations within business and industry, and rising costs of living, collectively have contributed to a rather severe compression of American economy. One major result of these economic conditions has been a change in "payors"–buyers, purchasers and consumers, in general, have become more cautious and more demanding. This, in turn, has led to increasingly more competitive business practices which have led to dramatic changes in modern business and industry. For example: (1) there have been many cost-cutting and cost-saving initiatives (e.g., businesses are wanting their employees to assume more responsibilities for their own health care costs); and reductions in personnel costs (e.g., employees are being expected to "do more or less"). To assure cost savings with increased worker productivity, coupled with enhanced computer capabilities, businesses and industries are engaging in hypervigilant monitoring, in general, and more centralized monitoring (e.g., micromanagement) from the top down. As one worker recently said, "No matter what I say or do, I constantly feel that big brother in the front office is watching every move I make." These changes in the basic infrastructure of most large businesses and industries have had, in turn, many understandable outcome effects on the modern work environment, employees, and employee assistance programs (EAPs):

Work Environment:
- worker behavior is being highly monitored, job tasks are being tightly controlled
- there are more rigid rules for individual behavior (e.g., political correctness)
- there is increased pressure on workers for "doing more"

Employees:
- workers are feeling more suspicious and fearful of losing their jobs
- the "survival mode" has meaningfully lowered employees' job satisfaction
- there is increased job frustration (and lowered levels of worker autonomy)
- workers have increased feelings of paranoia

Note: This chapter is reprinted from *Employee Assistance Programs: A Basic Text,* Second Edition (1997) with permission of the author, the book's editors (W.S. Hutchison, Jr. & W.G. Emener) and the publisher (Charles C Thomas, Publisher, Ltd.).

EAPs:
- EAP will be attending to an increased amount of "work-related" problems and difficulties (along with the typical "personal" kinds of problems and difficulties)
- EAPs will feel pressured to do more (for less) as a result of the managed care model of human service delivery, companies' cost-cutting efforts, and increased competitiveness with the overall health care industry
- EAP professionals will increasingly feel "in the middle" (e.g., the company will want more specific outcomes for the benefit of the company and the EAP professional will feel more compelled to do what's best for the individual employee)

Overall, these scenarios do not necessarily paint the most exciting and inviting picture for the future of EAPs. The decade ahead will most certainly be extremely challenging!

CONCLUDING COMMENT

For companies (1) to continue to be profitable and therefore viable in the highly competitive business world of the nineties, *AND* (2) to continue to provide efficient and effective EAPs for their employees, indeed constitutes an extremely demanding set of challenges. Likewise, for EAP professionals (1) to continue to provide efficient and effective EAP ser- vices to their clients, *AND* (2) to continue to be professional and ethical in the process, also constitutes an extremely demanding set of challenges.

Hopefully, companies, unions, and EAP professionals will continue to work together cooperatively and successfully in aiding and assisting troubled employees (in spite of the respective challenges facing them).

Chapter 36

EMPLOYEE ASSISTANCE PROGRAMS: CHALLENGES FOR THE NEW MILLENNIUM

WILLIAM G. EMENER, WILLIAM S. HUTCHISON, JR., and MICHAEL A. RICHARD

*Forecasting the future includes appreciating the past
and understanding the present.*

There are several critical factors which have affected the development of employee assistance programs (EAPs), and are likely to continue to influence their prevalence, structure and operation as we continue our journey into the new millennium. These factors can be roughly divided into three groups: (1) influences internal to the EAP enterprise; (2) those within the workplace as a whole; and (3) those in the broader society beyond the workplace.

The EAP Enterprise

One of these factors is the assessment of EAPs by managed care organizations (MCOs), individual employers and labor groups. EAPs and their predecessors historically have "sold" themselves to employers on assertions of their effectiveness in returning valued employees to productive employment (e.g., Trice & Beyer, 1984). However, EAPs often are difficult to assess (e.g., Normand, et al., 1994) due in part to the fact that they typically are only part of a larger intervention system which also includes treatment providers, MCOs, employers and others. Changes in any of these groups could positively or negatively affect treatment costs, employer savings, worker rehabilitation, and consequently the acceptance of EAPs as a component in the overall intervention system.

Second, intense market competition among external EAP providers, either as independent companies or as divisions of larger MCOs, has driven the development and availability of services in this field. According to Oss and Clary (1998), the EAP field is likely to evolve in several directions.

One growth direction is the expansion of the EAP market through the coverage of a larger number of workers and proportion of the labor force. A second area of growth could be in the form of external purveyors continuing to increase their market share at the expense of internal programs. While external EAPs are a cost-effective option for particular types of companies (i.e., smaller, geographically dispersed, governmentally-regulated, etc.), they often gain their cost savings by limiting the range of core technologies offered to those associated with employee services and have little structural impact on conditions within the workplace. However, market expansion is unlikely to accommodate all purveyor organizations to their individual satisfaction. Oss and Clary (1998) document an ongoing process of the consolidation of EAP organizations. The effect of this consolidation was that the large organizations serve a larger proportion of EAP enrollees. For example, at the beginning of 1997, the 20 largest purveyor organizations covered 85.9 percent of all EAP enrollees (approximately 33.5 million lives). During 1997, several large purveyors merged, resulting in a consolidation of 88.5 percent of covered lives in the largest 20 organizations. As of

November, 1997, one organization (Magellan Health Services, Inc.) controlled 34.1 percent of the market share, covering 13,291,822 lives. Further, Oss and Clary (1998) predict that EAPs will evolve into three tiers of organizations: (1) large national programs serving in excess of 800,000 covered employees; (2) mid-sized regional programs serving between 60,000 and 800,000 employees; and (3) smaller local programs serving fewer than 60,000 employees. The largest providers have the economic advantage of scale in administrative and technical support, while smaller EAPs have the advantage of local support and personal relationships with employers and employee groups. In the future, intermediate EAPs are likely to feel pressure from both ends of this continuum, and feel pressure to consolidate with larger purveyor organizations. The predicted consequence will be that companies will have increasingly fewer choices when selecting an EAP provider. Given increasing costs of full service EAP programs and limited choices in EAP provider groups, internal and peer-assistance programs could gain support in specific service niches in the future.

The Workplace

Another influence on the growth and development of EAPs is the real and perceived need for such services. For example, after the Vietnam conflict, employers widely believed that returning veterans were likely to import their substance abuse patterns into the workplace (Robins, 1974). Also, the significant increase in the utilization of MCO services and benefits has paralleled the growth of labor force participation of among women since the 1980s. Similar changes in the needs of labor force participants precipitated by demographic and other social forces could continue to influence the growth and direction of EAP services. Workplace characteristics, in terms of stress and cultural influence to participate in the use of alcohol and illicit drugs, could impact the continuing need for EAP services. For many years, researchers have attributed some of the cause for behavioral health problems to the workplace (consult Trice and Sonnenstuhl, 1988, for a conceptual overview of these influences). EAPs historically have worked with troubled individual workers and supervisors on how to manage such workers, but have participated only marginally in the structural redesign of the labor process (Steele, 1989). However, EAP professionals have expressed interest in becoming more involved in the prevention of alcohol misuse and drug abuse by participating in workplace risk management activities, attempting to mitigate the workplace risk factors.

The Society

As indicated by the various types of EAP programs emerging in recent years, the field is quite sensitive to changes in managed care practices. In 1997, approximately 168.5 million of an estimated 223.7 million Americans with health insurance were enrolled in some type of managed behavioral health care program (75%). Of the 168.5 million, 149 million are enrolled in specialty managed behavioral care programs and 19.5 percent receive benefits through programs internally managed within HMOs. This latter number represents a 19 percent increase from 1996. Thus, one arguable prediction for the future is that EAPs could become more involved in MCO oversight activities (EAPA, 1997).

OVERVIEW

The health care industry is only one institution that has made inroads into the workplace. Other social institutions are interested as well in the issues that bring workers to EAPs for services. For example, criminal justice agencies are interested in issues of illicit drug abuse (U.S. Department of Justice, 1997), inappropriate use of alcohol, domestic violence, illegal gambling, violence in the workplace and sexual misconduct. Detection devices and procedures developed by criminal justice agencies are increasingly being utilized by workplace (particularly drug testing) programs.

Ethical and legal issues of mandatory crime reporting, such as in the case of child abuse, are under greater scrutiny by law enforcement professionals. Finally, various EAP, insurance, workplace health, civil rights and substance control legislation has influenced the direction of EAP models and practices. For example, the state licensing of employee assistance programs has influenced their development. Particular Federal legislation which has impacted EAPs includes the Americans with Disabilities Act, the Health Insurance Portability and Accessibility Act, the Mental Health Parity Act, the Employee Retirement Income Security Act, the Comprehensive Omnibus Budget Rehabilitation Act, and the Federal Employee Health Benefit Act. In addition, health care reform applicable to HMOs and other MCOs, if enacted, could influence the future growth and development of EAPs.

CONCLUDING COMMENT

If there is any one phenomenon being witnessed in the first two years of the new millennium, it is the spiraling rate of change. Things, locally as well as on a global scale, are changing faster than ever. Unethical and illegal actions by government officials, illegal activities by CEOs, nosedives in the national economy, and the pervasive threat of international terrorism collectively have translated into a state of instability in almost every facet of life. Increasingly, industries, businesses and employees have become more and more fragile, and if there ever was a time in history when the United States needed efficient and effective employee assistance programs, it is now.

The founders, developers and leaders of many of today's EAPs, started EAPs via the "learn as you go" method. They were what could be considered the first generation EAP professionals. However, most of the recent graduates of counseling, rehabilitation counseling, social work, and psychology programs (to name a few), have had coursework and specialized training in EAPs and indeed are in a much better position to continue to develop, lead, and work in the EAPs of tomorrow (Dixon & Emener, 1999). Fittingly, when we look down the road into this emerging new millennium, we shudder at all of the societal vicissitudes forecasting an escalating need for EAPs. Therefore, when we look at the new breed of EAP professionals coming out of our colleges and universities who will pick up the reins and take on the challenges of the new millennium, we feel much relieved and optimistically confident.

REFERENCES

Dixon, C. G., & Emener, W. G. (1999). *Professional counseling: Transitioning into the next millennium.* Springfield, IL: Charles C. Thomas, Publisher, Ltd.

Employee Assistance Professionals Association (1997). *EAPA Model Employee Assistance Professional Licensure Act.* Arlington, VA: Employee Assistance Professionals Association.

Normand, J., Lempert, R. O., & O'Brien, C. P. (eds.) (1994). *Under the influence: Drugs and the American workforce.* Washington, DC: National Academy Press.

Oss, M. E., & Clary, J. (1998). EAPs are evolving to meet changing employer needs. *Open Minds,* January, 4–10.

Robins, L. N. (1974). *The Vietnam drug user returns.* Washington, DC: Special Action Office on Drug Abuse Prevention; Monograph Series A, Number 2, May.

Steele, P. D. (1989). A history of job-based alcoholism programs: 1955–1972. *Journal of Drug Issues, 19* (4), 511–532.

Trice, H. M., & Beyer, J. (1984). Employee assistance programs: Blending performance-oriented and humanitarian ideologies to assist emotionally disturbed employees. In Greenley, J. R., ed., *Research in community and mental health.* Greenwich, CN: JAI

Press, 4, 245–297.

Trice, H. M., & Sonnenstuhl, W. J. (1988). Drinking behavior and risk factors related to the workplace: Implications for research and prevention. *Journal of*

Applied Behavioral Health, 24 (4), 327–346.

U.S. Department of Justice. (1997). *Combating workplace drug crimes.* Washington, DC: Office of Justice.

INDEX

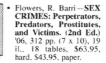

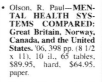

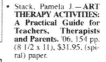